IN THE FELLOWSHIP
OF HIS SUFFERING

IN THE FELLOWSHIP
OF HIS SUFFERING

*A Theological Interpretation of Mental Illness
— A Focus on "Schizophrenia"*

Elahe Hessamfar

Foreword by John Swinton

The Lutterworth Press

Dedicated to Helia

"All this," said David, "the Lord made me understand in writing by His hand upon me, all the details of this pattern."
1 Chronicles 28:19

The Lutterworth Press
P.O. Box 60
Cambridge
CB1 2NT
United Kingdom

www.lutterworth.com
publishing@lutterworth.com

ISBN: 978 0 7188 9382 8

British Library Cataloguing in Publication Data
A record is available from the British Library

First published by The Lutterworth Press, 2015

Copyright © Elahe Hessamfar, 2014

Published by arrangement with Cascade Books

Unless otherwise indicated, all Scripture quotations are taken from the New American Standard Bible®, Copyright © 1960, 1962, 1963, 1968, 1971, 1972, 1973, 1975, 1977, 1995 by The Lockman Foundation Used by permission. (www.Lockman.org)
I would like to thank the following publishers and authors for their kind permission to reprint quotations from their publications: Publishers: The Edwin Mellen Press, NY; Hachette Book Group, NY; Oxford University Press; Penguin Books, London; Peter Lehmann Publishing, Berlin; St Vladimir's Seminary Press , NY; Taylor & Francis Group; Wesleyan University Press, CT; Xlibris, IN.
Authors: Daniel J. Carlat, Unhinged; Isabel Clarke, Madness, Mystery and the Survival of God; Carina Håkansson, Ordinary Life Therapy; Larry Merkel, "The History of Psychiatry"; Robert Whitaker, Mad in America and Anatomy of an Epidemic.

Contents

Foreword by John Swinton ix

Acknowledgments xiii

Introduction 1

1   A Theological Anthropology 19

2   The Historical Contexts of Psychiatry
     and Mental Illness 66

3   A Theology of Illness 142

4   A Path Forward: *Healing Together* 244

5   Conclusion 303

Bibliography 315

Subject Index 335

Scripture Index 371

Foreword

The world of mental health and illness is a strange place. It is strange, not because people are strange, but because it is essentially mysterious. What exactly do we mean by mental illness? How can a mind be ill? Indeed, how can something immaterial be either broken or mended? It is clear that whatever mental illness is, it is not the same as measles or influenza. It may be that some claim to have tracked down biological, neurological, or genetic causes for our psychological disturbances. But such explanations, whilst arguably telling us from where such experiences come from, do little to inform us of what they actually are. Asking the question "what does it mean to experience schizophrenia" is a quite different question from asking what causes it. The mistake we often make in relation to understanding mental illness is allowing ourselves to be convinced that once we think that we have discovered the pathological root of the condition, we know what it is. It's really not as simple as that.

It is only relatively recently that the types of experiences that we now describe in terms of mental illness have come to be defined purely in pathological, bodily terms. If we trace the history of what has come to be known as mental illness, it becomes quite clear that the experiences that we now describe in terms of diagnoses and symptoms have been open to a multitude of different interpretations. At one point in history strange and mysterious experiences, behaviors, and ways of talking about the world were considered gifts from the gods, leading to respect, reverence and awe. At another point such experiences were assumed to be the product of demons, leading to exorcism and exclusion. Later the cause of such experiences came to be located in such things as poor parenting, pathological families, sexual abuse, and difficult social conditions, thus moving the mystery outwards into family and community. Nowadays we are taught that we should interpret unusual experiences in terms of biology, neurology, and genetics, thus turning the locus of interest inwards towards the individual. So we are constantly shifting the causes and outcomes of mental illness upwards, outwards, inwards. Each of our explanations requires of us a different set of understandings, and each of our interpretations has a profound effect on how we choose to live with those who experience things that are different from the accepted norm.

But the problem with any kind of explanatory framework is that whilst it allows you to see some things it inevitably prevents you from seeing other things. If we choose to interpret those clusters of experiences that make up the concepts of mental illness as pathology, then that is what we will see. But humans are much more than predetermined biological units. Even if the causes of mental illness were conclusively shown to be biological in nature (and Elahe Hessamfar in this book makes a strong case that this cannot be done), there would still be deep and profound issues that would require to be explored deeply before any claim of understanding mental illness could find justification. I repeat, finding the cause of something does not tell us what it is or what it means. That takes a different set of skills and a whole new way of looking at people. Mental illnesses are not biological entities any more that they are social, psychological, theological, or spiritual entities. They are occurrences that happen within the life narratives of real individuals in real situations who require to be recognized as whole persons within whom each of these aspects—biological, psychosocial, theological, spiritual—need to be recognized as fundamental building blocks that are necessary in order that we can truly discover what mental illness is, rather than what may or may not be its root cause. Working out what mental illness is and what it means requires a complex interdisciplinary conversation that simply cannot and must not be dominated by any single perspective.

One of the problems for the church is the temptation to overly prioritize one particular way of seeing and interpreting mental illness and to take that as its beginning point for pastoral care and understanding. Arguably this is precisely what has happened over the past forty years or so as psychology and psychological explanations for mental health issues has taken priority over the theological. We might choose to take psychiatric definitions as the beginning point of our theological and pastoral reflections. In that case we take common assumptions and interpretations of human behaviors that are classified by psychiatrists as illness and try to develop theological understandings and pastoral strategies accordingly. That is fine, except that psychiatric diagnoses and definitions are intended for psychiatrists, to enable them to carry out the particular tasks that they have been trained to do. It may be that within the realm of psychiatry understandings of mental illness that focus on neurology, genetics, and pharmacology are perceived as the right place to begin. However, is that the right place of the church to begin? Elahe Hessamfar challenges the church to begin from a different place; to recognize the hermeneutical complexities of mental health and illness and to boldly enter the conversation as theologians who may well challenge established understandings, rather than as neutral bystanders who assume that conformation to established wisdom is the safest place to stand.

For Elahe the place to begin to understand mental illness and the nature of the churches response to it lies deep within Scripture and theology. There, alongside of some fascinating and I imagine, controversial, critiques of contemporary mental health care, she finds a new interpretation of mental illness. This new way of seeing mental illness will be deeply challenging to many. Some will see it as liberating, some will see it as threatening. Either way, Elahe's important book opens up some fresh, critical, and very important theological space within which new conversations can be begun which will undoubtedly lead to a deeper understanding of the role of the church in mental health care, alongside of new ways in which we can offer care which is truly theological and faithful. This is a deeply theological book that brings with it a new perspective and a new world within which we can seek to understand the mystery of mental health and illness. Whether you agree with it or not, this book will certainly challenge you and leave you with no choice other than to respond.

John Swinton
University of Aberdeen
January 2014

Acknowledgments

This book is birthed out of my PhD thesis, which was completed in September, 2013. My PhD research, like that of most others, required passion, focus, hard work, and more than anything, time. I could not have been given that gift of time away from my home without the support of many friends and family. I cannot name everyone who, during the three years of my research and under some difficult circumstances, gave my family a helping hand so that I could focus on my research. However, a few people have to be named, who made it possible for me to go to Scotland to work on this project. My friends Massoud Nicokar, Nasrin and Shahram Zaboli, Jaleh Kashi Brock, and my mother-in-law Maryam Riazi-Sadri, were devoted and compassionate angels who helped with caring for my family in my absence. I am indebted to them.

This whole project would have never taken off had it not been for the unmatched support and encouragement of my remarkable husband, Shariar Makarechi, whose unconditional love has been and continues to be the source of my strength. My precious daughter Tara, who makes me so proud, was and continues to be my sounding board for my thoughts and the editor of many draft versions and revisions of my dissertation. Tara, I love you beyond what words can explain. You are one of a kind!

I wish to express my deep appreciation for Professor John Swinton's supervision of my thesis. While John's wisdom and insight guided me, helped me shape my vision, and guarded me against falling into traps of my own creation, he gave me enough space to find my own voice in this noisy, chaotic, and hotly debated realm of mental health. I thank you, John, for your patience and your help in getting this project to land.

In my research, I was helped by the work of many scholars who influenced my thinking and led me to great sources of information. I am intellectually indebted to many scholars cited in this book, particularly to Jean-Claude Larchet, Aarne Siirala, Shirley Sugerman, and Robert Whitaker, who, in my opinion, has done more to give a voice to the mentally ill than any other contemporary scholar. Their research paved the way for my work.

Acknowledgments

I would like to express my gratitude to those who read portions of my thesis and commented on it. Thank you, Sharoz Makarechi, Pastor John On-wuchekwa, Cathy Price, Veronica Rogers, Donnell Shariat, and Jon Temple. I am especially grateful to Drs. Brian Brock and Edward Welch for their support and insightful comments on my thesis. I am also thankful to Ulrike Guthrie who helped me with editing my dissertation to convert it to this book.

Last but not least I am in deep emotional debt to my precious daughter Helia who is truly a gift from heaven. Helia, you have inspired me with your endurance, sense of sacrifice, and submission under the providential hand of our awesome God. I would not be the person I am today if it were not for the lessons I have learned from you and through you. You are an amazing instrument in the hand of our loving Redeemer. It was through you that I learned how to love selflessly. Please know that I love you with every fiber of my being.

Elahe Hessamfar
January 2014

Introduction

Look to the right and see; For there is no one who regards me;
There is no escape for me; No one cares for my soul.

—Psalm 142:4

The spirit of a man can endure his sickness,
but a broken spirit who can bear?

Proverbs 18:14

Suffering ceases to be suffering in some way
at the moment it finds a meaning.

—Viktor Frankl[1]

The ubiquity of mental illness and its exponential growth in the US has made it the primary "medical disability" of our time. This pervasiveness and the destructive force behind it to destroy human spirit demands an urgent attention not only from medical community and social policy makers, but also from the church. In the history of Christian communities, mental illness has tended to be viewed as some form of malignant manifestation that stands against the will and rule of God. It has thus tended to evoke a response from within the church. Today, for the most part, that response has been delegated to the medical profession and the state. I hope that by the end of this book you will understand why the church is so well placed to reassume most of that responsibility.

---

1. A Country Doctor, "Treating Pain," Lines 1–2.

The issue of mental illness has invited and ignited many debates in the current philosophical and scientific realms. In this book I show how we have come to frame mental illness in contemporary America. The twentieth century saw an astronomical rise in the popularity of the biological sciences as explanatory frameworks for everything related to human beings. Psychiatry has attempted to develop a scientific context to capitalize on that success and create a framework for how we view and name those experiences that make up the criteria "mental illness." Here, I evaluate those attempts and explore the challenges of modern psychiatry in normalizing human behavior based on scientific theories. The intention of this study is to determine whether the church could or should intervene in such encounters, and if so, what such an intervention might look like.

Mental anguish can cripple individuals in variety of ways. Among all manifestations of distress, anxiety, fear, and mental confusion, nothing can be more destructive than what psychiatry has called "schizophrenia." This has been the most elusive, cruel, and puzzling "mental disorder" of all times, leading to prolonged disability and intense personal suffering. Furthermore, it attacks the core of a person's consciousness, sense of identity, humanity and ability to relate to others and to God. In this book I propose a biblically based Christian framework for interpreting the phenomenon of "schizophrenia" by reflecting theologically on the experience quite apart from what psychiatry may or may not have to say. I argue that not only is "schizophrenia" not pathological, but rather it touches on the most fundamental fragilities of the human soul—hence, it is a very critical pastoral issue. I suggest that madness ought to be recognized as a phenomenon, both *theological* and *teleological*, with a deep prophetic voice, exposing our state of sinfulness, calling the church into repentance. Given that, we will explore how the church ought to encounter it effectively and faithfully.

Every research project is justified by a problem that demands an answer; a problem that baffles the mind and emerges from an experience that challenges existing understandings. At times the questions need to be asked in new ways and the accepted theories may need to be reexamined fundamentally. It was such an experience that motivated this research and that is perhaps motivating your reading of it. What follows is a summary of my personal experience with my daughter's mental illness, which is vital for understanding the shape and texture of this study. That being so, and in line with the method and approach of my chosen discipline of practical theology, I will begin by laying out the issues I intend to address in this study via my own story.

In this study my intention is to expose the reader to some of the best research in the field of mental health, spanning a variety of disciplines. However, reflection on my experience with my daughter Helia will help to locate the study and offer some provisional pointers as to the issues I intend to focus on in this book. In writing this book I have benefitted from a wealth of wisdom and insight given by many psychiatrists, scientists, journalists, and theologians. To avoid cluttering the message, I have kept the footnotes to a minimum, but an extensive bibliography is provided to guide readers to sources that have influenced my thinking and my writing.

In the middle of 2000, after an intense religious experience, my 22-year-old daughter, Helia, began a journey of madness. She was a healthy, well-educated, stunningly beautiful girl at the prime of her life—a recent graduate of one of the top universities in the country, and was about to be engaged to the love of her life. Helia was a devout Christian, and her life was centered on her faith. By all standards she was blessed beyond measure.

It is an underestimation to say that her illness "caught everyone by a surprise." The girl who was known to be fun, happy, talkative, and the center of attention in every room she entered had suddenly become removed and self-reflective. She was no longer participating in life. Instead, she spent her days on her knees praying and fasting. This change marked the beginning of what became a downward spiral into an abyss of darkness.

My husband and I, like any "good" American parents, took charge and by force and against her will put her under psychiatric treatment. But regardless of our ardent efforts to bring her back to "normal," she was not getting "better." In fact her condition worsened with each and every new treatment. In order to care for her, I gave up my career as a successful senior executive in corporate America. Having come from the business world, my expectations were quite logical. I expected the physicians to have answers to my most basic questions: "What had happened to her?"; "What is the prognosis for her illness?"; "How long will her condition last?"; etc. To my surprise, the physicians offered no convincing answers. In fact, Helia's diagnosis changed every few months and so did the treatments. She was hospitalized several times against her will and the explanations and the manifestation of her illness were getting more confusing and stranger every day. All our efforts to save our daughter were to no avail. We were losing her and we weren't sure to whom or what.

The psychiatrists could never settle on a concrete diagnosis for her, mostly because her condition was changing all the time. We had embarked on a long journey with no clue about the nature of the encounter. Every year we would change to a new psychiatrist, hoping that maybe this new psychiatrist—who always came with the highest of recommendations—would know what was wrong with Helia. Every one would start with confidence, but when faced with a mixture of "symptoms" that seemed to cross many conditions, from depression to "mania," to catatonia, to "schizophrenia," and faced with the ineffectiveness of the treatment, they would wonder whether the problem was something else, or just how to proceed. I was often baffled by the confusion I witnessed among the psychiatrists. After all, I was living in the most technologically advanced country in the world. My child was receiving the most expensive treatments. Why was she getting worse? There was no explanation.

Over the next many years she was seen by several Christian and non-Christian psychiatrists and psychologists. Her diagnosis changed from Psychotic Depression to Anxiety Disorder to Bipolar Disorder to Obsessive Compulsive Disorder (OCD), to Schizoaffective Disorder, and finally to schizophrenia. But none of the diagnoses would ultimately explain the complexity of Helia's condition. And none of the physicians could fully explain the rationale behind their diagnosis. For example, they thought she suffered from OCD because she was praying too much, or that she was depressed because of her sudden turn toward reclusive-like behavior, but that only touched on a few of her "symptoms" and behaviors.

With each new diagnosis, Helia was subjected to an array of treatment plans. She was given a dozen different psychiatric drugs, including some of the best-known antipsychotic, antidepressant, and anti-anxiety medication. Helia felt the impact of each drug. Some had a positive impact, but most impacted her negatively—her beautiful face became covered with blistering pimples; she gained weight; her cholesterol skyrocketed; she was losing her hair; and, most of the time, she was very irritated. Her facial expression screamed fear, anger, confusion, and death. There was a dark frown covering her face all the time. She did not look like our daughter anymore!

It was so easy to think that God had forsaken us. Regrettably, the church was of no help in the midst of this intense suffering. Most Christians were either at one end of the spectrum, thinking this was a demonic attack, which caused them to want to stay away, or they were at the other end, perceiving this to be purely a biological phenomenon, which rendered them helpless, because then it was the purview of the medical sciences. Helia was dying before our eyes and we could not help her. The situation felt so hopeless. We were scared of what we were witnessing. She had gone down so deep that we could not reach her anymore. We could not love her enough to overcome the power of evil that had taken her away from us. Her body was lying on the bed, frail, pale, with few signs of life. Her eyes were glazed over; she seemed to be gazing at something far away. We could not get her to look at us; we were not even sure if she heard us when we talked.

Helia's condition continued to worsen. Her behavior had become very scary. She would not eat or drink for days or weeks and was becoming less mobile. She would freeze in strange postures for hours and sometimes days, and then, suddenly, she would transform back to normal postures and movements. There were times when she would keep her mouth open and stare at a single point for many hours without the slightest movement. She did not even seem to blink! She would stand in one location with her body twisted and her fingers twisted, her head held in strange ways as if she were staring at something through the wall! It was as if her twisted body was a picture of her twisted soul. She was driven mad by the sight of what she was seeing. She was speechless, motionless, and seemingly lifeless. Her twisted body in her strange frozen postures was more reminiscent of a piece of dark cubist art than the body of a stunning twenty-something-year-old.

The days and weeks and months and years were passing. Her condition was regressing. Our lives were completely changed. The whole family was pulled into darkness with her.

She was frozen in her bed, not moving, and had lost a lot of weight due to starvation. Though Helia is about five feet, ten inches tall, at one point she weighed only eighty-five pounds. She was appallingly emaciated—we could virtually see her ribs from under her skin. We were very concerned about her physical health. Though she was showing no signs of discomfort, it was very scary to watch her melt away before our eyes. As a caregiver, I was witnessing a phenomenon beyond that which words could describe. Her condition had consumed our family and had transformed us beyond our wildest imaginations. It was obvious to all of us that this was far more than a "brain disease." It was as if she was speaking to us through every "sign" and "symptom."[2] Her condition was deeper and darker than

---

2. We, like most Americans, had been convinced of the medical model of "schizophrenia." It was only after much research that we came to comprehend the hermeneutical nature of this phenomenon and the fact that psychiatric diagnosis is only one frame in which such experiences can be understood. This construction is true and real insofar as it helps with research, but other discourses construct illness through other images that are harder to grasp and yet are exceedingly powerful. Our encounter was bound to take us beyond the medical to social, political, ethical, and certainly theological areas

what medical science could explain. It was only when we started really listening to Helia's silent communication that we decided to abandon our quest for medical answers and start exploring a different route.

Suffice it to say that her condition lasted many years. She was mute, catatonic, starving, completely out of this world. Her journey of madness changed everyone around her. It was by the grace of the amazing God she worshiped that one day she rose up and walked out of that grave that had swallowed her in for more than seven years. She got up and came back to this world. That was in 2008. Today, she suffers from many residual problems; by no Western standards can she be considered functional. Though we lost forever the person she was before her illness, we are grateful that she is alive and engaged with life despite all her challenges.

John Foskett, who was the chaplain at Bethlem Royal and Maudsley Hospitals, speaks to the significance of madness: "'Madness' is an important matter. Words about it are not adequate even to capture its mysteries let alone to reveal its meaning. To understand it one has, incarnate like, to enter into it—into one's own and other people's madness. It is my experience and conviction that there is meaning to be found there."[3] I entered into Helia's madness during the years I cared for her. What I witnessed there shattered me into dust and has changed me forever. In search of answers, I worked among mentally ill persons for several years. Helia's hospitalizations also brought me into contact with people suffering from mental illness and their families. I spent countless days and hours sitting in the dark and hopeless corridors of mental hospitals conversing with those who were forgotten by their society. Through them, I recognized that what I had experienced and what I had learned had to be exposed and shared with others.

This research and subsequent writing that underlies this book was birthed out of my ardent pursuit of answers to the mysteries of madness. What follows is the result of a very personal and passionate exploration and investigation, one that literally became a matter of life and death for my beloved child. This book is a testimony to her and a challenge to assumptions behind the contemporary Western explanations of mental

---

where different meanings were formed; and no one model alone could speak the truth. Bradley Lewis, himself a psychiatrist, explains that alternative interpretive "models of madness" can "counterbalance the dominant-hegemonic psychiatric readings," and they are legitimately developed, not based on science, "but on the perspectives and values of the person and persons involved." Lewis, *Moving Beyond Prozac, DSM, & the New Psychiatry*, 96, 108.

3. Foskett, *Meaning in Madness*, xi.

illness. My experience with Helia is that there is a spiritual dimension to her experience and indeed to that of many others like her. That spiritual dimension not only needs to be brought to light, but actually needs to be allowed to shift, change, and transform both understanding and practice, beginning with the church.

The aim of my research was to investigate the deeper meaning behind "mental illness"—and specifically "schizophrenia"—and to evaluate the related care practices from a Christian perspective.[4] As such, it is necessary to evaluate this phenomenon by reflecting on the manifestation of it through a theological lens. Doing so will help to discern how God is active in the midst of it and, more importantly, what he intends to accomplish through it in his ongoing work of redemption. By discerning meaning in madness, we can then formulate strategies for actions and practices that will enable the church to respond to the call of God. It is important to note that defining a particular form of "mental illness" such as "schizophrenia" with any level of precision is very difficult. In fact, some "symptoms" of "schizophrenia" are shared among several other mental illnesses catalogued in the *Diagnostic and Statistical Manual of Mental Disorders (DSM)*. For that reason, the terms "madness" or "insanity" are often used to bundle manifestations that project a subjective reality different from what is perceived or experienced by most others in the community.

Although this study will benefit from global research, my primary focus is the American system of mental health care, for this is the context from which my experience with Helia and the church comes and back into which my findings will feed. According to a report published by the National Institute of Mental Health (NIMH), one out of every seventeen Americans suffers from a debilitating mental illness at some point in their lifetime. Mental illness does not discriminate against age, race, gender, or social class. It can and does afflict anyone. Moreover, they claim, "an estimated four million American children and adolescents suffer from a severe mental illness."[5] The lack of knowledge about the etiology of mental illness has made the treatment challenging and subject to trial and error

---

4. For the official categorization of "schizophrenia" in American Psychiatric Associations (APA)'s *Diagnostic and Statistical Manual of Mental Disorders (DSM)*, see DNA Learning Center, "DSM-IV Criteria," 1–18. Also see Brown University, "Schizophrenia (DSM-IV-TR)." It explains: "Schizophrenia is a chronic, more or less debilitating illness characterized by perturbations in cognition, affect and behavior, all of which have a bizarre aspect. Delusions, also generally bizarre, and hallucinations, generally auditory in type, also typically occur." I will be developing and criticizing such definitions later in the book.

5. Levitt and March, *Transformative Neurodevelopmental Research in Mental Illness*.

and therefore the cause of incomprehensible levels of suffering. Furthermore, it attacks the core of a person's consciousness, sense of identity, humanity and ability to relate to others and to God. Stephen Pattison believes, "Mental illness will continue to present an enormous, perpetual but hidden challenge to all healing systems for the foreseeable future."[6]

The issue of mental illness has invited many debates in the current philosophical and scientific realms. Some have completely denied its existence.[7] Others, such as American Psychiatric Association (APA), consider it to be a physical (i.e., brain) disease. This position stems from a belief that the mental phenomenon is the byproduct or outworking of the neurology of the brain. In short, there has yet to be a consensus on what constitutes mental illness. Arthur Kleinman, a psychiatrist at Harvard Medical School and a professor of anthropology at Harvard University, defines illness as the innate "human experience of symptoms and suffering." Illness, for him, points to "the principal difficulties that symptoms and disability create in our lives." For Kleinman, illness is "always culturally shaped" and may vary in different contexts. He views an "illness" as distinctly different from a "disease," which refers to "an alteration in biological structure or functioning."[8] Notwithstanding the current debates, the phenomena known as mental illness cause personal and social disruption and have been an integral part of all societies and cultures. George Rosen states:

> Every society recognizes certain extreme forms of aberrant behavior as mental derangement or insanity. In other words, along the range of human behavior, from that which a society considers normal to that which it regards as abnormal, there is some point or section at which a social judgement is made and an individual comes to be regarded as mad.[9]

The ubiquity of this illness and the destructive force behind it to destroy human spirit demands an urgent attention from all involved. I agree with Pattison's claim that, "In many ways, there is no more important disorder for Christians to study and respond to than mental illness."[10] Along the same line, Aarne Siirala points to the importance of "the conquest of the powers which cause mental illness," in Scripture, "as a sign of the messianic

6. Pattison, *Alive and Kicking*, 104.

7. Szasz, *The Myth of Mental Illness*, 329.

8. Kleinman, *The Illness Narratives*, 3–6.

9. Rosen, *Madness in Society*, 101.

10. Pattison, *Alive and Kicking*, 103.

age," and the coming of God's kingdom.[11] Given such an intense impact on the human spirit, the intent of this study is to determine whether the church could or should intervene in such encounters, and if so, what such an intervention might look like.

Mental anguish can cripple individuals in variety of ways. Among all manifestations of mental distress, nothing can be more destructive than what psychiatry has called "schizophrenia." This has been the most soul-wrenching and mysterious "mental disorder" of all times, leading to prolonged disability and intense personal misery. The term "schizophrenia," coined by Eugen Bleuler, a Swiss psychiatrist, has a Greek root and its literal translation means "split mind." Popularly, the term is known to refer to "split personality." However, most people diagnosed with "schizophrenia" do not suffer from split personalities at all.[12] Bleuler came up with the schizophrenia label not implying a double consciousness that would control the person alternately, but rather he meant to point at "the 'splitting' of psychic functions." There was a chasm between that part of a person's consciousness that knew what was happening, versus another part that experientially felt what was happening—what Ian Hacking calls "a split between sense and sensibility."[13] Hacking explains,

> Schizophrenia is an absolutely dreadful condition. There are those who urge that it is the worst illness that is now rampant in the Western industrial world. You can think of schizophrenia, rather than cancer, say, as the worst disease of prosperity because it so often strikes at young people just as they are about to enter adult life. The impact on families is horrible. One of the worst things about severe episodes in the life of schizophrenics is that other people are terrified as they see good sense and order turned upside down, chains of ideas turned into threatening parodies of ordinary life. The withdrawal, the indifference, the fascinations; speech awry, glances blocked, feelings inverted—above all strangeness.[14]

People diagnosed with "schizophrenia" are "besieged by auditory hallucinations, persecutory delusions, confused thinking, and mood swings."[15] It is the severity of this illness and its damaging blow at the spiritual life

11. Siirala, *The Voice of Illness*, 51.

12. Andreasen, *Understanding Mental Illness*, 19.

13. Hacking, *Rewriting the Soul*, 130.

14. Ibid., 138.

15. Patterson, *The Therapist's Guide to Psychopharmacology*, 105.

of the individual and the family that demands a practical solution. How might we understand this illness and its influence on the lives of God's people?

Before delving any further, it should be noted that in this study I have chosen to not use gender inclusive language in general and in particular in reference to God. Since God is generally referred to in Scripture with the pronoun *he*, this pronouncement is respected in this book. Many might object to my use of male pronoun in all my references. For simplicity of writing, instead of using she/he, or referring to the person in neutral ways, as "the one"—which would make the writing convoluted on many occasions—I have chosen to consistently use the male gender as my primary grammatical device. This is by no means intended to offer any hidden meanings to the significance of one gender over the other in relation to the particular subject being discussed.

Methodology

The discipline within which this study is located is practical theology. Practical theology aids the church in reflecting theologically on life situations in order to facilitate a faithful Christian understanding and response to the problems of the world. There are different schools of thought led by prominent practical theologians. However, what they have in common is that they all advocate the importance of integration of theory and practice. They all want theology, in general, and practical theology, in particular, to be a *reflective* discipline that wrestles with the application of faith to the world and engages in dialogue with other sources of knowledge.

According to James Fowler, "The way forward in practical theology involves placing more radical trust in God's self-disclosure and promises found in our traditions of revelation"; more intentional involvement in our social-historical contexts in anticipation of the inbreaking of God's love, and a greater commitment "through present action and prayer, to make us partners in God's work of creation, governance, and liberation/redemption."[16]

As a result of the influence that social sciences have played on the nature of practical theological studies, Scripture has tended to take a back seat. Can theological formulation afford to play down the role of Scripture? The Christian tradition claims to have received *special* revelation from God and that *special* revelation is the inspired Scripture that points to the

16. Fowler, "Practical Theology and Theological Education," 58.

soteriological Truth, and, as such, that Truth is *accessible.* "Were there no 'general revelation' there would be no religion in the world of any kind," says B. B. Warfield, "were there no 'special revelation' there would be no Christianity." In other words, God's general revelation in nature is almost indisputable (Rom 1), but it is the special *salvific* revelation, revealed only in Scripture, that is unique to Christianity.[17]

The exalted position of Scripture as the master guide in pastoral ministry becomes in focus when we ask: "Is the person in ministry the 'mouth-piece of the Most High' to do God's work among his creation, to bring healing to the oppressed and wholeness to the broken"? "Is he standing on behalf of God before the world which is in pain to make known to them who this God is and what his purposes of grace are, and how he might be accomplishing his purposes"? If the answer to these questions is "yes," then the nature of theological studies is forced to change. Then it is the knowledge of God that is revealed by him through Scripture that becomes the guiding light in that ministry. As Warfield reminds us, if the aim is to lead people into the *saving* hand of God and to build them up into a true knowledge of their Creator, to know his will for their lives, "which will be unassailable in the face of fiercest assault," no second-hand rationalistic knowledge of the revelation can suffice the needs of a ruined world.[18]

Faced with incomprehensible mysteries of madness, we are confronted with the challenge of doing the practical theological work with methods that align with a Christian epistemological framework as revealed to us in Scripture empowered by the Holy Spirit. Otherwise, our ministry is not powered by the revealed ways of God, and instead of working toward transformational healing, as Andrew Purves points out, it "languishes in the pride of our own attempts to storm heaven."[19] In order to ensure the centrality of Scripture, and a theological foundation that is faithful to the Christian tradition, I have aligned my methodology with the work of John Frame, a leading conservative systematic theologian and a Christian philosopher with Calvinistic views. Frame's commitment to the doctrine of divine sovereignty and covenant theology brings particular sensitivity to God's workings in the lives of his people. His central focus is on Scripture as the Word of God, which drives all theological work. In that context, he offers a methodological framework for doing faithful Christian theological work without being overrun by secular views. He allows the voice of

17. Warfield, *Selected Shorter Writings of Benjamin B. Warfield*, 25–27.

18. Ibid., 369–76.

19. Purves, *Reconstructing Pastoral Theology*, ix

other sciences to be heard, but always in submission to Scripture through the use of a "hermeneutical circle." He explains:

> We come to know Scripture through our senses and minds (self) and through Scripture's relations with the rest of the world. . . . But then what we read in Scripture must be allowed to correct the ideas we have formed about these other areas. Then as we understand the other areas better, we understand Scripture better. There is a kind of circularity here, a "hermeneutical circle" if you will, but that does not prevent Scripture from ruling our thoughts; it merely describes the process by which that rule takes place.[20]

Frame points at a series of triads in the Bible (referred to as triperspectivalism), which all represent significant perspectives on a unified entity, on top of which is the concept of Trinity. The concept of Trinity has been a source of mystery and challenge for Christians throughout the history of Christian faith. The Christian God is one God who comprises three persons: Father, Son, and Holy Spirit. The three persons are divine and participate in every act of God. They may have distinct roles in every divine act, yet they make up one God, not three gods. Scripture points at different activities for each person in the fulfillment of God's plans. Frame explains that in every divine act *all* three persons are present; even when one has a distinct role the other two are participating toward the fulfillment of plan. The Scripture emphasizes that "the Father and Spirit are 'in' the Son; the Son is 'in' the Father; and the Spirit is the Spirit of the Son and of the Father" (John 10:38, 14:10, 15:26; Rom 8:9). Now, since each person is "in" the other two, we cannot know each person without knowing the other two, and we cannot know God without knowing all three and their correlations. This Trinitarian model is the foundation for Frame's triperspectival method.[21]

Frame's theological formulation is informed by three perspectives on knowledge: 1) it attempts to apply Scripture (*normative perspective*); 2) by persons who bring their own reason, emotion, experience, and faith into the theological work (*existential perspective*); 3) applied to circumstances (*situational perspective*).[22] God's knowledge is the absolute Truth. Frame explains that "knowledge of God involves (and is involved in) knowledge of His law, the world, and ourselves." Therefore, these three perspectives

20. Frame, *Knowledge of God*, 89.

21. Frame, "A Primer on Perspectivalism."

22. Frame, *Knowledge of God*, 80.

are *correlational* and *coexistent*; they "are involved in one another because of their mutual coordination in God's plan."[23] In this triperspectival method, Frame affirms the idea that human beings are finite creatures and as such their knowledge is limited to their personal perspectives. It is only God who is omniscient and knows everything there is to know about anything. Therefore, for people to develop an enhanced understanding of any topic, it requires that multiple *perspectives* come into play to create a fuller picture of that reality. This finitude of human knowledge, and our fallibility due to sin, makes it necessary for us to be open and humble before other perspectives. We bring our backgrounds, our education, emotions, our reason and our faith amongst other attributes into our perspectives. Because of God's sovereignty over all elements in creation, all finite perspectives are interdependent; and God's perspective governs and includes all other finite perspectives. The process of gaining knowledge is always "communal." The importance of this communal interdependence for discovery of truth is affirmed by God when he reveals his truth to us by human authors with multiple perspectives (i.e., the four Gospels within the context of the unity of Scripture).[24]

Frame sees the work of theology to transcend the statement of biblical doctrines and to engage in questioning us, commanding us, inspiring us to worship and giving us a sense of awe. For this reason he suggests "adopting new forms of expression," to engage the world and existential experiences with the fullness of God's revelation in Scripture.[25] As an example, he draws on the work of Richard Pratt, suggesting that Scripture can be looked at through metaphors of "picture," "window," and "mirror." Scripture as the *canon* is the "object of literary analysis," in the same way that a piece of art is analyzed by an art critic—a symbol of "Scripture-as-'picture.'" "Scripture-as-window" functions as "a portal to events through *historical analysis*."[26] This way, looking through Scripture one would come to see something else, such as learning about the redemption of our souls through God's acts. Finally, and most relevant to our study, "Scripture-as-mirror," mirroring "our own lives," helps us to look at Scripture in search of answers to human questions, that we may find ways to meet personal

---

23. Ibid., 65.

24. Frame, "A Primer on Perspectivalism."

25. Frame, *Knowledge of God*, 202. Frame's contextual interpretation of Scripture is in line with the traditional appeal to *sensus plenior* ("fuller meaning,") as God's voice is heard into his people's lives. Kaiser and Silva, *Hermeneutics*, 336.

26. Pratt, "Pictures, Windows, and Mirrors in Old Testament Exegesis," 156–67.

needs. Frame sees Pratt's "picture," "window," and "mirror," respectively to correspond to his "normative," "situational," and "existential" perspectives.[27]

The *normative* perspective is about the authority of God's law, but this law can be understood only in "its relations to the world and the self." In other words, its application and meaning are identical. Frame says:

> Thus all knowledge is a knowledge of the law. All knowledge also is a knowledge of the world, since all our knowledge (of God or the world) comes through created media. And all knowledge is of self, because we know all things by means of our own experience and thoughts.[28]

Therefore, these "three kinds of knowledge" are the same knowledge, understood from three different "perspectives," each perspective being dependent on the other two.

The *situational* perspective highlights life circumstances, and uses extra-biblical data from a variety of sources, such as language, logic and science, to bring a situation before Scripture. Sciences used for such analyses will function as "tools of theology."[29] Therefore, the church achieves "theological progress" only when she "creatively and faithfully responds to difficult situations on the basis of Scripture." As a Calvinist with belief in the sovereignty of God, Frame explains that every situation reveals God; "for everything is under His control, authority [and] presence."[30] As the theologian brings situations of life before Scripture, it is under the guidance of the Holy Spirit that God's mysteries are revealed in new ways. In regards to sciences as "tools of theology," he values how by "describing the situation," they can aid the church to reconsider her "*interpretations of Scripture*," and yet cautions the church to guard against "unbelieving presuppositions."[31]

Under this perspective, we will look at the content of the experience of mental illness and see how it manifests in the real world. How do all parties involved view the situation? What is the problem with the situation that demands some corrective actions? The intent is to suspend all non-biblical presuppositions and just observe and listen carefully to the actual lived experience of a person, and other forces at work, so that we can truly

27. Frame, *Knowledge of God*, 204–5.

28. Ibid., 89.

29. Ibid., 215.

30. Ibid., 307.

31. Ibid., 313–15.

understand the situation. Additionally, we will look upon extra-biblical sources of knowledge about mental illness, such as psychiatry, psychology, anthropology, with the intent to create a rich, thick description to deepen the key themes that emerge from the original experience. John Swinton and Harriet Mowat explain:

> To complexify something is to take that which at first glance appears normal and uncomplicated and through a process of critical reflection at various levels, reveal that it is in fact complex and polyvalent.[32]

By complexifying the situation, we seek to answer the following questions: What are the cultural contexts that impact the way "mental illness" is perceived? How does that perception influence the treatment options? What are the historical and political dimensions of this phenomenon? Who is benefiting from it and who are the victims? What are the real barriers to recovery? Is there a common theme behind the cases of those who have recovered? Can analyzing those recovered cases lead us to a systematic thought about the true dynamics that are at work? How has the church dealt with this phenomenon historically and why? This will open a "window" into the inner texture of the experience separate from any theoretical overlays imposed on it by the outside world. Situations never happen in abstraction. They always happen in a context and have different forces affecting them. Our task is to expose these hidden dimensions.

We will be concerned to learn how the experience of "schizophrenia" might fit within God's redemptive plan and what the theological implications of our findings might be. If God has revealed himself to man by speaking to him, can his voice be heard in this particular situation? How might this experience and all we have learned about it challenge our faith and vise versa? Are there deeper purposes and hidden meanings that will come to focus through our faith magnifying lenses? Is there a prophetic insight and wisdom that should be brought to bear on the experience? Are the practices involved with the care of the "mentally ill" appropriate in the context of Christian faith? The attempt is to figure out what is going on and what needs to be changed moving forward. This work is critical, analytical, and aimed at challenging us to abandon current false assumptions and beliefs and embody faithful Christian practices.

Frame puts a great emphasis on the "intensely personal nature of theology"—hence the significance of the *existential* perspective. He perceives

---

32. Swinton and Mowat, *Practical Theology and Qualitative Research*, 13.

theology to be the application of one's "deepest convictions," and "his presuppositions." Therefore, inevitably, the theologian will share "*himself*" with others at some intimate level.[33] This is a very different view of theology than one depicted by those who conceive of theology as an objective academic exercise. For Frame, impersonal theology is an outright impossibility since theology must address the deepest issues of human life in relation to God. Since God cannot be detected empirically, the knowledge of God cannot be reached "by the experimental methods of natural science." He affirms the value of propositional language to convey information *about* God, but stresses that knowing God is a *personal* journey led by the Holy Spirit. Frame notes that people's ideas are not separable from who they are, as "God's Word is one with God himself." A theology not touched by personal experiences is "a theology without a soul."[34] In fact, the divine authority of Scripture encounters a person in his concrete circumstances, as it did for me in my personal experience with Helia's illness. It allowed me to enter into God's story of redemption.

It is Frame's high regard for the authority of Scripture, his belief in theology's role to "*meet human needs*" through "reinterpretation and re-proclamation of Scripture"—that they may come to know God and his revealed Truth—and his triperspectival approach to knowledge, that makes his methodology attractive for this study. He rejects the application of theology as "a narrowly intellectualist or academic discipline"; it is always about the use of Scripture "in the situations of human life." His theologian is always a *practical* theologian.[35]

The Outline of the Chapters

In the *first* chapter, I will develop a contextually-driven theological anthropological model, which will provide a lens through which the experience of insanity/madness will be evaluated. I will explore how our anthropological assumptions may shape our views of the phenomenon of mental illness and guide our practices of how to deal with it. I suggest how we

33. Frame, *Knowledge of God*, 319. John Colwell, a theologian who has struggled with bipolar disorder, stresses that all theology is done within a certain context: "Objective detachment is a foolish delusion that is neither desirable nor achievable; there is no theological reflection without a person reflecting, and that person has a story that has shaped them: a story that, in turn and inevitably, shapes their reflection, their speaking, and their writing." See Colwell, *Why Have You Forsaken Me?*, xi.

34. Frame, *Knowledge of God*, 321–22.

35. Ibid., 78–81.

might understand the role of intense suffering in human spirit and how that might shape a Christian soul.

In the *second* chapter, I will examine the principal theories underpinning the medical model of psychiatry (biopsychiatry), in which all problems are diagnosed and treated primarily as physical problems such as other disciplines in medicine. We will examine how well this system of care has been serving the sufferers of mental distress by allowing its scientific findings to inform our critical analysis.

In the *third* chapter, we will try to understand whether an illness has meanings beyond its physical manifestation. We will look beyond the biological and medical model of diagnosis towards what the *voice* of illness might be from a *theological* perspective. We will focus on "schizophrenia" through theological reflection, attempting to discern the voice of this illness through the guidance of Scripture and the Holy Spirit. The author's personal experience and other scholarly views will be incorporated in this theological reflection.

In the *fourth* chapter, our theological understanding of "schizophrenia" from previous chapters will guide us to proceed on a path that would be glorifying God, faithful to God's call on church's ministry and responsive to the needs of the individuals. Thinking more deeply and more theologically on the complexities of illness and healing, how should we formulate meaningful and practical approaches for care? What is the required role played by different parties (i.e., family, the church, pastoral office, psychiatry, and local community)? The proposed solutions will be built on the work of organizations that have applied some of the basic principles behind the arguments of this study and have enjoyed success in helping people with severe mental distress.

In *conclusion* we will summarize the study by highlighting its new findings and the general arguments supporting them, reiterate the case for action, and offer some personal reflections.

1

A Theological Anthropology

*"What is man, that . . . Thou has made him a little lower
than God, and dost crown him with glory and majesty!"*

Psalm 8:4–5

It is the Spirit who gives life; the flesh profits nothing

John 6:63

In this chapter we will lay down our anthropological foundation, which
will shape our analysis of mental illness as a human phenomenon.
Throughout history man has been an enigma, and a paradox, not only in
the pages of Scripture, but also to himself and his fellow human beings.
Although there have been many studies on every detail of a human's life
concerning his social, psychological, economical, political, physiological,
and cultural status in life, one seemingly trivial question that has puzzled
philosophers, scientists, and laymen alike, driving the fundamental answer to all aforementioned categories, is *What is a human being?* The
answer to this question is fundamental to our understanding of madness.
The implied anthropological assumptions we bring to all contemporary
settings not only affect our treatment of our modern challenges—whether
sociological, economical, psychological, ethical, or even physical—but
they also have a profound impact on the formulation of our fundamental

theological understanding.[1] As Barth commented, "One cannot speak of God without speaking of man."[2]

The way we understand the nature of humankind is not merely a product of historical philosophical reflection or a phenomenon emerging out of contemporary scientific and technological debates. In fact, for Christians, these questions are "deeply rooted in the biblical traditions of the people of God."[3] The biblical writers' focus on human nature primarily pointed the reader toward humanity's covenantal relationship with God. They did not perceive humanity as an ambiguous entity awaiting conceptual clarity by scientific discoveries. Instead, they pointed to a creature clearly distinguished by his standing in relation to his Creator. A "real man," says Barth, "is the being determined by God for life with God and existing in the history of the covenant which God has established with him."[4] Our study is guided by this covenantal anthropological picture that receives a greater clarity in the person of Jesus in the New Testament.[5] Based on this, we will offer, not a full blown but a contextually-driven, theological anthropology, which will inform our analysis of key issues with regard to how the church should understand and frame "schizophrenia." While dealing with the subject of mental illness and what a person is experiencing in the midst of madness, the questions about the essence and nature of the human being, *who* he is, *why* he is who he is, and whether there are any meanings in the events surrounding his life, make a significant difference as to *how* his particular situation should be treated.

Scientists such as Bill Joy, Stephen Hawking, and Ray Kurzweil predict that it is conceivable for computer technology to displace human species. They predict that without genetic modification, humans will not be able to keep ahead of technological advancements.[6] Are humans merely primitive machines that soon will be replaced with newer and more advanced models? Ray Kurzweil, the famous inventor and technology futurist, predicts that in a few decades, "nanobots will roam our blood streams

1. Anderson, *On Being Human*, viii.

2. Barth, *The Humanity of God*, 56. Likewise, Calvin asserts that without knowledge of self, no one can have any knowledge of God (Calvin, *Institutes*, 1/1.1).

3. Green, "Bodies—that is, Human Lives," 149.

4. Barth, *Church Dogmatics*, 3/2:204.

5. For a detailed Christ-based theological anthropology, see Cortez, "Embodied Souls, Ensouled Bodies."

6. Joy, "Why the Future Doesn't Need Us"; Herzfeld, "Creating in our Own Image," 303–4.

fixing diseased or aging organs." He believes it is only a matter of time before humans and computers will intermingle with nanobots—blood cell-sized robots—that will be integrated into our bodies and brains. So, if something goes wrong, the damaged cells can be amended or replaced with the right technology that will correct the problem. It is merely a matter of technical repair! Thus, those who manage to survive for another fifteen to thirty years, Kurzweil predicts, will never die but will have an "eternal life."[7]

These predictions bring hope and excitement to many people and fear and despair to many others. But what do these projections mean? Are our lives so meaningless that they could easily be replaced with robots? Are we beings devoid of purpose beyond our physical manifestation? We are reminded by the evidence that technologists in the field of Artificial Intelligence (AI) have traditionally over-claimed and under-delivered. AI has faltered in the past not because of difficult challenges such as solving an astrophysics problem, but it has failed in mimicking what a young child can do, such as identifying a face in a crowd, or appreciating nuances in a simple story requiring a common sense, or experiencing the emotional effects of such a story. It is that level of consciousness, which is able to experience love and hate and beauty of a sunrise, that has been problematic for AI to figure out.[8]

Then there are those materialists who view humans through a somatic lens made of chemical substances. Not only is a person's bodily existence dependent on a tiny thyroid-gland secretion, so too is his or her sanity and psycho-spiritual life determined by it. A minor blow on the right spot upon the head, which is considered purely physical damage, could turn a "genius" into an "idiot," and bring a fruitful life down to a mere survival. It is easy to understand, as Brunner suggests, how a physician who is limited by this reductionist view of human existence, finding that to be the only sphere of influence for him, "constantly falls a prey to the temptation to ignore other aspects" of a person's being.[9] Based on all these scientific observations, are we to accept that we are reduced to mere structured aggregates of physical parts?

The presuppositions about the constitutional nature of human beings that a psychiatrist brings into the treatment determine a great deal. In the

7. Kurzweil, *The Singularity Is Near*; Gaudin, "Kurzweil: Computers Will Enable People to Live Forever."

8. Herzfeld, "Creating in our Own Image," 304–6.

9. Brunner, *Man in Revolt*, 40–41.

absence of a correct conceptual model of a human being, psychiatrists, psychologists, and all those in the field of mental health, are bound to "run up against an inadequate framework for treating" the person as he actually is.[10] Andrew Sims, the former president of the Royal College of Psychiatrists, a supporter of biopsychiatry, points to the "unhealthy situation" created in modern times where "psychiatry denies the significance, and even existence, of soul or spirit." This has been "disastrous for all those involved," he claims.[11]

When many theologians in the latter part of the twentieth century rejected the idea of the existence of the soul, the soul did not disappear as some might have expected. According to Jeffrey Boyd, a distinguished psychiatrist, it only "got uncoupled from religion." Today the soul is as talked about and analyzed as it ever was in the history of humanity. The difference is that now it is called by different names: "self," "personality," "mind," "I," or even "*psyche*." The new soul experts, according to Boyd, are those in the mental health profession who treat and analyze the soul through various procedures, "without ever mentioning God." Throughout history, the question "who am I?" was always treated as a religious reflection. But twenty-first-century Western culture considers it to be a "psychological question." From Boyd's perspective, this question that the popular culture is consumed with can only be answered if we start with God and with why Christ had to die in our place.[12]

Warren Kinghorn, a psychiatrist and theologian himself, believes that the church has assumed that "mental illness" is a "given," and as a result it has failed to build a theological response to concepts that are not only "not givens," but are badly in need of some interpretive help. The longstanding questions and doubts about a psychiatric diagnosis "can be solved *not* by more and more research but rather *only* by a theology, or something like a theology," claims Kinghorn.[13] This is where anthropology can adjudicate the debate on the best course of action for treating mental illness; a "properly nuanced Christian anthropology" would provide a "more complex account of human agency" than is being advertised by

---

10. Moreland, "Restoring the Substance to the Soul of Psychology," 30.

11. Sims, *Is Faith Delusion?*, 2.

12. Jeffrey Boyd points to Oscar Cullman's seminal essay challenging the concept of an immortal soul as a turning point in this debate; Boyd, "Losing Soul," 472–74, 479; and Cullmann, *Immortality of the Soul Or Resurrection of the Dead?*

13. Kinghorn, "Ordering 'Mental Disorder.'" Emphasis mine.

some consumer advocacy groups[14] and would provide psychiatry with "a much needed aesthetic and eschatological context" to perform its challenging task.[15]

This is the challenge that this chapter will take up: to understand the true nature of the human being as revealed within Scripture, but in so doing to focus not only on what a human *is*, but also on what a human *can be* or *ought to be*.

A Theological Framework

There is a long tradition of inquiry into the nature and constitution of the human person in the history of the church. Different theologians and philosophers have attempted to determine the proper way to construe the elemental construct (i.e., mental, physical, spiritual) of a human person. Some see the human as a single physical substance (physicalism), others as a single non-physical/spiritual substance (idealism), some as two distinct substances (dualism), and others as consisting of three distinct substances (trichotomism). There also are a variety of positions within each one of these categories. This debate usually structured as the body/soul, or brain/mind has engaged philosophers and theologians for centuries. But, in the past two centuries, due to the implications raised by dramatic developments in the neurosciences, this debate has received vitality and intensity beyond what was experienced in earlier times. Advancements of imaging technologies have opened up unparalleled windows to the brain.

The advances in neurosciences, plus great challenges and opportunities presented by technological developments in artificial intelligence, human cloning, and DNA discoveries have caused theologians and philosophers to rethink their theological anthropologies. They are asking new questions about how we should make sense of biblical revelations in light of scientific developments, questions about how to address a wide range of issues, including distinguishing humans, animals, and machines; the role of human agency, free will, moral responsibility; and making sense of our traditional values for human significance.

14. Ibid., 16. He points to NAMI (National Alliance on Mental Illness), which, in an attempt to fight stigmatization of those suffering from mental illness, promotes mental illness as "no-fault brain disorders." See www.nami.org.

15. Kinghorn has addressed these issues in greater details in his own doctoral dissertation, "Medicating the Eschatalogical Body."

Our definition of the human constitution has great implications for our traditional Christian doctrines. What does it mean that we are sinners before God? What is the hope of salvation in Christ? What is it that is being saved? What does it mean that we are made in the image of God? What is spiritual growth? What is sanctification, and *who* or *what* is being sanctified? Are prayer and worship byproducts of our brain chemical stimulations? What does death mean? What does Scripture say about who we are and how we are made? A proper understanding of what it means to be a human has significant implications on these fundamental questions answered by Christian tradition.[16]

A Trinitarian Framework

In theological anthropology, the relationship between God and humans takes precedence over any other issue and will inform all other determinations that we may make. God displays His "ownership of the world and of the human race" through the act of creation. He is not only the "power behind creation", but also, "its authoritative interpreter," and its "faithful maintainer." Frame notes that since God's Wisdom was "his agent of creation (Prov 8)," it is impossible for us to make sense of the mysteries of creation—human creation being the climactic act—without seeking God's Wisdom.[17]

Since, in biblical teachings, humans are primarily presented in the context of the covenantal relationship with God, I will define our theological anthropology within the paradigm of the *economic* Trinity. Frame claims that the whole Bible is about God's story of redeeming His people. Since, God chose the name *Yahweh* (Lord) for Himself, and that name is "at the heart of the fundamental confession of faith of God's people," he wants his people to know him primarily as a covenantal Lord.[18] *Economic* Trinity speaks of how the triune God relates to creatures, centered on the distinct roles played by the Father, the Son, and the Spirit in regards to creation, providence, and redemption.[19]

16. Ibid., 3; Cortez's dissertation ("Embodied Souls, Ensouled Bodies") raises these fundamental questions.

17. Frame, *Doctrine of God*, 296, 298.

18. Deut 6:4–5; Rom 10:9. Frame has written a multi-volume exposition of God's covenantal Lordship. See ibid., 12.

19. Ibid., 706.

We can only understand the human person in relationship to the God who is Creator, Redeemer, and Life-giver/Sanctifier. God is thus "the answer to questions about the ultimate origin, meaning, and goal of life which lie behind all other problems and questions." An anthropology based on faith in the triune God explores all events of life—including "mental illness"—through the interpretative lens of this Creator-creature relationship.[20] The human being is thus understood from a threefold perspective: first, based on the knowledge of God the Creator—the human is made by the Father in his image; second, based on the knowledge of God the Redeemer—the human is one who as a sinner cannot fulfill God's purposes for his life alone and is in need of redemption by the Son; and finally, based on the knowledge of God the Lifegiver/Sanctifier—the human is in need of regeneration to become "alive" in Christ and grow in conformity to his image. The act of regeneration, though mysterious to us, causes one to be born of the Spirit of God—a true union between the Spirit of God/ Christ and the human spirit.[21]

The Father and the Creation of Human Being

In the book of Genesis, following the creation of light, heaven, earth, seas, vegetation, and animals, God on the sixth day created Adam, the first man, from the dirt of the earth. Wayne Grudem explains that the creation text brings to light God's lordship over his creation, and highlights the fact that creation came to being because of God's free will, and "it is to be used solely for His purposes, and that is to glorify Him."[22] Therefore, all our lives and circumstances that we encounter will providentially point to God's glory and his lordship over his creation (Isa 43:21; Eph 1:11–12; 1 Cor 10:31). This fact highlights that human lives have purpose and significance.

The first creation account introduces the human person as the pinnacle of God's creative activity. Moreover, it affirms human beings' unique

---

20. Shirley Guthrie is a systematic theologian who has developed a strategy for pastoral counseling drawing on central insights from Barth's theological anthropology. He presents a helpful example of how economic Trinity can be used as a model to deal with human issues in counseling. Guthrie, Jr., "Pastoral Counseling, Trinitarian Theology, and Christian Anthropology," 132; see also Hunsinger, *Theology and Pastoral Counseling*, 18.

21. For explanation of regeneration, see Frame, *Doctrine of God*, 74–75; Grudem, *Bible Doctrine*, 301–2; Berkhof, *Systematic Theology*, 468.

22. Grudem, *Bible Doctrine*, 129.

significance and dignity as created in the image of God himself.[23] Consider the following relevant texts from the first chapter of Genesis:

> Then God said, "Let Us make man in Our image, according to Our likeness; and let them rule." . . . And God created [*bara*] man in His own image, in the image of God He created him; male and female He created them. (Gen 1:26–27)

By "divine fiat," God created *adam*—"generic humanity." The verb used here for act of creating is *bara*. *Bara* stresses "the initiation of the object," not any manipulative act that may be necessary afterwards.[24] Clearly, the verse emphasizes God's creation of the essence of man, his inner person, and marks this creature—*adam*—as something special, resembling God. Created to reflect God's likeness, man stands out in distinction and superior to other creatures made on the same sixth day. Verse 27 shows that humankind was created as two sexes. James Beck and Bruce Demarest state, "The repeated affirmation that God created persons in His image signifies that both male and female possess a remarkable resemblance to Himself" in their inner persons, and both are "endowed with unparalleled dignity and worth."[25]

> And God saw all that He had made, and behold, it was very good (Gen 1:31).

Is this an absolute pronouncement about the nature of creation? Beck and Demarest claim, "The descriptor, 'very good,' denotes that the entire creation, including human persons, perfectly conforms to the divine will and is ideally suited to the purpose for which God created it." If God created the universe including persons for his own glory then it is expected that their design, whether we approve of that design or not, would ultimately fulfill God's purpose.[26]

In Genesis 2, God formed the human person from the dust of the earth, and breathed life into his material frame:

> Then the LORD God formed [*yatsar*] man of dust from ground, and breathed into his nostrils the breath of life [*nismat hayyim*]; and man became a living being [*nephes hayya*] (Gen 2:7).

---

23. Beck and Demarest, *The Human Person in Theology and Psychology*, 39.

24. Zodhiates, *Hebrew-Greek Key Word Study Bible*, 1716.

25. Beck and Demarest, *The Human Person in Theology and Psychology*, 39–40.

26. Ibid., 40.

This was not a mechanical act as if "He first formed a body of clay and then put a soul into it," explains Louis Berkhof; "When God formed the body, He formed it so that by the breath of His Spirit man at once became a living soul."[27] Here the verb *yatsar* (to form, to sculpt) is used in contrast to *bara* in verse 1:27, emphasizing that the act of creation took place once. Here, the emphasis is on how God formed man's structure and made him to become a living being, where in 1:27 the focus was on man's inner person to be a reflection of God's image. Although *nsama* ("breath") is also used of the life force that animates animals (Gen 7:22), according to Walther Eichrodt, "animals are produced and brought to life simply, so to speak, by the universal divine breath blowing through the whole of Nature." However, only in the case of the man is there recorded "a direct transfer of the divine breath" that constitutes the man "an independent spiritual I" and unique image of God.[28]

The body was made out of the dust of the ground, but the soul of the man came to life through a new substance, the breath of God. Berkhof believes that in these simple words—distinguishing the "dust" from ground and the "breath" of the living God—the twofold nature of man is clearly pronounced, and corroborated by other passages in Scripture (Eccl 12:7; Matt 10:28; Luke 8:55; 2 Cor 5:1–8; 1 Pet 3:19). The two elements are the "body" and the "spirit of life," and by the combination of the two, "man" became a "living soul." In fact, from Berkhof's perspective, man is a living soul who has a body and a spirit; "Thus, it may be said that man *has* spirit, but *is* soul."[29]

HUMAN ONTOLOGY—Considering the variety of positions in regards to the human constitution in contemporary debates, one could arrange them in three distinct broad categories: *monism, dualism,* and *trichotomism.*[30]

Broadly speaking, influenced by biblical references such as 1 Thessalonians 5:23 and Hebrews 4:12, Christian *Trichotomists*[31] see the three distinct components of the human to consist of: (1) a physical body—the source of all passions; (2) a soul—as the seat of rationality with reason,

---

27. Berkhof, *Systematic Theology*, 192.

28. Eichrodt, *Theology of the Old Testament*, 2:121.

29. Berkhof, *Systematic Theology*, 183, 194.

30. Beck and Demarest, *The Human Person in Theology and Psychology*, 120.

31. For examples of the trichotomist position, see Nee, *The Spiritual Man* and van Kooten, *Paul's Anthropology in Context*.

affection, and will; (3) a spirit—as the center of connection with God.[32] In this view, all people have a soul, and different faculties of the soul can either serve God or yield to sin. They argue that as the consequence of sin, the spirit of the human is dead before faith, and it comes to life when one receives the new life.[33]

In the *dualistic* views, soul (Heb. *nephesh* and Gk. *psyche*) and spirit (Heb. *ruach* and Gk. *pneuma*) both refer to the immaterial part of the human, and in many biblical texts it appears that they are used interchangeably. "This is the part that lives on after our bodies die," says Grudem. He emphasizes, "Those who hold this view often agree that Scripture uses the word 'spirit' . . . more frequently when referring to our relationship to God." Many people with dualistic views affirm that the biblical text portrays the human as a unified entity with a constant interaction between the "material" and the "immaterial" parts of which the person is made.[34] This interaction is of a great significance in the manifestation of "mental illness."

Until the early part of twentieth century, according to J. P. Moreland, the vast majority of Christian thinkers believed in substance dualism—body and soul/spirit. He states that "the mind[35]and spirit are faculties of the soul and the soul is an immaterial substantial reality that contains a person's various faculties of consciousness." Moreover, the soul is what "animates . . . and makes the body human."[36] Thomas Aquinas claimed, "we now proceed to treat of man, who is composed of a spiritual and corporeal substance."[37] Although humans are created as holistic unified persons, Moreland asserts that most Christians "ought to" believe in the preservation of "personal identity" in a "disembodied intermediate state."[38] The

32. Beck and Demarest, *The Human Person in Theology and Psychology*, 127.

33. The text used for this argument is Romans 8:10: "And if Christ is in you, though the body is dead because of sin, yet the spirit is alive because of righteousness." See Grudem, *Bible Doctrine*, 193.

34. Ibid., 193–94. Grudem points out: "in John 12:27, Jesus says, 'Now is my *soul* troubled,' whereas in a very similar context in the next chapter John says that Jesus was 'troubled in *spirit*' (John 13:21)."

35. The Old Testament does not have a specific word for mind; it is usually referred to by *leb* (heart), or *kilya* (kidney) or *ruach* (spirit), always referring to the innermost part of the person, Gk. *nous, dianoia, phronema*. Beck and Demarest, *The Human Person in Theology and Psychology*, 132–34.

36. Moreland, "Restoring the Soul to Christianity," 23–27.

37. Thomas Aquinas, *Summa Theologica*.

38. Moreland, "Restoring the Soul to Christianity," 23–27.

doctrine of intermediate state has been part of the faith of many Christians since the inception of the tradition. John Cooper, who has done a detailed exposition of this doctrine, points out that not everyone who advocates the "traditional view of the afterlife" is necessarily a dualist. For example, both G. C. Berkouwer and Herman Ridderbos strongly defend Pauline teaching of the intermediate state, yet both vehemently reject dualism.[39]

Nevertheless, according to Moreland, most people, Christian or non-Christian, consider dualism to be the natural response to how they perceive themselves. Many philosophers who reject the dualistic view, even, admit that it is "the common sense view."[40] Today, the concept of dualism is being challenged, not by atheists or non-believers who might consider Christianity to be very archaic, but rather by some sincere Christian theologians or philosophers. These people are pointing to scientific findings in brain sciences and making a case that "mind is something that matter *does.*" The mind emerges out of chemical interactions and electrical stimulations within the brain.[41] For many theologians and philosophers, this reliance of the mind on the brain has made the existence of a distinct self-activating entity such as the soul/mind questionable. This has serious implication for how psychiatrists treat mental illness, for it has caused them to embrace a reductionist view of human being, an entity that is only as good as its physical parts and its chemical construct.

Those who propose a holistic portrait of human nature and insist on the physicalness of its constitution insist that since "science has not yet discovered empirical evidence for the existence of the soul," we cannot assume that there is a reality distinct from the physical body. These *monists* claim that terms such as *mind, soul,* and *spirit* depict human beings from different perspectives, and have no bearing on the constitution of one's nature. Philosophically, *monism* consists of supporters of both *materialism* (also called *physicalism*), and *idealism or panpsychism* (contending that all is spiritual).[42] In today's contemporary debates, monists with a variety of views are presenting a challenge to the historical dualism of Christian faith.

39. Cooper, *Body, Soul, and Life Everlasting,* 159.

40. Moreland, "Restoring the Soul to Christianity," 23.

41. Welch, *Blame it on the Brain?,* 29–30.

42. Beck and Demarest, *The Human Person in Theology and Psychology,* 120–22; Cooper, *Body, Soul, and Life Everlasting,* 20 n.36. For detailed views in support of materialism, see Bultmann and Grobel, *Theology of the New Testament,* 1:209; Berkouwer, *Man,* 203; and Robinson, *The Body,* 16.

Joel Green is a New Testament theologian who argues for *ontological monism*. He admits that there is enough textual evidence in the New Testament for the dualistic reading to have gained support, but he dismisses that as "conceptual glossolalia."[43] Green is primarily concerned to take a stand against the Gnostic denigration of the body and individualistic spirituality and soteriology to the exclusion of relational issues of present life in the community of God's people. Yet Cooper, who has developed a cogent and popularly received position called "holistic dualism,"[44] considers Green's argumentations for an "alternative to the traditional position" to be "incomplete and unsound."[45] Green rejects the idea that Luke 16 has anything to do with an intermediate state and sees the characters acting as "human agents with a corporeal existence."[46] Cooper objects to this position and suggests that Green "avoids the topic" of intermediate state even when he comments on Luke 23:43—Jesus' conversation with the thief on the cross—and fails to "engage the debate about this important aspect of Luke's eschatology."[47] Green deals lightly with his alternative reading of 2 Corinthians 5:1–10 and admits that this text is "the most pressing evidence in Paul for a body-soul dualism," but argues that irrespective of Paul's inconsistent language, for him, "embodied existence is the norm."[48] Cooper notes that in an effort to avoid the debate about the disembodied intermediate state, Green "fails to consider" 2 Corinthians 5:6–9, 12:2–4 and Philippians 1:20–24—where Paul points to a separation from his body. In Cooper's view, Green brushes over evidence related to the intermediate state instead of directly "refuting it" or arguing for an alternative interpretation that would be "as comprehensive and coherent" as the traditional readings. Nonetheless, many Christian monists consider Green's exegetical reading of a materialistic human nature not only acceptable, but rather convincing.

One of the more vocal advocates of monism is Christian philosopher Nancey Murphy. Murphy advocates *non-reductive physicalism*, defining the person as "a physical organism whose complex functioning, both in society and in relation to God, gives rise to 'higher' human capacities

---

43. Green, "Bodies—that is, Human Lives," 173.

44. Cooper, *Body, Soul, and Life Everlasting*, 108.

45. Ibid., xxii.

46. Green, "Bodies—that is, Human Lives," 168.

47. Cooper, *Body, Soul, and Life Everlasting*, xxii.

48. Green, "Bodies—that is, Human Lives," 171–72.

such as morality and spirituality."[49] Murphy contends that Christians can remain faithful "with a view of the human being as a purely physical creation," because, "In the Hebrew Bible, human life is regularly understood monistically rather than dualistically, and this unified being is a physical being." She is not as concrete about the portrayal of humans in the New Testament, and perceives that those writers "recognize a variety of conceptions of the composition or makeup of the human being." However, she assures us, that they "do not *teach* body-soul dualism."[50]

It seems that Murphy et al. in their attempt to describe the "human nature that would allow for greater resonance between science and faith,"[51] have concluded that "humans are what you see," and nothing more; that is "there is not another invisible, non-material part of the individual that must be factored into the formula of understanding."[52] Warren Brown concludes that they see value in this position because it "allows one to accept and profit from both scientific and theological accounts of humankind." This is essential for reconciling theological and scientific accounts. Brown says: "If the human being is not divided into parts, such as body and soul, then explanations given by different disciplines and from difference [*sic*] perspectives must ultimately be seen as noncontradictory." It also seems that by reducing humans to one substance, they seek to remove some complexity. The "understanding of human nature," says Brown, is a "grandiose" task that they are trying to simplify, and make it "at least theoretically possible." But what if in their noble cause to reduce complexity, they destroy the identity of what they're studying? The aforementioned objectives run the risk of sacrificing theology at the altar of science in a realm that science is not well-equipped to address.

A. Pedro Barrajon skillfully challenges Murphy's and Brown's arguments, contending that if the spiritual realm cannot be detected by scientific methods, "that does not mean that [it does] not exist nor that there be not a form of knowledge different from that proposed by experimental sciences. . . . The soul cannot in effect be experienced by science, except by its spiritual activity." The question is whether we accept the existence of the

---

49. Murphy, "Human Nature," 25. Murphy has co-edited and contributed two chapters to *Whatever Happened to the Soul?*, which is a collection of articles by Christians from different walks of life, including some prominent biologists, psychologists, ethicists, philosophers, and theologians, all advocating for physicalism.

50. Murphy, "I Celebrate Myself," 24–25, cited in Cooper, *Body, Soul, and Life Everlasting*, xxiv–xxv..

51. Murphy, "Human Nature," xiii.

52. Brown, "Conclusion," 228.

spiritual realm or not, a concept which admittedly is culturally dissonant, but not necessarily philosophically obtuse. If the metaphysical level is not accepted, then everything has to be studied by empirical methods. But if the spiritual realm, as clearly presented in Scripture, is a reality, then it has to be studied by appropriate methods relevant to that realm. None of the hard sciences are able to study or handle the soul/spirit, because it is not conducive to their methodologies and falls outside of their field of investigation.[53]

Now, with all these debates, are recent philosophical and scientific developments sufficient for the "wholesale revisionism" or agnostic positions that some theologians advocate? "No," strongly responds Cooper. He points out that, like himself, the dualists are not caving in and theologians, philosophers, and scientists alike—such as J. P. Moreland, Scott Rae, Alvin Plantinga, Richard Swinburne, Jeffrey Boyd, Sir John Eccles (the Nobel Laureate for his work in brain physiology), and many others—strongly argue for the biblical evidence in support of dualism.[54] Cooper believes that none of the advancements in brain sciences and our understanding of the correlation of mental states and the brain functions justify favoring monism over "a doctrinally required dualism." He points to Nancey Murphy's candid statement about this. After researching the advances in brain sciences, she admits: "It is still possible to claim that there is a substantial

53. Barrajon, "The Soul in Theology," 462–63.

54. Moreland argues that regardless of how "widespread Christian monism" is, a careful exegetical reading of Scripture cannot sustain it. "Holy Scripture clearly teaches some form of anthropological dualism" (Moreland and Rae, *Body & Soul*, 23). Alvin C. Plantinga, "On Heresy, Mind, and Truth," 186: "Now I should confess upfront that I confess dualism." He continues to emphasize that dualism was accepted by Paul and is what the Christian creeds teach; Cooper, *Body, Soul, and Life Everlasting*, xviii.n9; and Swinburne, *The Evolution of the Soul*, 174, 310–11. Swinburne defends an anthropology in which humans are made of two substances, body and soul, which causally interact with each other, hence, "*dualistic interactionism*." He says, "A man's having a mental life must be understood as a non-bodily part of the man, his soul, having a mental life." Swinburne uses an analogy of a light bulb and a socket to argue that soul (like a light bulb) needs the brain (similar to a socket) to turn on and work. Thus, the breakage of either the bulb or the socket eliminates the light. He points out that it is the omnipotent God who sustains the soul, and even if the brain stops working, he is able to keep the soul alive. Boyd advocates a dualistic model of human constitution and believes that complexity of human characteristics such as consciousness, free will and sinful tendencies cannot be supported through materialistic models. See also Boyd, "What DNA Tells Us about the Human Soul," 142–59 and Eccles, *Facing Reality*, 173–74; he believes in Cartesian *dualistic interactionism*. He identifies "the subjective component of each of us," which is "the conscious self" as the soul. He believes that the soul "is non-material and hence is not subject in death to disintegration that affects all components of the individual . . . both the body and the brain."

mind and that its operations are neatly *correlated* with brain events. . . . It follows, then, that no amount of evidence from neuroscience can *prove* a physicalist view of the mental."[55]

As was previously explained, the body/soul debate is structured as brain/mind debate among neuroscientists and psychiatrists. For decades many brain scientists have hoped that sooner or later they will map a one-on-one causal connection between specific brain states and particular functions of the mind. According to Cooper, "science has not turned out that way."[56] It has not been easy to find a complete correlation between brain events and particular states of consciousness. The brain seems to function like a major network in which millions of inter-connected events have to work together to bring about a single thought or emotion. This does not mean that if one experiences the same thought or emotion repeatedly, the brain cells will go through the same connections every single time. In fact in some cases of those who have suffered from strokes or other damages, other parts of brain can take over to compensate for the damaged parts.[57] Furthermore, the complexity of interactions among brain cells specific to any mental state make it prohibitive to map the relation between the two. Thus, the "thesis that all mental events are correlated with specific kinds of brain events" is just a thesis that has not been proven.[58]

Even if a strict and consistent correlation between mental states and changes in the brain could be observed, this would not prove that the brain events were the cause of mental states. In fact the experience demonstrates that *brain states could easily be the effect of mental states*. This theory plays a big role in how mental illness should be evaluated. Brain scientists have observed that a person could easily generate complex brain events, for example, by visualizing an image, meditating on God, being anxious, or fearing something. In these cases it is clearly the mind that affects the brain; thus, *it is very possible that mental turmoil causes changes in the brain*. Therefore, according to neuroscience research, based on "hard empirical data," we can see two distinct "kinds of events—mental and physiological—each of which appears to be able to affect the other."

55. Cooper, *Body, Soul, and Life Everlasting*, xxvi; Murphy, *Human Nature*, 139.

56. Cooper, *Body, Soul, and Life Everlasting*, 206.

57. Jill Bolte Taylor is a neuroanatomist who experienced a massive stroke, and explains how her brain was retrained to relearn the functions it had lost resulted from her brain damage. Taylor, *My Stroke of Insight*.

58. Cooper, *Body, Soul, and Life Everlasting*, 206.

The actual mechanism behind this correlation is not detectable.[59] The famous brain surgeon and neurophysiologist Wilder Penfield declared:

> The nature of the mind presents . . . perhaps the most difficult and most important of all problems. For myself, after a professional lifetime spent in trying to discover how the brain accounts for the mind, it comes as a surprise now to discover . . . that the dualist hypothesis seems the more reasonable of the two possible explanations. . . . In the end I conclude that there is no good evidence, in spite of new methods . . . that the brain alone can carry out the work that the mind does. I conclude that it is easier to rationalize man's being on the basis of two elements than on the basis of one.[60]

Despite all of the advancements in brain sciences, Herman van Praag, the Emeritus Professor of Psychiatry at the universities of Groningen, Utrecht, and Maastricht, the Netherlands, and the Albert Einstein College of Medicine, New York, recently wrote:

> Today the brain reigns supreme in psychiatry at the expense of the mind. The mind is in danger to be usurped by the brain. Mind, so it is rumored in neurobiological circles, will eventually and probably pretty soon reveal its secrets via the study of the brain. . . . For the future of psychiatry, this reductionist viewpoint is risky. Psychiatrists cannot, with impunity, disregard an important domain of man's personality makeup. . . . It seems highly unlikely that in the foreseeable future, brain studies will provide useful information about the appearance of individual minds. As psychiatrists, we should continue to honor the mind in its own right. Let's not quench its luster by reducing it to sheer matter.[61]

Andrew Sims reiterates this point by explaining why spiritual experiences are more than mere "irritation of the brain." Even if a scientist can pinpoint all mental states and visions and beliefs to specific localities in the brain, this only explains where in the brain the experience was mediated. "[W]hen I look at and see a cherry tree," Sims explains, "there is electrical activity in my occipital cortex at the back of my brain." This does not mean that the cherry tree is not real and is only the effect of Sims's brain state.

59. Newberg et al., *Why God Won't Go Away*, 7, 36–37; Cooper, *Body, Soul, and Life Everlasting*, 207; and Clarke, *Madness, Mystery and the Survival of God*, 21.

60. Penfield, *The Mystery of the Mind*, 85, 114.

61. Van Praag, "Enlightenment and Dimmed Enlightenment."

Identifying brain locality of an experience does not *"explain away"* that experience, any more than "an analysis of the wood fiber *explains away* the meaning of what is written on this page."[62] Consequently, the argument that brain causes "mental illness" merely due to observation of changes in the brain is questionable. The changes could very well be the byproduct of the turbulence in a person's soul, spirit, and mind.

Kenneth Kendler, a psychiatrist and a philosopher, a hard-core biological/genetic researcher, attempts to offer a "coherent conceptual and philosophical framework for psychiatry." He claims that psychiatry needs to go beyond the "temptations of simplistic reductionist models" and "embrace complexity" of mind-brain interrelationship and accept that, "In ways we can observe but not yet fully understand, subjective, first-person mental phenomena have causal efficacy in the world. They affect our brains and our bodies and through them the outside world." For him, "both brain → mind and mind → brain causality are real," and psychiatrists who reject this reality are doing it to their own and their patient's peril.[63]

As demonstrated here, the brain/mind (or body/soul) relations continue to be hotly debated not only among theologians but among neuroscientists and psychiatrists as well. However, regardless of distinct perspectives on human ontology, there seems to be an emerging consensus among most theologians that God created humans as holistic entities. Cooper offers a distinction between "functional holism" and "ontological holism" to drive at his model of "holistic dualism." In *functional holism* "the body-soul complex is a deeply integrated unity with a vastly complicated, intricate array of mutual functional dependence and causal connections." Functional holism allows for the soul to exist independent from the body, but certainly sustained by God at all times. *Ontological holism* argues that "mental constituents" of a person are "ontologically dependent" on a properly functioning brain and thus no disembodiment is possible. In Cooper's model, "A holistic entity could conceivably be constituted out of any number of metaphysical substances or principles." These distinct substances of a whole may exist independent from each other, yet "without all the properties and capacities they had when integrated within the whole." Thus, there is a "phenomenological," "functional," and "existential" unity, yet the "whole" at the bottom is not a "single homogeneous substance."[64]

62. Sims, *Is Faith Delusion?*, 111.

63. Kendler, "Toward a Philosophical Structure for Psychiatry," 433–40.

64. Cooper, *Body, Soul, and Life Everlasting*, xxvii, 45–46; Moreland and Rae, *Body & Soul*, 21.

It is striking that, despite the widespread consensus that Jesus Christ is the ultimate model for humanity, much of the contemporary theological anthropology has failed to center its formulations of human ontology in a Christocentric context. If Christ is the perfect human person, what must we believe about human ontology? The analysis of scientific and philosophical investigations into the nature of the brain and mind are rarely done through the christological lens.[65] For example, Nancey Murphy has stated that the emerging positions on the mind/brain debates may have "implications for thinking about the person of Christ," but she fails to reverse the direction of her analysis to evaluate how human constitution ought to be perceived in light of who Jesus was. In fact, she goes as far as saying that with recent scientific findings, and the "recognition of the continuity of humans with the whole of nature," it is time for "reconsideration of the scope of God's final transformative act."[66] She is so certain of human understanding of self that she is willing to fundamentally question the history of revelation in the Christian tradition.

In fact most christological models used for understanding human beings are limited to Jesus' actions and behaviors and what he "reveals as the *exemplar* of true human living."[67] Regardless of the value of such models, it is a very limited lens through which to understand the nature of a human person christologically. Nellas argues for *imitatio Christi* to be understood as an internal mode of "*Christification*" to be transformed to his likeness rather than a mere "external imitation." This ontological likeness will lead to moral imitation.[68]

For Barth, the priority of Jesus' subjective experience over any physical agents is of "decisive importance . . . in the anthropology of Jesus."

65. Cortez makes a point that, even when a theologian is clearly committed to the Christocentric approach to anthropology, such as Ray Anderson who makes his anthropological arguments based on Barth's Christocentric anthropology, he never addresses what implications this christological model has on human ontology. Cortez, "Embodied Souls, Ensouled Bodies," 6.

66. Murphy, "Human Nature," 23.

67. Cortez, "Embodied Souls, Ensouled Bodies," 6.

68. Nellas and Russell, *Deification in Christ*, 39, 136–39, 153–54; cited in Cortez, "Embodied Souls, Ensouled Bodies," 7 n. 14. It seems as if Nellas is arguing that imitation is more ontological than moral. The question one should ask is: What is the relationship between Christ's ontology and his morality? Could it be that it is the abundance of Divine Spirit in him that brings his perfection? John Owen argues that the Holy Spirit is what caused the Son's *imaging of God* in Jesus' humanity. See Owen, *The Works*, 3:168–69, cited in McDonald, "The Pneumatology of the 'Lost' Image in John Owen," 327.

When man "thinks and wills," claims Barth, "the soul proceeds," and "the body follows."[69] But stressing the holistic nature of Christ as the model of humanity, he points to the fact that Christ's body and soul are inseparable; yet, it is *always* the spiritual realm that is directing him, and interestingly, this invisible reality always manifests in a physical form. Barth says:

> He does not fulfill His office and His work from His miraculous annunciation to His fulfillment in such a way that we can separate His outer form from His inner or His inner form from His outer. *Everything* is the revelation of an inner, invisible, *spiritual* plane of life. But it is almost more striking and characteristic that everything has an outer, visible, bodily form.[70]

According to Cortez, "Any view of the human person, on Barth's account, that gave primacy to the body in the activity of the person, would, therefore, undermine the biblical account of Jesus' person and work." For Barth, it is "a series of key christological principles from which anthropological reflection must begin." However, it must always be done in a way that "anthropology is not reduced *to* Christology." We should avoid collapsing the two into one another.[71]

IN THE IMAGE OF GOD — Throughout the church ages the portrayal of humanity as being in the image of God has been intensively analyzed, resulting in varied and diverse hypotheses and sentiments concerning the meaning of *imago Dei* in Scripture. From ancient Jews to contemporary theologians, from philosophers to psychologists, scholars have debated for centuries about God's statement, "Let Us make man in our image, according to our likeness," leading to various conclusions.

The significance of the topic invites renewed attention any time we gaze at profound human challenges (e.g., deep suffering caused by mental illness) and seek to understand them in the context of God's image in the human person. We will not attempt a comprehensive survey and synthesis of *imago Dei* here, but will focus upon those elements that will have direct impact on questions with which this study is concerned.[72] There is little exegetical consensus about the phrase in Genesis 1:26, so that it plays vir-

---

69. Barth, *Church Dogmatics*, 3/2:418.

70. Ibid., 3/2:327; emphasis mine.

71. Cortez, "Embodied Souls, Ensouled Bodies," 99, 217.

72. Overstreet has developed a detailed historical survey of well-known theologians' perspectives on the *image of God*. See Overstreet, "Man in the Image of God."

tually no role in theological formulations of the Old Testament. However, it dominates the anthropology of the New Testament, and there is almost a universal agreement that in the New Testament it is clearly identified with the person of Jesus Christ as the true image of the invisible God (2 Cor 4:4; Col 1:15).

LeRon Shults points out that the significance of *imago Dei* for Christians comes from the fact that it points to Jesus. Since Jesus is the true *imago Dei*, then the "ultimate reality" of being "human" requires partaking of His life.[73] Van Hyssteen echoes the significance of humanity sharing in the life of God revealed in Christ. Humanity, he says, "is intrinsically oriented to life with God in the Spirit as disclosed in Jesus Christ who alone is the true image of God."[74] Thus, in our anthropological formulation, *imago Dei* plays a vital role. After all, if Jesus, the perfect human person, is the true image of God, what does that say about the rest of humanity? How might God be transforming humanity to that true *imago*?[75]

While affirming the true reflection of *imago Dei* in the person of Jesus, how should one interpret the chasm between the image emanating from Him, in contrast to the rest of humanity? Where does this likeness lie between God and humans, or God and Jesus? Did humans totally lose the image as a result of sin? Or is it merely marred and defaced? Was the image meant to be shared among all humanity, or was it a special gift for people of faith? What is the mystery behind restoration of the image if it is lost or damaged? What does it mean to our daily lives? Have we mixed up the specific identification of the image with the implications resulting from it? Is the image part of our ontology (*substantive* interpretation), or is it about our role and functionality in life on earth (*functional* interpretation), or is it about our relational capacities (*relational* interpretation)?[76]

Many theologians, ancient and modern, see the image of God in humans as the capacity to imitate God and grow to be more and more in His likeness. Nonna Verna Harrison emphasizes that for the early church fathers "there is no imitation except through participation in the

73. Shults, *Reforming Theological Anthropology*, 220.

74. Van Huyssteen, *Alone in the World?*, 125.

75. See further explanation of a Christological perspective of the *imago Dei*: Watson, *Text and Truth*, 277–304; Marshall, "Being Human: Made in the Image of God," 55; and McFarland, *The Divine Image*, 4.

76. Some have added other categories to these commonly used groupings, such as *existential* (closely associated with the relational view of neo-orthodoxy) and *eschatological* interpretations (e.g., Moltmann's). See Shults, *Reforming Theological Anthropology*, 233–40, and Van Huyssteen, *Alone in the World?*, 126.

archetype," which can only be granted through God's gracious gift of Self.[77] Thus, bearing God's image necessarily meant *participating* in the life of the Trinity. Therefore, *theosis* played a key role in the Patristic foundation of any anthropological formulation. This did not necessarily mean "a glorious transfiguration of the human person"; but it was about sharing in and having union with the Spirit of God and the "communal life" of the Trinity. The common belief tends to limit this understanding of *imago Dei* to the Greek fathers or Cappadocians in particular. Harrison makes a case that "recent patristic scholarship has shown that the Cappadocians and Augustine agree . . . more than is sometimes supposed." The fathers understood "*imago Dei* primarily in Christological" terms.[78] According to this view, without faith in Christ the image cannot be manifested in the person. Moreover, "the *imago Dei* means . . . the inmost core of the human person is ontologically connected to God. This point of contact enables us to enter into communion with God and participate in divine life."[79]

Some of the fathers distinguished between image and likeness. Irenaeus is considered to be the "earliest significant" commentator on the doctrine of *Imago*, which the church took henceforth as standard. He held that man, after the Fall, continued to possess the image (*tselem*) of God, but lost his likeness (*demuth*). From an etymological perspective, *tselem* meant representation, and *demuth* meant imitation. Thus the "image was construed to be the basic natural *form* of the human, while likeness was taken to mean the supernaturally endowed *function* of existing in right relation to the Creator."[80] It is only through the work of Christ that man can receive the "robe of sanctity," which is the likeness of God and it is granted *only* through the *Spirit*. Thus, "likeness" comes by the work of the Spirit as mediator of righteousness. This was a promise seed in Adam that anticipated the work of Christ, and Adam lost it as a result of the Fall. For

77. Harrison, "Greek Patristic Foundations of Trinitarian Anthropology," 399.

78. Ibid., 400. The Greek fathers and Augustine alike strongly advocated the relationship between participation in the Spirit of Christ and formation of *imago*. Augustine wrote: "But the soul's beatitude, by which it is made happy, cannot be, except by participation of that ever-living life and unchanging and eternal substance which is God. . . . It is made blessed by participation in God." For him this is possible only because of Christ's Incarnation and by grace. According to Bonner, Augustine was "prepared to equate justification and deification, regarding both as the consequence of man's adoption," and insisted that "our renewal and reform to the image of God is a process which, begun in baptism, is the work of a lifetime." See Bonner, "Augustine's Conception of Deification," 373, 384, 381.

79. Harrison, "Greek Patristic Foundations of Trinitarian Anthropology," 401.

80. Anderson, *On Being Human*, 216–17.

Irenaeus, there was a clear distinction between a human's natural nature (image) and the supernatural nature (likeness) potentially endowed by the Spirit consequent to the work of Christ.[81]

Augustine continued with Irenaeus' view of separation between image and likeness, yet for him the "Primitive State" was a state of perfection. In Irenaeus's view *likeness* grew as the person matured spiritually; but in Augustine Adam was created with an "original state of perfection." Augustine was influenced by Neo-Platonist concepts and had a "mystical concept of *imago*," which was the essence of a "person in love and knowledge of God," but his commitment to Scripture and Trinitarian self-love made his approach to *imago* very *pneumatological*. Andrew Louth remarks, for Augustine, "An image is like that of which it is the image, but less than it. . . . The image seeks to return to that of which it is the image—it longs for its archetype." Augustine created a dichotomy between the rational soul and spiritual soul; the former holding a lower level of knowledge, and the latter holding knowledge of God. The Fall virtually destroyed the image with the loss of true knowledge and love of God. As a result of the Fall the soul has turned away from eternal truths to engagement in corporeal realities. Augustine's views strongly influenced Aquinas, Luther, and Calvin.[82]

Thomas Aquinas defined the image as the rational soul and identified it as being about how humans relate to God. Drawing on Aristotalian concepts of human nature, he defined the progression of image through three stages: (1) common to all men and inherent to their nature is the intellectual *aptitude to understand* God and love God; (2) those who have been justified by grace *actually understand* who God is and love him, though not perfectly; (3) finally, those who are blessed enough to *know and love God perfectly*, carry the image that is "in the likeness of glory." In a sense, there is an image at the time of *creation*, another one at the time of *regeneration*, and yet another one (that is a perfect likeness) at the time of *glorification*.[83]

With the Reformation, both Luther and Calvin built their anthropological models on an Augustinian foundation, each adding their own emphasis. Luther broke with the thirteen-centuries-old tradition of distinction between image and likeness. He pointed out that if the image was about the natural soul, then this meant that Satan carried the image of

---

81. Irenaeus, "Church Fathers."

82. Anderson, *On Being Human*, 217–18; Brunner, *Man in Revolt*, 506; Louth, *Christian Mystical Tradition*, 153, 147.

83. Aquinas, *Summa Theologica*.

God, since he was given the same natural qualities—a scenario he force-fully rejected. To Luther man was a "theological being" who could only be understood in the light of Scripture. His challenge was to explain the relationship of the image to a fallen man. His answer to what remains was "*Relics of imago.*"[84] For Luther, the significance of the image was to show that humans "were created 'by a special plan and providence of God' for a better spiritual life in the future," which would come through the gospel of Christ.[85]

While Luther believed that the *imago* was virtually destroyed as a consequence of the fall, Calvin believed that despite total "defacing" of the *imago*, God bestowed his "common grace" upon humanity, such that they can continue their human existence—though in sin—distinct from other animals. While this vestige of the image has no soteriological relevance, it is nevertheless fundamental to what it means to be human. Calvin took Paul's references to image in Colossians 3:10 and Ephesians 4:24 and in-terpreted them as the image referring to *knowledge* (of God), *righteousness* and, *holiness*. Even though Calvin granted that the *imago* "was not totally annihilated" in Adam, he still saw it to be "so corrupted" that whatever had survived was "frightful deformity."[86] Calvin, like Luther, centered the *imago* in relation to God rather than in an intrinsic natural reason.[87]

To Calvin, it was a "settled principle" that the image of God was "spiritual." He attacked those who attributed image to anything other than man's soul or spirit and accused them of mingling "heaven and earth." Therefore it is only at "the end of regeneration" that Christ will "reform us to God's image." The progressive process is shown when Paul teaches: "we . . . with unveiled face beholding as in a mirror the glory of the Lord are being transformed into the same image" (2 Cor 3:18). Thus it is the image of Christ as the perfect human that is the image of God to which we are *being* conformed.[88]

John Owen is another Reformed theologian who emphasizes the loss of image through sin, such that it is only present in the person of Jesus as the perfect human, and "derivatively" in those who are united to him by his Spirit. McDonald points out, "On the whole, the historic Reformed

---

84. Brunner, *Man in Revolt*, 507–8; Anderson, *On Being Human*, 218–19.

85. Van Huyssteen, *Alone in the World?*, 129.

86. Calvin, *Institutes*, 1/15.4.

87. Anderson, *On Being Human*, 219; Brunner, *Man in Revolt*, 508–9; Shults, *Reforming Theological Anthropology*, 227–29.

88. Calvin, *Institutes*, 1/15.3–4.

tradition attempts to eschew an absolute either/or on this question for a nuanced both/and." Representatives of the tradition usually do this by distinguishing the "creational" aspect of image representing a "facultative emphasis" against the "soteriological" aspect reflecting "relational emphasis." This allows the sustenance of image as "an abiding, albeit distorted and misdirected" character of the creation of a human person. Owen "severely minimizes" this division of facultative and relational aspects of image, and his overall outlook places him further on the spectrum, toward the "utter loss" of the image. The image, for Owen, is centered on holiness and righteousness, as it is for Calvin.[89] Wherefore, lacking this holiness and "*conformity* unto God," we have lost the capacity to "stand in that relation unto God which was designed us in our creation." We lost all that "blessedness" and "pre-eminence" of our original state "by the entrance of sin."[90]

Owen goes on to emphasize that if we do not acquire the image again, we will "always come short," and will not be able to fulfill the "end of our creation." We are called unto a true "*intercourse*" and a real "*communion with God.*" One must endeavor to attain this by surrendering to the sanctifying work of the Spirit unto holiness. He who fails in this will "always misseth both of his end, his rule, and his way."[91] Even when he speaks of those who have been justified, and regenerated, he says:

> [T]hough all children do partake of the nature of their parents, yet they may be . . . very deformed and bear very little of their likeness. So . . . we may have the image of God and yet come short of that likeness unto him, in its degrees and improvements that we ought to aim at.[92]

Many of those "who have had extraordinary gifts of the Spirit," or are living in "rigid austerities," or "renunciation of the world," or "outward works of charity," are even considered "vessels of wood and stone," who being "not purged from sin," cannot be used by God for purposes they were created.[93] The answer consists, therefore, "alone in that likeness unto God,"

89. McDonald, "The Pneumatology of the 'Lost' Image in John Owen," 324–25.

90. John Owen et al., *The Works of John Owen*, 3:129.

91. Ibid., 3:129–30.

92. Owen, *The Works*, 3:578 as cited in McDonald, "The Pneumatology of the 'Lost' Image in John Owen," 325.

93. He refers to Matthew 7:22–23, saying: "Many will say to Me on that day, Lord, Lord, did we not prophesy in Your name, and in Your name cast out demons, and in Your name perform many miracles? And then I will declare to them, 'I never knew you; Depart from Me, you who practice lawlessness.'"

which can be restored, by the grace of God, through the work of the Spirit, in union with Christ.[94]

Owen places tremendous emphasis on the work of the Spirit as the "efficient cause of all external divine operations" in our lives; so, "all our ascending towards Him" begins in our spirit connecting to his Spirit. Thus, "the restoration of the image" can only happen when people grow in the likeness to Christ through the "mortification" of their flesh, which is the sanctifying work of the Holy Spirit.[95] "Indwelling sin always abides whilst we are in the world; therefore it is always to be mortified," says Owen. It seems like, for Owen, faith in Christ is the beginning of the process, which reorients the person toward God. But only as sin is "mortified," through an *ongoing* and *progressive* work of sanctification by the Spirit, can conformity to Christ—the true image—begin to appear.[96]

In the post-Reformation era there were not any essential contributions to the doctrine of the *imago Dei*. Most everyone continued with teachings of Luther, Calvin, and Augustine. With the growth of humanism taught by the Enlightenment, many returned to the scholastic notion of a rational soul representing the image of God. Because of biblical and scientific criticism the questions about "the primitive state of human prior to the fall" fell off scholarly radars. Later theologians have not generated ideas that would address the traditional issues; they have been mostly absorbed in questions raised with the scientific advancements.[97]

The view espoused by Karl Barth, and shared by several contemporary theologians, is that image has to do with man's capacity for personal *relationship*.[98] Humans can reflect God's image only in community and as God is relational in himself, so has he created humans to be. Barth originally believed with Luther that the *imago* was totally lost with the Fall, but later modified his position by insisting that a human person could not lose what he never owned.[99] Drawing on Barth, Anderson says, "The human

---

94. Owen et al., *The Works of John Owen*, 3:140–41.

95. Ibid., 3:161, 200, 386 as cited in McDonald, "The Pneumatology of the 'Lost' Image in John Owen," 326, 331.

96. One of Owen's most influential works in the Reformed tradition has been his treatise on *The Mortification of Sin*, which he wrote in 1656 while he was the Dean of Christ Church and Vice-Chancellor of the University of Oxford; it is in this treatise that he deals in great exegetical detail with how fleshly sin will be mortified by the power of the Holy Spirit unto holiness. Owen, *The Mortification of Sin*, 13.

97. Anderson, *On Being Human*, 220.

98. Ibid., 76.

99. Barth, *Church Dogmatics*, 3/1:200.

person is not created to *be* the image and likeness of God, but rather created *in* the image of God." This means that human identity is defined by its intrinsic constitution as a communion among human beings, which is their interrelatedness. Barth believes that Genesis 1:27 is a commentary on Genesis 1:26. The fact that God made humans as male and female in His own image points to the fact that "co-humanity is itself the *imago*." He argued that the image was to be seen in the man-woman relationship as a type for all other relationships in community.[100]

The prevailing view among contemporary theologians is that *imago Dei* describes humans in their current state, and that it must not be applied to an aspect of human existence that was lost as a result of the Fall. These theologians mostly give the biblical image an existential interpretation with a "relational" twist. In their view, biblical language must be applied to current human existence, rather than focusing on the first man and woman. Niebuhr and Tillich are examples of theologians who believe that humans are relational beings, longing for a relationship with a God who has set human beings apart from other beings, to love and be loved.[101] Likewise, there seems to be a general agreement that the fact that man and woman were created in the image of God is primarily pointing to—even if the image does not consist in this—the human's exalted position in the created world and his preeminence in the eyes of God. Many theologians point to the redeeming sacrifice of Christ to argue the value and eminence of humans in God's economy.

Of this variety of conclusions about what constitutes the image of God in the human person, the view shared by conservative theologians who have an exalted view of Scripture as the word of God points to a profound corruption of the image as a result of the Fall. Moreover, they agree that the restoration of *imago Dei* is an essential element of God's redemptive act through Christ. How shall this lost or damaged image be restored? How might this loss of image influence our understanding of insanity? Where is the image of God in the midst of madness? The concept of *imago Dei* will inform our anthropological framework as we move forward in search of answers to these questions.

100. Anderson, *On Being Human*, 221–23; Brunner, *Man in Revolt*, 514.

101. Tillich, *Systematic Theology*, and Niebuhr, *The Nature and Destiny of Man*, 1:161–65. For an analysis of contemporary views see Shults, *Reforming Theological Anthropology*, 233–42.

The Redeeming Son and the Human Being

It is in the person and the work of Jesus Christ that the nature of the human being is truly revealed. In an economic Trinitarian picture of God, we know him not only as our Creator, but also as our Redeemer. According to Frame, the act of redemption is "to rescue or deliver from bondage" through a payment. He points to Leviticus 25:47–53, where a poor man faced with his inability to pay his debt may "sell himself into slavery." He can redeem himself later—if he prospers—or he can be redeemed by a blood relative who is willing to pay his debt.[102]

The biblical narrative portrays the human person in the bondage of sin, with an inner struggle that he cannot overcome on his own. Frame says: "Scripture is a book about redemption from sin. Contrary to many false religions and philosophies, our problem is sin, not finitude."[103] Paul portrays the human person as one with constant struggle between his nature and the will of God (Rom 7:14–19). Brunner points out that "man" can only be understood in terms of the contradiction he is in: "the contradiction between Creation and Sin"; and this is not "'something in' the actual man; it is himself." Furthermore, this contradiction can only be understood from "the standpoint of faith . . . namely, in the Word of God," and never from "the point of view of an *a priori* philosophy."[104]

In this study we accept the historicity of the Fall of Adam as articulated in the orthodox Reformed tradition.[105] All those who affirm the historicity of the Fall agree that something destructive happened to the human person. The teaching of Scripture realistically points to diminished functioning of the humankind by the effects of sin. All humans with their fallen nature are impaired and not able to know God and to live their lives in ways intended for them by their Creator. The human mind is distorted by sin impacting one's perception of reality. Sin has affected the human's affections, longings, understanding, values, sense of right and wrong and personal functioning. The book of James refers to the worldly wisdom, void of spiritual sight, as "earthly, natural, [and] demonic" (Jas 3:15). The unregenerate boast of their freedom, but Berkouwer asserts that "the call

102. Frame, *Doctrine of God*, 373–74.

103. Ibid., 401.

104. Brunner, *Man in Revolt*, 478.

105. Calvin, *Institutes*, 1/15.4,6–8; Grudem, *Bible Doctrine*, 210–18; Berkhof, *Systematic Theology*, 223–64; Frame, *Doctrine of God*, 339; Boice and Ryken, *The Doctrines of Grace*, 71–73; Beck and Demarest, *The Human Person in Theology and Psychology*, 230–45.

for freedom, which can be heard in all ages . . . is nothing but the lust for lawlessness."[106] The fallen human is not even able to love according to God's plan and suffers from a distorted love: his love is for self (2 Tim 3:2), the world (1 John 2:15), wickedness (2 Pet 2:15), money (1 Tim 6:10; 2 Tim 3:2; Heb 13:5), and pleasure (2 Tim 3:4). According to the words of the Preacher, all of humankind suffers from "insanity . . . in their hearts throughout their lives" (Eccl 9:3). From a scriptural perspective, natural man is truly "insane." By appropriating the new life, Christ offers a renewal to all aspects of the human's existence.[107]

The goal of this segment is to focus on the person of the Redeemer, and the solution God offered humanity to bring them out of bondage and out of their fallen state into the right relationship with him. The lifelong process of reviving the *imago Dei*—severely damaged by sin—begins with the new birth. Through the work of the Holy Spirit those grafted into Christ can enjoy a union with him and be renewed by the life that flows through him. This is what Peter referred to as "partaking of the divine nature" (2 Pet 1:4). Through regeneration and lifelong sanctification, people of God are transformed to the image of Christ, who is the true image of God (2 Cor 3:18, 4:4). Christ is the ideal and perfect human (John 19:5), the Last Adam who is also "the Life-giving Spirit" (1 Cor 15:45), and the model for the new humanity that God is bringing into existence. The Scriptures from Genesis to Revelation reveal a redemptive narrative, established by the Father, as the *goal of humanity*: to be conformed to the image of his Son (Rom 8:29).

Considering the significance of this redeeming transformation, how *ought we* to view this "conforming to the image of Christ"? What are the changes that happen in the human nature for it to be changed? Referring to Ezekiel 11:20 and 36:26–27, Frame points out that God regenerates his people by putting his own Spirit *in* them, and giving them a new heart.[108] Grudem expands on the same text:

> Through [Ezekiel] God promised a time in the future when he
> would give new spiritual life to his people: "A *new heart* I will
> give you, and a *new spirit I will put within you*; and I will take
> out of your flesh the heart of stone and give you a heart of flesh.
> And I will put my spirit within you, and cause you to walk in

106. Berkouwer, *Man*, 330.

107. For a more detailed exposition of the effects of sin, see, Beck and Demarest, *The Human Person in Theology and Psychology*, 238–43.

108. Frame, *Doctrine of God*, 50.

my statutes and be careful to observe my ordinances" (Ezek 36:26–27 [RSV]).[109]

God the Father, through the redeeming work of Christ, puts his Spirit *in* the sinners and changes their nature—a true Trinitarian work of salvation and regeneration.

Our focus in this study is the anthropological dimension of this soteriological process—the *transformation of the human condition* that believers experience. How is it that the *imago Dei* is restored in the person? How is a person engrafted into Christ and become a partaker of his Spirit? How does one escape the corruption of his nature and becomes a "partaker of divine nature" as God promised through Peter?[110] What is the appropriate anthropological framework for understanding the human experience in this transformation? How might that anthropological framework inform our understanding of the journey through madness?

Norman Russell argues that "attainting *likeness*" (*homoiosis*) to God and participation (*methexis*) in God are the foundational elements upon which the Patristic tradition developed the concept of *deification* or *theosis*. These concepts represent "the relationship between Being and becoming, between that which exists in an absolute sense and that which exists contingently." Thus, references to deification are about restoring the image and participating in the divine life.[111] Benjamin Blackwell, building on Russell's "twin pillars," describes deification "as the process of restoring likeness to God, primarily experienced as incorruption and sanctification, through a participatory relationship with God mediated by Christ and the Spirit." It is through this process that "believers become adopted sons of God, even gods, by grace and not by nature."[112]

Drawing on both Irenaeus and Cyril of Alexandria, Blackwell points to their notion of deification as a way to explain restoration of likeness to God and partaking in his divine life, and their use of Pauline texts to support their conclusions. In the context of Psalm 82, both men recognize believers with the "appellation of 'gods,'" and they relate that to Pauline texts in regards to union with Christ, immortality, sanctification, and adoption as sons of God. Blackwell writes: "As believers experience this deifying

109. Grudem, *Bible Doctrine*, 300.

110. "For by these He has granted to us His precious and magnificent promises, in order that by them you might become *partakers of the divine nature*, having escaped the corruption that is in the world by lust" (2 Pet 1:4).

111. Russell, *The Doctrine of Deification*, 1–2.

112. Blackwell, "Christosis," 234–35.

move the image and likeness of God is restored through a participatory relationship with God mediated by Christ and the Spirit." He points out that this aspect of Pauline soteriology has been "routinely missed or underplayed" by Western theologians; he renames the phenomenon "*Christosis*" to highlight deification through participation *in* Christ.[113] Based on his analysis of the soteriological language used by church fathers such as Irenaeus and Cyril of Alexandria (e.g., "union," "communion," "participation," and "deification") in contrast to Paul's, he states, "we conclude that the anthropological dimension of Paul's soteriology is equivalent to deification."[114]

Paul's "image language" often "refers to the telos of humanity"— believers are set to become conformed to the image of Christ. Blackwell points to Paul's use of "variety of 'morphic' terms" to describe the way believers become like Christ—union with Christ, to be in Christ, incorporation into Christ, conforming to Christ, etc.[115] Paul also puts great emphasis on suffering as a condition for conforming to Christ and participating in his life (Rom 6:5). Blackwell explains Paul's view on the *necessity* of suffering:

> Suffering is not merely an instantiation of corruption from which the gift of eschatological incorruption will bring release (Rom 8:18–23). It also allows believers to embody the narrative of Christ. This metaphorical death with Christ is regularly associated with a corresponding experience of life as the result or outcome.[116]

We must not minimize the significance of Paul's calling the believers to conform not only to Christ's life, but also to his death. In regards to knowing Christ, Paul states that he has given up everything that he "may know Him, and the power of His resurrection and the fellowship of His sufferings, being conformed to His death," in order that he "may attain to the resurrection from the dead" (Phil 3:10–11). It is only through "fellowship of Christ's sufferings" that believers can experience the power of his resurrection. It is embodying his death and life that will culminate in an experience of divine and heavenly glory and immortality. According to

113. Ibid., i–1.

114. Ibid., 239–45. As stated earlier, according to Bonner, this appears to have been Augustine's view too.

115. Ibid., 238.

116. Ibid., 242.

Blackwell, "Paul makes conformation to Christ's suffering and death as central as conformation to His resurrection life."[117] Anderson notes that our point of departure has to be "crucified humanity of Christ," for us to grasp "true order of humanity" as revealed through Jesus' resurrection. The link between "Jesus of Nazareth as the crucified one" and "Christ the Lord as the resurrected one" is an "indispensible foundation" for formulation of any theological anthropology.[118] In the course of our investigation, we will be guided by this transformation of the human condition that believers in Christ will experience. We will focus on what it means to share in Christ's death and life. If the prerequisite for knowing the power of Christ's resurrection, and "the fellowship of His sufferings," is to "count all things to be loss" (Phil 3:8, 10), as Paul proclaimed, how does this inform our understanding of insanity?

Jesus told Nicodemus that unless one is "born of Spirit" he cannot enter the kingdom of God (John 3:5). What does the process of new birth of the Spirit entail? If this is a true process, and not metaphorical, how are we to understand it? How does one who is *dead* in sin partake in the life of Christ and become a "living being"? If the restoration of the image and the transformation of the human condition depend on the union with Christ and participation in his Life through the Spirit, then we should attempt to understand how this is achieved.

The Life-Giving Spirit and the Human Being

The doctrine of union with Christ—through which his life flows into the members of his mystical body, by the power of his Spirit—has been very prominent in Eastern Christianity.[119] In the East, several individuals have extensively and directly addressed the divine participation and union with Christ. Athanasius is the one who popularized the phrase, "He became human, in order that we might be divinized."[120] John Piper, the influential Reformed theologian and clergyman, has written concerning Athanasius's view of soteriology: "It's true that Athanasius deals with salvation mainly in terms of restoring the image of God in man by Christ's taking human nature into union with the divine nature." Piper does not deny that

117. Ibid, 243.

118. Anderson, *On Being Human*, 18.

119. Louth, "The Place of Theosis in Orthodox Theology," 33–34.

120. Swope, "Spirit-to-Spirit Model of Christian Union with God," 20 n. 5; the phrase was originally coined by Irenaeus.

Athanasius's language about deification is quite mysterious to contemporary Western ears. "But what he saw we may be blind to," Piper admits. "The implications of the incarnation are vast, and one reads Athanasius with the sense that we are paupers in our perception of what he saw."[121] For Athanasius, Louth explains, soul is not an eternal entity that can connect to God by nature. It is only by God's grace that "soul is divinized, or better, man is divinized, as he is restored to conformity with the image of God." Soul is like a "mirror" that when it "has put off every stain of sin," becomes "pure" enough to reflect the image of God, or "becomes more truly that image."[122]

Throughout the centuries, theologians, pastors, and philosophers alike have been challenged to understand divine union precisely. John Swope has developed an anthropological model based on Paul's view of union with Christ as depicted in 1 Corinthians 6:17: "But he who unites himself with the Lord is one with Him in spirit."[123] He points to the Scriptural teaching that by the work of Jesus a true union—not metaphorical, or moral, or symbolic—happens between a believer and the person of Christ. This "Spirit-to-spirit" union is how the life of Christ flows into the deadness of the fallen human, regenerates him and makes "the dry bones" come back to life.[124] This union is to be understood not as one in which the human person or Christ are "ontologically confused or absorbed," but rather, as a "mutual indwelling" in which the two persons by the way of their spirits "form a durative bond of unity." This union takes place merely by the grace of God; there is nothing an individual can do to bring it about on his own; it is given as a gift. Union with Christ covers the whole person but Swope points at the scriptural emphasis on the "innermost" part of humans—which is mostly referred to by the term "spirit"—as the medium.[125] In his historical survey of the concept, like Blackwell, Swope proposes two "intertwined concepts" to be the most relevant to the formulations of this

121. Piper, *Contending for Our All*, 59, 61.

122. Louth, *Christian Mystical Tradition*, 79–80.

123. This is the NIV translation. In NASB it says, "But the one who joins himself to the Lord is one spirit *with Him*."

124. Ezek 37.

125. Swope, "Spirit-to-Spirit Model of Christian Union with God," iv, 16. He defines this innermost place within a person as the center of one's relationship with God, which is often referred to by terms like the "soul," "heart," "kidney," (mostly in the Old Testament), and "spirit" (in the New Testament). The human spirit is "construed as a dynamic deep within the human being," it is the "'core' of the person," more than any faculties of the mind—"cognitive, affective, conscious, subconscious, etc."

doctrine in the church: "union as participation" and "union as sharing in the divine image."[126]

Irenaeus saw union with God in the context of being transformed to His likeness. He says: "For as those who see the light are within the light and partake of its brilliancy; even so, those who see God, are in God and receive of His splendor."[127] Irenaeus's emphasis on the intimacy of the divine Spirit with the human spirit is to show that when a person *sees* God in his inner spirit, he is changed by the image. Demetrios Constantelos points to Irenaeus's writing to confirm this meaning: "The *substance of life* is participation in God. But to participate in God is to know God and enjoy his goodness. Men therefore shall *see* God that they may live, being made immortal by the *vision* and attaining even unto God." Constantelos is bringing together both aspects of union—participation in the Spirit and sharing in the *imago*—and explains that for Irenaeus,

> Salvation as participation in God implies the transformation of human nature into divine where mortal becomes immortal. Since immortality is the distinguishing quality of the deity, human nature that participates in God becomes immortal.[128]

These representations point to the "interconnectedness" of *union as image* and *union as participation* in the Eastern theology. In the writings of most fathers and the Eastern scholars, the two are often used interchangeably.[129] It is important to note that in the case of the fathers, their view of participation was very different than their contemporary Greek philosophies of Platonism or Stoicism or mystery religions, which viewed divine participation as pantheistic. According to Constantelos, participation in the view of Patristic thinkers "includes the total person . . . but not in a pantheistic manner which would mean absorption of the human by the divine."[130] In

126. Ibid., 38.

127. Irenaeus, "Church Fathers."

128. Constantelos, "Irenaeus of Lyons," 354; emphasis mine.

129. Harrison referring to St. Basil's views explains how "participation in divine life" was seen in the East: "According to the Cappadocians, human knowledge of God and participation in divine life also follows a sequential order; we ascend by the same path on which God descended to us. As the Father is manifest through the Son in the Holy Spirit, it is in the Spirit that we come through the Son to the Father. In this manner . . . we encounter each of the three persons in a distinctive way. The Holy Spirit dwells in the faithful and unites them to Christ as members of His body, which brings them to the Father as His adopted children." See Harrison, "Greek Patristic Foundations of Trinitarian Anthropology," 408.

130. Constantelos, "Irenaeus of Lyons," 355.

fact, Swope points out, Athanasius was careful to emphasize participation with God as an act of "assimilation" and not "identification." The human and the Divine stayed as two distinct natures. It was only by grace, and through the indwelling of the Spirit in the believer, that one becomes not only the adoptive child of God, but also "restored to the place for which humanity was originally intended." Thus, for the Eastern church, *one is truly human only when one partakes of the divine Spirit.*[131]

Although the doctrine of union with Christ has not been at the forefront of doctrinal debates in Western Christianity, many influential theologians have pointed to its significance and mysterious nature. There is a long history of Christian mysticism in the Roman Catholic tradition, with a strong belief in authentic experiential encounter of the faithful with the Spirit of the Lord.[132] Augustine also saw human transformation taking place via "participation" in the "substance of God," which is accomplished by the Spirit of God through grace. This transformation of human nature requires brokenness and the emptying of self to facilitate the Spirit of God to break in. Christ as the mediator between human and God makes possible the union with divine Spirit. He does this as the "sharer (*particeps*) of our infirmity, giving us participation of His divinity." It is also the participation in his crucifixion that leads us to sharing of his divinity.[133]

Even Thomas Aquinas brought partaking of the divine into his soteriological discussion. For Aquinas, divine participation is clearly beyond the "created nature" and can be brought to human nature by God's grace. According to A. N. Williams, Aquinas saw this partaking as a result of an act of contemplation, a "form of prayer," in which one participates in "God's self-knowledge," which in reality is "God's own self." The transformation brought about by grace is not to produce "better or happier human beings" but "that we might be made deiform."[134]

Many Reformed and evangelical theologians also have identified union with Christ as a significant condition for a sanctifying Christian life. Calvin is the foremost figure who has given great significance to this doctrine. He refers to Plato as the only ancient philosopher who recognized

131. Swope, "Spirit-to-Spirit Model of Christian Union with God," 40–41. This is certainly modeling after the person of Jesus, the true *image of God*.

132. Underhill, *Mysticism*, 279–304; Teresa, *The Interior Castle*; Louth, *Christian Mystical Tradition*, 215. For a more recent discussion from an evangelical perspective, see Corduan, *Mysticism*, 150.

133. Bonner, "Augustine's Conception of Deification," 373–74.

134. Williams, "Mystical Theology Redux," 58, 69.

"man's highest good as union with God," yet he could not "even dimly sense its nature," for he knew "nothing of the sacred bond of that union." Calvin believes it is that goal Paul holds out as something he was striving for and had not achieved yet (Phil 3:12–13).[135] The "sacred wedlock," Calvin claims, is that "through which we are made flesh of his flesh and bone of his bone . . . and thus one with him." Christ "unites himself to us by the Spirit alone." Through this union, we are made "his members," and in turn we will "possess Him."[136] Calvin states that without the "mystical union" the believer will not be able to enjoy the true benefits of salvation. He says:

> I confess that we are deprived of this utterly incomparable good until Christ is made ours. Therefore, that joining together of Head and members, that indwelling of Christ in our hearts—in short, that mystical union—are accorded by us the highest degree of importance, so that Christ, having been made ours, makes us sharers with Him in the gifts with which He has been endowed. We do not, therefore, contemplate him outside ourselves from afar in order that his righteousness may be imputed to us but because we put on Christ and are engrafted into his body—in short, because he deigns to make us one with him.[137]

Additionally, Calvin is giving us some insight into the concept of the "mystical body" of Christ. He suggests that union with Christ and sharing of his Spirit is what connects all believers to each other and makes them members of one another (1 Cor 12:12–20).

In addition to other Reformed theologians, such as Luther[138] and Edwards,[139] many contemporary Christians have articulated the

---

135. Calvin, *Institutes*, 3/25.2.

136. Ibid., 3/1.3.

137. Ibid., 3/11.10.

138. For analysis of Luther's view of union, see Bakken, "Holy Spirit and Theosis," 410: "in justification . . . Christ comes into the person"; Carlson, "Luther and the Doctrine of the Holy Spirit," 137: Luther "makes the Holy Spirit the active subject, working within man to conform him to Christ" and "This is accomplished by conforming man to Christ's death and resurrection"; and Purves, *Reconstructing Pastoral Theology*, 87: "Luther compared union with Christ to a marriage between Christ and the soul of the believer, which is his bride"; therefore by marriage the two become one.

139. Youngs, "The Place of Spiritual Union," 27. Youngs argues from Edwards's writings that "the doctrine of spiritual union is not only the biblical foundation of his spirituality but also the point of contact between his formal theology and his strong emphasis upon religious experience."

significance of union with Christ, e.g., Grudem, Ferguson,[140] and Erickson. Grudem focuses on Pauline expressions of "being in Christ" and "Christ in us." He says: "[T]here is a real, personal dwelling of Christ in us, and that this does not mean that we merely agree with Christ or that his ideas are in us. Rather, *he* is in us and remains in us through faith (Eph 3:[16]–17; 2 Cor 13:5)."[141] In fact, Paul challenges the believers to examine themselves and see if they truly have Christ *in* them, otherwise their faith is a mere deception. Grudem does not get into mystical mysteries of this indwelling, but argues for the fact that Christ's Spirit truly dwells in the Christian believer.

Likewise, Millard Erickson has done significant analysis of the doctrine of union. He addresses the main question central to any study of this doctrine: "In what sense can Christ be said to be in us, and we in Him? Are these expressions completely metaphorical, or is there some literal referent?"[142] He identifies four models applied by the various church traditions that he considers faulty. The four models are called (1) *metaphysical* (humans have the same essence as God—a form of pantheism); (2) *mystical* (a human is absorbed into God's essence); (3) *Psychological* (one is influenced by the teachings of Christ, like two friends; indwelling is just a figure of speech); and (4) *sacramental* (a mystical union through administration of sacrament—the model used by the Roman Catholic Church).[143]

Echoing Paul in his epistle to the church in Colossae (Col 1:26–27), Erickson reminds his readers that union with Christ is a "mystery" before he moves on to identify his *"adequate"* models of union: (1) *Judicial* (in oneness with the believer, Christ took God's judgment on behalf of his church); (2) *Vital* (Christ renews the "inner nature" as a vine renews branches; the union impregnates the believer with *life*); (3) *Spiritual*.[144] Erickson portrays this spiritual union as:

> Not only is our union with Christ brought about by the Holy Spirit, it is a union of spirits. It is not a union of persons in one essence, as in the Trinity, or of natures in one person, as the

140. Ferguson, "The Reformed View," 47–76: "it is through union with Christ that sanctification is accomplished in us." Cited in Swope, "Spirit-to-Spirit Model of Christian Union with God," 50, n. 95.

141. Grudem, *Systematic Theology*, 845.

142. Erickson, *Christian Theology*, 949.

143. Ibid., 949–51.

144. Ibid., 951–52. Erickson defines the union as trinitarian, based on Paul's interchangeable language of *God, Christ* and *Spirit*. See Rom 8:9–11.

incarnation of Jesus Christ. It is not a physical bonding, as in the welding of two pieces of metal. It is in some way a union of two spirits that does not extinguish either of them. It does not make the believer physically stronger or more intelligent. Rather, what the union produces is a new spiritual vitality within the human.[145]

Erickson clearly identifies the union as a "Spirit-to-spirit" connection that is essential to the believer's new life. He highlights the christological and Trinitarian nature of the union and at all times maintains the Creator-creature distinction.[146]

As articulated in Romans 8, Galatians 3–4, and 2 Corinthians 3, the Spirit plays a crucial role in Paul's soteriology. It is the Spirit that gives life and is "the instantiation of the divine, glorifying presence." The Spirit aims at transforming humans to the likeness of Christ (2 Cor 3:17–18). It is, again, through the Spirit's presence that believers experience God, are united to him and become adopted children of God—co-heirs with Christ. Thus, the Spirit plays a central and distinct role in Paul's portrayal of the human encounter with God. Blackwell notes that this experience is "christo-telic in nature," meaning, in the process believers will "embody Christ-narrative in death and life."[147]

As we have seen, the models of union with God that are recognized to be an "actual union," are always considered to be done in the realm of the human spirit—"Spirit-to-spirit."[148] Due to this significant anthropological dimension of the union, it is vital to gain some clarity around the substance of the "human spirit" in the work of these theologians. Starting from the person of Jesus, the role of the spirit in human ontology cannot be overestimated. It is through the human spirit that the life of God flows in. According to Barth, we cannot lose sight of the "human person of Jesus" and the "absolutely unique relation" he had with the Holy Spirit. "He is to be a man who is pervasively and constantly, intensively and totally filled and governed" by the power of the Holy Spirit.[149] However, in the case of Jesus, he "does not have the Holy Spirit in the way in which it can be said of any man." Jesus "does not have Him only in virtue of an occasional,

145. Ibid., 952–53.

146. For further analysis of the perspectives of the aforementioned theologians and many others on the spiritual union as a "Spirit-to-spirit" connection see: Swope, "Spirit-to-Spirit Model of Christian Union with God," iv–290.

147. Blackwell, "Christosis," 227.

148. Swope, "Spirit-to-Spirit Model of Christian Union with God," 6.

149. John 1:32, 3:34; Luke 1:35, 4:1, 18; Matt 1:20, 12:18.

transitory and partial bestowal," but, rather has him "lastingly and totally
. . . He not only has the Spirit, but primarily and basically He is Spirit." Yet
as "the new man," Jesus revealed the "true nature of man" as intended by
God—one which is intimately tied to the Holy Spirit to receive life.[150]

In the patristic theology, the fathers stressed the connection between
the body and the soul as the two components of the person. They usually
distinguished three "powers" in the soul: (1) *vegetative/vital power*—necessary for survival, source of life shared among all living creatures, applied to
growth, nutrition, and procreation; (2) *animal/ appetitive power*—shared
among mankind and animals, the irrational part of the soul; it comprised
of "irascibility" and "ardor"; (3) *power of reason*—the unique principal
characteristic of human nature. The two primary faculties here are *reason*, the source of thinking, judgment, reflection, memory, and language;
and, "at an even higher level, the spirit (*pneuma*) or intellect (*nous*) which
is the principle of consciousness," the highest faculty in man. *Pneuma/
nous* is the source of "intuitive intelligence," the "faculty of contemplation
. . . and the source of all knowledge." In this lies the human capacity for
"self-determination." The fathers used *nous* and *pneuma* interchangeably,
referring to that innermost intuitive part of the person.[151]

It is this *nous* or *pneuma* that is the seat of union for Swope in his
"Spirit-to-spirit" model. *Nous* is often translated as "mind" or "intellect."
For the fathers, it always referred to the "deepest part of the human person," and it was commonly used in relation to union with God. Swope
points out that the essence of *nous* for Eastern theologians was very different than the English terms *mind* or *intellect*. He cites Gregory of Nazianus
speaking in regards to the union of God and human: "The point of union
is the mind [*nous*], that which in the thought of the Cappadocians is the
most essential part of man."[152] Louth explains that when the fathers used
the term *nous*, they meant "mind" in a special way and a much deeper way
than we Westerners refer to the term. He says:

> *Nous* is usually translated as "mind" or "intellect." Part of the
> problem is that neither of these words is as rich in derived forms
> as the Greek *nous*. . . . The most fundamental reason for this is

150. Barth, *Church Dogmatics*, 3/2:332–334.

151. Larchet, *Mental Disorders*, 26–28. According to Larchet, "the authors of the
first centuries (for example St. Ignatius of Antioch, *To The Philadelphians*, XII, 2; St.
Irenaeus, *Against the Heresies*, V, 6, 1) utilized the word *pneuma*, following the practice
of St. Paul (1 Thess. 5:23). The Fathers of the fourth century and the Byzantine Fathers
of the later centuries adopted and preferred the word *nous*."

152. Swope, "Spirit-to-Spirit Model of Christian Union with God," 63–64.

a cultural one: the Greeks were pre-Cartesian, we are all post-Cartesian. We say, 'I think, therefore I am,' that is, thinking is an *activity* I engage in. . . . The Greeks would say, "I think therefore there is that which I think—*to noeta*." What I think is something going on in my head; what the Greek thinks, *to noeta*, are the objects of thought that (for example, for Plato) exist in a higher, more real world. This means that *nous* and its derivatives have a quite different *feel* from our words, mind, mental, intellect, intellection, etc. Our words suggest our reasoning, our thinking; *nous*, *noesis*, etc. suggest an almost intuitive grasp of reality. . . . *Nous*, then, is more like an organ of mystical union than anything suggested by our words "mind" or "intellect."[153]

"Because of the *nous*," Jean-Claude Larchet claims, "man has the possibility to situate, master, and transcend himself"; this is where all "contemplative possibilities" lie. For the fathers, it is *nous* that essentially is a link between the human person and God; it is *nous* that "leads him towards and unites him with God." Larchet builds on the work of fathers such as Athanasius, St. Basil, and Clement of Alexandria, to claim: "The *nous* is in effect the image of God in man."[154] According to the fathers *nous* is where the personhood resides; this *nous* has the possibility "of being deified" through grace, after it has been conformed to the likeness of God. Although deification applies to the whole person, it is *nous* that first receives grace and is transformed; "it is by means of its intermediary function that grace is communicated to the rest of the human composite."[155] Larchet points to Vladimir Lossky, saying, "it is the seat of the person, of the human hypostasis which contains in itself the whole of man's nature—spirit, soul and body." So, *what happens in nous happens to the person, and what happens to the person is experienced most of all in nous.*[156]

Tom Marshall points out that because this innermost place is the key to one's relationship with God, it becomes "the fundamental objective" of the demonic powers to "gain access" to it so that they might "draw life from it." It is this inner part of the human being that ought to go through major metamorphosis to gain new life, and the deeper the journey, the more exposed, naked, and vulnerable the person is to spiritual attacks. He explains that a spirit that is oppressed and under evil attack cannot reach

153. Louth, *Christian Mystical Tradition*, xv–xvi.

154. Larchet, *Mental Disorders*, 28–29.

155. Ibid., 29 n. 5.

156. Lossky, *The Mystical Theology*, 201; cited in Larchet, *Mental Disorders*, 29.

out to God, and a "Spiritual dryness" engulfs the person. For an oppressed spirit, God becomes hidden, because it is only through his spirit that man can connect to God.[157] This is very relevant to the phenomenon of "mental illness." John Colwell, a theologian who suffers from "bipolar disorder," admits that the circumstances of his illness are far more bearable for him than the "distress at the perceived absence of God."[158] God is seemingly nowhere to be found to the one who suffers from "mental illness" and is being oppressed in his spirit.

The concept of innermost faculty is highlighted by Paul in 2 Corinthians 4:16, in which he puts the external being of the person in contrast to his inner being: "Therefore we do not lose heart, but though our outer man is decaying, yet our inner man is being renewed day by day." Thus there is an inner man that is distinct from the physical outer man and that is where the connection with God takes place. It should be noted that in regards to this text, a variety of interpretations have been offered. For example, Bultmann, who is a monist, affirms that Paul's language sounds dualistic. He dismisses Paul's dualistic expression and claims that it is "derived from the anthropology of Hellenistic dualism," and it has a "purely formal meaning" for the "subject-self."[159] In Bultmann's opinion, Paul's different terminologies always refer to the self from various perspectives. Man is about his *soma*: "we can say man does not *have a soma*; he *is soma*."[160] In distinction to Bultmann, trichotomists such as van Kooten and Watchman Nee, argue that Paul's language represents a strict material-immaterial dualism. Van Kooten believes that the immaterial dimension is the focal point of Pauline anthropology.[161] Watchman Nee argues that those who are united to Christ are led and ruled by the power of the Spirit within them. Paul's focus is to highlight the significance of the role of the Spirit in living a life that is pleasing to God. The breaking of the outer man is necessary for the release of the power of the Spirit hidden within.[162]

---

157. Marshall, *Healing from the Inside Out*, 117–18, 107.

158. Colwell, *Why Have You Forsaken Me?*, 48.

159. Bultmann, *Theology of the New Testament*, 1:203.

160. Ibid., 1:194.

161. Van Kooten, *Paul's Anthropology*, 298–308.

162. Watchman Nee (1903–1972) was a very popular author and leader of the "little Flock" movement in China. He believed: "New birth is something which happens entirely within the spirit; it has no relation to soul or body." See Nee, *The Spiritual Man*, 1:61; Nee, *The Breaking of the Outer Man and the Release of the Spirit*, 116.

The middle ground is the position taken by theologians such as Blackwell and Swope. They are both interpreting the text from a holistic-dualistic position. Man is a holistic entity, but here, Paul is referring to the deepest part of man inside him, i.e., his *spirit*. Blackwell argues that Paul is making a "bold declaration about life in the midst of death." Here Paul is clarifying how the image of Christ—referred to in 2 Corinthian 3:18—is actually formed: "believers experience this life [the new life] in the somatic context of suffering so that Christ's image, characterized by death and resurrection, is formed in them." Thus, it is deep inside the human being, in the core of his being, that one's suffering "acts as a mirror polish" to surface "the image of Christ" and bring about the transformation to the new life.[163]

Could it then be that the "mental illness" that affects one's sense of self and consciousness is the illness of *nous*, the *spirit*, the innermost part of the human? Could this be a "spiritual" phenomenon and not pathology? From the writings of the great Christian mystics we learn that it is the spirit, the inner man that is subject to great turmoil and attack as one travels through the journey of abandonment toward a union with God. We will discuss this phenomenon in greater detail in chapter 3: "A Theology of Illness."

A Theological Anthropology of Suffering

In constructing a theological anthropological model for this study, we draw from the wealth of insights we've received from the theologians of the past and present, synthesizing various positions laid out thus far. This synthesis is an original contribution to the anthropological debates, guided by the person of Christ as the true image of God and the reflection of true humanity. Jesus Christ is our chief exemplar, in whose likeness we are being transformed, "with ever-increasing glory, which comes from the Lord, who is the Spirit" (2 Cor 3:18, NIV). Both Calvin and Blackwell reminded us that "as believers encounter the Spirit in 2 Cor 3:18, they reflect the image of Christ as they are transformed."[164] In our formulation, we are guided by the following questions:

---

163. Blackwell, "Christosis," 184.

164. Calvin, *Institutes*, 1/15.4; Blackwell, "Christosis," 247.

1. Given the fallen nature of humanity, the redeeming work of Christ, and the promised renewal through the work of the Spirit, what must we believe about the human being?

2. Given that Christ is the true *imago Dei* and the perfect exemplar of humanity, what is it that a human being *ought to be*?

3. Given the Fall and the effect of it on *imago Dei*, how is the image to be restored in the human being?

4. Given what we know of Jesus as the perfect human, what can we make of the human being's ontological constitution?

First, as Calvin has said, there is "a sense of divinity," given by God's common grace, engraved upon the human soul that "can never be effaced." In fact, if anything, the human being does not have the choice to run away from God; and the struggle within his soul points to his fear of God and his judgment, which "is naturally inborn in all" and is "fixed deep within." All of humanity is born to live for the one end that "they may know God." Yet, because of the Fall, humankind is "so damaged" by the effect of sin that it has lost the ability and capacity to know God.[165] Thus, *the human being, created to know God intimately, has fallen into sin, and is caught in bondage of fear, guilt, and shame that he cannot release himself from.*

But God has not abandoned humanity in this plight. God sent forth his Son, Jesus Christ, to die on behalf of humanity for its sins. Because "the whole world lies in the power of the evil one" (1 John 5:19), through the person of Christ, God the Father "has delivered us from the domain of darkness and transferred us to the kingdom of His beloved Son" (Col 1:13). Thus, by the sacrificial work of Christ, *those who put their faith in him have been delivered from bondage to the guilt of sin and bondage to its ruling power in their lives.*

Frame says: "To say that 'God is Spirit' then . . . means not only that God is invisible and immaterial, but that he bears all the characteristics of the Spirit who dwells with his people."[166] It is through the medium of the Spirit that God's people are "washed, sanctified, and justified," and come to know God.[167] Through the work of the Spirit, God brings new life into his people and regenerates their nature. The "new birth marks the beginning of spiritual understanding as well as the beginning of obedient

165. Calvin, *Institutes*, 1/3.3, liii.

166. Frame, *Doctrine of God*, 599.

167. Ibid., 687.

discipleship."[168] According to Blackwell, the transformation taking shape in the life of the believer that Paul espoused, in 2 Corinthians 3:18, "functions as the climax of the life-giving work of the Spirit."[169] Thus, *God bestows his grace upon his people by the power of his Spirit, transforming their nature and bringing them to a new life of spiritual abundance.*

Second, if humans are to model their lives after Christ, as the true image of God and the perfect human, then accordingly, Timothy Savage writes:

> Paul seems to be drawing attention to the visible character, the salient image, of Jesus Christ. He is underscoring the fact that Christ, in his resolve to live for God's glory and not his own, and in his act of consummate self-sacrifice on the cross, demonstrates not only what God is like, but also, dramatically, what humans *ought to be* like. They ought to manifest the same self-emptying character which Christ displayed on the cross. They ought to be "transformed into the same image."[170]

Drawing on Savage, Blackwell emphasizes the narrative of Christ's death and life as the model of human existence, by pointing to Paul's claim: "always carrying in the body the dying of Jesus, that the life of Jesus also may be manifested in our body" (2 Cor 4:10). Blackwell says: "Therefore, this image that believers are transformed into is not merely some abstract replication" of Christ, but rather it is "one of the dying and rising Christ."[171] Calvin points out that "THE SUM OF THE CHRISTIAN LIFE" is about "THE DENIAL OF OURSELVES." Because after redemption, *"we are not our own"* any longer, *"we are God's."*[172] By focusing on him, "when the soul has grasped the knowledge of God, it is wholly transformed into his likeness."[173] As Christ lived for the glory of the Father, we too must live for God's glory and surrender to his will. It is self-denial, and living for God's pleasure, that motivates us to "esteem" others "above ourselves" and faithfully serve them.[174] Thus, *modeling Christ means the embodiment of*

168. Ibid., 74.

169. Blackwell, "Christosis," 170–71. Blackwell says: "More than any other verse in the Pauline corpus, the transformation in 2 Cor 3.18 has attracted comments about deification in modern literature."

170. Savage, *Power through Weakness*, 151–52. Emphasis is mine.

171. Blackwell, "Christosis," 168.

172. Calvin, *Institutes*, 3/7.1.

173. Ibid., 1/3.3.

174. Ibid., 3/7.4.

the dying and rising of Christ, living a life of self-sacrifice to the point of death, and devotion to God and fellow humans. When the self is dead, then Christ's image will emanate from the person; without crucifixion, there is no experience of resurrection (Rom 6:5).

Third, it is one thing to know what constitutes a Christ-like life; it is another to embody that life. As we have heard from many theologians, the human person cannot accomplish this feat on his or her own. It is only by God's grace that this capacity can be bestowed upon the person through the work of the Spirit. According to John Owen, the natural faculties of even the most righteous person are "not enough to enable any rational creature to live to God"—to model the devoted life that is Christ's *imaging of God* in his humanity. This "was wrought in Christ by the Holy Spirit." For Owen, *imago Dei* is "only a Spirit-enabled possibility," even in the case of the man Jesus Christ.[175] Calvin stresses that transformation of the soul—regeneration—is achieved through sincere repentance (*metanoia*) which involves "mortification of the flesh" and "vivification of the spirit." Both things only happen through "participation in Christ." As one participates in Christ's death the old nature is crucified, and as one shares in his life, then the *imago Dei* is renewed.[176] Both Calvin and Owen use the word "mortification" to point to the difficulty of the task. The "common nature must die"; it must be "violently slain by the sword of the Spirit."[177] Blackwell stresses that it is the embodiment of Christ's death and life that constitutes the *imago Dei* in Christ. And it is by participation in Christ "through the Spirit that believers are transformed into the image of Christ."[178] Thus, *the human person will be conformed to imago Dei as God had always intended, through union with (or participation in) Christ. This will be mediated by the work of the Holy Spirit on the human spirit—a "Spirit-to-spirit" connection. The manifested image in the human person is characterized by the embodiment of the death and the life of Christ.*

Finally, in the spirit of Calvin, Owen, Berkhof, Grudem, Plantinga, Moreland, Cooper, and many other great theologians of the past and present, I believe that the human person is a holistic entity who has been created by God in a dualistic fashion. He or she is made of a material body and an immaterial part that is referred to by many names, primarily

175. Owen, *The Works*, 3:168–69, 284–85, cited in McDonald, "The Pneumatology of the 'Lost' Image in John Owen," 327.

176. Calvin, *Institutes*, 3/3.8–9.

177. Calvin, *Institutes*, 3/3.8; Owen, *The Mortification of Sin*, 83.

178. Blackwell, "Christosis," 238.

soul/spirit.[179] According to Scripture, God is Spirit, and angels are spirits. Since God is Spirit, he will indwell his people in the realm of their spirit. Since Jesus Christ, the chief exemplar of personhood is made of body and Spirit, so are humans.[180] Most importantly, personhood is not about functionality in this world, as is espoused by those who advocate any form of physicalism. Personhood is about being created by God for his purposes, to know him (not necessarily intellectually, but rather spiritually, through a "Spirit-to-spirit" connection) and to bring glory to him by fulfilling his plans for one's life. Luke writes about Anna, a prophetess who had dedicated her life to fasting and prayer in the temple. Anna had been married for merely seven years before she was widowed, and for the rest of her life to the age of eighty-four, she spent all her time "serving night and day with fasting and prayer" (Luke 2:36–37). Her vocation and calling by God was clearly different than what one might consider a productive life based on contemporary Western mentality. Let us remember that it is holiness, and not "happiness," that Scripture claims is the chief end of man. For it is from holiness that the true joy of the Lord flows (Lev 20:26; Psalm 32:11; Matt 5:6, 8; Rom 14:17; 1 Thess 1:6).

The human soul is an "immaterial substantial reality" that consists of the person's distinct "faculties of consciousness." A person is "identical" to his soul—a psychophysical unity. In fact he is a "living soul" who has a body. Mind and spirit are faculties of the soul. According to Berkhof: "The word 'spirit' designates the spiritual element in man as the principle of life and action which controls the body," whereas, *soul* "denominates the same element as the *subject* of action in man." Therefore, often it is used for the personal pronoun. While personal identity can be sustained without a body—in a disembodied state while awaiting the resurrection—full human functioning in this world is achieved through a holistic integration of the body and the soul. Because of this holistic integration, there is a correlation of cause and effect between the body and the soul. Changes in one can cause effects in the other.[181]

It is the soul that thinks and acts; but the soul cannot be reduced to either the mind or the body. Therefore if one loses a limb, or suffers

179. It is not within the scope of this book to engage in debates with various particularities of distinct dualist position. For our purposes, it is sufficient to acknowledge the holistic-dualism of human ontology.

180. Moreland and Rae, *Body & Soul*, 24.

181. Moreland, "Restoring the Soul to Christianity," 24; Swope, "Spirit-to-Spirit Model of Christian Union with God," 100–101; and Berkhof, *Systematic Theology*, 194 (emphasis mine).

brain damage, the "self" remains constant as the identity of the person. In fact as Blackwell interprets Paul, for the believing Christian, while the "outer man" is decaying, the "inner man" is being renewed (2 Cor 4:16). It is through that inner man, the deepest part of the soul (usually referred to as the spirit), that God's Spirit connects to the human, communicates to him, and brings about a transformation in his character. Thus, *the human person is a "living soul" created by God, who has a body—that visibly reflects and interacts with the material world. The soul as the "self" is what represents the individual identity and includes "interaction within the physiological world (through the body) and the immaterial world (through the spirit)."*[182] *The soul and the body are strongly integrated in this life, such that there is a correlation of cause and effect between the two.*

Summary

Behind Western concepts of mental health and illness lie a collection of assumptions about the nature of human beings rooted in varied worldviews. These anthropological assumptions have shaped our views of the phenomenon of mental illness and have guided our practices of how to deal with it. In order to evaluate the current practices in mental health, we need a biblically valid framework to understand human beings. The Trinitarian anthropological model defined in this chapter will set the context within which we will look at the phenomenon of "schizophrenia." Different facets of this model inform our analysis of those who are created, loved, and used by God in their insanity. We have seen through the course of this chapter that our anthropological perspectives can have a major influence on how we perceive our lives, our purposes on earth, and God's relationship with humanity.

We have followed the steps of great theologians of the past and the present to open up the complexity of humanness. Right where the puzzle seems impervious, where the confusion and fear overwhelms, where human nature is immersed in disgrace and manifests chaos, we encounter the divine revelation pointing not to dysfunctional creatureliness, but to personal sin as the root of humanity's contradiction.[183] It is precisely for this reason that effectively addressing any dimension of human pain, suffering, and distress can only be done through an anthropology informed by God's special grace revealed in Scripture. Therefore, we built our anthropologi-

182. Swope, "Spirit-to-Spirit Model of Christian Union with God," 98.

183. Anderson, *On Being Human*, 30.

cal model within the paradigm of the *economic* Trinity, with an emphasis on how the triune God relates to creatures, centered on the distinct roles played by the Father, the Son, and the Spirit throughout the redemptive history.

To the extent that we view a human's problems as sin versus some creaturely dysfunctionality, we will deal objectively and not merely subjectively with "distortion." This is of critical importance for our study of mental illness.[184] I raised the question that "mental illness," affecting one's sense of self and consciousness could be the illness of *nous*, the *spirit*—the innermost part of a human. We will further evaluate this hypothesis in the following chapters and ask whether the evidence points to pathology or to a "spiritual" phenomenon. Potentially, a change in our perspective about the etiology of the disorder could open up the door to the possibility of radical deliverance, restoration, and redemption.[185] If the essence of the illness is such that a more drastic encounter with the very being of the person is necessary before true wholeness can be restored, eyes must turn to Christ and the promise of his radical new Life.

In our journey of encounter with madness, the person of Christ as the true *imago Dei* and the perfect man is our guide into how we should understand the human being. We saw that it is the *crucified* Christ who will lead us to the *exalted* One. The promised ongoing metamorphosis in human nature, brought forth by grace, through the work of God's Spirit, leads us into a journey of "christoformity" that entails "both suffering and death, but also future glorious resurrection."[186]

With this in mind, we now turn to a critical analysis of the experience of mental illness in our contemporary world in order to develop a rich *situational* perspective. The anthropological framework I developed in this chapter will be kept in sight normatively as we evaluate the assumptions and forces that have shaped our view of the phenomenon of "schizophrenia" and guided our respective practices.

184. The famous psychologist, O. Hobart Mowrer, notes, "So long as we subscribe to the view that neurosis is a bona fide 'illness,' without moral implications or dimensions, our position will, of necessity, continue to be an awkward one. And it is here I suggest that, as between the concept of sin (however unsatisfactory it may in some ways be) and that of sickness, sin is indeed the lesser of two evils. We have tried the sickness horn of this dilemma and impaled ourselves upon it. Perhaps, despite our erstwhile protestations, we shall yet find sin more congenial." Mowrer, *The Crisis in Psychiatry and Religion*, 50–51.

185. This sentiment has been echoed by the famous psychiatrist Karl Menninger who makes the radical statement that "sin is the only hopeful view." Menninger, *Whatever Became of Sin?*, 188.

186. Blackwell, "Christosis," 171.

2

The Historical Contexts of Psychiatry and Mental Illness

For the love of money is the root of all sorts of evil.

1 Tim 6:10

It has been said that how a society treats its least well-off members says a lot about its humanity. Our treatment of the mentally ill says that American society is inhumane.

—Elyn Saks[1]

In this chapter, we will begin to develop a rich *situational* perspective to further our investigation. In order to grasp the reality behind the phenomenon of mental illness, we need to contextualize it within its historical framework and understand why and how it is culturally perceived, and how that perception has influenced the treatment options. What are the historical and political dimensions of this phenomenon? Who is benefiting from it, and who are the victims? What are the real barriers to recovery? Situations, including illness, never happen in abstraction; they always happen in a context and have different forces affecting them. Our task is to expose these hidden dimensions to lead us to greater clarity.

Historically, the experiences that we have come to name as mental illness have evoked in us a wide range of responses, from bafflement, disgust

1. Saks, *Refusing Care*, 1

and fear, to a sense of awe and wonder. We have given them wide range of names and meanings in hope of better understanding and controlling them. Ian Hacking claims, "Sometimes, our sciences create kinds of people that in a certain sense did not exist before."[2] He calls this "making up people," and highlights the fact that "naming" and "classifying" people into boxes changes them. They become who we have defined them to be, which in turn confirms our classification, which in turn leads to further classification. He calls this the "looping effect," and notes that it occurs widely in "human sciences," including psychology, psychiatry, and "a good deal of clinical medicine." According to Hacking, "The engines used in these sciences are engines of discovery but also engines for making up people."[3]

Psychiatry, by some accounts, has taken it upon itself to explain the "normal and abnormal functioning of the personality modeled on medicine."[4] One of the main claims of Scripture is to transform the personality of the people of God that they might be conformed to the image of Christ. Thus, both psychiatry and Christianity are in the business of changing personalities: the former according to the standards of a culture and the societal norms by attempting to eliminate "mental disorders" in the medical context, and the latter according to the image of God by the power of God's grace.

The twentieth century saw an astronomical rise in the popularity of the biological sciences as explanatory frameworks for everything related to human beings. Psychiatry has attempted to develop a scientific context to capitalize on that success and create a framework for how we view and name those experiences that make up the criteria "mental illness." We will evaluate those attempts and seek to explore the challenges of modern psychiatry in normalizing human behavior based on scientific theories.

We will begin with a historical analysis that outlines something of the roots of how we have come to frame mental illness in contemporary times. Historically, how the experiences are named determined the type of treatment that was deemed to be appropriate. Of course, any historical presentation is undoubtedly discriminating, stressing some events and disregarding others in order to construct a coherent narrative. Edward Shorter, a prominent psychiatric historian and a staunch proponent of modern biological psychiatry, warns: "The history of psychiatry is a

---

2. Hacking, "Making Up People."

3. Ibid.

4. Dreyfus, "Foucault's Critique of Psychiatric Medicine," 311.

minefield. Both the revisionists and neoapologists such as myself risk being blown up by uncharted pieces of evidence."[5]

Keeping that in mind, we focus here on the elements of history that inform our understanding of "mental disorder" as a medical phenomenon with a focus on "schizophrenia" as the crown-prince of all "mental disorders," the treatment of the mentally ill within the psychiatric framework, and the questions that the foregoing analyses raise for the church. The aim is to contextualize our contemporary experience of mental illness, as we seek to understand this most mysterious phenomenon of human history called *insanity*.

A Historical Analysis: Roots of Psychiatry

There is a burgeoning body of literature devoted to the history of psychiatry. Here, we will devote most of our attention to the nature and character of post-World War II psychiatric developments through psychopharmacology, and homogenizing diagnostic techniques based on the American Psychiatric Association's (APA) *Diagnostic and Statistical Manual for Mental Disorders* (DSM), which has shaped today's Western psychiatry.[6] However, in order to put things in the right perspective, we will look briefly at the development of psychiatric history from earlier times.

The evidence indicates that from the pre-classical and the classical periods onwards most societies recognized episodes of extremely aberrant behavior as madness or insanity. Some saw these as sacred behavior and others as the result of failure to uphold ritual prescriptions and, most importantly, as a punishment from gods that was brought upon directly or through the agency of demons and evil spirits.[7]

The increasing emphasis on natural knowledge in the fifth and sixth centuries BC led to theories of Hippocrates in the fourth century BC, who explained illness as a consequence of an imbalance between the four bodily humors (basic fluids): blood, black bile, yellow bile, and phlegm. These corresponded to the four underlying qualities of matter: heat, cold, moisture, and dryness. The harmony among these humors brought health to the body and the mind. The predominance of one of these humors determined a person's character type. Medicine was now excluding the

5. Shorter, *A History of Psychiatry*, ix.

6. The European counterpart for DSM is the World Health Organization's *International Classification of Diseases*, now in its 10th edition.

7. Merkel, "The History," 1.

supernatural influences and health and illness could only be understood in naturalistic terms.[8] One of the Hippocratic texts confirms this view:

> Men ought to know that from the brain, and from the brain only, arise our pleasures, joys, laughter, and jests, as well as our sorrows, pains, griefs and tears. Through it, in particular, we think, see, hear, and distinguish the ugly from the beautiful, the bad from the good, the pleasant from the unpleasant. . . . It is the same thing which makes us mad or delirious, inspires us with dread and fear, whether by night or by day, brings sleeplessness, inopportune mistakes, aimless anxieties, absentmindedness, and acts that are contrary to habit.[9]

This text clearly suggests that from the fourth century BC the biological concept of madness was pervasive in medicine. In this model, excesses of blood and of yellow bile could cause mania, whereas a surplus of black bile (*melaina chole*)—or later called *melancholia*, which was a dark fluid that darkened other fluids in the body—could result in melancholy and depression. One of the ways to deal with the polluted blood was for the person to undergo *blood-letting* (also called *phlebotomy* or *venesection*). There was an ever-increasing acceptance of the natural law and the rejection of the supernatural. Within humoralism, it was easy to understand mental conditions as byproducts of physical states.[10]

The ascendancy of Christianity and the fall of the Roman Empire placed Christian doctrines at the center of intellectual dialogue in the West. Larry Merkel explains:

> Medieval concepts of mental illness stressed that individuals had free will and were responsible for their actions, but that illness (including mental illness) came from sin and resulting punishment from God or possession by the devil. Theological and humoral concepts were not incompatible in that theological precepts addressed ultimate causes of illness, i.e., why a certain person became ill, rather than specific mechanisms of illness. Thus melancholia was seen as a trial of faith. Mental illness was seen as either the result of sin or as a test of faith. For instance of the seven deadly sins . . . sloth (*acedia*) had a clinical profile, presenting with boredom, depression, obsessions, anxiety, and a variety of psychosomatic symptoms. . . . Since sin was central

8. Porter, *Madness*, 36–37.

9. Ibid., 37.

10. Ibid., 38, 41–42; Merkel, "The History," 2.

to mental illness, religious activity was central to cure. Mental illness was seen as alienation from God, thus return to God was essential for cure.[11]

In this period, the church developed Christian-based therapeutic processes and certain monasteries were engaged in the treatment of mental illness through prayer, Bible reading, and counsel. In many Catholic nations, the care of the mentally ill remained in the custody of religious orders, a practice that continued into the twentieth century. However, the application of clinical treatments such as bloodletting and purgatives continued to be common.[12]

Greek thoughts retained their validity and acceptance through the Renaissance. From the fifteenth and sixteenth centuries on secularism increased and the church declined in power. Advancements in mathematics, physics, and experimental sciences often opposed the beliefs of the church. The consequent dichotomy between the church teachings and science resulted in a growing humanism and took the attention away from God and turned it toward man, who became the center of attention and the subject of inquiries. Nonetheless, the illness model based on humoral concepts given by Hippocrates and Galen persisted until the eighteenth century.[13]

With the Reformation, many believers started experiencing severe emotional turmoil that they recognized as a spiritual experience, and the medical community regarded as psychopathology. Autobiographical depiction of madness by saints such as Margery Kempe, John Perceval, and George Trosse pointed to their major conversions with a coherent and meaningful religious experience of madness. These cases portrayed madness as a "desperate, acute phase in the trial and redemption of souls, because it brought a sinner into a state of crisis, and provided the prelude to recovery." During this period over 200,000 people, mainly women, were executed as witches. This excessive bloodshed eventually prompted public objection and skepticism about demon possession.[14]

In 1648, the famous physician, Thomas Willis, who believed in devils and in the effectiveness of harsh treatment of the mentally ill, wrote an influential book on insanity, which set the stage for the work of many mad

11. Merkel, "The History," 3.

12. Porter, *Madness*, 92.

13. Ibid., 49–50; Merkel, "The History," 4.

14. Porter, *Madness*, 21–25. Kempe et al., *The Book of Margery Kempe*; Perceval, *Perceval's Narrative*; Trosse and Brink, *The Life of the Reverend Mr. George Trosse*.

doctors that followed him: *The Practice of Physick: Two Discourses Concerning the Soul of Brutes*. He believed that the insane were animal-like fierce creatures who enjoyed superhuman strength. Since reason, as advocated by Locke, Newton, and other seventeenth-century philosophers, was what made man superior to animals, then the loss of reason would bring him to a beastly level. Willis stressed that if the insane were to be cured, they needed to revere their physicians and regard them as their "tormentors."[15] He believed they should be "treated with torture and torments in a hovel instead of with medicament."[16] This perspective reinforced the natural inclination of the attendants to break down the insane at any cost and bring them under control. Bloodletting, powerful purges, emetics, and blistering therefore continued to be regularly applied for many years.[17]

In the seventeenth and eighteenth centuries the numbers of the insane greatly increased. Various theories explain this increase. One suggests it was the result of the loss of traditional support by extended families as a result of industrialization and urbanization. Foucault states that the seventeenth century was the age of "the great confinement," and that "more than one out of every hundred inhabitants of the city of Paris found themselves confined."[18] But those who were confined were not necessarily mentally ill; many of them were poor, unemployed, criminals, or other outcasts who were nuisances to society.[19] Andrew Scull, who is in agreement with Foucault's basic philosophy, blames capitalism and points to a "humanitarian and scientific gloss on the community's behavior" to legitimize the confinement of "troublesome people."[20]

While Shorter challenges Foucault's numbers of the confined, he affirms that historically it has been common practice to put the "homeless psychotics" in "hospices for the sick, the criminal and vagrant," and at times "in jails and workhouses." He believes, ultimately, it was the private madhouses that gave rise and prominence to modern psychiatry and not

---

15. Andrew Scull explains how English doctors perceived the insane as wild animals: Scull, *Social Order/mental Disorder*, 54–79; cited in Whitaker, *Mad in America*, 6.

16. Quoted in Zilboorg and Henry, *Medical Psychology*, 261.

17. Whitaker, *Mad in America*, 6–8.

18. Foucault, *Madness and Civilization*, 38.

19. Ibid., 39.

20. Scull, *The Most Solitary of Afflictions*, 245–46. It should be noted that Scull, who agreed with the overall assertions of Foucault, found his work "riddled with errors of fact and interpretation." Scull is quoted in Gutting, "Foucault and the History of Madness," 48.

the state confinement places.[21] Roy Porter regarded Foucault's claim as simplistic, and pointed to market economy as the facilitator of the growth in the numbers of those deemed insane and of their confinement, which he perceived to be more the "product of complex bargaining between families, communities, local officials, magistrates, and the superintendents themselves" than the byproduct of a "central policy."[22] Whitaker claims that madness became a great business in England. Most of the "well-to-do" from London "shipped their family lunatics" to privately owned madhouses.[23]

All over Europe, the condition of the insane kept at home was horrific and unfathomable, and families, overwhelmed by their insane members, would ship them away. Shorter cites writings by Müller,[24] who gave an account of the condition of some of those coming to his hospital: "A youth of sixteen, who for years had lain in a pigpen in the hut of his father, a shepherd, had so lost the use of his limbs and his mind that he would lap the food from his bowl with his mouth just like an animal." Another man had been tied up by his wife for five years so that he had lost the use of his legs.[25]

Merkel explains that the church too was not much help in that period. Protestant ethics valued a person's productive life and ability to work; riches and wealth were perceived as divine favor. In contrast, insanity and poverty were seen as a sign of God's abandonment and loss of grace. The insane were mostly neglected, ridiculed, and mistreated as less-than-human.[26]

The treatment was grossly dehumanizing to the point that Bethlem[27] hospital in England, which was almost entirely dedicated to the poor insane, was included on the list of "shows of London," and would place the inmates on display for the outsider's entertainment.[28] In France also, the

21. Shorter, *A History of Psychiatry*, 4, 16–17.

22. Porter, *Madness*, 98–99.

23. Whitaker, *Mad in America*, 8.

24. Müller became chief of psychiatry at the Royal Julius Hospital in Würzberg in 1798.

25. Shorter, *A History of Psychiatry*, 2–3.

26. Merkel, "The History," 7.

27. Bethlem was founded in the thirteenth century as the Priory of St. Mary of Bethlehem. Over time, the name corrupted itself to Bethlem, or Bedlam, which "resonates as a synonym for chaotic madness." See Shorter, *A History of Psychiatry*, 4–5.

28. Porter, *Madness*, 70.

excursion to Bicêtre and viewing of the insane by the "Left Bank Bourgeoisie" as a Sunday entertainment continued until the Revolution.[29] Later, in the American Pennsylvania Hospital, visiting the lunatics was so popular that the hospital started "charging a visitor's fee of four pence."[30]

At the close of the eighteenth century, the fertile ground created by the French Revolution's call for "liberty, equality, and fraternity" set the stage for asylum reform in France. The greatest and most publicized reforms took place at Salpêtrière and Bicêtre hospitals in Paris, led by Philippe Pinel, who was appointed by the revolutionary government.[31] Prior to the revolution, Foucault explains how the cells of Bicêtre were furnished with only a straw pallet on which the lunatics would lie with their "head, feet, and body pressed against the wall . . . soaked by the water that trickled from that mass of stone."[32] Whitaker citing Pinel explains that men were fed only one pound of bread daily given to them in the morning, leaving them to spend the rest of the day "in a delirium of hunger." The mortality rate was very high: "[m]ore than half of the men admitted to the asylums died within a year from starvation, cold, and disease."[33]

Likewise, La Salpêtrière's horrific treatment of madwomen led to misery and death at times. When the waters of the Seine rose in the winter, the dungeons that were at the level of the sewers would not only stink and cause serious health problems, but became "a refuge for a swarm of huge rats," which bit the women severely and would leave them "with feet, hands, and faces torn by bites," which were often fatal. Everywhere the more dangerous lunatics were usually chained to the walls or to the beds if they had any. The depth and intensity of evil, and the beastly spirit that haunted the asylums of that period were daunting.[34]

In 1793, when Pinel took over Bicêtre and La Salpêtrière, he built upon the reform that had just begun by his predecessor Jean Baptiste Pussin. He took the chains off the patients and freed them; all physical restraints were abandoned and he noticed that many of the insane started behaving in a more orderly fashion when the cruelty stopped. He was very skeptical of the medical practices prescribed in medical texts and considered

29. Foucault, *Madness and Civilization*, 68.

30. Whitaker, *Mad in America*, 5.

31. Porter, *Madness*, 104–5.

32. Foucault, *Madness and Civilization*, 71.

33. Philippe Pinel and David Daniel Davis, *A Treatise on Insanity*, 32. Cited in Whitaker, *Mad in America*, 20.

34. Foucault, *Madness and Civilization*, 71–72.

them "rarely useful and frequently injurious." In place of barbaric treatments or "pharmaceutic preparations," he started reviewing the patient's case histories carefully and focused on "management of the mind," which he called "*traitement morale*." He advocated psychological and humane treatments, talked to the patients, and addressed their complaints.[35] Pinel also stressed the significance of the patient's life history in "understanding their symptoms."[36] As he got to know his patients personally he developed affection and appreciation for them:

> I have nowhere met, except in romances, with fonder husbands, more affectionate parents, more impassioned lovers, more pure and exalted patriots, than in the lunatic asylum, during their intervals of calmness and reason. A man of sensibility may go there every day of his life, and witness scenes of indescribable tenderness to a most estimable virtue.[37]

Andrew Sims, the prominent British psychiatrist, regards Pinel as the "father" of psychiatry. To him one of Pinel's great contributions to psychiatry was the emphasis on "observing and listening to the patient."[38] The success of Pinel's moral treatment was so vivid that some patients were considered healthy enough to be discharged. This convinced Pinel that the prevailing scientific theories of madness were wrong, and since a "nurturing environment" had the potential for healing, then insanity most likely was not due to an "organic lesion of the brain," but instead was a mental disorder. Consequently it only made sense for the treatment to consist of mental approaches.[39] Comparable developments took place in Italy, led by Vicenzio Chiarugi, a twenty-six-year-old Florentine psychiatrist, who criticized "custodialism," and the use of medication and restraints. He instead advocated humane treatments of the insane to lead them toward healing—treatments described in his three-volume work, *On Insanity*.[40]

In England, an attempt was made to separate the insane from other inmates in all institutions. William Battie, the eighteenth-century owner of two private madhouses, and the founding medical officer of St. Luke Hospital in London, was the first physician who argued that all the insane

35. Whitaker, *Mad in America*, 21; Porter, *Madness*, 104–5.

36. Merkel, "The History," 8.

37. Quoted in Whitaker, *Mad in America*, 21.

38. Sims, *Is Faith Delusion?*, 56.

39. Whitaker, *Mad in America*, 21–22.

40. Porter, *Madness*, 104; Shorter, *A History of Psychiatry*, 10.

are not the same and argued for early diagnosis, confinement, and individualistic treatment design. Battie advocated the curability of mental disorder, through isolation from family and friends, decreased stimuli, orderly routines, and a strong doctor-patient relationship—his own version of moral treatment in England. Shorter claims it was with Battie that "the birth of psychiatry commenced."[41]

In 1796, the local Quaker community in York, led by a tea merchant, William Tuke, established the York Retreat as a counter model to the York Asylum in which they had witnessed scandalous treatment of other Quakers. In 1791, Hannah Mills, a young Quaker woman, died of harsh treatment and neglect at the York asylum. Instead of protesting against her death, they quietly set up the Retreat based on their religious values so that their mentally ill would never again have to go through such abuse. They considered the mad as "brethren."[42] This is where moral therapy with its emphasis upon community life was developed and practiced. Porter explains:

> It was modeled on the ideal of bourgeois family life, and restraint was minimized. Patients and staff lived, worked, and dined together in an environment where recovery was encouraged through praise and blame, rewards and punishment, the goal being the restoration of self-control.[43]

Medical treatments had been tried at the Retreat with little success. Thus all medical means had been put aside and were replaced with "kindness, mildness, reason, and humanity, all within a family atmosphere—and with excellent results."[44] Pinel and Battie were both physicians who tried managing their patients through helping their *psyche* and had a key role in changing the way physicians and society treated the insane, but they never questioned whether the insane should be put under the care of medical doctors. It was the Quakers who "presented a much more vigorous challenge to the medical establishment." And while Pinel is recognized as the father of moral therapy, Whitaker believes it was the Quaker's reformed model of care, "rooted in religious beliefs," that shaped the future care of the mad in America. In its first fifteen years, York Retreat witnessed a re-

41. Porter, *Madness*, 100–102; Merkel, "The History," 7; Shorter, *A History of Psychiatry*, 9–10.

42. Whitaker, *Mad in America*, 23.

43. Porter, *Madness*, 104.

44. Ibid.

markable recovery rate of 70 percent among the patients who showed up in the first year of their illness.[45]

Pinel, Battie, and the York Quakers had changed the image of the insane from animals to members of the human family, one of the "brethren." They showed European society that for the insane, the ultimate source of recovery lay within their soul and "not in the external powers of medicine." This was a revolutionary image—one that the nineteenth-century America with its "democratic ideals" was poised to embrace.[46] Shorter notes, "What the English called moral therapy and the French 'le traitement moral' thus became the gold standard of enlightened asylum administration."[47] It was evident to everyone that patients responded to compassion, words of comfort, and caring physicians. Shorter, speaking of moral therapy, points out, "What is astonishing is not that it was discovered, but that it was later lost so completely from view in asylum life."[48]

In the United States, European models of care for the insane were retained until the 1930s. Before the nineteenth century, harsh treatment of the insane was pervasive in the US. In 1756, the first general hospital (Pennsylvania Hospital) was founded at the instigation of the Religious Society of Friends and Benjamin Franklin, who were interested in importing concepts of Quaker-developed moral therapy into the colonies. They also were concerned about too many "lunatics" roaming around the roads and bringing terror to their neighbors, and it was this second concern of using the hospital as jail that took precedence. Whitaker explains, "In those early years, the lunatics were kept in gloomy, foul smelling cells and were ruled over by 'keepers' who used their whips freely."[49]

The prominent and influential period for American psychiatry started with the attending physician in Pennsylvania Hospital, Benjamin Rush (1745–1813), who was officially crowned by the APA in 1965 with the title of "father of American psychiatry" and believed that all mental illnesses were "due to vitiated blood."[50] Rush agreed with the European physicians who preceded him that the brain drove mental disorders. In his famous psychiatry textbook, he stated, "The cause of madness is seated primarily in the blood-vessels of the brain, and it depends upon the same kind of

45. Whitaker, *Mad in America*, 22–24.

46. Ibid., 22, 25.

47. Shorter, *A History of Psychiatry*, 21.

48. Ibid, 22.

49. Whitaker, *Mad in America*, 4.

50. Shorter, *A History of Psychiatry*, 15; Porter, *Madness*, 126–27.

morbid and irregular actions that continues other arterial diseases."[51] It was this medical viewpoint that guided him to continue with practices such as bloodletting, purges, and emetics as systematic remedies for the disorder.

Rush, born of Quaker parents and influenced by Pinel and the Quakers, spoke of moral therapy and humane application of medicine, and he advocated "kindness and respect" toward the insane in his hospital. Shorter, who finds inconsistencies in stories about how the insane were treated under Rush's rule, says, "As a founder of psychiatry therefore, Rush is a bit of a sham."[52] He cites a visitor to the Pennsylvania Hospital in 1787 recounting, "cells were . . . partly underground . . . about 10 feet square, and made as strong as a prison . . . In each door is a hole, large enough to give them food . . . Some of them were extremely fierce . . . nearly or quite naked."[53] Rush also took advantage of "spinning therapy" and the "Tranquilizer Chair," which was his proud invention.[54] Unfortunately, most of those highly acclaimed procedures brought forth nothing but additional pain and trauma for the sufferers.

But it was in 1817 that Philadelphia Quakers opened the first non-medical asylum purely based on the concept of moral therapy. This was the first of many asylums operated in different states by the Quakers, and their approach was different from Rush's. By 1841, there was a total of sixteen private and public asylums in the US that treated the insane based on moral therapy. All these facilities were built in the country, with manicured gardens, and kept small (with a maximum of 250 people) to offer individual attention in a humane and compassionate environment. The key was to treat the patients as "rational beings" by expecting them to behave rationally and by helping them to overcome their personal stumbling blocks. The results were remarkable. Hartford Retreat reported recovery of twenty-one of twenty-three patients that came to them in their first three years. McLean Hospital reported a recovery rate (including those who were "improved") of 59 percent among the 732 patients they received between 1818 and 1830. The numbers were as impressive in all asylums built on moral therapy principles.[55]

51. Rush, *Medical Inquiries and Observations upon the Diseases of the Mind*, 15; cited in Shorter, *A History of Psychiatry*, 15.

52. Shorter, *A History of Psychiatry*, 16; and Whitaker, *Mad in America*, 5.

53. Shorter, *A History of Psychiatry*, 16.

54. Whitaker, *Mad in America*, 16.

55. Ibid., 25–27.

In the Fellowship of His Suffering

The great rate of recovery generated considerable excitement and optimism that in the right environment insanity was treatable. "I think it is not too much to assume that insanity," said Worcester Superintendent Samuel Woodward in 1843, "is more curable than any other disease of equal severity; more likely to be cured than intermittent fever; pneumonia, or rheumatism."[56] The obvious question, then, is what happened? As Shorter pointed out earlier, how could something this successful disappear from the scene? What made society drift away from what seemingly had revolutionized the treatment of the insane and had led to such remarkable outcomes? According to Whitaker, it is the story of how medicine grabbed hold of moral treatment and enslaved it to its own theories.

Scull explains that the first asylums in the US were modeled after the York Retreat and were run by superintendents who gave medicine a secondary role in the treatment of the insane. These leaders considered physical remedies for madness to be of no value and deemed them to be at best useless and at worst "injurious and frequently fatal."[57] One asylum director confessed that "he and his colleagues were so prejudiced against the use of medical measures, as to object even to the election of physicians in their board, being fearful they might effect some innovation."[58] Whitaker claims that "moral treatment . . . had presented physicians with a clear threat." It was obvious to them that as the asylums run by the Quakers and civic groups flourished the physicians were left behind with no role to play. In order to stop this threat, The Connecticut State Medical Society lobbied the state and civic groups to build a local asylum; in return for all its efforts it demanded the right to assign the superintendent that was guaranteed to be a physician. Hartford Retreat in Connecticut was opened in 1824 with Dr. Eli Todd as its superintendent. He immediately claimed that this new asylum was going to offer "superior care to the insane," and take advantage of "lofty conceptions of truly combined medical and moral management."[59] Although in York the original movement started as "a backlash against medical practices," medicine was now claiming these "retreats" to be its own. With the Hartford asylum and the idea that physicians are best suited

56. Quoted in ibid., 27.

57. Scull, *Social Order/mental Disorder*, 103; cited in Whitaker, *Mad in America*, 28, 307 n. 11.

58. Quoted in Whitaker, *Mad in America*, 28.

59. Scull, *Social Order/mental Disorder*, 106; cited in ibid.

to be superintendents, moral therapy in the United States took an unquestionable turn, one with profound repercussions as we shall see.[60]

Soon after, asylum medicine became a specialty and in 1844, the Association of Medical Superintendents of American Institutions for the Insane (AMSAII) was founded by thirteen asylum superintendents who passed a resolution indicating that every asylum would have a physician as its Chief Executive Officer and superintendent. Medical remedies were brought back and the use of sedatives such as morphine and opium and application of cathartics such as bloodletting again became acceptable. Whitaker states, "Their use of such chemical 'restraints,' in turn, made them more receptive to the use of physical restraints," such as straitjackets, which became increasingly in demand as the asylum population grew.[61]

Even though the intrusion of medical doctors into asylums brought the forces that led to the downfall of moral treatment, one must remember that there were physicians who devoutly followed the inner principles of moral therapy and produced great results. One such physician was Thomas Kirkbride, who was born and raised in a Quaker religious home. His personal character of humility and faithfulness were planted in him through his upbringing. He governed the asylum at the Pennsylvania Hospital from 1841 to 1883, which were the glorious years of that asylum, run in an opulent setting, with meticulous landscaping, a beautiful dining room, and facilities for entertainment and education—an environment conducive to healing. He hired only loving, patient, and compassionate attendants who would spend personal time with the patients. He argued that it was the way the society reacted to insanity that made it such a horrific experience. "More than half of these horrors will be destroyed, and the chances of recovery increased," he wrote, "whenever the whole community can look upon the insane as upon other sick."[62]

Kirkbride became renowned for his "skill as a healer." He pastorally and gently counseled his patients and helped them to develop "a sense of guilt and even shame for one's misbehavior." He sought a lasting inner change in them.[63] His patients admired him, and many sought his counsel even after they were discharged. The letters that came to him from his former patients expressed fervent emotions of gratitude and love. They thought of their hospital stay as a "green spot" in their past that built their

60. Whitaker, *Mad in America*, 28.

61. Ibid., 29.

62. Tomes, *A Generous Confidence*, 234.

63. Whitaker, *Mad in America*, 32.

character. One man wrote that the asylum was "the finest place in the world to get well."[64] In fact, patients' sanity appeared to depend in large part upon how successfully they internalized the "love and sympathizing care" they received from Kirkbride.[65] Yet although Kirkbride helped many patients and led them not only to recovery from their illness but also to a lasting inner change, loads of people remained in the hospital as chronic cases.

A key principle in the success of moral therapy was the creation of a home-like environment with a maximum population of 250. By 1874, the average number of patients in state hospitals had grown to 432, and in some places the number was more than 1,000.[66] The "empathy" and "guidance" were gone. The recruitment of attendants could not be as selective as earlier times; "They had to settle instead for staff drawn from the lowest rungs of society, 'criminals and vagrants' in the words of one superintendent."[67] The skyrocketing growth in the number of the insane was not unique to the US, but was seen all across Europe. Porter notes that, "Positivistic, bureaucratic, utilitarian, and professional mentalities vested great faith in institutional solutions in general."[68] The new environment was no longer conducive to moral treatment principles. The management of large number of insane people demanded new procedures.

The new environment brought back the old order: "coercion, brute force, and the liberal use of restrains." Treatment outcomes were becoming more disappointing every day. As an example, Worcester asylum had claimed that in its first decade, 80 percent of its patients who were newly ill had either "recovered or improved." After the expansion of the asylum, that number dropped to 67 percent and continued falling further and further. In 1892, the asylum superintendents officially changed their name from AMSAII to the American Medico-Psychological Association (later

64. Tomes, *A Generous Confidence*, 226.

65. Ibid., 224.

66. In 1931, Pilgrim State Psychiatric Hospital opened up with the purpose of holding all the mentally ill in the state of New York. Its eventual population reached 14,000 patients and it became "the largest psychiatric institution in the world." The hospital had its own fire and police department, power plant, and cemetery. See Bentall, *Doctoring the Mind*, 34–35.

67. Whitaker, *Mad in America*, 35.

68. Porter, *Madness*, 112.

called the American Psychiatric Association), threw away the foundational principles of moral therapy and vowed to pursue science and medicine.[69]

An important question is whether moral therapy was truly a failure or whether it was the circumstances and political motives that brought it to its end. Notwithstanding Foucault's criticism of moral therapy, most assessments point to a radical approach to madness that was fruitful.[70] Whitaker claims, "Modern historians have concluded that it did indeed produce surprisingly good results."[71] During Kirkbride's management, from a group of 8,546 "insane" patients, 45 percent were released as "cured," and another 25 percent as "improved." On a more general basis, the first decade of moral therapy in the US saw a discharge rate of 35 to 80 percent for the newly admitted patients within their first year of treatment, of which the majority were released as "cured."

Shorter believes that the defeat of the asylum reform was not because of faulty ideas, but because of the increasing number of patients who flooded these places. These warehouses were filled with "chronic paretics, dements, and catatonic schizophrenics." As the numbers grew, the treatments increased in violence to tame the patients. Quality care became only a memory of the past. By the beginning of the twentieth century, psychiatry was at a "dead end." Psychiatrists themselves suffered from low self-esteem, since the rest of the medical profession perceived them as "the dull and the second-rate, just a step, if that, above the spa-doctors and the homeopaths."[72]

Porter believes that psychiatrists, in some ways, were the "victims of their own propaganda." They had advertised that they were able to address many human problems that were normally labeled as "sin," "vice," or even "crime" by suggesting that all those who suffered in these ways needed was good medical treatment in an asylum. When the magistrates, the community, and the state leaders believed them and "deflected difficult cases from the workhouse or jail," superintendents of asylums discovered to their disappointment and cost that "rehabilitation posed more problems

69. Whitaker, *Mad in America*, 35–38.

70. Foucault, who does not deny that moral therapy brought sanity back to many of the patients, considers religion to be "a constant principle of coercion." In his view the person who was freed from external chains became a prisoner of internal "stifling anguish of responsibility" based on religious moral principles, which gave birth to inner fears that "now raged under the seals of conscience": Foucault, *Madness and Civilization*, 244, 247.

71. Whitaker, *Mad in America,*, 36.

72. Shorter, *A History of Psychiatry*, 65.

than anticipated." Psychiatry took a new posture in response to the new environment: the reason that "moral therapy" failed is because much of insanity is, "after all, chronic, indeed ingrained, constitutional, and probably hereditary" and there was little that could be done for these people other than controlling them, stopping them from hurting their neighbors and breeding future generations.[73]

The first half of the twentieth century probably marks some of the darkest chapters in psychiatry's history, not only for the patients, but also for the physicians. Many intellectuals, such as Dr. Alexis Carrel, the Nobel Prize winner, in support of eugenics, demanded that society should "dispose of the criminals and insane in a more economical manner."[74] In the eyes of most people, the psychiatrists had been reduced to acting as society's policemen, or gatekeepers who handled the insane and protected the population from them. They performed this bestowed responsibility, if necessary, in the severest and harshest ways. As Shorter says, "A profession composed of practitioners who did this kind of thing for a living would not hold its head up."[75]

The institutionalization paradigm was a reflection of the times. It grew out of the "imperatives of a rational state" combined with capitalizing on a market economy, masked in a desire on the part of the social elites to help the unfortunate. Porter says:

> Not least, the asylum idea reflected the long-term cultural shift from religion to scientific secularism. In traditional Christendom, it was the distinction between believers and heretics, saints and sinners, which had been crucial—that between the sane and the crazy had counted for little. This change and the great divide, since the "age of reason," became that between the rational and the rest, demarcated and enforced at bottom by the asylum walls. The keys of St. Peter had been replaced by the keys of psychiatry.[76]

Indeed the asylums of this era separated the "normal" from the "mad," and emphasized their "otherhood," and created a managerial ambiance in which that otherness could be controlled. This also planted the seeds of an ideology in the Western church to abandon her most unfortunate and oppressed and allow the society not only to label them as aliens, but also

73. Porter, *Madness*, 119.

74. Carrel, *Man the Unknown*, 318–19; cited in Whitaker, *Mad in America*, 66.

75. Shorter, *A History of Psychiatry*, 65.

76. Porter, *Madness*, 122.

for the church herself to marginalize them and question how they could possibly be the children of the Most High.

The Rise of Modern Psychiatry

The initial optimism to find the biological root of mental illness ended in the realm of degeneration, the notion that the illness passed down through the generations and worsened continually. With the failures of the nineteenth century, psychiatry had to assess its direction in a new paradigm. Set on proclaiming its position among the reputable biomedical disciplines, alongside neurology, and "utterly distinct from such quackish and fringy embarrassments as mesmerism and spiritualism," psychiatry could no longer find its answers in the noisy and stinky asylum halls, but in the research laboratories of the universities, with a mission to "lay bare the relationship between mind and brain." It is this goal to develop a systematic approach that set the new paradigm for psychiatry of the twentieth century.[77]

One of the most influential people to define the direction for the modern psychiatry was German Emil Kraepelin (1856–1926). For Kraepelin, it was essential to "shed the unscientific dross which had gathered around psychiatry," with unfounded diagnoses such as "old maid's insanity," "erotomania," and "masturbatory psychosis."[78] Kraepelin's contributions are recognized through a century of *descriptive clinical psychiatry* and psychiatric *nosology*. For more than a decade he analyzed the course of illness rather than the momentary symptoms for the patients under his care—a longitudinal method to diagnosis, versus a cross-sectional approach. He then categorized the various mental disorders through clinical description of "symptoms," rather than neuroanatomical explanation, and related them to predicted outcomes. Kraepelin is remembered mostly for dividing psychotic illnesses into two categories: 1) *manic-depressive illness*, which consisted of emotional disturbances along with psychotic episodes of mania, which had a positive prognosis for recovery; 2) *dementia praecox*, which was exhibited in "atrophy of the emotions," and "vitiation of the will," as if the person had "forsaken his humanity." He conveyed the sense that these people were "moral perverts, psychopaths, almost a species apart." His prognosis for this illness was very gloomy, projecting that more than 75 percent of them would steadily degenerate

77. Porter, *Madness*, 183; Shorter, *A History of Psychiatry*, 69–70.

78. Porter, *Madness*, 184; Whitaker, *Mad in America*, 165.

into an "end-stage dementia."[79] Kraepelin's *dementia praecox*, which was later called "schizophrenia" by Swiss psychiatrist Eugen Bleuler, has left an indelible mark on modern psychiatry. It is Kraepelin's work that set the foundation for the current *descriptive psychiatry*.

Kraepelin's gloomy prognosis about "schizophrenia" later fed into concepts of eugenism and degenerationism, and led to psychiatric politics in which the very lives of the mentally ill were conceived as not worth living. In fact, in the 1930s, "Nazi psychiatry deemed schizophrenics, no less than Jews, ripe for elimination."[80] The aggressive treatments of people suffering from "schizophrenia" with little regard to the side effects on their lives have been justified by this pessimistic view of the illness. At best, psychiatrists decided that if these people had no likely chance for a normal life, and not much to lose, then even the most severe treatments such as a brain lobotomy made sense if they brought some relief.[81]

It is of great significance that English historian Mary Boyle has so convincingly argued that among Kraepelin's psychotic patients, some undoubtedly were suffering from *encephalitis lethargica (EL)*, an organic and infectious brain disease discovered in later years by Austrian neurologist Constantin von Economo, and which in many cases damaged the brain.[82] When Kraepelin came up with his description of *dementia praecox*, anybody suffering from *encephalitis lethargica* would have been grouped with the lunatics in the asylums. He and Blueler identified a common type of patient with a peculiar set of physical symptoms, such as "spasmodic phenomena in the musculature of the face," "disorders of equilibrium," unequal pupils, sudden bouts of sleepiness after a good night of sleep, etc.[83]

Boyle demonstrates with great detail that the descriptions of alleged cases of dementia praecox/schizophrenia given by Kraepelin and Blueler are "virtually identical" to those of encephalitis lethargica and its "Parkinsonian sequelae."[84] In some of his patient's brains, Kraepelin had found serious nerve damage along with "the proliferation of abnormal glial cells," which was exactly the same kind of damage found by von Economo in his

79. Porter, *Madness*, 185; Whitaker, *Mad in America*, 165.

80. Porter, *Madness*, 186.

81. Whitaker, *Mad in America*, 165.

82. Boyle, "The Non-Discovery of Schizophrenia?," 3–22. The resemblance is confirmed in Gelder et al., *Shorter Oxford Textbook of Psychiatry*, 426.

83. Boyle, "The Non-Discovery of Schizophrenia?," 16–17.

84. Ibid., 15.

patients.[85] Von Economo declared, "some people said to be suffering from dementia praecox, were in fact cases of encephalitis lethargica." Others also confirmed the diagnosis of EL at post-mortem examination of brains originally thought to have had *dementia praecox*.[86] Furthermore, it was noticed that when the worldwide pandemic of the disease ended around 1927, there were no longer a supply of "schizophrenics" who fit Kraepelin's list of symptoms of patients who had the unfortunate hopeless outcomes.[87]

Regrettably, Kraepelin's view of the gloomy outcome that he attached to *dementia praecox* has shaped the philosophy of treatments in the past 100 years; and psychiatry has not gone back to revisit Kraepelin's work in a fundamental way. If it is true that Kraepelin and Blueler were the first to describe "schizophrenia" "so thoroughly and sensitively,"[88] it is quite noteworthy, as Boyle has observed, that apart from delusions and hallucinations, today's "schizophrenia" does not share any of the original phenomena described by them. The kinds of cases seen by Kraepelin and Blueler are almost nonexistent today.[89]

What would Kraepelin have thought of sufferers of psychotic symptoms if those with EL had been removed from his pool? Would he still have attached a gloomy prognosis to those who had no biological brain pathology? Was his pessimism about "schizophrenia" justified after psychiatry has seen many global studies of people who have recovered?[90] As Whitaker discovered in his research, the concept of "schizophrenia" was "too vital to the profession's claim of medical legitimacy" to be easily let go. Instead of dropping the whole concept, psychiatry just limited the diagnostic criteria to elusive mental symptoms, including unusual thoughts, delusions, and hallucinations. This categorization severely complicated the diagnostic process.[91]

The question that continues to be debated is whether one could consider unusual thoughts pathological. Undoubtedly, many biblical experiences of prophetic visions or inspirations can be considered "abnormal

---

85. Whitaker, *Mad in America*, 167.

86. Boyle, "The Non-Discovery of Schizophrenia?," 18.

87. Whitaker, *Mad in America*, 167.

88. Gottesman et al., *Schizophrenia, the Epigenetic Puzzle*, 258; cited in Boyle, "The Non-Discovery of Schizophrenia?," 17.

89. Boyle, "The Non-Discovery of Schizophrenia?," 17.

90. For an inspiring story of recovery, see the TED Talk: Longden, "Eleanor Longden: The Voices in my Head."

91. Whitaker, *Mad in America*, 167.

thoughts." These experiences are meant to be "abnormal," because they are unique bestowment of grace on certain individuals. When do such experiences become pathological? John Mirowsky, of the University of Illinois, explains that psychotic symptoms are exaggerations and distortions of normal functions. He reports on a study conducted on 463 people in El Paso, Texas, to evaluate their thought processes. The findings pointed to the commonality of abnormal thoughts. They found that "[m]ost people in the community" had experienced thoughts that could "range in severity." Many experienced what might be considered as "symptoms" of "schizophrenia," such as being dominated by forces beyond their power, seeing things that others did not see, or feeling they had special powers.[92]

Gordon Claridge, the British psychologist from Oxford University, disagreeing with the extreme position taken by organic psychiatry that psychotic disorders are "entirely discontinuous with healthy functioning," suggests that "schizophrenia" is a *psychobiological* disturbance of function," which stems from "a disposition to react to events in a particular way and the impact of those events on a vulnerable individual."[93] Claridge is basically confirming that we are all created uniquely and we react differently to various conditions. The reactions might differ from societal norms, but nevertheless their seeds are built into the individual humanness.

American psychiatrists have been very aggressive in diagnosing people as "schizophrenics." Indeed, in an alarming experiment, David Rosenhan in 1973 from Stanford University proved how easily American psychiatrists diagnosed people with "schizophrenia." A team made up of Rosenhan himself and seven other "normal" people showed up at twelve different mental hospitals, some showing up at more than one place, claiming they were hearing vague voices telling them things such as "thugs," "empty," or "hollow." Rosenhan explains that, "Beyond alleging

92. Mirowsky, "Subjective Boundaries and Combinations in Psychiatric Diagnosis," 407–24, 161–78; Theodore Sarbin also demonstrates that schizophrenia symptoms "are not uncommon among the general population." He asserts, "The failure of eight decades of research to produce a reliable marker leads to the conclusion that schizophrenia is an obsolescent hypothesis and should be abandoned." Sarbin, "Toward the Obsolescence of the Schizophrenia Hypothesis," 259–84, 13–38. On the other hand, Shitij Kapur explains, "So long as these events (delusions and hallucinations) remain private affairs, they are not an illness by society's standards. . . . It is only when the patient chooses to share these mental experiences with others, or when these thoughts and percepts become so salient that they start affecting the behavior of the individual, that they cross over into the domain of clinical psychosis." Kapur, "Psychosis as a State of Aberrant Salience," 16.

93. Claridge, "Can a Disease Model of Schizophrenia Survive?," 160, 173.

the symptoms and falsifying name, vocation, and employment, no further alterations of person, history, or circumstances were made."[94] Remarkably, in every case, these "pseudopatients" were admitted into mental hospitals, and all except one were diagnosed with "schizophrenia." After admission, the "pseudopatients" never complained of voices, and acted as normally as they could. They were never detected as "imposters." Among the eight of them they were given a total of 2,100 neuroleptic pills—which they threw away—and the range of their hospital confinement was from seven to fifty-two days, with an average of nineteen days. Rosenhan and his colleagues also experienced how it felt to be carrying the label of "schizophrenia" in the eyes of the others. Doctors and nurses never took them seriously, and nothing that came out of their mouths had any meaning deemed worth attention. The "pseudopatients" felt they were "invisible" and "unworthy of account."[95] Regardless of how "normal" they continued to behave, it seemed as if, "Having once been labeled schizophrenic, there is nothing the pseudopatient can do to overcome the tag. . . . Once a person is designated abnormal, all of his other behaviors and characteristics are colored by that label."[96] This study is a remarkable reflection on how difficult it is to distinguish "sanity" from "insanity." After all, we all can be seen as "insane" in the "right" context.

Beginning in the 1930s and building on Kraepelin's gloomy theories, along with eugenic beliefs, psychiatry began to embrace remedies such as "insulin coma, metrazol convulsive therapy, electroshock, and prefrontal lobotomy," all of which working by harming the brain.[97] The age of physical force and restraint was gone, and with the downfall of moral therapy, psychiatry had vowed to pursue scientific and medical treatments. Although Freudian psychotherapy had played a key role in psychiatry in the beginning of the twentieth century, it was not deemed effective enough for the large number of patients kept in institutions. Considering the medical advancements toward the end of the nineteenth century in treating tuberculosis, cholera, typhoid, and diphtheria, it only made sense for psychiatry to follow the same route. However, most of the psychiatric therapeutic techniques were designed to dull the intellect. Harry Stack Sullivan, a leading psychoanalyst at the time, said, "The sundry procedures, to my way of thinking, produce 'beneficial' results by reducing the patient's ca-

94. Rosenhan, "On being Sane in Insane Places," 251.

95. Ibid., 256.

96. Ibid., 253.

97. Whitaker, *Mad in America*, 73–74.

pacity for being human. The philosophy is something to the effect that it is better to be a contented imbecile than a schizophrenic." Another physician commented, "The greater the damage, the more likely the remission of psychotic symptoms."[98] Most of these harmful remedies started fading away due to the arrival of antipsychotic drugs.

The Age of Psychopharmacology

As the above historical analysis shows, psychiatry has had a checkered past and has been the location for various political, economic, and professional power struggles as the discipline has developed and has sought to offer a rationale for its existence. With the colossal rise in the popularity of the biological sciences as explanatory frameworks for everything, psychiatry in most parts has come to use this perspective as a primary lens through which it views itself and its patients. It is the advent of psychopharmacology that has solidified this desired stature. In order to evaluate the scientific basis of organic psychiatry invigorated by psychopharmacology, we will explore the foundational elements upon which this discipline has been built.

The modern era of psychopharmacology "began with systematic experimentation into the chemistry of the brain."[99] Brain chemistry is centered on *neurotransmitters*, which is the medium for the transmission of nerve impulses in the brain. The human brain is made of 100 billion nerve cells called *neurons*. These are electrically excitable cells and they communicate to each other through a very complex network. Each neuron can be pictured like an electric wire called an *axon*, with many branches called *dendrites*. There are fluid-filled gaps about twenty nanometers wide between neurons and these are called *synapses* or *synaptic clefts*. There are about 150 trillion synapses in an adult brain. In each cell, chemicals called *neurotransmitters* are made, which carry the electric impulse for communication between the two neighboring neurons. When one neuron sends an electric impulse to another neuron, the *presynaptic*—the sending—neuron manufactures the neurotransmitters, puts them inside little sacs called *vesicles* and moves the filled vesicle to its web of dendrites, into a synapse and then finally activates or inhibits the receiving—*postsynaptic*—neuron. The postsynaptic neuron takes in the neurotransmitter when the neurotransmitter attaches a receptor site on the receiving dendrites.

98. Quoted in ibid., 98–99.

99. Shorter, *A History of Psychiatry*, 246.

There are unique types of neurotransmitters and receptor sites that bind together "similar to a lock and key." There are a variety of neurotransmitters with different functions travelling between cells, but it has been hypothesized that serotonin, dopamine, and norepinephrine are the three that are commonly involved in mental illness.[100]

After neurotransmitters have influenced the firing of a postsynaptic neuron, some are taken back by the presynaptic neuron in a process called *reuptake*. Sometimes the extra neurotransmitters are destroyed by enzymes in the synaptic cleft, while some will continue to sit in the synaptic cleft. It is by interfering with this process of communication among neurons that psychiatric drugs affect feelings, thoughts, and behavior.[101] Kirsch explains, "The chemical-imbalance hypothesis is that there is not enough serotonin, norepinephrine, and/or dopamine in the synapses of the brain."[102]

While depression was framed as lack of serotonin or norepinephrine in the brain, "schizophrenia" or other psychotic illnesses were claimed to have resulted from "overactive dopaminergic pathways"—either the presynaptic neurons were firing too much dopamine into the synaptic cleft, or the postsynaptic neuron had an "abnormally high density of dopamine receptors."[103] This theory arose from efforts to figure out the therapeutic effects of the first antipsychotic: Chlorpromazine (brand name Thorazine). Antipsychotics were supposed to put a brake on this system and to normalize the level of dopamine neurotransmitters in the brain.

It was through the discovery of metabolites—neurotransmitter breakdown products, e.g., Homovanillic acid (HVA) for dopamine—in the spinal fluid, that the theory arose that mental illness is caused by an abnormality in the concentration of these chemicals in the brain, which could be countered by a specific drug. In other words, by figuring out how these drugs worked, scientists speculated, it was possible to identify what was wrong with the brains of the mentally ill. "For example," says Angell, "because Thorazine was found to lower dopamine levels in the brain, it was postulated that psychoses like schizophrenia are caused by too much dopamine."[104] The same logic applied to the theory of too little serotonin

100. Kirsch, *The Emperor's New Drugs*, 82; Patterson, *The Therapist's Guide to Psychopharmacology*, 15–16; and Whitaker, *Anatomy of an Epidemic*, 67–68.

101. Bentall, *Doctoring the Mind*, 76.

102. Kirsch, *The Emperor's New Drugs*, 82.

103. Whitaker, *Anatomy of an Epidemic*, 70.

104. Angell, "The Epidemic of Mental Illness." Marcia Angell is an American

causing depression. In other words, "instead of developing a drug to treat an abnormality, an abnormality was postulated to fit a drug. . . . Similarly, one could argue that fevers are caused by too little aspirin."[105]

Drug Revolution and the Outcome

The introduction of Lithium—a mood stabilizer—in 1949 for managing manic-depression and the subsequent arrival of antipsychotics (notably Chlorpromazine, called by critics the "liquid cosh") and antidepressants, revolutionized the psychiatric industry. It was the introduction of Chlor-promazine in 1952 that facilitated the beginning of de-institutionalization of the insane and the hope that they could be integrated back into the community. The prominent British psychiatrist William Sargant saw these drugs as "a blessed deliverance" that would finally free the insane not only from imprisonment in the asylum, but also from the "follies of Freud." He proudly predicted that these drugs "would eliminate mental illness by the year 2000."[106] This false optimism has been an iconic symbol of psychiatric history.

The term *antipsychotic* is applied to drugs that reduce and control symptoms of psychosis. These drugs in their first generation were referred to as *neuroleptic* and *major tranquillizer*, none of which fully reflected the purpose for which they were being prescribed. Neuroleptic points to the side-effects of these drugs rather than any potential therapeutic effects. Major tranquilizers emphasize the numbing and dulling effect of the drug. Atypical antipsychotics are the second generation of these drugs and are claimed to have fewer side effects. Antidepressants are mostly used to manage the symptoms of *depression*, and at times for the management of *generalized anxiety* and *panic disorder*. There are other families of psychiatric drugs commonly prescribed as well, such as mood stabilizers, stimulants and hypnotics.[107]

This drug revolution was a great morale boost for the profession. It had the promise of a "cost-effective" method of treatment without lengthy

---

physician, author, and the first woman to serve as editor-in-chief of the prestigious *New England Journal of Medicine* (NEJM). She is a Senior Lecturer in the Department of Social Medicine at Harvard Medical School.

105. Ibid.

106. Porter, *Madness*, 205–6.

107. Gelder et al., *Shorter Oxford Textbook of Psychiatry*, 658; Sinaikin, *Psychiatry-land*, 110.

hospitalizations, psychoanalysis, or dangerous psychosurgeries. Additionally, Porter notes, "It would also promote psychiatry's wishful identity as a branch of general medicine."[108] The introduction of Chlorpromazine, the leader of this revolution, was compared by Edward Shorter to "the introduction of penicillin in general medicine," and this was in spite of it lacking any curative effect![109]

The "era of psychopharmacology" had begun. English psychiatrist Henry Rollin saw psychiatrists' "morale" charged up by "the most important revolution in the history of treatment in psychiatry."[110] Chlorpromazine was given to an estimated two million American patients within eight months of its introduction in May 1954. This was the beginning of an era in which a steady stream of psychotropic drugs kept flowing from the pharmaceutical production lines. "And still, they come!"[111]

The new drugs created a phenomenal market. The results were beyond anyone's wildest imaginations. Porter explains:

> The tranquillizer Valium (diazepam) became the world's most widely prescribed medication in the 1960s; by 1970 one American woman in five was using minor tranquillizers; and by 1980 American Physicians were writing ten million prescriptions a year for antidepressants alone. . . . Introduced in 1987, Prozac, which raises serotonin levels and so enhances a "feelgood" sense of security and assertiveness, was being prescribed almost ad lib for depression; within five years, eight million people had taken that "designer" antidepressant, said to make people feel "better than well."[112]

Regardless of all the excitement, at best the benefits of drugs for "schizophrenia" are still quite limited, and at worst, the outcomes are horrendous. As an illustration, an antipsychotic drug can receive regulatory approval from FDA if it can show 20–30 percent reduction in symptoms relative to a placebo. People suffering from "schizophrenia" are often on a complex multi-medication regimen. In addition to antipsychotics, these "drug cocktails" usually include antidepressants, anticonvulsants, benzodiazepines (with sedative, hypnotic, anti-anxiety, muscle relaxant, and amnesic effects), and anticholinergic medications to manage side

108. Porter, *Madness*, 206.

109. Shorter, *A History of Psychiatry*, 255.

110. Rollin, "The Dark before the Dawn," 113.

111. Ibid.

112. Porter, *Madness*, 206.

effects of movement abnormalities created by the other drugs. Of course, anticholinergic drugs have side effects of their own, which require other drugs to suppress them, and soon one would get into cascading effects of medication upon medication. This long list of psychotropic medications "reflects both the unique characteristics of the patient and our rather limited understanding of the disorder and its treatment," claims Patterson.[113]

The first generation of antipsychotics, led by the introduction of Chlorpromazine, is believed to block the dopamine receptor. One of the unintended and undesirable consequences is that they also affect other parts of the brain and thus cause a great number of side effects. These drugs block the dopamine receptors wherever they exist, and through this blockade, though positive symptoms—hallucination, paranoia, and delusion—are reduced, a host of other traits that depend on the functionality of dopamine pathways are damaged. For example, the negative symptoms in "schizophrenia"—affective flattening, avolition, social withdrawal—are not only not improved by dopamine blockade, "If anything, the medication is likely to make negative symptoms worse."[114] These kinds of assessments are well known and shared by the whole profession. Additionally, this dopamine blockade in the "nigrostriatal pathway" induces severe "motor symptoms like muscle rigidity, inexpressive facial features, and tremors, reminiscent of the manifestations of Parkinson's disease." These are the side effects that are usually referred to as *parkinsonian* and *extrapyramidal symptoms*. Another undesirable side effect is the increase in "the production and release of a hormone called prolactin . . . normally elevated in pregnancy . . . responsible for breast enlargement and milk production." This is an even more distressing problem when it happens to male patients. Other effects of abnormally elevated prolactin levels include menstrual dysfunction, sexual dysfunction, and decreased bone density. One of the most dreaded side effects of these drugs is *Tardive Dyskinesia* (TD), which causes "Protrusion of tongue, puffing of cheeks, chewing movement, involuntary movements of extremities and trunk."[115] Some patients also develop *Neuroleptic Malignant Syndrome*, a life-threatening neurological disorder, which is accompanied by muscle rigidity, fever, autonomic instability and cognitive changes such as delirium.[116]

113. Patterson, *The Therapist's Guide to Psychopharmacology*, 115. We will show later that the margin of improvement has been trending downward in recent years.

114. Ibid., 116.

115. Ibid., 117.

116. Ibid., 119.

It was in the late 1980s that the second generation of antipsychotics was kicked off with Clozapine (trade name Clozaril). The new generation called "atypical" antipsychotics were believed to reduce the incidence of extrapyramidal symptoms and TD. However, Clozapine had its own "disturbing side effects and dangerous adverse reactions," notably, severe seizures, and "an increased risk of potentially fatal agranulocytosis," a serious acute blood disease accompanied by "a severe drop in white blood cell count."[117] To manage this potential risk, patients are required to take weekly blood tests for the first six months and with a decreased frequency thereafter, which is even extended for a period of time after they stop the medication. Clozaril was the first of many atypical antipsychotics—e.g., Risperidone (Risperdal), Olanzapine (Zyprexa), Quetiapine (Seroquel)—which became blockbuster drugs, in the sense of earning the pharmaceutical companies billions of dollars. Although it is believed that the rate of extrapyramidal effects and TD are lower in atypical antipsychotics, they appear to have their own bag of major side effects, such as elevated prolactin, metabolic syndrome, obesity, heart disease, hyperglycemia (elevated blood sugar), diabetes, high cholesterol, hyperlipidemia (elevated blood fats), which all lead to a much "shorter life expectancy."[118]

Additionally, the great market success of psychotropic drugs has generated new treatment problems. Organic psychiatry, particularly in the United States, has become so medication driven that in most cases psychiatrists know very little about the personal lives of their patients. In the words of Roy Porter, it is "a case of the tail wagging the dog." It is true that these drugs have significantly increased the number of mentally ill persons sent back into their communities, but "problems of side-effects and dependency are perennial, and their long-term effects are necessarily unknown."[119]

Whitaker, who has done a detailed historical analysis of antipsychotic drugs, notes that the positive view espoused by historians and psychiatrists toward the end of the twentieth century is not necessarily how Chlorpromazine was perceived while it was in use: "It was seen at that time as a pill that hindered brain function, much in the same manner that lobotomy did." Chlorpromazine was part of a group of compounds called phenothiazines, developed in 1800 as synthetic dyes. According to Whitaker, "In the 1930s, the U.S. Department of Agriculture employed

117. Ibid., 119–21; See also Novartis, "Highlights of Prescribing Information."

118. Ibid., 121.

119. Porter, *Madness*, 207.

phenothiazine compounds for use as an insecticide and to kill swine parasites." Later, in the 1940s, it was realized that the compound "sharply limit[s] locomotor activity in mammals." This enabled French surgeons to do surgery without the use of anesthesia. In 1952, French psychiatrists Jean Delay and Pierre Deniker used Chlorpromazine to "calm manic patients" at St. Anne's Hospital in Paris. As expected, the drug induced a "profound indifference," and made the patients feel "an invisible wall" that separated them from the world around them. Delay and Deniker named their new procedure "hibernation therapy." Life was becoming much more controllable in the asylums with this drug induced "vegetative syndrome." The psychotic patients did not rant and rave anymore. Instead, they became "completely immobile" and were easily "moved about like puppets."[120]

Deniker and Delay coined the name "neuroleptic" to reflect the adverse effects of the drug, because it would "take hold of the nervous system" and it could restrain the brain chemically.[121] It was also soon discovered that Chlorpromazine induced Parkinson's disease symptoms. More important, psychiatrists did not find the drug to have any antipsychotic effects. "It is important to stress that in no case was the content of psychosis changed," noted Joel Elkes, recognized as one of the pioneers of psychopharmacology. "The schizophrenic and paraphrenic patients continued to be subject to delusions and hallucinations, though they appeared to be less disturbed by them."[122] Chlorpromazine worked for the staff of the asylums who had to deal with the unruly patients, and for the psychiatrists who saw these patients as hopeless and saw the drug as a comforter to redeem these people from their turbulent minds, but it did not work for the patients themselves.

In a study, the California Mental Hygiene Department reviewed 1413 first-episode male "schizophrenics" who were treated in California hospitals between 1956 and 1957. They discovered that neuroleptics seemed to delay recovery and extend the length of hospitalization. In their analysis, those who had never been put on the drug had a greater chance of getting back to their communities. The new paradigm of releasing patients into community meant, it was thought, that they had to be controlled by the drugs continuously. They were no longer simply short-term remedies that

120. Whitaker, *Mad in America*, 141–44.

121. Deniker, "From Chlorpromazine to Tardive Dyskinesia," 254; cited in Shorter, *A History of Psychiatry*, 255.

122. Healy, "Pioneers in Psychopharmacology," 191. Elkes, "Effects of Chlorpromazine," 560–65; cited in Whitaker, *Mad in America*, 145.

would calm patients down within the walls of the institutions. Instead, "Pharmaceutical firms had lifelong customers for their drugs, and a society poised to insist that such drugs be taken."[123]

The perceived success of Chlorpromazine paved the way for other "me-too" neuroleptics to be put in wide use. Daniel Carlat states, "Whether we are talking about depression, schizophrenia, or bipolar disorder, the new drugs introduced over the past fifty years are no more effective than the original prototypes."[124] This disappointing reality has recently been publicized by several large objective studies, known as STAR-D, STEP-BD, and CATIE, conducted by the NIMH in the United States, studies that show that the newer drugs for depression, bipolar disorder, and schizophrenia generally are not more effective than the older drugs.[125] More surprisingly, even the concept of "fewer side effects" is being called into question. The report on CATIE indicates, "Overall, the medications were comparably effective but were associated with high rates of discontinuation due to intolerable side effects or failure to adequately control symptoms. . . . Surprisingly, the older, less expensive medication (perphenazine) used in the study generally performed as well as the four newer medications."

Deniker and Delay, as the original advocates of neuroleptics, knew very well that these drugs worked not by curing the illness but by disrupting some brain functionality. This knowledge began to be widely understood in 1963. Up to that point, it was not clear how neuroleptics accomplished the effects that patients experienced. It was the Swedish pharmacologist Arvid Carlsson who claimed that "neuroleptics inhibit the activity of a chemical messenger in the brain, dopamine." Later technologies, such as Positron Emission Tomography (PET), made it easier to understand that inhibition.[126]

Today "most antipsychotics are believed to produce their therapeutic effects through the blockade of dopamine D2 receptors," but that is not a confirmed scientific understanding.[127] There are drugs such as Clozapine, which is widely believed to be effective in suppressing the "symptoms" of

123. Epstein et al., "An Approach to the Effect of Ataraxic Drugs on Hospital Release Rates," 36–47; Whitaker, *Mad in America*, 157–58.

124. Carlat, *Unhinged*, 10–11.

125. For a study of 4,000 patients with depression see: NIMH, "STAR*D." For a study of 4,300 patients with bipolar disorder see: NIMH, "STEP-BD." For a study of 1,460 patients with schizophrenia see: NIMH, "CATIE."

126. Whitaker, *Mad in America*, 162.

127. Gelder et al., *Shorter Oxford Textbook of Psychiatry*, 135.

"schizophrenia" and has a "weak affinity" for binding the D2 receptors. Even though the therapeutic mechanism of antipsychotics is not scientifically confirmed, the damaging side effects have been verified through several studies. In a study of twenty-two people with "schizophrenia," it was discovered through PET scans that in patients treated with conventional dosages of classical neuroleptics, the D2 occupancy was 70 percent to 89 percent, causing a "blockade" of the dopaminergic pathways in the brain. The level of the D2 occupancy was directly related to the intensity of extra-pyramidal syndromes (EPS), which before the advent of neuroleptics were associated with "degenerative disorders of the basal ganglia" in the brain. Farde et al. claim, "Neuroleptic-induced EPS are generally believed to be mediated by drug interference with dopamine transmission in the basal ganglia."[128] This way the person's thinking and behavior is changed "by partially shutting down vital dopaminergic nerve pathways." In fact, this is why neuroleptics induce symptoms similar to Parkinson's disease, because the disease is the result of "the death of dopamine-producing neurons." Neuroleptics also tranquilize people by "impairing the limbic system" from where "we *feel* the world." This feeling is critical to the "sense of self" and to one's "conceptions of reality." This blunting effect is what has made these compounds "useful in veterinary medicine for taming animals."[129]

Peter Breggin, a former fellow at Harvard Medical School, is a psychiatrist who is well known for his criticism of psychiatric drugs. He points to a study that was sponsored by the US government to evaluate the effects of multiple street drugs on the brain. He points out that, "A serendipitous finding came up in the mental patient control group: *the consumption of neuroleptic drugs was directly associated with a permanent loss of overall mental function.*"[130] He believes that for political reasons the findings were not publicized. One of the authors of the unpublished report was Lewis Judd, the former Director of the NIMH. In the unpublished report, presented in some professional conferences, the authors highlighted a "statistical correlation" between "lifetime ingestion of neuroleptic drugs and persistent mental dysfunction." None of the patients in the study had been treated with the drugs for more than five years. Judd et al. declared, "We were struck that the deficit frequently occurred in psychiatric patients," and "[i]t is also clear that the antipsychotic drugs must continue to

---

128. Farde et al., "Positron Emission Tomographic Analysis," 538.

129. Whitaker, *Mad in America*, 162–63.

130. Breggin, *Toxic Psychiatry*, 82.

be scrutinized for the possibility that their extensive consumption might cause general cerebral dysfunction."[131]

If these reports are accurate, then antipsychotics seem to control some "symptoms" of psychosis by inducing "a *pathological* deficiency in dopamine transmission."[132] As Deniker put it, these medications produced a "therapeutic Parkinsonism."[133] With the pervasive use of these medications in psychiatric treatments madness found a new pathological image. In the Western world, as Whitaker puts it:

> The image we have today of schizophrenia is not that of madness—whatever that might be—in its natural state. All of the traits that we have come to associate with schizophrenia—the awkward gait, the jerking arm movements, the vacant facial expression, the sleepiness, the lack of initiative—are symptoms due, at least in large part, to a drug-induced deficiency in dopamine transmission.[134]

The question is how we could understand the natural progression of the illness, if we never allow it to progress naturally. Our conception of people with "schizophrenia" is filtered by how the medications have shaped their personalities, image, and behavior. We have lost them in their true selves as created by God from our circle of humanity. In our pursuit of removing what is bothersome, difficult, and challenging, we have lost the opportunity to unravel one of the greatest mysteries of being human. What did we gain in return? Possibly a sense of false security!

The Myth of "Chemical Imbalance"

The widely advertised idea that mental illness is the result of a chemical imbalance in the brain is "a rather controversial theory," says Kirsch, and "there is not much scientific evidence to support it . . . rather, there is a ton of data indicating that the chemical-imbalance theory is simply wrong."[135]

131. Ibid.

132. Whitaker, *Mad in America*, 164.

133. Deniker, "From Chlorpromazine to Tardive Dyskinesia," 253–59, cited in ibid.

134. Whitaker, *Mad in America*, 164.

135. Kirsch, *The Emperor's New Drugs*, 5–6. Kirsch, Associate Director of the Program in Placebo Studies and a lecturer in medicine at the Harvard Medical School, and professor emeritus of psychology at the University of Hull, United Kingdom, has been widely recognized for his seminal research, which unraveled the story about the

The dopamine imbalance theory of "schizophrenia" was developed in a backward way. In the 1950s, Swedish scientist Arvid Carlsson—who won the 2000 Noble prize in physiology for his work on the dopaminergic system—suggested that a deficiency of dopamine might be the reason for Parkinson's disease, and the theory was tested and verified by Oleh Hornykiewicz in Vienna. Psychiatric researchers took this information and hypothesized that since neuroleptics commonly produced Parkinsonian symptoms in "schizophrenic" patients, and if the deficiency of dopamine is the cause of Parkinson's, one could conclude that the neuroleptics possibly frustrated dopamine transmission and/or killed dopaminergic neurons, which resulted in "dopamine malfunction." Around the same time, it was reported that amphetamines—which can induce hallucination and delusions—increased the dopamine level in the brain. These findings collectively gave birth to the hypothesis that an excessive level of dopamine in the brain is the cause of psychosis, which neuroleptics could bring back to balance.[136]

Carlsson soon reported that indeed all neuroleptics did produce a dopamine malfunction in the brain. This finding "told of drugs that 'disconnected' certain brain regions. They weren't normalizing brain function; they were creating a profound pathology," says Whitaker.[137] Thus, these drugs would be categorically antipsychotic and this led to Dutch scientist Jacques Van Rossum to formally put forth the dopamine hypothesis of "schizophrenia" in 1967: "*When* the hypothesis of dopamine blockade by neuroleptic agents can be *further substantiated*, it may have fargoing consequences for the pathophysiology of schizophrenia. Overstimulation of dopamine receptors could then be part of the etiology. Obviously such an overstimulation might be caused by overproduction of dopamine."[138] Van Rosuum's statement was very conditional, but it was taken as a fact and

---

efficacy of anti-depressants in comparison to placebos. He concludes his fifteen years of scientific quest to understand how antidepressants work, stating, "antidepressants are little more than active placebos, drugs with very little specific therapeutic benefit, but with serious side effects. . . . The belief that antidepressants can cure depression chemically is simply wrong. . . . Depression is not caused by a chemical imbalance in the brain, and it is not cured by medication. Depression may not even be an illness at all. Often, it can be a normal reaction to abnormal situations. . . . Depression is a serious problem, but drugs are not the answer." See 4, 5, 177.

136. Bentall, *Doctoring the Mind*, 76. Whitaker, *Anatomy of an Epidemic*, 63–64.

137. Whitaker, *Anatomy of an Epidemic*, 63–64.

138. Baumeister and Francis, "Historical Development of the Dopamine Hypothesis of Schizophrenia," 272; emphasis mine.

became the basis for the treatment of "schizophrenia" for the next four decades or so on to this day.

In 1974, Malcolm Bowers raised questions about the validity of the dopamine hypothesis. He reported that in his tests, unmedicated "schizophrenics" had a normal level of dopamine metabolites in their cerebrospinal fluid.[139] In fact in some cases "net increases in HVA were produced by antipsychotic drug administration."[140] In 1975, this was followed by Robert Post from NIMH, who reported that in a study of "[t]he metabolites of serotonin, dopamine and norepinephrine," of twenty unmedicated acute "schizophrenic" patients, no significant difference was found between the "normal" and the "affectively ill" people.[141] There was also no abnormal level of dopamine detected in autopsy of the brain tissue of unmedicated schizophrenic patients.[142] Again, in 1982, John Haracz of UCLA reviewed the existing body of research on dopamine hypothesis of "schizophrenia" and reported: "Drug free schizophrenics and controls were reported to have similar DA [dopamine] and HVA concentrations in several brain regions. . . . Preliminary studies indicated that schizophrenics and non-schizophrenics did not differ in the post mortem fluorescence[143] histochemistry of catecholamine neurons. . . . These findings do not support the presence of elevated dopamine turnover in the brains of schizophrenics."[144]

When it became clear that "schizophrenics" who had never been medicated had normal dopamine levels, the researchers turned their attention to a second possibility. Now the search was on to see if the "schizophrenics" suffered from an "overabundance of dopamine receptors," which would imply that postsynaptic neurons are "hypersensitive" to dopamine and "this would cause the dopaminergic pathways to be overstimulated."[145] This hypothesis was confirmed by Phillip Seeman in 1978. In an autopsy of twenty "schizophrenic" brains, it was discovered that they contained

139. Bowers, Jr., "Central Dopamine Turnover in Schizophrenic Syndromes," 53.

140. Ibid., 50.

141. Post et al., "Cerebrospinal Fluid Amine Metabolites in Acute Schizophrenia," 1063.

142. Whitaker, *Anatomy of an Epidemic*, 75.

143. Scientists had discovered that different neurotransmitters fluoresced different colors when they are exposed to formaldehyde vapors. This characteristic makes it possible to trace neurotransmitter pathways in the brain. See ibid., 68.

144. Haracz, "The Dopamine Hypothesis," 440.

145. Seeman and Snyder identified two distinct dopamine receptors, D1 and D2, based on Van Rossum's hypothesis; Whitaker, *Anatomy of an Epidemic*, 76.

"70 percent more D2 receptors than normal." Lest some people would assume that the cause of "schizophrenia" had finally been discovered, Seeman cautioned that the long-term administration of neuroleptic drugs may have had an influence on this evidence.[146]

Further research quickly demonstrated that "the drugs were indeed the culprit." Burt et al. demonstrated that *"chronic treatment of rats with the neuroleptic drugs . . . elicits a 20 to 25 percent increase in striatal dopamine receptor binding. . . . This increase in receptor sites may account for behavioral supersensitivity to dopamine receptor stimulants in such animals and for tardive dyskinesia in patients treated with these drugs."*[147] Furthermore, these researchers emphasized, "Our data indicate that the motor changes seen after chronic neuroleptic treatment are associated with an increase in the number of dopamine receptors."[148] In other words, *the problems that were initially thought to be inherent in "schizophrenia" are in reality created by the drugs.* In each case, as the drug blocked the transmission of dopamine, the brain compensated for that lack by elevating the supersensitivity of the postsynaptic receptors by increasing their density.

Further proof of this evidence came in 1982, when after examining the brain tissue of forty-eight deceased patients with "schizophrenia," Mackay et al. reported: "The increase in receptors were seen only in patients in whom neuroleptic medication had been maintained until the time of death, indicating that they may be entirely *iatrogenic*."[149] Nevertheless, researchers continued to seek abnormalities within dopaminergic pathways to make sense of the prevailing theories. By the end of the 1980s, "it was clear that the chemical-imbalance hypothesis of schizophrenia— that this was a disease characterized by a hyperactive dopamine system that was then put somewhat back into balance by drugs—had come to a crashing end."[150]

The low-serotonin theory of depression and the high-dopamine theory of "schizophrenia" had been hypothesized for decades. These made the "twin pillars of the chemical-imbalance theory" of mental illness, and by the late 1980s, all researchers in the field knew that neither of the two

146. Lee et al., "Binding of 3H-Neuroleptics and 3H-Apomorphine in Schizophrenic Brains," 897–900, cited in Whitaker, *Anatomy of an Epidemic*, 76.

147. Burt et al., "Antischizophrenic Drugs," 326.

148. Ibid., 327.

149. Mackay et al., "Increased Brain Dopamine and Dopamine Receptors in Schizophrenia," 991.

150. Whitaker, *Anatomy of an Epidemic*, 77.

theories had any credibility anymore.[151] But in our collective consciousness those theories persisted. The question is why our collective beliefs are so misdirected and get ahead of the evidence. This is partially due to advertising techniques by pharmaceutical companies, who continue to attach mental illness to a chemical imbalance, because it is a graspable concept for the public and it sells drugs. Unfortunately, until recently, the physicians have had little reason to question it. According to Kirsch, most doctors don't have the time to "carefully sift through the data," and they are influenced by drug advertisements they see in their trade journals.[152] But now the data has become so strong that it can no longer be avoided.

Peter Kramer, drawing on the work of Carl Degler, the Stanford professor who analyzed the fall and rise of social Darwinism, contends that "cultural needs influence the evidence scientists attend to."[153] For a society that does not want to face its personal flaws and relational dysfunction, and for a society intrigued by miraculous advancements of biological medicine, the proposition that "biology is destiny" seems "incontrovertible." Now that it was clear to the researchers that the "chemical imbalance" theory was dead, therefore, psychiatry turned to other dimensions of science in search of finding a biological answer for insanity.

The Genetics of Mental Illness

Neuroscientists are enthusiastic and well-intentioned to move the "science" of mental disorders forward. But it is critical to be honest about how much we do not know. Carlat, a renowned psychiatrist, says, "In virtually all of the psychiatric disorders—including depression, schizophrenia, bipolar disorder, and anxiety disorders—the shadow of our ignorance overwhelms the few dim lights of our knowledge."[154]

However, Carlat is certain that psychiatric disorders can be inherited; his certainty comes from studies that have compared identical twins (those who share 100 percent of their DNA) with fraternal twins (those who share fifty percent of their DNA). Studies that examined the concordance rate of "schizophrenia" between twins have identified a concordance rate of 40 percent in the former group, and a rate of 10 percent in the latter.

151. Ibid.

152. Kirsch, *The Emperor's New Drugs*, 92.

153. Kramer, *Listening to Prozac*, xiv.

154. Carlat, *Unhinged*, 80.

Carlat believes that this implies a significant role for genetics in the development of schizophrenia. Of course, this has never been proven.[155] And the question arises that, if genes play such a primary role, why then do only 40 percent of identical twins that suffer from "schizophrenia" share the illness and not 100 percent? Carlat admits that finding an answer to the genetic puzzle of "schizophrenia" has been "devilishly hard" and that "the latest landmark study found that we are much further away from identifying such genes than we thought."[156]

The "landmark" study that Carlat is referencing is a genome-wide study, in which they examined the genetic sequences of 10,000 people who were diagnosed with "schizophrenia" and compared those against 20,000 controls—"normal" people—from multiple European locations. In this genome-wide study they found more than 10,000 gene variants "to have a role in 'causing' schizophrenia." This was an "embarrassment of riches," says Carlat.[157] Interestingly, "A fundamental message emerging from genome-wide association studies of copy number variations (CNVs) associated with the disease is that its genetic basis does not necessarily conform to classical nosological disease boundaries."[158] Based on this analysis, it appears that "schizophrenia" is not a single disease, but a manifestation of a variety of "symptoms" in different people for reasons yet unknown.

Nicholas Wade, the science writer for *The New York Times,* sarcastically wrote: "Schizophrenia . . . seems to be not a single disease, but the end point of 10,000 different disruptions to the delicate architecture of the human brain. Yes, that discovery is a landmark. The kind that says you have 10,000 miles yet to go." He called the findings "a historic defeat, a Pearl Harbor of schizophrenia research." He noted that his comments are no reflection of the quality of the research methods, or the researchers themselves, but that "The defeat points solely to the daunting nature of the adversary."[159] If a study shows that among 10,000 "subjects," there are 10,000 gene variants, this is pointing to the complexity of the individuality of these people, and how their manifestation of the illness has a unique voice.

155. For an evaluation of the problems associated with the Twin Studies, see Joseph, "The 'Missing Heritability,'" 69–70.

156. Carlat, *Unhinged*, 81.

157. Ibid.

158. Stefansson et al., "Common Variants Conferring Risk of Schizophrenia," 744.

159. Wade, "Hoopla, and Disappointment in Schizophrenia Research."

As Wade remarks, "The march of science is not direct but two steps forward, one step back."[160] The anatomy of madness could possibly be revealed over time, but, for now, insanity appears to be as mysterious as it has been throughout the ages. In the twenty-first century there has been a "remarkable resurgence" of research into psychosocial risk elements in the development of insanity. Indeed, by some accounts, "psychiatry has been in the process (again) of changing its mind."[161] Now the study of genetics in psychiatry is shifting slowly toward the field of epigenetics, which focuses on the "interplay between environment and genetic susceptibility." Psychiatrists seem to be more willing to accept that "genetics is not destiny," that someone's life history, circumstances, and environmental elements can "regulate the expression of heritable genes," and the brain development has a lot to do with the environmental factors beyond genetics. In *Psychiatric News*, published by the APA, Jun Yun wrote, "After 20 years of genetic research on psychiatric disorders, scientists have not pinned down a specific genetic cause or risk factor for most patients. . . . The molecular basis of psychiatric disorders has turned out to be far more complex."[162]

The research in epigenetics is indeed a turn in the right direction. But the hoopla around the genetics of mental illness and daily pronouncements in media, and even scientific literature, about advancements in the treatments of serious mental disorders such as "schizophrenia" fall short of producing meaningful outcomes. The people afflicted with these illnesses continue to suffer deeply and live semi-functional lives. A very recent review of scientific findings published since the beginning of the twenty-first century shows that the picture is far less promising than the public is led to believe. After looking at 103 published studies on issues of linkage between environmental variables and genetics, the reviewers, Laramie Duncan from Harvard Medical School and Matthew Keller from the University of Colorado, said in an interview: "Based on our calculations and the date [*sic*] from related fields, we estimate that many of the positive findings in this particular area of research may, unintentionally, be incorrect." According to their analysis, it seems that novel findings make

160. Ibid.

161. Staub, *Madness is Civilization*, 190.

162. Yan, "Epigenetics Links Nature and Nurture," 12. Likewise, in a review of psychiatric genetic studies over the past decades, Joseph concludes "that decades of negative results support a finding that genes for the major psychiatric disorders do not appear to exist, and that research attention should be directed away . . . toward environmental factors." Joseph, "The 'Missing Heritability'," 65.

it into publication before the findings are consistently proven through replicable research.[163]

The Epidemic and Chronicity of Mental Illness

As we have already seen, the research findings speak to the ability of psychiatric drugs to control some of the "symptoms," while causing deeply damaging side effects. Some have even argued that pharmacological intervention *causes* mental distress and neurological damage rather than offers healing towards it. "More people seem to be diagnosed as suffering from more psychiatric disorders than ever: is that progress?" asks Porter.[164] If the history that we have reviewed in this chapter is a reflection of reality and the biological causes of mental illness remain to be discovered, then Whitaker believes a picture is emerging of a society "led horribly astray," and one might say "betrayed," suffering from the "epidemic of disabling mental illness" fueled by psychiatric drugs.[165] Although many mainstream psychiatrists may disagree with Whitaker's conclusions, many researchers also have noted this "epidemic of mental illness."[166]

Thomas Insel of NIMH highlights the findings of the World Health Organization Global Burden of Disease study, which identified mental illness as the primary cause of disability among Americans and Canadians aged fifteen to forty-four years, "accounting for nearly 40 percent of all medical disability in this age range."[167] As shown by the government disability data, the number of those who are disabled due to mental disorders in the United States, has "increased nearly two and a half times between 1987 and 2007—from one in 184 Americans to one in seventy-six." The tally is even more alarming in the case of children—"a thirty-five-fold increase in the same two decades"—and the number seems to be on the rise. In the National Survey of Children's Health conducted by the Center for Disease Control (CDC) in February 2011 and June 2012, it was reported that 6.4 million kids aged between four and seventeen—11 percent of kids

163. Duncan and Keller, "A Critical Review of the First 10 Years of Candidate Gene-by-Environment Interaction Research in Psychiatry," 1041–49. For the interview see: Lockhart, "More replication study needs to be carried out."

164. Porter, *Madness*, 214.

165. Whitaker, *Anatomy of an Epidemic*, 11.

166. Torrey and Miller, *The Invisible Plague*, 416; cited in Bentall, *Doctoring the Mind*, 18.

167. Insel, "Translating Scientific Opportunity into Public Health Impact," 129.

in this age group—are diagnosed to have ADHD. This is an increase of two million more kids than in 2007. According to Marcia Angell, "Mental illness is now the leading cause of disability in children, well ahead of physical disabilities like cerebral palsy or Down syndrome."[168]

Most alarming is that as the treatments increase so does the disability numbers. Insel, perplexed by the data, notes, "Curiously, despite increased treatment, there was no evidence for decreased disability. . . . While more people are receiving treatment, fewer than half of those who are treated receive treatments for which there is any evidence base."[169] Insel, as the director of NIMH, is the man in charge of funding research and implementing strategies and policies that would improve the state of mental health in the US. However, his honest assessment points to the gravity of the situation at hand and raises hope that if we all see and admit that "the emperor has no clothes on," something might finally be changed. Insel says:

> Given the limited improvements associated with current treatments, it is not surprising that the outcome data for serious mental illness in 2008 are disappointing. Today, mental disorders are the largest diagnostic category for those receiving disability . . . at a cost of almost $25 billion per year. Of those with schizophrenia, roughly 80 percent remain unemployed, and relatively few will marry. Despite five decades of antipsychotic medication and deinstitutionalization, there is little evidence that the prospects for recovery have changed substantially in the past century.[170]

The actual numbers are much higher, since indirect costs such as costs related to the loss of economic productivity by patients and their caregivers are not reflected here. Bentall estimates the true annual cost of "schizophrenia" to be more than sixty-two billion dollars in the US, and four billion pounds in the UK.[171]

In the US, the number of people taking antidepressants has increased to a startling 10 percent of the population. The use of antipsychotics is even more "dramatic." Angell says, "The new generation of antipsychotics,

168. Angell, "The Epidemic of Mental Illness." For the report on the escalation of ADHD diagnosis see: www.firstcoastnews.com/news/article/336557/10/ADHD-diagnoses-rise-to-11-of-kids.

169. Insel, "Translating Scientific Opportunity into Public Health Impact," 129.

170. Ibid.

171. Bentall, *Doctoring the Mind*, 9.

such as Risperdal, Zyprexa, and Seroquel, has replaced cholesterol-lowering agents as the top-selling class of drugs in the US."[172] What could be behind this alarming increase? How could it be that although many people claim to have been helped by their psychotropic drugs, the number of those disabled by mental illness is growing out of control? Whitaker asks a "heretical" question: "Could our drug-based paradigm of care, in some unforeseen way, be fueling this modern-day plague?"[173] His assertion is that this epidemic is *iatrogenic* in kind and to support this assertion he points to the following studies.[174]

In the late 1970s, Guy Chouinard and Barry Jones at McGill University offered an explanation for why relapse rate was so high among those diagnosed with "schizophrenia," and why they became chronically ill for life. Their theory was based on studies on the dopamine hypothesis of the illness which had shown that these drugs agitated the neurotransmitter system. The standard antipsychotics obstruct 70 to 90 percent of all D2 presynaptic receptors. This causes the postsynaptic neurons to gear up to compensate for the blockage by increasing the density of their D2 receptors by at least 30 percent. This scheme makes the brain supersensitive to dopamine, which is believed to be the pathway to psychosis. This means that anytime the drug is stopped, the blockage is removed from presynaptic neurons; the dopamine is fired up in an accelerated fashion, and the increased density of the D2 receptors in postsynaptic neurons already ingrained in the brain cannot be changed. Thus, "The system is now widely out of balance." The dopaminergic neurons are firing up so out of control that it may lead to "psychotic relapse or deterioration."[175] In other words, because of the biological changes in the neurotransmitter system caused by the medication, psychosis settles into the brain and the person has no choice but to stay on the drugs—and live with the side effects—and changing or adding other drugs as the old ones lose their effect.

172. Angell, "The Epidemic of Mental Illness."

173. Whitaker, *Anatomy of an Epidemic*, 9. Several studies have pointed to positive correlations between increased mental health treatment and suicide rates in the population. In a recent study, Rajkumar et al. concluded that "Countries with better psychiatric services experience higher suicide rates." They stress that these associations are quite complex and must be analyzed with caution and care. See Rajkumar et al., "National Suicide Rates."

174. Whitaker, *Anatomy of an Epidemic*, 208.

175. Chouinard and Jones, "Neuroleptic-Induced Supersensitivity Psychosis," 16–21; cited in Whitaker, *Anatomy of an Epidemic*, 105–6.

In 1996, Steve Hyman, the former director of NIMH, reported that psychiatric drugs "produce long-lived alterations in brain function," and basically confirmed what Chouinard and Jones had shown decades past. He highlighted the "molecular and cellular changes in neural function" caused by natural brain adaptations to chronic drug consumption. These changes, Hyman noted, "are rooted in homeostatic mechanisms that exist, presumably, to permit cells to maintain their equilibrium in the face of alterations in the environment or changes in the internal milieu." These compensatory mechanisms cannot last forever and after a while they will fall apart. This is why the "chronic administration" of the medication can cause "substantial and long-lasting alterations in neural functions." After a short few weeks on the drug, the person's brain will be functioning "qualitatively as well as quantitatively different from the normal state."[176]

This was an eye-opening analysis of many years of research. It appears that the drugs change the course of illness and as Whitaker explains, "once a person is put on a psychiatric medication, which, in one manner or another, throws a wrench into the usual mechanics of a neuronal pathway, his or her brain begins to function, as Hyman observed, *abnormally*."[177] What this analysis is not answering, is, why then some patients after several years of treatment can still recover from their insanity. If the biology of their neurotransmitter system is permanently damaged, can the brain recover over time? Does the recovery take place only after the person has been off medication for a while? What is the point of no return? The present research does not appear to have clear answers to these questions.

The advancements in imaging technologies have made it possible to evaluate the brains of people with "schizophrenia" more thoroughly. Nancy Andreasen, the former editor-in-chief of the *American Journal of Psychiatry* began a long term study of 538 people diagnosed with first-episode "schizophrenia" in 1989.[178] Eighteen years later, Andreasen, commented to a *New York Times* reporter about her team's longitudinal learning. Speaking of 305 patients that they were still monitoring, she explained, the "thing we've discovered is that the more drugs you've been given, the more brain tissue you lose." This is because, "They block basal ganglia activity. The prefrontal cortex doesn't get the input it needs and is being shut

176. Hyman, "Initiation and Adaptation," 151–62; and Whitaker, *Anatomy of an Epidemic*, 83.

177. Whitaker, *Anatomy of an Epidemic*, 84.

178. Ho et al., "Progressive Structural Brain Abnormalities and their Relationship to Clinical Outcome," 585–94.

down by drugs. That reduces the psychotic symptoms. It also causes the prefrontal cortex to slowly atrophy."[179] In other words, the treatment has an iatrogenic effect, managing some of the positive symptoms (e.g., hallucination), but worsening the negative symptoms (e.g., relational capacity), impairing cognitive ability, and leading to brain shrinkage.

In a recent reporting of their study about 211 of their patients, Andreasen and her team noted that although "[p]rogressive brain volume changes in schizophrenia" may be an outcome of the disease itself, animal studies indicate that antipsychotics "also contribute to brain tissue volume decrement." To validate this finding in humans, they measured the effect of brain reduction as a result of four potential contributors: "illness duration, antipsychotic treatment, illness severity and substance abuse." Their evaluation resulted in the following statement:

> Longer follow-up correlated with smaller brain tissue volumes and larger cerebrospinal fluid volumes. Greater intensity of antipsychotic treatment was associated with indicators of generalized and specific brain tissue reduction after controlling for effects of the other 3 predictors. More antipsychotic treatment was associated with smaller gray matter volumes. Progressive decrement in white matter volume was most evident among patients who received more antipsychotic treatment.[180]

179. Dreifus, "Using Imaging to Look at Changes in the Brain."

180. Ho et al., "Long-Term Antipsychotic Treatment and Brain Volumes," 128. For a broader review of research on relationship between use of antipsychotics and brain shrinkage see Goff, "Antipsychotics and the Shrinking Brain." See also an editorial written for *The British Journal of Psychiatry* by Anthony Morrison, professor of clinical psychology at the University of Manchester, stating that "Recent evidence from systematic reviews and meta-analyses suggests that the efficacy and effectiveness of antipsychotics to produce clinically meaningful benefits for people with psychotic disorders have been overestimated. . . . There is also evidence, again from systematic reviews and meta-analyses as well as from large controlled studies, to suggest that the adverse effects of antipsychotics have been underestimated. For example, a recent systematic review concluded that some of the structural abnormalities in brain volume previously attributed to the syndrome of schizophrenia may be the result of antipsychotic medication." Morrison et al., "Antipsychotics: Is it Time to Introduce Patient Choice?," 83. See also Brennand et al., "Modelling Schizophrenia using Human Induced Pluripotent Stem Cells," 221–25; in this study, neurobiologists using skin cells of patients diagnosed with "schizophrenia" produced stem cells suffering from "schizophrenia" in a petri dish. Their unexpected findings pointed to the *structural changes* of the brain neurons after they are exposed to antipsychotic drugs, which affected the course of illness. They think that the next generation of drugs will leave dopamine or serotonin concentrations alone and will focus on basic structural issues in the neurons. See an interview conducted with the researchers: Melville, "Schizophrenia created in a petri dish."

Moreover, a recent remarkable research finding comparing the outcome of antipsychotic dose-reduction/discontinuation strategies in patients with remitted first-episode psychosis against those maintained on medication shows that though those who discontinued their medication had a higher relapse rate in short term, their long term recovery rate was twice the recovery rate of the latter group (40.4 percent versus 17.6 percent) at seven years.[181] Those who stayed off medication became far more functional in the long term, perhaps because they were not exposed to long-term damages caused by these drugs and their natural healing mechanisms kicked in.

As is demonstrated in study after study, these drugs cause permanent damage in the brain. It appears that the patients on these drugs are on a downward spiral, risking loss of cognitive abilities, emotional capacity, ability to relate to others, and faculties that make them a human. Moreover, after structural changes in their brain, they may have no choice but to live their whole lives depending on these drugs, with all sorts of physical and emotional side effects that will shorten their lifespan. An iatrogenic process might be acceptable when benefits outweigh the losses and the person has no access to any alternative treatments. Since all these studies again and again raise questions about the entire paradigm of medical care for human mental distress, in absence of any biological tests to confirm these phenomena as biological diseases, it behooves us to weigh the evidence when deciding how to treat a sufferer of mental affliction and more importantly to abstain from forced treatments against one's will when nothing less than their personhood and consciousness are at stake.

The "Science" of Psychiatry: What Has Gone Wrong?

We have argued that the scientific basis of psychiatry is not as firm as is often claimed. Kraepelin's gloomy prognosis of "schizophrenia" has not proved to reflect reality. The theories of "chemical imbalance" and the "genetics of mental illness" have fallen short of producing convincing results as to the etiology of mental illness. Meanwhile, it appears that a "hidden epidemic" is destroying the lives of millions of adults and children around the globe. If the challenge of mental illness is a medical problem, then one wonders, contrary to all astronomical advancements in medicine, why can we not make any progress with madness?

---

181. Wunderink et al, "Recovery in Remitted First-episode Psychosis."

Simon Sobo, an American psychiatrist, questions the validity of "scientific" framework in dealing with mental illness in clinical settings. He warns against waving the banner of science in a quest for credibility and warns that science's "virtues can act as a smokescreen," to the extent that its "prestige" and "trappings" would distract clinicians from the reality of "what is known and not known." Sobo is concerned that the psychiatric treatments developed out of the paradigm of Evidence-Based Medicine (EBM) "too often are ineffective." He stresses, "Considering how much we still don't understand, our steps forward should be exploratory, investigative, and not closed off." Also, he points out the fallacy of scientific research based on DSM classifications of "disorders." He sees DSM-based diagnoses as mere "operational definitions," a "best attempt by committees of experts to group manifestations of psychopathology into 'disorders.'" He reminds his colleagues that, "This cataloguing is not the same thing as understanding cause and effect. We haven't yet discovered the etiology of any DSM-IV diagnosis."[182]

In order to understand the dynamics underpinning the "science" of psychiatry, we need to explore how these "disorders" are classified. What is the science behind cataloguing a certain phenomenon as a "psychiatric disorder"? Also, how are the treatments for these "disorders" researched, approved and marketed? It is only after understanding these foundational elements upon which the "science" of psychiatry has been built that we may be able to make sense of why we are where we are. These explorations may reveal why the "science" behind psychiatry has not fulfilled its promises.

"The Bible of Psychiatry"

It is difficult to understand how psychiatry is influencing our societal lives without understanding the nature of DSM, an American venture, through which psychiatry defines which behavior is "normal" and sets the standards by which "abnormality" is understood. Psychiatry, through its nearly 400 psychiatric diagnoses in DSM—now in its fifth edition—categorizes mental suffering into groups of disorders, such as those of anxiety, mood, and psychosis. Each disorder is given a name and a number—a diagnostic code that is necessary for communication in the mental health

---

182. Sobo, "Does Evidence-Based Medicine Discourage Richer Assessment of Psychopathology and Treatment?"

care industry and certainly for reimbursement from insurance companies in the United States. Carlat says:

> Naming psychiatric disorders reassures patients, who often improve markedly just by hearing that they have a condition that is well-organized and treatable. But just because it has a name, is it actually a disease? We commonly think of diseases as collections of symptoms with clear biological origins. Psychiatric diseases are similar but different. They are indeed collections of symptoms, but without any clear biological cause.[183]

Phillip Sinaikin, a practicing American psychiatrist, claims that whether the DSM diagnostic criteria to *"describe an **actual cellular mediated human disease**"* are "valid" categories has never been the "primary focus" of its authors. The original framers of the system "did not prioritize the question of the validity of psychiatric diagnoses, they prioritized reliability."[184] The intent of the system was to ensure the same diagnosis for a given phenomenon among a multitude of psychiatrists. Sinaikin stresses that DSM has been an indisputable success in "commodifying" mental and behavioral problems. He believes this is behind "the lasting success and unassailable dominance of the medical model in psychiatry" that "has rendered its failure" in its "clinical usefulness or theoretical validity" completely "irrelevant."[185]

In the past, most psychiatrists were psychoanalysts and were curious about the "why" behind a person's behavior. According to Carlat, nowadays, psychiatrists pay more attention to "what" symptoms the person is experiencing to put him in the box defined by DSM. If a woman complains of sadness, insomnia, lack of concentration, and low energy, because she had only four and not five out of nine symptoms for major depression, then she will not qualify for that disorder. Again, Carlat remarks:

> Four out of thirteen panic symptoms equals panic disorder; five of nine depressive symptoms equals depression; and so on through the dozens of other disorders listed in our peculiar bible. Is there something in the human brain that dictates these numbering rules? Of course not. The modern criteria for depression and other diagnoses are human constructions.[186]

183. Carlat, *Unhinged*, 44.

184. Sinaikin, *Psychiatryland*, 59.

185. Ibid., 104–5.

186. Carlat, *Unhinged*, 47.

The root of this construction goes back in history as far as the late 1800s when, as we have seen, Emil Kraepelin came into the mainstream of psychiatry. At that time mental illness was widely divided into insanity and "mental deficiency"; and there was a great effort on the part of neurologists to find the "presumed defects" behind mental illness. This quest was fueled by the excitement of the discovery of one type of insanity—neurosyphilis. Kraepelin saw in neurosyphilis a viable model for "a form of insanity with an identifiable neuropathological explanation." If all mental illnesses followed the same model, then they were all "discrete diseases with yet-to-be-discovered biological roots." He decided that he first had to classify these illnesses, based on common trends. Kraepelin believed that "if a group of patients shared the same course and prognosis," most probably they "shared the same biological cause." This systematic categorization of insanity "kick-started the process of searching for biologically based treatments."[187]

After the Second World War, in order to address the inconsistencies surfaced by the psychiatric problems encountered by the armed forces, a task force was formed with the mission to assemble a new standardized diagnostic system. The result of their work was the first version of the APA's *Diagnostic and Statistical Manual of Mental Disorders (DSM-I)*, which was published in 1952. This "was a triumph of the doctrine of truth by agreement," says Bentall. The influence of DSM was as great outside the United States as it was inside. It triggered an effort by the World Health Organization to achieve an international agreement about psychiatric classifications. An earlier attempt by WHO to classify psychiatric illnesses in their sixth edition of International Classification of Diseases (ICD-6) had been received unenthusiastically, partly because psychiatrists could not agree on etiologies. After the publication of DSM, it was decided to produce the eighth edition of ICD without any mention of etiology. This version was the byproduct of the cooperation among psychiatrists from many countries. Even the APA chose to revise their DSM based on ICD-8, and this resulted in publication of DSM-II in 1968 "as a spiral-bound notebook, 150 pages in length, available to clinicians for $3.50."[188]

It soon became apparent that the agreement around taxonomies did not guarantee that "diagnoses were reliable, let alone scientifically meaningful."[189] Many studies showed that patients would get different

187. Ibid., 48–51.

188. Bentall, *Madness Explained*, 46–47.

189. Ibid., 47.

diagnoses from different psychiatrists for the same problem, and more importantly, there were wide discrepancies in the diagnoses given in different countries. This was clearly demonstrated in the famous US-UK Diagnostic Project conducted by Kendell et al.[190] Subsequently the International Pilot Study of Schizophrenia (IPSS), conducted by WHO, highlighted the differences in local practices among nine countries. Again it was discovered that the concept of "schizophrenia" was much broader in the US and the Soviet Union than other countries.[191] Multiple studies exploring the level of diagnostic agreement between psychiatrists resulted in an astonishingly low rate of 32 to 42 percent.[192]

These were unacceptable and demoralizing results for many psychiatrists. It signaled "a crisis in the theory and practice of psychiatry." Some felt these diagnoses were "meaningless" and "dehumanizing" and called for the discontinuation of such practices. Others considered the problem to be rooted in the lack of rigor and an insufficient "medical approach."[193] One of the leaders of the second position was Robert Spitzer, who is credited with influencing the American *psyche* to accept psychiatric diagnoses in the latter decades of the twentieth century. Spitzer was hired by the APA to lead the development of DSM-III with the goal to solve the reliability problem. In this effort, Spitzer and his team allocated a list of symptoms to each diagnosis, and gave each diagnosis a "numerical threshold." The patient who "met the minimum threshold number of symptoms" was "qualified" to receive that diagnosis. The committee not only expanded the existing definition of the disorders, it also added new disorders. "The book increased in girth from 100 pages to 494 pages, and from 182 diagnoses to 265," says Carlat.[194] The estimated revenue for the APA selling just the main book and not counting the variety of pocket guides was over $9.8 million.[195] According to Sinaikin, DSM-III, "promoting a pseudo-scientific medical-model for psychiatry, would literally change the world and the lives of everyone in it."[196] Spitzer and his team took "the floundering and

---

190. Kendell et al., "Diagnostic Criteria of American and British Psychiatrists," 123–30.

191. Bentall, *Madness Explained*, 50–53.

192. Spitzer et al., "DSM-III Field Trials: I. Initial Interrater Diagnostic Reliability," 815–17; cited in Carlat, *Unhinged*, 52.

193. Bentall, *Madness Explained*, 53.

194. Carlat, *Unhinged*, 52.

195. Bentall, *Madness Explained*, 62.

196. Sinaikin, *Psychiatryland*, xvii.

unfocused specialty of psychiatry" and connected it skillfully to the "*awesome* power of the 'regime of truth' we call medicine." Sinaikin believes it is in meeting that responsibility of acting as a true medical discipline that "psychiatry has spun so wildly and dangerously off course."[197]

In a personal interview conducted by Carlat, in response to how all these decisions were made, Spitzer said:

> Ultimately . . . they were made by votes of a committee. We started with the categories that were already listed in DSM-II, and we brainstormed about other disorders that were being discussed in the psychiatric literature but which had not yet been formally defined. . . . It was just a consensus. . . . We would ask clinicians and researchers, "How many symptoms do you think patients ought to have before you would give the diagnosis of depression?" And we came up with the arbitrary number of five.[198]

This is how psychiatry came up with criteria for diagnosing approximately 300 "sources of suffering."[199] DSM-III was the beginning of the "Industrialization of Psychiatry." Psychiatrists started shifting their view of the disorders; they no longer represented Freudian theories. To those who were disenchanted with psychoanalysis—partly because it had failed to produce the desired results, but also because it was not "medical" enough—DSM-III held tremendous promise. At last, the industry was placing all its hope in a complete biological approach to mental illness.[200]

Stuart Kirk called the development of DSM-III in 1980 "one of the most significant events in psychiatry in the last half of the 20th century."[201] Many called this a revolution for psychiatry. What was the nature of that revolution? DSM-III put the nails in the coffin of psychoanalysis. "What was at stake was the fate of the psychiatric profession and the enormous, multibillion dollar mental health industry." The new descriptive psychiatry in Kraepelin's shadow, opened the door for a new generation of psychiatrists to "gain control over the infrastructure" of their profession and

197. Ibid., 68.

198. Carlat, *Unhinged*, 53.

199. Ibid., 55.

200. Bentall, *Madness Explained*, 57–58.

201. Kirk and Kutchins, *The Selling of DSM*, 5–6.

to abolish any opportunity for "diffusion of power" to others in the mental health enterprise.[202]

DSM-III was followed by DSM-III-R (revised) in 1987, which was followed by DSM-IV in 1994, and followed by DSM-IV-TR (text revised) in 2000. DSM-IV ensured that the classifications of disorders were consistent with the psychiatric disorders in the ICD-10, to be used internationally.[203] DSM-IV, under the chairmanship of Allen Frances, became one of the most powerful publications of the twentieth century. The pervasive use of DSM-IV around the globe truly made it "the bible of psychiatry." DSM-IV became the worldwide standard for psychiatric diagnosis and treatment, and through it American values about human nature have been imported to other nations across the globe.[204]

Part medical manual, part legal reference, DSM is the authority on human behavior embraced by both state and industry. It determines whether insurers, including government supported Medicare and Medicaid, will pay for treatment, and whether children will qualify for "special needs" education and whether the schools will provide financial aid for such services. Courts apply it to evaluate the extent of mental impairment of a criminal defendant; pharmaceutical companies depend on it to set direction for their research; and regulatory bodies use it to approve of treatments. The influence of psychiatry through DSM is so pervasive on the societal and cultural dynamics that everything from taxes, to education, to personal liberty, to health, to spirituality, to our relationships to our family, our neighbors, and even God is indirectly dictated by it.[205]

This level of control has created a wave of protest in and outside of the psychiatric community. Paula J. Caplan, a clinical and research psychologist, and a fellow in the Women in Public Policy Program at Harvard's Kennedy School of Government, who served on and subsequently resigned from two committees that worked on the DSM-IV, writes: "I used to believe that the manual was scientific and that it helped patients and therapists. But after seeing its editors using poor-quality studies to support categories they wanted to include and ignoring or distorting high-quality research, I now believe that the DSM should be thrown out." She writes about the irreversible damages caused by "snap-judgment diagnoses" based on the DSM criteria, which has replaced "listening to

202. Ibid., 7–8.

203. Bentall, *Madness Explained*, 62.

204. Watters, *Crazy Like Us*, 3.

205. Urbina, "Addiction Diagnoses may Rise Under Guideline Changes."

patients respectfully to understand their suffering" and how lives have been permanently damaged because of it.[206] Investigating the value of DSM, sociologists Herb Kutchins and Stuart Kirk, have written two books criticizing DSM, where they have bluntly called DSM "a book of tentatively assembled agreements."[207] They refer to "unpleasant and distressing experiences,"[208] such as smoking, shoplifting, hangover, shyness, menstrual discomfort, etc., that ordinary people encounter, but in DSM they are all listed as "criterion for one or more mental disorders." They argue that DSM has found a diagnosis for everybody: "Where you thought your friends were just having normal troubles, the developers of the American Psychiatric Association's diagnostic bible raise the possibility that you are surrounded by the mentally ill. Equally disconcerting to you, you may be among them."[209]

The next version of DSM—its 5th edition—originally scheduled to be released in 2010, mired in controversy and was finally published in May 2013. DSM-5[210] was initially promised to offer a "paradigm shift" compared to the previous editions. In their published *Research Agenda*, the editorial committee suggested that the new edition would be taking advantage of the latest findings in neuroscience to categorize the disorders in a more scientific way based on neurobiology and/or genetics.[211] The psychiatric blogosphere was swamped with editorials from world-renowned psychiatrists questioning the value of DSM-5 and its direction. Among them, the influential voices of Spitzer and Frances, the former DSM chairpersons, demanded change. Frances declared that "the work on *DSM-V* has displayed the most unhappy combination of soaring ambition and weak methodology."[212] He said, "There can be no dramatic improvements in psychiatric diagnosis until we make a fundamental leap in our understanding of what causes mental disorders." He declared that a "real paradigm shift of basing diagnosis on biological findings" is "years (if not decades) from fruition." He criticized categories that justify medicating people as a preventive measure in an attempt to keep them from ever

---

206. Caplan, "Psychiatry's Bible, the DSM, is Doing More Harm than Good."

207. Kutchins and Kirk, *Making Us Crazy*, 28.

208. Ibid., 21.

209. Ibid., 22.

210. APA has abandoned Roman numerals. DSM-V is now changed to DSM-5.

211. Kupfer et al., *A Research Agenda for DSM-V*, 307.

212. Frances, "A Warning Sign on the Road to DSM-V."

developing a mental disorder. He called that "a wholesale imperial medicalization of normality," and a great prize to the pharmaceutical industry. He argued the patients "will pay a high price in adverse effects, dollars, and stigma, not to mention the unpredictable impact on insurability, disability, and forensics." He warned about "false epidemics," and criticized his own work in DSM-IV: "the sudden increase in the diagnosis of autistic, attention-deficit/hyperactivity, and bipolar disorders may in part reflect changes made in the *DSM-IV* definitions."[213] In a broader sense he questioned the basic concept of psychiatric "disorders." Frances said, in a colorful language, to the *Wired* magazine: "[T]here is no definition of a mental disorder. It's bullshit. I mean, you just can't define it. . . . These concepts are virtually impossible to define precisely with bright lines at the boundaries."[214]

In 1997, Edward Shorter proudly defended the track record of organic psychiatry: "If there is one central intellectual reality at the end of the twentieth century, it is that the biological approach to psychiatry—treating mental illness as a genetically influenced disorder of brain chemistry—has been a smashing success."[215] In what appears to be a striking shift in perspective, even a staunch supporter such as Shorter is now raising questions about the direction of psychopharmacology. In anticipation of the upcoming revision of DSM manual in 2013, he wrote a piece for the *Scientific American* blog, saying:

> There has been almost no progress in psychopharmacology for the last thirty years. . . . Among antipsychotics (with the possible exception of clozapine, an effective but dangerous agent), none is superior to the first antipsychotic ever launched, chlorpromazine, marketed as Thorazine in the United States in 1955. Why this lack of progress? You can't develop drugs for diseases that don't exist. And in U.S. psychiatry today the principal diagnoses are comparable to a handful of smoke. Will DSM-5 fix this? Don't count on it.[216]

It appears that the fifth edition included "no paradigm shift after all." In a personal interview, Darrel Regier, the Vice-chair of DSM-5, told Carlat that "their initial hope of adding the neurobiological criteria to the diseases would not happen." After all, "It's not clear that there is enough evidence,"

213. Ibid.

214. Greenberg, "Inside the Battle to Define Mental Illness."

215. Shorter, *A History of Psychiatry*, vii.

216. Shorter, "Trouble at the Heart of Psychiatry's Revised Rule Book."

he said.[217] All of these contradictions raise a fundamental ethical question as to whether a private association, whose members stand to benefit from creating more diseases, is morally positioned to write the manual, rather than an independent group with no direct interest, or a federal agency not under the influence of pharmaceutical money—albeit, that may be hard to find.

For authors of DSM, life seemingly has no meaning but empirical sensations through our biology. They have rejected any possibility that there might be unique "models of the world" that "their patients have created," and it is these models that lead to certain behaviors. Kutchins and Kirk remind us, "As it is for all of us, what determines our behavior is not events but how we have interpreted events." In the world of DSM, the question of interpretation behind aberrant behaviors is never raised. Kutchins and Kirk point out: "These behaviors are described in terms which make them appear to be unusual, strange, even bizarre. Yet, if the interpretations which led to the behavior are examined they can be seen to be ordinary interpretations, well within the range of most people's experience."[218] In other words, it is all in the "eye of the beholder." Unless those inner interpretations are normalized against some meaningful standards, the behaviors can merely be controlled superficially, maybe by paralyzing the part of the brain that can react and engage in those interpretations. Isn't this where the church is called to act? To proclaim the good news of God's grace and the redemption by Christ is the framework within which a lens can be provided for the interpretation of life events. This is how the seemingly meaningless can be impregnated with meaning that can be life-changing.

The Quality and the Reliability of Psychiatric Trials

Building on the DSM foundation, all psychiatric drugs will receive their approval to market based on clinical trials. In order to understand why these drugs have not fulfilled their stated promise, we need to understand the nature of the evaluation behind such trials. In celebration of the fiftieth birthday of the introduction of neuroleptics into psychiatry, Emmanuel Stip—who later was appointed as the head of the department of psychiatry

217. Carlat, *Unhinged*, 66. For a review of "the APA's final decisions about some of the most controversial new disorders as well as hotly debated changes to existing ones," see Jabr, "The Newest Edition of Psychiatry's 'Bible,' the *DSM-5*, is Complete."

218. Kutchins and Kirk, *Making Us Crazy*, xvii.

at the University of Montreal—took a look at results related to therapeutic practices with these drugs in treating "schizophrenia." After more than fifty years of treatments by neuroleptic drugs, however, Stip wonders whether the discipline of psychiatry is able to answer the following simple questions: "Are neuroleptics effective in treating schizophrenia? Is there a difference between atypical and conventional neuroleptics?"[219]

He wondered if a review of the research results in the past fifty years or so would demonstrate the efficacy and safety of newer antipsychotic drugs to be superior to the older drugs. Evidence-based medicine (EBM) is "medicine resting on strong scientific proof." Psychiatry, like other medical disciplines, embraces EBM to rationalize its clinical practices. In that light, it often resorts to meta-analysis, "a procedure for statistically processing studies as data." In other words, it reviews and evaluates *all* published research literature on a given topic as pieces of data and makes the appropriate statistical analysis to arrive at interpretations and conclusions leading to clinical practices. "In a sense," says Stip, "meta-analysis is analogous to experimental research in its aim to statistically integrate and analyze results."[220]

A meta-analysis completed by Thornley and Adams evaluated 2,000 controlled trials conducted from 1948 to 1997.[221] In total, it consisted of 30,000 reports and 6,000 articles. In their examination, "only 1% of the studies was deemed to be of good quality . . . only 1% of the studies had sufficient statistical power," and the poorest studies were generated within the United States. The length of the trials for 54 percent of research was less than six weeks; only one-fifth of them lasted to about six months. The authors stressed that the limited length of the study has the potential for misleading conclusions. This is an astounding data that exposes the vulnerability of psychiatric practice, which is based on any of the research included in meta-analysis in isolation from the rest. The other glaring question arises in the face of low quality studies conducted in the US. Could this be due to the tremendous influence that the pharmaceutical industry exercises over the research structure in the US? We will address this issue later in this chapter. Thornley and Adams concluded,

219. Stip, "Happy Birthday Neuroleptics!," 115.

220. Ibid., 116.

221. Thornley and Adams, "Content and Quality of 2000 Controlled Trials in Schizophrenia Over 50 Years," 1181–84; cited in Stip, "Happy Birthday Neuroleptics!" 116.

"The consistently poor quality of reporting is likely to have resulted in an overoptimistic estimation of the effects of treatment."[222]

In search of understanding if the atypical antipsychotics are more effective than conventional neuroleptics, Leucht, et al. published a meta-analysis "on efficacy and extrapyramidal side effects of the new antipsychotics."[223] The result of their examination presented the new drugs with improvement over a placebo, but only with moderate effect.[224] The authors further noted the clearest superiority were in cases where the old drug such as Haldol were given at a much higher dosage comparable to the new antipsychotics. This biased the results against the old drugs and created an illusion that the new atypicals have fewer side effects, where in reality the super-dosage of the old drug was the culprit behind the misleading results and the severe side effects. The same conclusions were confirmed in another meta-analysis conducted by Geddes et al., examining fifty-two "controlled trials" involving 12,649 patients.[225] Of course, it is in the best interest of the pharmaceutical companies to sell the new drugs, since they bring in far greater revenues than the old drugs, which have lost their patents and are mostly produced in generic form at very low prices.

These meta-analyses highlight the importance of guarded examinations to ensure that pharmacological trials are "clinically meaningful." Stip points out that "despite the long-term course of schizophrenia" the duration of the treatments in the aforementioned meta-analyses were very short. Therefore, "there is currently no compelling evidence on the matter, where 'long-term' is concerned."[226] These reviews emphasize the critical

222. Ibid.

223. Leucht et al., "Efficacy and Extrapyramidal Side-Effects of the New Antipsychotics," 51–68; cited in Stip, "Happy Birthday Neuroleptics!," 117.

224. In a recent meta-analysis conducted by FDA, the clinical trial data submitted to FDA as part of New Drug Applications (NDAs) for the treatment of "schizophrenia" between 1991 and 2009 were reviewed. Interestingly, the researchers noticed that in later years the patients were responding far more favorably to placebos in contrast to earlier years. This caused "great concern" for them. The report says, "A high and increasing placebo response and a declining treatment effect are of great concern in schizophrenia trials conducted in North America." FDA's concern is that the drug companies may stop making these drugs. The question is whether these findings are the result of greater scrutiny on pharmaceutical companies. See Khin et al., "Exploratory Analyses of Efficacy Data from Schizophrenia Trials," 856–64.

225. Geddes et al., "Atypical Antipsychotics in the Treatment of Schizophrenia," 1371–76; cited in Stip, "Happy Birthday Neuroleptics!," 117.

226. Ibid.; For a cautionary analysis of these drugs on people over forty, see Jin et al., "Comparison of Longer-Term Safety and Effectiveness of 4 Atypical Antipsychotics in Patients Over Age 40."

need for trials with longer duration to measure the impact of the drugs on patients' lives and their health in the long term. Actually, the answers yielded by these meta-analyses "should elicit in us a good deal of humility," says Stip.[227] He warns his colleagues: "One thing is certain: if we wish to base psychiatry on EBM, we run the genuine risk of taking a closer look at what has long been considered fact." Moreover, these meta-analyses show that none of these drugs "causes schizophrenia to go into remission, so there is still a long way to go on efficacy."

In a recent study, Jose Miyar and Clive Adams, of the University of Nottingham, conducted a broad assessment of 10,000 controlled trials done in the past sixty years, evaluating their content and quality in regards to the treatment of people with "schizophrenia." They raised concerns about the size of the trials being too small (median sixty people), and the employment of "nonvalidated outcomes scales." Apparently, they found 2194 different scales, "with every fifth trial introducing a new rating instrument." This complicates the comparison of multiple trials, and diminishes the collaborative value of the research. Also, they found the same trials being published commonly about thirty or forty times in different venues. In one particular case, the trial had been published "122 times in full articles." They raise the concern that "multiple publications serve only to confuse—often giving the impression that there are more data than there really are." Since most of the published data "highlight favorable findings of a treatment and hide disadvantageous facts," this can only confuse the practicing physicians leading them to believe the picture is far more hopeful than it really is. They raise awareness that these publication practices "are clearly corrupt and challenge the integrity of medical research." In most cases "financial incentives" are behind such practices.[228]

The problem of clinical research is not limited to antipsychotics, but it spans all areas of psychiatry. The *New England Journal of Medicine (NEJM)* is recognized as a medical publication with the staple of "research about causes of and treatments for disease." Marcia Angell, the former editor-in chief of the journal says:

> I witnessed firsthand the influence of the [pharmaceutical] industry on medical research. . . . Increasingly, this work is sponsored by drug companies. . . . The aim was clearly to load the dice to make sure their drugs looked good. . . . I became

227. Stip, "Happy Birthday Neuroleptics!," 118.

228. Miyar and Adams, "Content and Quality of 10000 Controlled Trials in Schizophrenia Over 60 Years."

increasingly troubled by the possibility that much published research is seriously flawed.[229]

For example, new drugs are only compared against placebos, and rarely against an older drug. This could make the new drug look good even though it might be far less effective than the older and cheaper drug; this embellishes the drug's apparent clinical effectiveness. Kirsch also points out the criticality of testing drugs not only against placebos, but also against unmedicated people; because without it one may contribute the recovery to the drug or the placebo effect, where it might be as a result of the passage of time and the natural healing work of the body: "It is rare for a study to focus on the placebo effect—or on the effect of the simple passage of time, for that matter."[230] Angell speaks about the research papers they rejected for publication due to the flaws in the trial design, just to see them show up in other medical literature with less stringent standards. In fact many journals refuse to publish articles criticizing drugs and the clinical trials in fear of losing advertisers.

Most of the psychiatric research is sponsored by the pharmaceutical companies. As expected, the studies "almost always" produce "positive results for the sponsor's drug." This is a well-known fact about a vast array of medications. Carlat notes that a "meta-analysis of all such studies found that drug company-sponsored studies were four times more likely to produce a favorable outcome for the sponsor's drug than studies with other funders." But the story is even more troublesome. The pharmaceutical companies not only control the design and writing of the results of studies, "they also routinely hide studies that don't look good for their drugs."[231] This practice, which is called "publication bias," had long been suspected by the medical industry, but the severity of the problem was exposed only after Erick Turner and his colleagues published an eye-opening paper in *NEJM* in 2008.[232]

Through intensive investigative work, Turner and his colleagues gained access to the results of studies about twelve antidepressants approved between 1987 and 2004. The pharmaceutical companies submitted seventy-four clinical studies to the FDA in order to get approval to market these drugs. Among the studies, thirty-eight of them were positive,

229. Angell, *The Truth About the Drug Companies*, xxvi.

230. Kirsch, *The Emperor's New Drugs*, 8.

231. Carlat, *Unhinged*, 115–16.

232. Turner et al., "Selective Publication of Antidepressant Trials," 252–60.

meaning the drug was more effective than the placebo, and thirty-six of them resulted in a negative or questionable outcome. Among the negative studies, twenty-two reports never made it to publication. The eleven negative studies that were published were presented in a way that "inaccurately conveyed a positive outcome ('spun' if you will)" and only three of the thirty-six studies with negative or questionable outcomes were accurately published. Carlat, who as a psychiatrist has to live with the reality of unreliable published data, states:

> If I relied on the published medical literature for information (and what else can I rely on?), it would appear that 94 percent of all antidepressant trials are positive. But if I had access to all the suppressed data, I would see that the truth is that only about half—51 percent—of trials are positive. Turner called this the "dirty little secret" of the psychiatric world.[233]

Kirsch claims that pharmaceutical companies have used questionable practices to shed a positive light on their drugs. In addition to withholding negative studies from publication, they also practice "salami slicing" (multiple presentations of the same data); use maneuvers such as "cherry picking" to publish only some of the data or only data from a few locations where the results are more positive; and publish "pooled analyses" of various trials to bundle data from multiple trials and reduce the effect of the negative data.[234] It is not difficult to understand the incentive behind such practices. With widely prescribed psychiatric drugs, "billions of dollars are at stake," so consequently drug companies have an instinctive bias to present their data favorably.

Marcia Angell, who as the editor-in-chief of *NEJM* for two decades, had a "front-row seat" on the increasing corruption of the pharmaceutical companies, describes that industry as:

> [A]n industry that over the past two decades has moved very far from its original high purpose of discovering and producing useful new drugs. Now primarily a marketing machine to sell drugs of dubious benefit, this industry uses its wealth and power to co-opt every institution that might stand in its way, including the U.S. Congress, the Food and Drug Administration, academic medical centers, and the medical profession itself. (Most

233. Carlat, *Unhinged*, 117.

234. Kirsch, *The Emperor's New Drugs*, 38–43.

of its marketing efforts are focused on influencing doctors, since they must write the prescriptions).[235]

The companies reward doctors who prescribe their new drugs with luxurious trips, dinners, gifts, and cash. In addition to paying doctors for offering their names on ghost-written articles, they also encourage the doctors to write "off-label" prescriptions—for treating cases that were not approved by the regulatory agencies. The renowned psychiatrist Giovanni Fava believes that the financial relationship between doctors and drug companies, and the influence these companies are exerting, have "brought the credibility of clinical medicine to an unprecedented crisis." He summed it up: "The game is clear: to get as close as possible to universal prescribing of a drug by manipulating evidence and withholding data."[236] And in this corporate culture of greed it is the unfortunate patients whose voices are silenced and whose lives are damaged forever.

Listening to Other Voices

I have argued that a deeper reflection on the practices of psychiatry reveals that the scientific basis of psychiatry is not as solid as is often claimed. That being so, in our quest for truth other voices need to be heard. If mental illness is as flexible as history and contemporary experience indicates, then there are good epistemological reasons for suggesting that the dissenting voices of experts in the field, people labeled "mentally ill," and the voice of theology should be considered significant in the understanding of "mental illness" for the church and indeed for society in general.

Antipsychiatry Movement

Madness as a medical phenomenon has had its challenges and opponents throughout history. This opposition has come from psychologists, anthropologists, sociologists, philosophers, but more often from other psychiatrists and certainly least often from theologians. Even Freud himself, who was trained as a psychiatrist, believed that medicine provided "a poor framework" for dealing with mental disorders. He advocated the practice of psychotherapy by "lay analysts" to be superior in the treatment of the mad. The concern about the efficacy of the medical approach and

235. Angell, *The Truth About the Drug Companies*, xxv–xxvi.

236. Fava, "Should the Drug Industry Work with Key Opinion Leaders? No," 1405.

the opposition of the counter movements reached "something of a crescendo during 1960s and 1970s."[237] These movements, generally grouped as *anti-psychiatry*—a term coined by the South African-born psychiatrist David Cooper—were mostly the result of the perceived dehumanizing and damaging treatments practiced by conventional psychiatry.[238] The critics argued passionately for the decisive role that the environment and the person's social context played in bringing mental distress and sought their transformation. Many of the populace "believed madness to be a plausible and sane reaction to insane social conditions," and that psychiatrists were primarily "agents of repression."[239]

Bentall believes this mistrust is due to psychiatry's unique power among all branches of medicine "to compel people to receive treatment," and not least because "some of the treatments inflicted on the mentally ill have seemed more terrifying than madness itself." Perhaps another reason behind opposition from the branches of human sciences is that traditionally they have offered alternative models for understanding mental distress.[240]

The leading figures associated with anti-psychiatry were dissident psychiatrists, Thomas Szasz in the US and Ronald D. Laing in the UK. The two men were often linked derisively with French philosopher Michael Foucault, whose masterpiece *Madness and Civilization* deliberated on how "our modern understanding of madness was *constituted* by the social policy of segregation."[241] All three men are identified as the products of their era and the popular success of their thoughts are attributed to the "feverish atmosphere" of their time. Michael Staub believes, "Foucault's questioning of reason's superiority to madness and his skepticism that enlightened treatments were more humane than early modern ones certainly lent additional cachet to antipsychiatric impulses."[242] However, this bundling of Foucault, Laing, and Szasz misses the point that all three men were very different and espoused a wide range of ideas, and the only common view among them was their objection to conventional psychiatry. Also, Laing and Szasz spoke from within the clinical psychiatric world where Foucault's views represented an outsider's assessment.

237. Bentall, *Madness Explained*, 116.

238. Cooper, *Psychiatry and Anti-Psychiatry*.

239. Staub, *Madness is Civilization*, 2.

240. Bentall, *Doctoring the Mind*, xv.

241. Pilgrim, "Competing Histories of Madness," 216.

242. Staub, *Madness is Civilization*, 3–4.

Foucault's *Madness* is a stunning and creative account of the critiques of psychiatry during the so-called classical age. The work is presented in a fresh and distinctively analytical way, by recreating mental illness from the original documents, as it must have existed in that period.[243] Foucault saw mental illness "as a cultural construct," which was kept alive by "a grid of administrative and medico-psychiatric practices." For him, the meaningful history of madness was about "questions of freedom and control, knowledge and power," and not about any disease or the variety of treatment methods.[244]

Following the publication of his book the *Divided Self*—by some accounts one of the most influential books of the sixties—Laing, the Scottish psychiatrist, became one of the most celebrated men in his field around the world. Laing, who had been trained in psychoanalysis, claimed that psychotic symptoms were impregnated with meaning, and therefore could not be understood as a medical phenomenon; he felt that an empathetic clinician could successfully decode a "psychotic speech."[245]

Later, in his book *Sanity, Madness and the Family*, he argued that dysfunctional families with their toxic dynamics drove their kids insane due to repetitive emotional injuries and inauthentic and conditional love.[246] Not surprisingly, this assertion was hard to receive by families who were already suffering because of their kid's afflictions with insanity, but it was "monumentally influential."[247] These theories were quite popular in the 1960s, but have been rejected with the influence of biological psychiatry. Although Laing mesmerized his fans with his talent and empathetic ability to observe "disturbed minds," Bentall notes that with "his unexpected celebrity," his views "became increasingly chaotic and inconsistent."[248]

However, family's potential negative influence on the *future* well-being of the person who is *already* suffering from "schizophrenia" has been scientifically established. It is not difficult to understand intuitively that those closest to the individual have the greatest emotional impact on one's state of mind. Studies evaluating the relapse rate of "schizophrenia patients" in the context of their living environment have shown that:

243. Foucault, *Madness and Civilization*, v.

244. Porter, *Madness*, 3. For a critical view of Foucault as a historian, see Gutting, "Foucault and the History of Madness," 47–70.

245. Laing, *The Divided Self*, 237. Bentall, *Madness Explained*, 116, 386.

246. Laing and Esterson, *Sanity, Madness, and the Family*.

247. Staub, *Madness is Civilization*, 40.

248. Bentall, *Doctoring the Mind*, 71.

[P]atients returning to live with their spouses and parents had higher readmission rates than those returning to live alone or in lodgings. . . . A number of studies have examined the predictive value of EE [Expressed Emotion], and the consistent finding that there is strong association between relapse and living with a High-EE relative has emerged across different cultural settings.[249]

It is of interest that this finding is true *only* for those diagnosed with "schizophrenia." This outcome is counter-intuitive. One would presume that a person living at home surrounded by family members would do a lot better compared to one living alone in a lodging facility. But clearly these studies indicate that family dynamics not only cannot be ignored, but rather they play a strong role in the outcome of the psychotic experience. This is an area that psychologists are turning to in search of some answers to the mystery of psychosis, and yet the church has ignored her responsibility to apply her gifts in the context of pastoral care. This presents a great opportunity for the church to make a difference in the lives of those suffering from insanity.

Laing was most probably on to something, but he might have gone too far. It is inherently difficult to point to families that are already under stress as contributors to their loved one's insanity; it is emotionally difficult and politically incorrect, and "many professionals treat it as taboo." Bentall claims that it is the "taboo" against regarding "the role of environmental influences" in the onset of psychosis that has upheld "exclusively biological accounts of madness."[250]

As other familial research influenced by Laing's work began to dominate the psychological scholarly world, it became apparent that qualities that Laing had pointed to as triggering insanity were common among all families. It was becoming harder to define a "normal" family and distinguish it from those who were considered "pathogenic." Laing wrote:

---

249. Tarrier, "The Family Management of Schizophrenia," 259.

250. Bentall, *Madness Explained*, 466. In a recent study, Bentall and his team analyzed thirty-six published studies on childhood maltreatments, covering about 80,000 people over the course of thirty years, and showed that people who suffered from childhood trauma such as sexual, physical and emotional abuse, death of a parent, school bullying and neglect, were between 2.7 and 3 times more likely to develop "schizophrenia" as adults. See Bentall et al., "Do Specific Early-Life Adversities Lead to Specific Symptoms of Psychosis?"

> Perhaps men and women were born to love one another, simply and genuinely, rather than to this travesty that we call love. If we can stop destroying ourselves, we may stop destroying others.[251]

Staub explains that Laing and his followers' works were not meant to be a "critique of the family as an institution." They were, rather, supportive of "strong and at once authoritative and caring fathers and of nurturing, self-sacrificial mothers."[252] It was only when these primary roles were abused intentionally or unintentionally that they led to injuries in the child. As it became increasingly apparent that the problem was not limited to some families, revisiting his theories, Laing moved the cause from family to the society and hoped that answers could be found in the societal dynamics. But neither he nor any of his admirers were able to "theorize social change at the level of the individual psyche." He could not define the interconnectedness between the individual psyche and the social structure surrounding it. Instead he seemed "unabashedly to have arrived at the limits of his own capacities for understanding." He could point to madness in "everyone everywhere."[253] It appeared as if he knew that something had fundamentally gone wrong, but, I suggest, because he had no theology of "sin" he had a hard time defining what or why.[254] "Our alienation goes to the roots," Laing wrote. "We are bemused and crazed creatures, strangers to our true selves, to one another, and to the spiritual and material world."[255]

Laing's views nonetheless continued to receive great admiration from a cadre of well-respected psychiatrists. In another one of his influential works, *The Politics of Experience*, Laing suggested that madness is a creative and mystical journey, leading to refinement, transcendence, and greater potential for creativity when one emerges at the other end.[256] In support of this theory, he helped found the Philadelphia Association, which consisted of a series of therapeutic communities. Kingsley Hall in

251. Laing, "Massacre of the Innocents," 7; cited in Staub, *Madness is Civilization*, 57.

252. Staub, *Madness is Civilization*, 42–43.

253. Ibid., 58.

254. Gavin Miller explains that Laing as a child went to Sunday Bible classes, was taught to do his nightly prayers, and went through a conversion experience in an evangelical camp in his mid-teens. But, he claims, Laing's theology that influenced his psychiatry was a mix of an existential mystical theology and a corporate theology. See Miller, "R. D. Laing's Theological Hinterland," 139–55.

255. Laing, *The Politics of Experience*, 12.

256. Ibid.

east London was the most famous among his communities, which attracted many "touring intellectuals." The residents were allowed to travel through their madness in any fashion they found helpful. The supportive environment gave them freedom to act out their inner impulses without being coerced.[257] It is becoming more apparent to the researchers that psychosis with all its mystery might be a very "normal" reaction to life. Bentall points to the "startling conclusion" of the research findings on the "continua between psychosis and normal functioning" to be consistent with Laing's philosophy.[258]

By 1964, Laing, with "his legendary inclination for overdrinking" was no longer just writing about madness, he was embodying his ideas. "Over time . . . [he] became increasingly intrigued to mimic (his version of) the inner workings of a schizophrenic mind," says Staub, "This meant that feelings of persecution and paranoia, for instance, as well as articulations of fractured logic, were no longer off limits as avenues of authorial expression."[259] These were no longer exclusive experiences of a "diseased mind." Laing was acting out his inner self, proving his theory that if we show ourselves authentically, there is no escape from insanity for any of us. We all are mad.

Another influential critic of conventional psychiatry was the Hungarian-born Thomas Szasz in the United States, who rejected the label of antipsychiatry with the same zeal as he criticized psychiatry itself. He considered the "antipsychiatry" movement as a "serious blow" to his work to "undermine the moral legitimacy of the alliance of psychiatry and the state."[260] Contrary to Laing, who believed that madness was quite real, Szasz spent no time offering insights into the nature of psychosis, or any other mental phenomenon. He fought against the claim that "mental illnesses are diagnosable disorders of the brain," because such claims are "not based on scientific research." He truculently called them "a lie" and "an error," because he saw mental distresses as "fictitious illnesses."[261] In fact, he considered mental illness nothing but a "myth," merely a "social con-

257. Bentall, *Doctoring the Mind*, 22, 71. One of the intellectuals who visited Kingsley Hall was Loren Mosher, who later became the chief of the Center for Studies of Schizophrenia at NIMH. Intrigued by Laing's vision, Mosher later established Soteria House in the San Francisco Bay area, where residents were cared for mostly without any medication.

258. Bentall, *Madness Explained*, 117.

259. Staub, *Madness is Civilization*, 56.

260. Szasz, *The Myth of Mental Illness*, xxviii.

261. Ibid., xii.

struct." He also felt psychiatry's assertions are incoherent, because even if its theory of mental illness as a brain disease proves to be correct, this falls under the purview of neurologists and has nothing to do with the mind and behavior. For him the term "mental illness" was an oxymoron and as meaningless as describing someone as a "married bachelor." The problem in Szasz's view was that "we have replaced the old religious-humanistic perspective on the tragic nature of life with a modern dehumanized pseudomedical perspective on it." We have accepted the "secularization of everyday life," which leads to "the medicalization of the soul and of suffering of all kinds."[262]

Szasz believed the theory of mental illness gave the state the ability to force the population to conform more fully to the social norms. He was a staunch defender of individual liberties to the point that he advocated "the right to commit suicide should be respected." Although he fought against compulsory treatments in psychiatry, to be consistent, he never objected to practice of psychiatry between consenting adults.[263] Szasz spoke vigorously against the "insanity defense" in the justice system, which acts at times as if "there are no more bad people in the world"; all we have to worry about are "mentally ill people."[264] He asserts, "This cultural transformation is driven mainly by the modern therapeutic ideology that has replaced the old theological worldview, and the political and professional interests it sets in motion."[265]

Szasz argued passionately several interwoven themes: the inappropriateness of a psychiatrist's testimony in court as "expert arbiter" to define someone as "ill" and evaluate his or her mental competence, the meaninglessness of psychiatric classifications, and the horror of compulsory commitment of individuals to mental hospitals. Szasz was vigorously denounced and dismissed by some of his colleagues, who objected to his definition of disease and his views on the differences between psychiatry and other branches of medicine. Rael Jean Isaac called Szasz's ideology "inhumane" with "devastating effect on families" who had to witness the deterioration of their loved ones over time.[266] The counterarguments pointed to his restrictive definition of disease as indicated by presence of a lesion; they argued that impairment in normal functionality, due to

262. Ibid., xiv.

263. Bentall, *Madness Explained*, 153.

264. Szasz, *The Myth of Mental Illness*, xvi.

265. Ibid., xvii.

266. Isaac, "Thomas Szasz: A Life in Error."

psychological problems, is as much disruptive to one's life as a physical problem and, therefore, requires treatment.[267]

Szasz's ideas were so offensive to his guild that the commissioner of the New York State Department of Mental Hygiene demanded that he should be expelled from his university teaching positions, because he did not believe in mental illness.[268] Nevertheless, his thoughtful and yet controversial views gained him prestige as a radical voice demanding social change. He has been recognized as a "renegade," an "iconoclast," and a "forerunner and progenitor" for antipsychiatric counterculture movements such as "psychiatric survivors" and alternative psychosocial movements.[269]

Staub points out that "none of the shortcomings of or difficulties encountered by antipsychiatry justify how it has been either derided, summarily ignored, or removed from its historical context." There is no doubt that some of the extreme views of antipsychiatry caused the subsequent backlash and "a near-total erasure" of some of their best ideas. Antipsychiatry as a movement failed partly because the methods offered were far more consuming of time, energy, and resources on the part of caregivers and the society at large. Also, advances in neurosciences generated enthusiasm about the possibilities of cure looming around the corner. Now, in the twenty-first century the wealth of evidence about the side effects of psychiatric drugs, the lack of cures and the poor long-term outcome of the current model has revived a new generation of critics of psychiatry. Although the term "antipsychiatry" carries baggage and is caricatured signifying the opposition as "crazy and outdated," the scientific studies have breathed life into those within and without psychiatry who are demanding fundamental change.[270]

267. Dammann, "The Myth of Mental Illness." Dammann has presented a summary of Szasz's views in contrast to many of his vocal critics. He shows that though arguments of substance have been expressed against Szasz and his controversial positions, the questions raised by him are yet worthy of serious attention. He says, "Although easy answers are not forthcoming, it is my contention that denial or ignorance of the importance of these issues is a potentially grave problem for mental health professionals" (734).

268. Ibid., 733.

269. Staub, *Madness is Civilization*, 91.

270. Ibid., 6. Bentall, *Doctoring the Mind*, xv.

The Voice of the "Patient"

The appropriate treatment for the mentally ill has become the purview of the state and the medical community. The mentally ill themselves are rarely asked and taken seriously about the way they are treated. The main objective has always been controlling the aberrant behavior and protecting the "normal" people from any discomfort or "danger" that the "abnormal" may present. In fact, the mentally ill are regularly dismissed as unreliable and therefore unable to make a judgment about their treatment or for that matter, anything else in life. Yet, the subjective experience is what can help or hurt these vulnerable souls and determine the outcome of their treatment. Their subjective experience rarely matches the assessment of their psychiatrists. In a study conducted by Karow et al., the researchers compared "symptomatic remission" as viewed by patients against the perception of their family members and psychiatrists. Their assessment showed that the patients' priority was on their "subjective well being." Moreover, only 18 percent of patients, relatives, and psychiatrists "agreed in their assessments" of the outcomes.[271] There is clearly a wide gap between the understanding of remission as perceived by the "experts" in contrast to the subjective assessment of the individual.

Mental distress, especially in the form of psychosis, and deeply felt expressions of inner conflicts, are uniquely personal in nature. Arthur Kleinman cautions the clinical researchers about evaluating suffering, noting that "it can only emerge from an entirely different way of obtaining valid information from illness narratives. Ethnography, biography, history, psychotherapy—these are the appropriate research methods to create knowledge about the personal world of suffering." These methods provide an opportunity to transcend reductionist psychiatric "symptoms" and to grasp the "complex inner language of hurt, desperation, and moral pain" of the experience.[272] It is the "reality" as experienced by those journeying into madness—not a "reality" imposed by others unto them—that matters most. Thus, it is instructive to listen to their voices.

Elyn Saks is Associate Dean and Professor of Law, Psychology, and Psychiatry and the Behavioral Sciences at the University of Southern California. She has suffered from "schizophrenia" most of her life and still has ongoing major episodes of the illness. Saks is a psychiatric success story

271. Karow et al., "Remission as Perceived by People with Schizophrenia, Family Members and Psychiatrists," 426.

272. Kleinman, *The Illness Narratives*, 28–29.

who found her way to recovery through a combination of antipsychotics, ongoing talk therapy, and most importantly, the love of her husband. She admits the "central role" that medication has played in the management of her psychosis, but notes, "What has allowed me to see the meaning in my struggles—to make sense of everything that happened before and during the course of my illness, and to mobilize what strengths I may possess into a rich and productive life—is talk therapy." She believes it is the relationships in one's life that are "at the heart of things," and her relationship with her therapist has been "the key to every other relationship" she holds "precious." Over time, she bounced between stunning accomplishments in her scholarly work and painful relapses and struggles with her illness. She says, "I'm navigating my life through uncertain, even threatening, waters—I need the people in my life to tell me what's safe, what's real, what's worth holding on to."[273]

Even though Saks' story is not common, her recovery gives hope to many of those who feel they will never have another chance in life. She writes,

> I . . . wanted to dispel the myths held by many mental-health professionals themselves—that people with a significant thought disorder cannot live independently, cannot work at challenging jobs, cannot have true friendships, cannot be in meaningful, sexually satisfying love relationships, cannot lead lives of intellectual, spiritual, or emotional richness.[274]

She also has used her platform to speak against forced treatment of the mentally ill.[275] She says:

> And I know, better than most, how the law treats mental patients, the degradation of being tied to a bed against your will and force-fed medicine you didn't ask for and do not understand. I want to see that change. . . . I want to bring hope to those who suffer from schizophrenia, and understanding to those who do not.[276]

Lori Schiller's is another successful story of recovery. Lori is the only daughter of an affluent family who experienced the horrifying world of insanity. Lori was seventeen years old when "uninvited and unannounced,

273. Saks, *The Center Cannot Hold*, 331.

274. Ibid.

275. Saks, *Refusing Care*, 304.

276. Saks, *The Center Cannot Hold*, 331–32.

the Voices took over [her] life."[277] This was the beginning of her ordeal of hospitalizations, suicide attempts, never-ending despair, and battles with those who were charged to care for her. Lori's mother explains that when Lori was put on psychiatric drugs, "her eyes became glassy and vacant, and she began to move like she was sleepwalking. She put on nearly twenty pounds. Her beautiful complexion began to break out, and her chestnut hair turned gray almost overnight."[278] Lori did not believe that these treatments were helping her at all; she was in a constant battle against the desires of her family and her psychiatrists to take medications. She claimed: "they don't help take away the voices."[279] Even when the drugs controlled her enough to be discharged from the hospital, her mother writes: "There was still something very wrong with this glazed, dazed stranger I saw before me. Thinking realistically, I could see that Lori was not better. She was drugged. . . . The fact I had to face was that this remote sleepwalking stranger was my daughter."[280] Lori did not want to be in the hospital and wanted to have her freedom back. She writes,

> Everything about the hospital infuriated me. I didn't know why I was there. . . . All I knew was that I was trapped. I felt like a prisoner doing my time. . . . There was nothing wrong with me. So why did they keep telling me there was? . . . They told me I was psychotic with hallucinations. I hated these two words. I knew they were not true. Psychotic meant like the movie *Psycho* and Norman Bates, and the Bates Motel. That was scary and sick. That wasn't me. I wasn't a *psycho*-tic woman with a butcher knife. . . . Hallucination meant that you were seeing something or hearing something that didn't really exist. But when I heard the Voices screaming at me, they were real. When the doctors and nurses challenged me, told me that I was out of reality, and hallucinating, I hated them. What made me the psychotic one? What about those judgmental people? What made them the experts?[281]

The hospital staff was not able to gain her trust, so she frequently told them what they wanted to hear to gain her release at any cost. She pretended that she wasn't hearing voices anymore. In reality, the voices were

277. Schiller and Bennett, *The Quiet Room*, 3.

278. Ibid., 66.

279. Ibid., 75.

280. Ibid., 85.

281. Ibid., 89–90.

much stronger when she was in treatment in the hospital, and they would lose their intensity when she lived at home.[282] Yet, even at home, the medication they gave her was making her feel worse. She writes:

> [T]he medication made me at once lethargic and restless, I often just stood in one spot, moving my weight back and forth from one foot to another. I was taking so much medicine that I found it difficult even to smile. I walked around the house sluggishly, doing what I had to do like a robot. . . . Those medications they gave me in the hospital were useless. I took them because people told me they would make me better. But lots of times I didn't know why I bothered. The only thing those fistfuls of stupid pills did was make me feel fuzzy and disoriented, as if I were at the bottom of a swimming pool. And the Voices still raged away at me, mocking the drugs, the doctors and me.[283]

Lori's intense battles continued for many years, until with the help of a caring psychiatrist and one determined psychotherapist she found her way back to recovery. After years of feeling like a "guinea pig"[284] and having gone through experimental procedures and medications, having lost all hope and left with nothing else to lose, she agreed to be put on a new experimental drug with potentially severe and fatal side effects. She says, "The first day I took Clozapine, I felt like I was stoned. An obscure feeling entered my body."[285] Finally changes began creeping up on her. The voices were getting softer. She wrote: "my prayers were finally being answered."[286] She contributes her recovery primarily to the work of Dr. Diane Fischer, her psychotherapist, whose care and attention left an indelible mark on Lori. She was finally ready to get back to the outside world with all its challenges. Life has not been that easy since then. She has had to relearn how to live in the world of "normal" people. She still hears voices here and there and she has learned to distract herself from them. At the end of her autobiography, she is living on her own in the community, going to work every day and enjoying a life of freedom that she so badly longed for. She writes,

282. Ibid., 95–96.
283. Ibid., 91, 107.
284. Ibid., 78.
285. Ibid., 249.
286. Ibid., 251.

> I meet with Dr. Doller twice a week. She helps me monitor my
> medication. I take twenty-six pills a day for my psychotic symp-
> toms, my mood swings, for anxiety and for the side effects that
> the drugs cause.[287]

She needs to continue to be under close psychiatric treatment for the rest
of her life; nevertheless, Lori's is a success story in the world of hopeless
"schizophrenics."

Another success story belongs to Cathy Levin, who was interviewed
by Whitaker. Her diagnosis originally was bipolar disorder and that was
later changed to "schizoaffective." By her own admission she was "saved"
by Risperdal, one of the leading antipsychotic medications. She had a difficult childhood and was "a difficult teenager, hostile, angry, withdrawn."
In college, she started acting in an "eccentric manner," smoking mari-
juana, and experiencing strange sexual fantasies. Her first encounter with
psychiatry was after she broke a glass object and recklessly walked on it,
which resulted in her being taken to a hospital by the local police. She was
told that she suffered from manic-depressive disorder and she was put on
Lithium and Haldol.[288]

She spent the next sixteen years going in and out of hospitals, never
feeling well, suffering from a variety of side effects resulting from a cock-
tail of drugs she was taking. She loved the feeling whenever she quit taking
her drugs: "When you go off meds it is like taking off a wet wool coat,
which you have been wearing even though it's a beautiful spring day, and
suddenly feeling so much better, freer, and nicer." However, she was not
able to handle anything without the aid of these drugs. In 1994, after her
fifteenth hospitalization, her psychiatrist put her on Risperdal, a newly
approved antipsychotic. "Three weeks later, my mind was much clearer,"
she says of her new experience. "The voices were going away. I got off the
other meds and took only this one drug. I got better. I could start to plan.
I wasn't talking to the devil anymore. Jesus and God weren't battling it out
in my head." According to her father, "Cathy [was] back."[289]

Cathy went back to school and earned a degree from the University
of Maryland, and got a part time job. But even today, she is on government
payroll as someone who is "disabled." Ironically, Risperdal, the very drug
that has helped her to get back to a "normal" life, has become a stumbling block for her full-time employment. The drug makes her sleepy,

287. Ibid., 267.

288. Whitaker, *Anatomy of an Epidemic*, 16–17.

289. Ibid., 16–18.

and affecting her emotions it makes it difficult for her to get along with other people. The drug has also caused her to gain sixty pounds more than her ideal weight, and develop metabolic problems with high cholesterol. Cathy says, "I can go toe-to-toe with an old lady with a recital of my physical problems. . . . My feet, my bladder, my heart, my sinuses, the weight gain—I have it all." Unfortunately, she has also developed symptoms of *tardive dyskinesia* (TD), causing her tongue to roll over in her mouth. TD is a side effect of antipsychotics' long-term use, which suggests her "basal ganglia, the part of the brain that controls motor movement, is becoming permanently dysfunctional."[290] In regards to TD, *The Oxford Textbook of Psychiatry* emphasizes: "it is important to reduce its incidence as far as possible by limiting long-term antipsychotic drug treatment to patients who really need it."[291] Indeed, Cathy as a chronically ill person is dependent on her drug, and cannot do without her antipsychotic.

Cathy, in spite of all her challenges is a "poster child for promoting the wonders" of Risperdal. After sixteen years of terrible hell, she has had fourteen years of stability. She wonders where she would be today if she had never been put on psychiatric drugs or if she had the support system in earlier years to wean herself off the medication. She expresses her sadness:

> [Y]ou lose your soul and you never get it back. I got stuck in the system and the struggle to take meds. . . . The thing I remember, looking back, is that I was not really that sick early on. I was really just confused. I had all these issues, but nobody talked to me about that. I wish I could go off meds even now, but there is nobody to help me do it.[292]

It is, of course, hard to judge what the course of her life would have been without being put on medication, an alternative that is almost never considered in today's American psychiatry.

Not all mental patients are as fortunate as Cathy, Lori, or Elyn Saks. Most of them will never see the light of stability and their adverse symptoms of their treatments overshadow any benefit that they may get. Traditionally, patients have fought against being medicated, because they "desire to be in complete control of their lives."[293] Many stop their medica-

---

290. Ibid., 18–19.

291. Gelder et al., *Shorter Oxford Textbook of Psychiatry*, 669.

292. Whitaker, *Anatomy of an Epidemic*, 20.

293. Theodore Van Putten, "Why do Schizophrenic Patients Refuse to Take their

tion due to a plethora of unpleasant subjective effects. Speaking of these effects, researchers have emphasized:

> [T]he sedative, extrapyramidal, or other physiologic effects of antipsychotic drugs can precipate panic reactions, further psychotic deterioration, and increased somatization. Extrapyramidal symptoms . . . are often subjectively very stressful and may be incompatible with clinical improvement.[294]

The medicated mentally ill regularly complain that their medication makes them "jittery-like," feeling "worse," and having "unbearable fatigue." One complained, "I want my own personality," while another one said, "It makes my eyes flip to the top of my head."[295] The patients seem to dread *akathisia*—an anxious restlessness—more than any other side effects that they have to endure. This effect is "entirely subjective," and prevents the person from performing any task or even resting. Van Putten citing other researchers states that the subjective experience of *akathisia* can be "more difficult to endure than any of the symptoms for which (the patient) was originally treated." This effect that has been referred to as "syndrome of impatience," is often associated with "severe anxiety," "peculiar bodily sensations," and "bizarre mentation." Highlighting this paralyzing side-effect of antipsychotics, Van Putten says, "A moderate akathisia can preclude sitting through the dinner hour or a movie—let alone a sedentary job."[296]

All these testimonies attest to the profound change that the psychotropic drugs produce in a person. The person's sense of being is altered. It becomes difficult to feel one's own mind. These experiences raise the question whether these treatments are targeted to help the insane, or to protect their "neighbors" from being offended by these troubled souls. Where is the church in all of this? Is the answer to all of life's distresses found in a pill? Jeffery Boyd, a prominent Christian psychiatrist, says, "In defense of psychiatrists, I might say that it is not entirely psychiatrist's fault that their theories are insufficient to fill the vacuum created by theologians."[297] Boyd believes that most of the problems in the mental health industry stem from their belief in materialistic monism, losing belief in the human's "soul," and understanding of the concept of the mind only in biological terms.

Drugs?" 68.

294. Ibid.

295. Ibid., 70.

296. Ibid., 71.

297. Boyd, "Losing Soul," 483.

Theologians have allowed the debate to focus on the "self" rather than God. Some of the theories of "mental illness" have often failed, not only because they are based on an unsubstantiated system of classification, but also because psychiatry has accepted, as self-evident, assumptions about the human nature and human mind that are scientifically questionable and biblically unsupportable.[298]

Summary

In this chapter we have traveled through the history of psychiatry to search for any evidence that psychiatry has helped in alleviating human emotional distress. Contrary to conventional wisdom, the evidence does not seem convincing. In comparison to other branches of medicine where remarkable achievements, from the discovery of penicillin to organ transplants, tell a story of breakthrough technologies and lifesaving progress, there is no evidence of similar advances in healing mental suffering. As psychiatry searches for some scientific explanations behind the etiology of mental illness, the debates about the success of psychopharmacology continue. Even though some people have been helped by medication in managing their symptoms, they continue to live a life with dire physical complications. After billions of dollars of investment in research and treatment development there is no "cure" looming in the foreseeable horizon.

In spite of the mysterious nature of "schizophrenia" and the incalculable personal and societal cost it entails, it has proven impossible for researchers to reliably identify the illness as a valid syndrome, distinguished from other forms of insanity. Moreover, the diagnosis has not been helpful in identifying etiology, predicting the outcome, or ensuring response to treatments.[299] The first step toward healing begins with the admission about how much we don't know and understand. Recently, none other than Thomas Insel, the United States' chief psychiatrist, spoke of psychiatry's scientific failures. Insel, who is the head of NIMH, wrote in a perspective piece for the *Archives of General Psychiatry*:

> Despite high expectations, neither genomics nor imaging has yet impacted the diagnosis or treatment of the 45 million Americans with serious or moderate mental illness each year. ... While we have seen profound progress in research ... the gap

298. See chapter 1, for issues related to human nature and human mind.

299. Bentall, "Concluding Remarks: Schizophrenia—A Suitable Case for Treatment?," 284.

> between the surge in basic biological knowledge and the state of
> mental health care in this country has not narrowed and may be
> *getting wider.* . . . In contrast to the steadily decreasing mortality
> rates of cardiovascular disease, stroke, and cancer, there is no
> evidence for reduced morbidity or mortality from any mental
> illness . . . individuals with serious mental illness die 13 to 32
> years earlier than those without mental illness. . . . Premature
> death related to mental illness were more often due to medical
> comorbidity, especially cardiovascular and pulmonary diseases,
> rather than suicide.[300]

Psychiatry may someday define the "pathophysiology of disorders from
genes to behavior," and define how to intervene to "preempt disability,"
but, in the absence of proven scientific approaches to the challenges of
mental illness, Insel himself suggests that it is time for psychiatrists to "develop new interventions based on a personalized approach to the diverse
needs and circumstances of people with mental illnesses."[301] Furthermore,
the scientific research has to be taken from under the control of drug companies, so that no conflict of interest would impact the future direction of
research and treatment.

In light of the failure of the body of research to provide conclusive
evidence in support of the madness-as-a-brain-disease hypothesis, after
listening to the voice of scientific studies, the putative patients, many renowned psychiatrists, psychologists, science journalists, and social scientists, I come to the conclusion that we should regard mental distress, even
at its ultimate intensity called "schizophrenia," as an expression of human
variation and not pathology. This does *not* imply that human biology is
not involved in the state of one's mind; indeed it almost always is. This
merely stresses the lack of scientific evidence in support of brain differences pointing to *etiology* of mental illness. We should keep in mind that
correlation is not the same as *causation.* Those who advocate a basic form
of biological reductionism have been left empty-handed. Moreover, their
anthropology, merely based on materialism, neither does justice to the
complexities of being a human, nor fits our biblical model.

The fact that the brains of people who suffer from "schizophrenia"
are different from the brains of ordinary people is not significant on its
own; the challenge is to discover what these differences mean. Researchers have yet to explain conclusively how the subjective experiences can

300. Insel, "Translating Scientific Opportunity into Public Health Impact," 128–29;
emphasis mine.

301. Ibid., 128.

be explained by brain "abnormalities" they have observed.[302] Also, the differences in the brain may be the consequence of environmental distress, spiritual turmoil, or life tribulations, rather than some lesion or genetic deformity.[303] Despite all the impressive progress in neuroimaging technologies, no consistent anatomical or functional brain alterations have been unequivocally related to psychosis or "schizophrenia."[304]

"We now know much more about psychiatric disorders," says Bentall. "Far from shoring up the medical approach, however, recent scientific research shows that it is fatally flawed."[305] Indeed, these flawed theories have yielded no progress in the treatment of psychiatric disorders since the time of Moral Therapy advocated by the Quakers. Thomas Kuhn in his seminal work on the philosophy of science describes how a paradigm shift takes place when a prevailing scientific theory is overthrown because of new understandings.[306] The trigger for this shift is the discovery of anomalies, which contradict the existing theories. As these anomalies multiply, the accepted theory is thrown into "a state of crisis," out of which arises a new theory, which gives fresh life to the field in a new paradigm. Although the medical model of insanity continues to persist for most psychiatrists, and certainly for the pharmaceutical companies, due to all anomalies and contradictions, many researchers are on a quest to offer up alternative models of mental illness.

Kenneth Kendler, a psychiatrist and a philosopher, a hard-core biological/genetic researcher, warns against giving in to "monistic explanatory approaches, especially biological reductionism," and explains that "Psychiatric disorders are, by their nature, complex multilevel phenomena. We need to keep our heads clear about their stunning complexity and realize, with humility, that their full understanding will require the rigorous integration of multiple disciplines and perspectives."[307] The proposition behind this chapter is that it is time to try to look at the concept of madness afresh, without the preconceptions given to us by the biological psychiatry and the prevailing flawed theories. It is within this historical context that we now turn to theology and allow a new picture of "schizophrenia" to emerge, offering a fresh perspective through theological reflection.

302. Bentall, *Doctoring the Mind*, 152.

303. Kirsch, *The Emperor's New Drugs*, 100.

304. Borgwardt and Fusar-Poli, "Third-Generation Neuroimaging in Early Schizophrenia," 270–72.

305. Bentall, *Doctoring the Mind*, xvi.

306. Thomas S. Kuhn, *The Structure of Scientific Revolutions*.

307. Kendler, "Toward a Philosophical Structure for Psychiatry," 433, 439.

3

A Theology of Illness

We need a life not correlated with death, a health not liable
to illness, a kind of good that will not perish, a good in fact
that flies beyond the Goods of nature.[1]

—William James

Bear one another's burden, and thus fulfill the law of Christ.

Galatians 6:2

This sickness is not unto death, but for the glory of God,
that the Son of God may be glorified by it.

John 11:4

In the previous chapter we evaluated the burgeoning psychiatric research to get a handle on the medical framing of madness. Our evaluation left us wanting. We realized that science with all its claims has yet to conquer the stunning complexities of this phenomenon. I argued, based on a variety of research findings, that "schizophrenia" should be regarded as a variation of human expression, rather than as pathology.[2] To unravel the

1. James, *The Varieties of Religious Experience*, 133.

2. Several researchers have outlined a substantial body of evidence establishing that psychosis and "normal" traits are distinct points on the spectrum of valid human behavior. See Claridge, "Can a Disease Model of Schizophrenia Survive?," 157–83; Kaplan and Murphy, *The Inner World of Mental Illness*, 467; Sarbin, "Toward the Obsolescence of the Schizophrenia Hypothesis," 259–84, 13–38 and Mirowsky, "Subjective

mystery of madness as a human phenomenon, I suggest that we need to shift our paradigm of understanding and appeal to biblical revelation for illumination. The broken voices of sufferers demand of us to look into this mysterious human expression in new and fresh ways under the direction of the Holy Spirit.

In an attempt to understand "schizophrenia" as a "mental illness," we will begin by looking into the nature of health and illness in a theological context, in order to establish an interpretative framework that can inform our analysis. The subject matter of illness speaks in many languages that demand attention: the languages of medicine, culture, psychology, and theology among others. Our interest is to look beyond the biological and medical model of diagnosis toward what the *voice* of illness might be from a *theological* perspective. If the God of the Bible is sovereign over all events of creation, surely there must be meaning behind the illnesses that affect our lives in such profound ways. Could God be speaking to us through our illnesses? Who might the expectant audience of this hidden voice be? Could God be targeting a wider community around a sufferer? Is there a role for an illness narrative that is internal to the illness itself?

In this chapter, we will expand on our findings from chapter 1 on "Theological Anthropology," and delve into the hypothesis that madness is an illness of *nous*, the *spirit*, the innermost part of the human being. We will scrutinize the work of a variety of scholars and theologians who have searched within the humanity of madness to find insights into its etiology. I will argue that not only is "schizophrenia" not pathological, it touches on the most fundamental fragilities of the human soul—hence, it is a very critical pastoral issue to be comprehended through a theological lens. In pursuit of hearing the voice of this illness, I will bring to bear the resources of the Christian tradition and my personal experience to give an alternative account of "schizophrenia" that emerges from a theological reflection on the experience quite apart from what psychiatry may or may not have to say. In one sense, we will create a new language or a new form of expressive/descriptive grammar to help Christians reframe "schizophrenia." There are crucial phenomenological insights that can be drawn from the experience of madness as a human spectacle through theological reflection. My goal is to develop a comprehensive, unifying interpretation that is biblically sound and would bring intelligible order to this seemingly meaningless jumble of chaotic behavior called *madness*.

Boundaries and Combinations in Psychiatric Diagnosis," 407–24, 161–78.

In this chapter, we learn from a few theologians and researchers who have studied the encounter with illness as a human reality beyond its medical nosology. Their observations will guide us in reframing "schizophrenia" theologically. Conceptually, we are defining illness based on Kleinman's definition given in the *Introduction* to this book. He views illness as the innate "human experience of symptoms and suffering," which points to "the principal difficulties that symptoms and disability create in our lives." For Kleinman, illness is "always culturally shaped" and may vary in different contexts. In his model, disease is "what the practitioner creates in the recasting of illness in terms of theories of disorder . . . within a particular nomenclature and taxonomy." Thus, in the biomedical model, "disease is reconfigured *only* as an alteration in biological structure or functioning." This means that the practitioner, whether a physician or a psychotherapist, takes the human illness and functional problems and maps them into a reductionist and narrow model of technical issues. In other words, diseases are always illnesses, but all illnesses are not necessarily diseases.[3]

Every human being will encounter illness at some point in his or her lifetime; it is an experience inescapably connected to the human condition. Health with its fragility is nothing but a temporary pause in a battle between forces of life and other powers opposing them. We all are in the grip of a "sickness unto death."[4] All illnesses bring about suffering. In most cases the suffering is both physical and psychological. Moreover, all illnesses create "spiritual suffering," by exposing the fragility of the human condition. We are continually reminded that health and biological life are not "goods" that we possess forever, but that we are mortal beings, destined for deterioration and eventual death. From the personal perspective, illness brings about inevitable questions such as: Why me? Why my loved one? What is this illness for? What will this do to me? Who can help me?[5]

The advancements of medical science and technology have resulted in remarkable benefits for the human race in terms of longer lives, overcoming complex diseases, and suppressing pain. Many illnesses that in the past centuries decimated populations have virtually been wiped out in our time. In light of these advancements, we face the temptation to allow science and technology to explain everything about our bodies and minds and name our experiences of illness within their technical language. The medical science with its foundation in natural sciences objectifies illness,

3. Kleinman, *The Illness Narratives*, 3–6.

4. Kierkegaard and Bretall, *A Kierkegaard Anthology*, 339–71.

5. Larchet, *Theology of Illness*, 9–10.

explaining it as a reality in itself, in isolation from the sufferer.[6] In the scientific/technical approach the body is regarded as a machine that is supposed to function based on the laws of physics and chemistry; "this automatically excludes personality from consideration," says Gotthard Booth.[7]

The history of the encounter with illness has proven that illnesses demand to be studied from different perspectives. Paul Tillich in his paper "The Meaning of Health"[8] explains that the human person is a "multidimensional unity," meaning that "in each dimension all other dimensions are potentially or actually present." He explains that from a physical perspective, health is seen as proper functioning of all biological organs; from a chemical perspective health constitutes the chemical balance in substances and processes of a living organism; and from a psychological perspective it is about emotional balance and harmony with the environment. Tillich points out that when one perspective alone controls the treatment approach, the outcome will be nothing but "an unhealthy health." For example, with the prevalence of medicalizing illnesses in the Western cultures, it is possible to remove with drugs some of the physical and psychological tensions that perhaps are meant to play a helpful function.[9] When health and sanity are reduced to chemistry, Tillich questions the chemistry of those who are in position to make such determinations. He concludes his paper by emphasizing that this "mutual within-each-otherness" of the different perspectives of illness is key to health and healing.[10]

Those in pastoral care ought to guard against surrendering to a medical model that objectifies the problems and looks for a technical solution without any regards for the complexities of human nature, journey of salvation, and natural struggles for existence independent from God. The words *sozo* and *soteria,* which mean "to save" and "salvation," occur in about 150 New Testament passages. Wheeler Robinson points out that about one third of these texts denote deliverance from captivity, disease, demon possession, or physical death. Deliverance from captivity and

6. Ibid., 11.

7. Gotthard Booth, "The Voice of the Body," 22.

8. The paper was presented to the New York Society for Clinical Psychiatry, January 1960, cited in Siirala, *The Voice of Illness*, 145.

9. For scientific argument of depression's evolutionary significance in helping the immune system to fight infection, see Raison and Miller, "The Evolutionary Significance of Depression in Pathogen Host Defense (PATHOS-D)."

10. Siirala, *The Voice of Illness*, 146.

illness was a foreshadowing of the ultimate eschatological salvation. Also, the reference to God or Christ in many of these passages reminds us that "save" points to a "Savior" and not a "moral development." The whole concept is much more related to a divine act than the modern mind is willing to accept.[11] However, despite the testimony of Scripture (Matt 10:7–8, 11:2–5; Luke 9:1–2, 6, 11; Acts 4:14, 30) that salvation and healing of the sick are mutually interrelated, church communities have rarely taken the encounter with illness as theologically significant.

Physical and mental health are desirable blessings; but should they be pursued absolutely? Ernest Becker, the Pulitzer Prize-winning cultural anthropologist, raises the concern that, "[M]an's natural and inevitable urge to deny mortality and achieve a heroic self-image are the root causes of human evil."[12] What matters when Christians are battling illness is not simply to defeat the problem and get back to one's daily chores. The victory does not lie in overcoming the germs or pain or forces of evil, but in perseverance in the face of such challenges and clinging to one's deep conviction of what it means to faithfully worship God and surrender to him while hanging on the cross. What matters mostly is that when Christians encounter the sick and dying, "they take it upon themselves," as Joel Shuman suggests, "to *make space* in their lives" to care for those persons as if they were caring for Christ himself; for in reality illness is more than an individualistic encounter.[13]

Building on the works of church fathers such as St. Basil, St. John Chrysostom, and St. Gregory of Nazianus, Larchet stresses that insofar as health does not serve one's relationship with God, it cannot be considered good by nature. In fact health could be evil if it causes one to turn away from God by giving a false impression of self-sufficiency, which could lead to arrogance, giving free rein to passion, and transgressions against God.[14] St. Gregory of Nazianus counsels the church "to despise an insidious health that leads to sin" and warns her to "not admire every form of health," and to "not condemn every illness."[15] This perspective brings our relationship with God in focus and minimizes all else in comparison.

Prior to the Enlightenment, James Woodward argues, most Christians "lived in a potentially miraculous world," under God's providential

11. Robinson, *Redemption and Revelation*, 232–34.

12. Becker, *Escape from Evil*, xvii.

13. Shuman, *The Body of Compassion*, xvi.

14. Larchet, *Theology of Illness*, 55.

15. St. Gregory of Nazianus, Discourse XIV.34, cited in ibid., 56–57.

and powerful hand. The Enlightenment has made people believe in a world trapped in a "closed system" governed by principles of cause and effect that can be observed and measured. "Mystery has not been banished from our world" and miracles still happen; the difference is that everything has to be explained by the physical laws, even at the cost of making the explanations nonsensical.[16]

Aarne Siirala claims that the theory of illness developed by natural sciences has fallen short in formulating the depth of the "character of illness."[17] In the case of our study, while the scientific community relentlessly pursues biological answers to the mystery of madness, which has haunted humanity for centuries, the church has been passive in finding her own theological answers to the dilemma, and worse still, she has bought in to the scenarios and solutions offered by the medical community, without any theological reflection. This appears to be because the church has consciously or unconsciously accepted a reductionist anthropology offered by medicine, and has uncritically made the pronouncements of psychiatry her own without any attempt to understand the processes of medicine behind such pronouncements.

As we discussed in chapter 1 on anthropology, there is an organic unity and harmony between the body and soul/spirit/mind; consequently, a problem with one will affect the other. Wittgenstein reminds us that "The human body is the best picture of the human soul."[18] Thus, what appears to be a physical aberration in many cases reflects a deeper inner wound within the human spirit. Humankind has always known "intuitively" that "the body speaks a very basic and very honest language through the healthy and unhealthy functioning of its organs," says Booth.[19] At times, our pathologies speak more prominently about our human condition than about the disorder itself. Booth believes that *illness* expresses the soul with greater depth than *health*. This is in the same way that "a good caricature" reveals essential aspects of personality much more precisely than a photograph taken under normal circumstances.[20]

---

16. Woodward, *Encountering Illness*, 93.

17. Siirala, *The Voice of Illness*, 32. Aarne Siirala is a Finnish theologian who has done extensive research in collaboration with his brother, Martti Siirala, a psychiatrist, in relating the work of the church to the task of healing.

18. Wittgenstein and Anscombe, *Philosophical Investigations*, 152e.

19. Booth, "The Voice of the Body," 1.

20. Ibid., 3.

Larchet says, "Rather than treat the person, many physicians today treat illnesses or organs" as autonomous entities of "a purely physiological character." He is pointing to depersonalization of medical practice. This has resulted in the patient taking very little or no responsibility for his illness and for the treatment becoming a matter of technical repair, denying the fact that illness is inherently personal. By neglecting the spiritual dimension of human beings when we work to diminish their physical ailments, says Larchet, "we do them immeasurable harm." This deprives the person of any real possibility to "assume their condition profitably" and to prevail over the various trials they have to encounter. Every illness touches us in our core and forces us to question ourselves, sometimes with a "tormenting attack on our very being." At times, it "plunges us into unfamiliar territory" forcing a different path upon our lives, shattering dreams and plans. It questions our way of life, the use of our body, our relationships, our system of values, and our priorities in life. Depending on the seriousness of illness the stark reality of death becomes more graspable. These questions are bound to result in spiritual struggles, and potentially lead to stress, fear, discouragement, anguish, and despair. Therefore, illness is very *theological* by nature.[21]

Due to his increased life span, Siirala argues, the contemporary person has a new attitude about physical existence, shaped by the prevailing "gospel of humanism," which rejects all theistic beliefs and is based on humankind taking full responsibility for his destiny and fulfillment.[22] Indeed, with advancements in the field of genetics and artificial intelligence, the scientific community looks to the possibility that by technical manipulations, it can biologically purify human nature of all its imperfections and that perhaps the true adversary, death, can finally be conquered.[23] The hope is that human beings might escape the limits of their present condition. In time, will science rise to this aspiration or it is just an illusion? Clearly for now, the enduring hope of perfect health is confronted with the reality of millions of lives buried in sickness, anguish, and pain.

Although medicine has successfully wiped out many illnesses in the Western world, in recent centuries new diseases have appeared to take their place.[24] Also, as we have seen, in a severe mental illness such

21. Larchet, *Theology of Illness*, 10–11, 14.

22. Siirala, *The Voice of Illness*, 18.

23. Larchet, *Theology of Illness*, 12–13. See the discussion around the aspirations of Artificial Intelligence and nanobot technologies to eliminate death, in chapter 1.

24. See Angell, *The Truth About the Drug Companies*, 25. In regards to cancer, Booth

as "schizophrenia," the common medical treatments cannot effectively reduce human suffering "without diminishing, modifying, or suppressing the patient's consciousness, thereby further limiting his or her personal freedom."[25] Indeed, John McNeill notes that many fervent and highly skilled men and women are undertaking the "reconstruction of personalities" damaged by stresses of life—what Peter Kramer calls "cosmetic psychopharmacology."[26] These are newly created challenges with ethical implications that the church cannot afford to disregard.

In the twenty-first century, the medical and scientific models consider the human person as purely a biological organism.[27] Even in cases where some attention is paid to the spirituality of a patient, it seems that this attention is superficial. Shuman points out that there is a trend in both popular and scholarly media to suggest "that God—like raw vegetables, regular exercise, and properly used seat belts—is an essential component of a healthy life." These articles usually point out that people who attend religious services or regularly pray or meditate live healthier lives than those who do not. In these presentations, the researcher explains in an intentional *non*-theological language, *why* religious activities are good and helpful to our health.[28]

Shuman observes that "this sort of facile, uncritical approach," that explains the positive causal link between health and certain religious practices, is highly problematic and misleading.[29] It fails to portray a true picture of biblical faith and the true character of the God of Scripture. In

---

explains that researchers noticed that with increasing success of overcoming infectious diseases, the rate of cancer was steadily increasing. Now it is understood that cancer is "directly related to the antibacterial defenses of the body." Booth, "The Voice of the Body," 14–15.

25. Larchet, *Theology of Illness*, 13.

26. McNeill, *A History of the Cure of Souls*, 319. See Kramer, *Listening to Prozac*, 97; Kramer (xviii) points to Prozac's "transformative powers" to provide more than a "cure" for a disease, and how it "went beyond treating illness to changing personality, how it entered into our struggle to understand the self."

27. We disputed this model in an elaborate fashion in chapter 1.

28. Shuman, *The Body of Compassion*, xv. Lowenthal makes a reference to a series of research that suggest that "religion may have a stress-buffering effect"; Loewenthal, "Religious Beliefs about Illness," 176. One of the best known research findings in this area is done by Harold Koenig of Duke University. His book is used widely by researchers in the Western world; Koenig et al., *Handbook of Religion and Health*. For a more recent study on the topic see Rosmarin et al., "Religious coping among psychotic patients," 182–87.

29. Shuman, *The Body of Compassion*, xv.

fact one of the frequently held presumptions of such studies is that in the end God's character is irrelevant, and must be left to individual choices, "since everything, including God, can be explained finally without reference to God."[30] This appears to be a spirituality centered on human beings' feelings and their personal desires for transcendence versus spirituality that is centered on the Most High God, and his plans for his creation. It is no surprise that this kind of spirituality is *not* concerned with *theology* at all.[31] Ethan Watters points out that although many treatments emphasize "psychosocial aid" and seek to support the person's spiritual needs, in reality "religions and forms of healing are given only lip service or, worse yet, are used as the proverbial spoonful of sugar that helps the Western medicine go down."[32]

John Frame believes, "There is nothing more important than knowing God." Indeed, it is the knowledge of God that can put our illnesses in the right perspective, such that we can make sense of them. In our contemporary time "the knowledge of God is rare," and many people "speak glibly" about their faith in some kind of god. Frame notes that fewer people "claim to know the true God, the God of the Bible."[33] This speaks to the image of the "wicked" that the psalmist portrays: "The wicked, in the haughtiness of his countenance does not seek Him; all his thoughts are, 'there is no God'" (Ps 10:4). Referring to the cultural drift that has overtaken the Christians' mentality, David Platt observes:

> The gospel reveals eternal realities about God that we would
> sometimes rather not face. We . . . enjoy our clichés, and picture
> God as a Father who might help us, all the while ignoring God
> as a judge who might damn us. . . . If we stop and really look at

30. Ibid., xvi.

31. In a book concerned with issues of *Spirituality and Psychiatry*, consisting of a collection of essays by some prominent psychiatrists, many of whom are professing Christians, the editors define "spirituality . . . with a view to inclusiveness," as that which "is concerned with human experience of relationship, meaning and purpose. This includes a transcendent, or transpersonal, dimension of experience that has traditionally been regarded as being more the domain of religion and theology than psychiatry. But it also encompasses experiences that are very familiar to psychiatry—life within family and society that have usually been viewed in a secular and non-spiritual sense." Cook et al., *Spirituality and Psychiatry*, xii.

32. Watters, *Crazy Like Us*, 98.

33. Frame, *Doctrine of God*, 1.

God in his Word, we might discover that he evokes greater awe
and demands deeper worship than we are ready to give him.[34]

Frame points out that in our time most people live "by the standards of
modern secular culture, rather than by the Word of God." They may speak
piously, "but he makes little real difference" to their daily encounters. "But
how can it be," asks Frame, "that the Lord of heaven and earth makes no
difference?"[35] Is this behavior something that God would ignore? Perhaps
humanity's pride and haughtiness should give us clues about what we
ought to learn from our illnesses.

The Original Cause of Illness

The majority of conservative theologians hold the view that the root of
all suffering in the world lies in Adam's disobedience, which led to his
separation from God and his ultimate removal from the Garden of Eden.
Prior to Adam's rebellion, there was no sin and no sign of suffering. God
had promised punishment—death—in case of Adam's disobedience and
his eating from the tree of the knowledge of good and evil. As Grudem
indicates, this death is "most fully understood to mean death in an extensive sense, physical, spiritual, and eternal death and separation from
God."[36] Throughout history, theologians have speculated on what might
have happened if Adam had fully obeyed God. Would he have died physically regardless? Was death part of the original creation? Grudem believes
that the presence of the tree of life in the midst of the Garden "signified the
promise of eternal life with God if Adam and Eve had met the conditions
of a covenant relationship by obeying God completely."[37]

34. Platt, *Radical*, 29.

35. Frame, *Doctrine of God*, 2.

36. Grudem, *Systematic Theology*, 516.

37. Ibid. Some theologians do not focus on the historicity of the Genesis message,
but rather on the existential message about our continued challenges in life. For example, Atkinson claims, instead of understanding Genesis 2 and 3 as "a logical statement
of causes and effects," we should receive them as a story that the author has "borrowed
various familiar mythological motifs, transformed them, and integrated them into a
fresh and original story of his own." He claims that in the story of our relationship to
God, we can learn how "beauty is turned to brokenness, unity to diversity, fellowship
to banishment, and life becomes overshadowed by death." Atkinson, who is *not* willing
to say that the events depicted in these chapters never happened, is more interested in
exploring how the twentieth-century humankind can find itself in the Garden. Atkinson, *The Message of Genesis 1–11*, 53. Tucker, also, calls into question the traditional

The ultimate reparation of the damage brought about at the beginning in the Garden manifests at the end of Scripture as "a new heaven and a new earth" (Rev 21:1), a place "in which righteousness dwells" (2 Pet 3:13). Then, God will dwell among his people and "they shall be His people. . . . He shall wipe away every tear from their eyes; and there shall no longer be any death . . . or crying, or pain; the first things have passed away" (Rev 21:3–4). This is not only the end of suffering, but also the end of sin: "and nothing unclean and no one who practices abomination and lying shall ever come into it" (Rev 21:27). Between Genesis and Revelation, there is endless evil, pain, illness, and suffering. From the perspective of Scripture's foundational narrative, D. A. Carson explains that these elements are profoundly related: "evil is the primal cause of suffering, rebellion is the root of pain, sin is the source of death."[38] Paul understood this principle when he said: "The wages of sin is death" (Rom 6:23).

The curse brought about pain, suffering, heartbreaks, and death. As a result of the Fall, humankind is destined to contend with nature for survival.[39] Ray Anderson offers a more nuanced expression of this principle. Although the natural consequence of sin is death and suffering, he believes that "God's judgment against sin . . . is itself a continued intervention of divine grace." He points out that if the sinner were left to the consequences of his "moral and spiritual disorientation," human personhood would not be able to bear the burden of "the sickness and turmoil of life." In that case human personhood would be destroyed. Thus, when God intervenes with his judgment upon Adam and Eve and stops them in their "fateful

---

reading of Genesis 1–3. He believes these narratives are about "a story not theology as such"; and "the story is a response to very serious questions about human nature and experience." Tucker, "Creation and the Fall," 113.

38. Carson, *How Long, O Lord?*, 40.

39. In regards to the curse, Bonhoeffer introduces an "unheard-of ambiguity." He interprets the curse as: "Now live in this destroyed world, you cannot escape it, live in it between curse and promise." Adam, as the serpent promised, has his way now, and "he must live like God in his *sicut deus* world." Bonhoeffer believes that this is the real curse: "Adam as man *sicut deus* has taken into himself death with the fruit of the tree of knowledge. Adam is dead before he dies. The serpent was right: you will be like God, you will not die; i.e. the death of non-being. But the Creator was right, too, '*for in the day that you eat of it you shall die*'; i.e., the death of being like God." Adam is permitted to live in this cursed world, but he has not been left without God's Word, "even though it is wrathful, repelling, cursing Word of God." He says, "In truth he lives in the world of the curse, but just because it is *God's* curse that burdens it, this world is not totally forsaken by God; it is the world of the preservation of life, blessed in God's curse, pacified in enmity, pain and work." Thus for Adam, both God's curse and promise continue. Bonhoeffer, *Creation and Fall*, 83–86.

situation," he is exercising grace and calling them back into relation with himself. Anderson suggests that those called to pastoral care must intervene similarly, "without being intimidated at the thought that a person's affliction or situation is the result of God's judgment against sin."[40]

It was common among the church fathers to attribute the root cause of illness to one's sinful nature. Irenaeus declared: "Because of the sin of disobedience, infirmities have come upon men."[41] The same concept is developed more explicitly by St. Gregory Palamas, who claims that "sickness, infirmities and the weight of all sorts of trials are the result of sin. ... Illness, as a result, is like a short and difficult pathway down which sin has led the human race."[42] Thus, if there had been no sin, humanity would not experience illness, which is "death's prelude." Darrel Amundsen, a historian of medicine in early Christianity, writes about St. Basil's views:

> While God will not allow the Christian to be tried more than he can bear, some are left to struggle against their afflictions, rendering them more worthy of reward because of these trials. Illness often is a punishment for sin that is imposed *for conversion*. Sometimes it is to keep the Christian from pride. Thus, when suffering calamity at God's hand, the Christian is admonished to ask two things of God: first, for understanding of the reason He has inflicted these blows; and second, for deliverance from these pains or for the capacity to endure them patiently.[43]

Illness and the resulting death are not the supreme instances of misfortune, but they are part of God's planned judgment against sin.[44] This principle is central to the Scriptural narrative from beginning to the end and must not be evaded. In Deuteronomy 32:39, the Lord says, "See now that I, I am He, and there is no God besides Me; It is I who put to death and give life. I have wounded, and it is I who heal; and there is no one who can deliver from My hand."[45] Carson notes, "Death is no accident; it is God's

---

40. Anderson, *The Shape of Practical Theology*, 224–25.

41. Irenaeus, "Church Fathers."

42. Quoted in Larchet, *Theology of Illness*, 27.

43. Amundsen, "Medicine and Faith in Early Christianity," 335; emphasis mine.

44. There are many scholars who oppose this view. For example, in regards to mental illness, Southard tries to make a distinction between "sinful behavior and behavior that is symptomatic of sickness." He finds it irresponsible to mix the two interpretations. Southard, "Sin Or Sickness," 147.

45. Interestingly, Gaiser claims that in their "contextual rhetoric," this and similar seemingly "dangerous and difficult" passages (e.g., Exod 4:11; 1 Sam 2:6; Job 2:10;

doing."[46] Thus, those who share the view of the Fall and the original sin, believe that their consequences touch the lives of everyone in this fallen world. Nevertheless, the fathers were focused on guiding the Christians to use illnesses "as an occasion to serve God and to grow in virtues." Like Anderson, they saw divine intervention as an act of grace to bring people back to the living God.[47]

At times, illness and death are the "immediate judicial consequence" of a particular sin, as was the case with the Judean king, Jehoram, and his severe sickness of the bowels, the paralyzed man by the pool of Bethesda, Gehazi and his leprosy, the sudden deaths of Ananias and Sapphira, and Herod, and the illness and subsequent death of some members of the Corinthian church.[48] Furthermore, as in the case of Jehoram's sons and wives, sometimes the consequences of personal sins manifest in the lives of others. In the book of Deuteronomy, the nation of Israel is warned beforehand that their sins will cause the Lord to bring "madness . . . blindness . . . bewilderment of heart . . . extraordinary plagues . . . and miserable and chronic sicknesses" (Deut 28:28, 59).

The church must be cautious not to conclude that the people who suffered in this way were the worst of the sinners among their contemporaries. Indeed, as seen above, at times people suffer for the sins of those around them. In fact Jesus warned against that kind of assessment. When someone asked him "about the Galileans whose blood Pilate had mingled with their sacrifices," he rejected the supposition that the incident had anything to do with personal sins (Luke 13:1b–3). Jesus was instructing them to look at the circumstance through a didactic lens, rather than a judgmental one. In the case of the man born blind, Jesus told his disciples that the man's congenital handicap had nothing to do with any specific sin that either he or his parents had committed, "but it was in order that the works of God might be displayed in him" (John 9:3). This last event was tied to Jesus' self-disclosure.

Isa 45:7; Lam 3:38) reveal that it is "absolutely clear that they are fundamentally understood as good news." These passages speak of Israel's strong monotheistic faith, where "demons and other divinities are excluded." More importantly, Israel's God is trustworthy, and Israel knows, "There is direction and purpose in Yahweh's activity, and it is marked not by wounding but by healing. . . . When Yahweh weighs everything in the balance, grace wins." Gaiser, *Healing in the Bible*, 26–27.

46. Carson, *How Long, O Lord?*, 98.

47. Boyd, "A Biblical Theology of Chronic Illness," 201.

48. Carson, *How Long, O Lord?*, 100.

It is also noteworthy that in Scripture many godly persons suffered illness and untimely death. The Apostle Paul, Timothy, Trophimus, and John the Baptist are among many characters whose ailment or death was not linked to a specific sin.[49] I agree with Carson that it is "pastorally insensitive" and "theologically stupid" to inflict immeasurable anguish on those who are already burdened with misfortunes in this life, by accusing them with either a hidden sin of which they have not repented, or worse, of lacking faith.[50] As shown above, both assumptions that 1) each ailment is linked to a specific sin and 2) that it is always God's will to heal every sickness, if only one could exercise sufficient faith, are scripturally unsupportable; this is the claim of those in "Word-Faith Movement."[51] God may have a variety of reasons for "sanctioning illness and sorrow." It is advisable instead for Christians to see the affliction of another member of the body of Christ as a blow on themselves; and at all times to resist the temptation to judge the sufferings of others.[52]

It is essential to understand that there are some illnesses and deaths that are not the results of sinful acts, but are "natural outworking of cause and effects, under *God's providence.*" Carson notes that many physical and emotional illnesses are caused by chaotic lifestyles, poor diet, lack of sleep, environmental pollution, dirty waters, sexual promiscuity, drug abuse, dysfunctional work places, and stressful relationships. There are hurtful and sometimes irreversible consequences to our sins in this life. At the same time, like many church fathers, Carson claims that pain and suffering borne by illness "may serve to bring about a good end, when they are *mingled with faith.*" From Scripture's position, "God disciplines His people—whether as chastening punishment or as the toughening up of a soldier." These experiences are never "intrinsically 'good.'" Moreover, they are not easy experientially, and we may not be able to perceive what good they are accomplishing in us or anyone else around us until a good chunk of time has elapsed.[53] That is why this kind of analysis is never helpful for someone in the midst of fire. However, a faithful person encounters

49. Because of surpassing greatness of revelations given to Paul, he was given a "thorn in the flesh" to keep him from exalting himself. But, it was certainly not to punish him for any particular sin (2 Cor 12:7). Timothy suffered from frequent illnesses (1 Tim 5:23); Paul had to leave the ill Trophimus behind in Miletus (2 Tim 4:20); John the Baptist was beheaded by Herod to please Herodias's daughter (Matt 14:1–12).

50. Carson, *How Long, O Lord*, 101.

51. Boyd, "A Biblical Theology of Chronic Illness," 199–200.

52. Carson, *How Long, O Lord?*, 101.

53. Ibid., 102–3; emphasis mine.

the experience of illness with an appeal to a merciful God expecting to hear from Him. The author of Hebrews reminds us: "All discipline for the moment seems not to be joyful, but sorrowful; yet to those who have been trained by it, afterwards it yields the peaceful fruit of righteousness" (Heb 12:8–11).

On the other hand, it is critical to remember that severe illness can make some people feel abandoned by God and cause them to lose faith in his mercies. John Colwell, a theologian who suffers from "bipolar disorder," identifies with the psalmist in Psalm 22. He claims that "the dominant distress of the psalm is . . . not distress at [the] circumstances but distress at the perceived absence of God." The psalmist feels "forsaken" by God. His experience of God's seeming absence is far more stressful than "the opposition, oppression, and suffering itself."[54] However, Colwell admits that for the psalmist, in the midst of despair, it was the "remembrance" of his "personal history" with God that issued "renewed prayer" and hope, knowing that "God will not remain distant" forever; he will "hear and answer" his prayer and will bring about his "deliverance."[55] John Swinton, referring to evil in general, points out that it has the potential to "separate human beings from their primary source of hope: *God*."[56] Therefore, it is crucial for the church to enable those who are hurt to "sustain faith even in the midst of evil and suffering."[57] Additionally, Atkinson sees a danger in viewing suffering to be purposeful and given by God, fearing that it has the potential to make the community dismiss their personal responsibility and feel more comfortable with one's pain.[58]

Nevertheless, based on Scriptural witness, all these illnesses, whether as a result of natural causes, or as a direct consequence of sins, are covered under the providence of God. Micah's prophecy, reflecting the state of humankind throughout generations, is an example of such providence:

> He has told you, O man, what is good;
> And what does the LORD require of you
> But to do justice, to love kindness,
> And to walk humbly with your God?
> The voice of the LORD will call to the city—

54. Colwell, *Why Have You Forsaken Me?*, 48.

55. Ibid., 53.

56. Swinton, *Raging with Compassion*, 44.

57. Ibid., 45.

58. Atkinson, "The Patient as Sufferer," cited in Loewenthal, "Religious Beliefs about Illness," 174. The church's responsibility toward her members' pain will be discussed in the next chapter.

For the rich men of the city are full of violence,
Her residents speak lies,
And their tongue is deceitful in their mouth;
So also *I will make you sick*, striking you down,
Desolating you *because of your sins*.
(Mic 6:8–9a, 12–13; emphasis mine)

The concept of God ordaining our illnesses is foreign to the Western cultural mentality. It is most natural for humans to project their own desires onto God and to create a God in their own image. David Leyshon sees this "propensity to think of God as one would like Him to be" to be a pervasive aspect of contemporary religious thought. He indicates that the most popular image in the West is "the 'God' of sentimentality who masquerades as 'love.'"[59] This is a God who could not possibly be behind any suffering. This assumption leads to more serious twisted portrayals of God. This God whose primary purpose is "to serve men" could not be the omnipotent God of Scripture. Indeed, "taking note of the pervasive nature of suffering in the world, this God clearly has a hard time coping with the power of evil."[60] Alongside the "reduction of God's love to a benign sentimentality," and the elimination of the truth of God's fierce anger toward sin, he believes, we find ourselves in a culture in which people are preoccupied with materialism and a pleasure-seeking lifestyle with an outlook on life that is totally earth-bound and focused on the present.[61]

Kathryn Greene-McCreight, who has suffered from bipolar disorder for many years, speaks of the sense of comfort in the midst of one's illness, knowing that God is the one who has brought the illness as a way of disciplining and refining his child. She points to Psalm 6 and how the psalmist understands his suffering as a sign of God's anger. "How unpopular such an understanding of the wrath of God is in our culture," says Greene-McCreight. "We prefer to see God as nice, indeed rather innocuous." She says, "To blame illness on the anger of God is to lay upon God perhaps too much power."[62] But what many in the Western cultures miss is that here, as in Psalm 22, God's sovereign power and providence is a source of comfort for the psalmist. The psalmist asks God for mercy knowing that he is a merciful God who hears the prayer of his people. After all, what is more

59. Leyshon, *Sickness, Suffering and Scripture*, 20.

60. Ibid.

61. Ibid., 54–55.

62. Greene-McCreight, *Darkness Is My Only Companion*, 103.

comforting: being subjected to random evil in a world where God has no power or inclination to stop such acts, or knowing that a sovereign and loving God who has a purposeful plan for all things is in control and nothing is in vain? Jeremiah laments, "For the Lord will not reject forever, for if he causes grief, then he will have compassion according to his abundant lovingkindness" (Lam 3:31–32). Greene-McCreight contrasts the reaction of the psalmist to that of William Styron, who suffered from depression. Styron says: "The pain is unrelenting, and what makes the condition intolerable is the foreknowledge that no remedy will come—not in a day, an hour, a month, or a minute."[63] Styron's pain and depression is meaningless, whereas the psalmist is drawn into a deeper relationship with God by his suffering. "There is a way out of this situation for the psalmist, while there is no way out of random suffering," says Greene-McCreight.[64]

Calvin also advocated the idea that the sinner can always rise above his affliction and have hope in Christ: "Christ as medicine for his wounds, comfort for his dread, the haven of his misery."[65] Carson points to Job as an example of a man who in the midst of his suffering, when accused by his friends that his sins and God's judgment have brought this disaster upon him, knows that even if that were true—Job disputes the accusation and knows that he will be vindicated—he would still trust God: "Though He slay me, yet will I hope in Him. . . . Indeed this will turn out for my deliverance."[66] Job knows that God is the source of goodness and mercy, and his eventual salvation; he can count on that. "Thus the godly mind," says Calvin, "however strange the ways in which it is vexed and troubled, finally surmounts all difficulties, and never allows itself to be deprived of assurance of divine mercy."[67]

Scripture speaks unambiguously about the "health-giving benefits of a well-ordered, God-fearing life" and the side effects of ignoring God's instructions (Prov 3, Ps 32). Leyshon notes that God employs illness along with other sufferings as fatherly discipline to bring his rebellious children back to their senses. He states the belief that God's chastisement may be present in our illnesses—as in the case of Corinthian church (1 Cor 11:27–31)—makes self-examination an essential response to the

63. William Styron, *Darkness Visible*, 62; cited in Greene-McCreight, *Darkness Is My Only Companion*, 39.

64. Ibid, 104.

65. Calvin, *Institutes*, 3/3.4.

66. Carson, *How Long, O Lord?*, 146.

67. Calvin, *Institutes*, 3/2.21.

onset of illness.[68] The sovereign, omnipotent God of Scripture who "works all things after the council of His will" (Eph 1:11) has his own good purposes in the afflictions we suffer in this life. Although the ways of God are ultimately mysterious and unfathomable, yet his ways, as revealed in Scripture, provide us a roadmap. First, it is a supreme belief of the Reformed tradition that God's rightful purpose in all things is his own glory. Leyshon points to Lazarus's illness and death, remembering the agony and grief of his sisters, "in order that God's glory might shine all the more brightly in the resurrection of the dead" (see John 11:4). Second, the eternal salvation of God's people, and their increasing conformity to the image of Christ, and thereby their union with Christ, is God's ultimate plan for his children. God accomplishes his good pleasure even if this should come at the cost of their earthly comfort. Leyshon believes that this is the reason that so many born-again Christians can trace the onset of their new life in Christ to some life crisis that involved brokenness, vulnerability, and affliction.[69] Indeed, even Jesus, "Although He was a Son, He learned obedience from the things which He suffered" (Heb 5:8; also see Heb 4:15).

According to Scripture, one's true strength has little to do with his natural faculties. It is neither his physical strength nor his intellectual capacity that brings him success. Rather, because the source of all power is in God, "human strength is dependent on the extent to which a man leans on God," says Leyshon. That is why Paul can claim: "I can do all things through Him who strengthens me" (Phil 4:13). Leyshon sees God energizing his people to lean on Him by "pruning" them. This pruning is essential to free one from that "innate self-reliance, pride, vainglory, and self-confidence which renders us weak."[70] What Leyshon, Carson, and others are emphasizing is that the source of *all things* is God, even if they are evil in themselves, and can be "portrayed as the effluent of a fallen world," or even "the work of the devil." Thus Paul "has no doubt," says Carson, "that his 'thorn in the flesh' is simultaneously 'a messenger of Satan' and something that God Himself sent Paul" to keep him from exalting himself.[71] Frame points to God's power and his perfect and unfathomable plan for his people to remind us that "God is at work in the ordinary, as

68. Leyshon, *Sickness, Suffering and Scripture*, 40–41.

69. Ibid., 59.

70. Ibid., 65.

71. Carson, *How Long, O Lord?*, 65.

much as in the extraordinary. He often works behind the scenes, and He often does His most wonderful works through apparent defeats."[72]

Erik H. Erikson, pointing to Otto Scheel's[73] "most soberly" biography of Luther, explains that he saw Luther's "attacks of unconsciousness and fits of overwhelming anxiety," and "delusional moments," and "states of brooding despair" as "genuinely inspired by a divine agency." To Scheel they were all "spiritual, not mental." Scheel insists that all attacks on Luther were "straight down from heaven." Erikson also points at the opposing view expressed by Roman Catholic priest, Dominican Heinrich Denifle, who believed the source of Luther's problems was his "abysmal depravity of character." To him Luther was a complete "psychopath" and no genuine mental or spiritual suffering should be attributed to him. He claimed it was only "the Bad One" who worked through Luther. Erikson finds it interesting that both views are structurally similar, although they differ in content. Common to both interpretations was attributing Luther's struggles to powers outside of him that had nothing to do with his psychology or biology.[74] Interestingly enough, Luther himself sees his struggles as liberating him and shaping his theology. He said, "I did not learn my theology all at once, but I had to search deeper for it, where my temptations took me." His dying to himself brought him life. Erikson says, "A theologian is born by living . . . not by thinking, reading, or speculating."[75]

Scripture clearly testifies to Satan's ability to cause diseases.[76] Acts 10:38 says that Jesus "went about doing good, and healing all who were

72. Frame, *Doctrine of God*, 527–28.

73. Otto Scheel, a Protestant professor of theology was "one of the most thorough editors of the early sources of Luther's life."

74. Erikson, *Young Man Luther*, 22–24.

75. Ibid., 245.

76. Piper and Taylor, *Suffering and the Sovereignty of God*, 24. Some theologians reject the fact that Satan is a real person that can cause anything. For example, Gaiser explains that demons are mostly absent from the Old Testament, not because the concepts were not known to Israel (in fact demons and spirits have been "common to religious worldviews everywhere") but rather, because such concepts were forbidden and "alien to faith in one God." He believes it was the influence of Persian Zoroastrianism, with a belief in the dualistic battle between "the supreme God Ahura Mazda" and Angra Mainyu ("the destructive spirit"), during the two centuries that Judah was a province of Persia, that made God's people accept that "there are chaotic forces out there beyond human control." These forces seemed "to be in opposition to the work of a good God." Gaiser argues, "Eventually, such forces became personified in biblical theology in the figure of Satan and the work of the demons." However, he admits that Jesus is "a healer" and that is "not just incidentally." Healing is a "characteristic of Jesus' ministry and identity." Pointing to Jesus' miracles and cures and exorcisms, he notes, "Surely, in New

oppressed by the devil, for God was with Him." Jesus encounters a woman who for eighteen years "had had a sickness caused by a spirit." He heals her on the Sabbath, and when he was criticized by the synagogue officials, he responds: "And this woman, a daughter of Abraham as she is, whom Satan has bound for eighteen long years, should she not have been released from this bond on the Sabbath day?" (Luke 13:16). Referring to these and other texts in Scripture, Piper asserts, "There is no doubt that Satan causes much disease. . . . This is why Christ's healings are a sign of the in-breaking of the Kingdom of God and its final victory over all disease and all the works of Satan."[77]

More important, Piper emphasizes that Satan might be an instrument used by God, but he is *never* sovereign in our diseases.[78] In the case of Job, when God gave Satan the permission to smite Job's body with boils, and Job's wife in despair asked him to "Curse God and die" (Job 2:9), Job looked past the finite "cause of Satan" to the "ultimate cause of God." Job referring to his wife as "foolish," and pointedly asked her, "Shall we indeed accept good from God and not accept adversity?" (Job 2:10). And lest we attribute ignorance to Job, the book comes to a close by speaking of Job's dramatic afflictions: "Then all his brothers, and all his sisters . . . came to him . . . and they consoled him and comforted him for *all the evil that the* LORD *had brought on him*" (Job 42:11; emphasis mine). Piper is pointing out that Satan is real and deceiving and desires destruction, but "he is not sovereign in sickness." Even though God uses him as an instrument in his hand, he will not attribute any sovereignty to Satan. As God asks Moses rhetorically at the burning bush: "Who has made man's mouth? Or who makes him dumb or deaf, or seeing or blind? Is it not I, the LORD?" (Exod 4:11). Piper sees God as the *ultimate cause* behind all illnesses.[79] In fact, he himself a cancer survivor, says:

> *You will waste your cancer if you do not believe it is designed for you by God. . . . You will waste your cancer if you believe it is a curse and not a gift. . . . You will waste your cancer if you think that "beating" cancer means staying alive rather than cherishing*

Testament perspective, Satan and the demons will always be lurking in the background of illness." Gaiser, *Healing in the Bible*, 128, 132, 135.

77. Piper and Taylor, *Suffering and the Sovereignty of God*, 24–25.

78. John Piper, *Spectacular Sins*, 107. See also Boyd, "A Biblical Theology of Chronic Illness," 202. Boyd claims, "The Bible does not present a radical dualism of Satan versus God. It presents God as almighty, with Satan on a short leash."

79. Piper and Taylor, *Suffering and the Sovereignty of God*, 25.

> *Christ. . . . You will waste your cancer if you treat sin as casually*
> *as before. . . . You will waste your cancer if you fail to use it as a*
> *means of witness to the truth and glory of Christ.*[80]

There is no doubt in Piper's mind that the hand of Almighty directs the course of an illness. Regardless of God's absolute sovereignty over our illnesses, it is a faithful act for Christians to pray for healing. It is in the process of praying and clinging to the hope of God's deliverance that he transforms us. God has promised that healing by the death of his Son on the cross. But we are not promised to receive all that inheritance in earthly life. We pray, and then have to trust his response.[81]

The Voice of Illness

The encounter with illness has a profound effect on the human soul and can teach us a lot about human condition. Under God's providence, anything that touches our lives in such a profound way cannot be void of meaning, and the interpretation of that meaning has to be undertaken by patients, families, and those who provide the care. As Kleinman explains, the way in which we interpret and respond to the experience of illness can "amplify or dampen symptoms" and "impede or facilitate treatment." Kleinman points out that medical practice with its "radically materialist pursuit of the biological mechanism of disease" fails to engage in this interpretative task.[82]

It is much easier to recognize the physical abnormality attached to a disease than to truly understand what it is representing. Booth points out that Inquisitors were quite able to describe the "disease" of witches; "they were only mistaken in their interpretations." In his view, modern medicine has followed the same mistake by defining disease as something destructive, "which attacks the otherwise healthy body," through birth defects, bad genes, germs, tumors, etc. Psychoanalysis also has added its own list of damages that civilization, particularly "religious moralism," brings about on the "normal instincts" that "seek oral, anal, and sexual gratifications." He points out that with careful analysis one can recognize that the

---

80. Ibid., 207–16.

81. Ibid., 25. See Matt 7:9–10; Rom 8:28.

82. Kleinman, *The Illness Narratives*, xiv, 9.

negative aspect of the illness as portrayed by medicine and psychology "does not exhaust the significance of sickness."[83]

Therefore, if our illnesses are designed by God for "good," and if they are a gift (in some unusual way) and not a curse—as Piper, Leyshon, Carson, and others have told us—such an attitude, however, dictates that we attribute to illness a purpose and *telos* that transcend physical manifestation. Then, how should one hear the voice of illness? What might our illnesses tell us? What might God be accomplishing through our illnesses? In the history of Christianity, the faithful particularly have wondered about the major illnesses and sufferings that afflict the people of God. The voice of illness is heard best when it is mingled with faith.

To consider illness strictly as a phenomenon unto itself forces one inevitably to experience it as a negative encounter, and this only brings on greater physical suffering, mental anguish, and weariness. This attitude leads to spiritual deterioration and compromises the soul perhaps even more than the body. To avoid this deterioration, we do well to turn our attention to discerning the "meaning" of illness in respect to one's relationship with God. The fathers encourage the person to be "philosophical" about his illness, beholding in the illness what might ultimately be good for the person. Larchet says, "To be philosophical about one's illness and suffering means above all for a person to consider what they reveal to him about his condition."[84] This may vary from one person to another, where both may suffer from the same medically identified disease. Similarly Gaiser suggests that time of illness "is inevitably a time of reflection, of searching for meaning, examining relationships, exploring theology, and actively seeking release." In fact, it is that active search for healing, especially in cases where "there is no clear and simple treatment," that transforms one's relationship with God, by exposing human limitation and our need for God's grace and mercy.[85]

Paul Tillich in his foreword to *The Voice of Illness*, which deals with the analysis of the relation of religion to psychotherapy and medicine, points out that illnesses always try to tell us something; and deciphering the message of illness is the first step in the "conquest of illness."[86] He believes that healing and salvation are interrelated; the healing points to and foreshadows salvation. Of course Tillich does not understand salvation in terms of

83. Booth, "The Voice of the Body," 5.

84. Ibid., 58.

85. Gaiser, *Healing in the Bible*, 74.

86. Tillich, Foreword, v.

"saving from hell and elevating to heaven." For him these concepts must be understood symbolically. He believes salvation consists of healing "in the ultimate dimension," which is made up of all other "dimensions of human existence." Therefore, he sees medical healing, including psychotherapy, as part of salvation in a more existential way. Tillich contends that theology must not be understood in traditional ways, and because of that, the concept of salvation is meaningless without understanding what healing means.[87] However, as Wheeler Robinson pointed out earlier, in the New Testament the whole idea of salvation is eschatological, and it is more an objective divine act, and much less related to a moral or psychological process, than the modern mind or Tillich's theology are ready to accept. Even though Tillich does not share the eschatological view of salvation from sin, his concept of healing as a foreshadowing of salvation—to "heal the split" between the "temporal order" and "the eternal"—is quite biblical. As Robinson points out, victory over evil—in the case of disease, captivity, or sin—was won by Christ on the cross.[88] Therefore, the principles at work in both healing from disease, and salvation from sin, are the same. One must keep those principles in sight.

Along the same lines, Siirala says, "Mankind, in the grasp of illness, encounters healing from within the illness. . . . We are compelled . . . to examine what the prophetic proclamation of salvation from sin means as we seek to listen to the message of illness." Siirala emphasizes the importance of listening to the message hidden in the illness, and understanding how healing might point to the ultimate Messianic salvation; the time when entire creation will experience healing. Siirala is very critical of the church in stifling the therapeutic process by having been too dogmatic and "inclined to exclude from church history the history of the encounter with illness." He attempts to address this impediment by bringing two traditions of healing—therapy and prophecy, as represented by works of Freud and Luther—into dialogue with each other; and through that dialogue, he shows that both medicine and the church have failed to understand "the reality of illness itself."[89]

Indeed, the methods of treatment and socially formed presumptions could deafen us to the voice of illness. Those who subscribe to the medical model of mental illness are in danger of losing the ability to interpret the

87. Ibid., vi.

88. Robinson, *Redemption and Revelation*, 232, 244.

89. Siirala, *The Voice of Illness*, 49–50, 53, 31.

phenomenon as something in relationship and unique to the particular individual. Laing says:

> It is just possible to have a thorough knowledge of what has been discovered about the hereditary or familial incidence of manic-depressive psychosis or schizophrenia, to have a facility in recognizing schizoid "ego distortion" . . . plus the various "disorders" of thought, memory, perceptions, etc., to know, in fact, just about everything that can be known about the psychopathology of schizophrenia . . . as a disease without being able to understand one single schizophrenic. Such data are all ways of *not* understanding him.[90]

Laing believes that the medical model distorts the picture. It will not allow one to hear the voice of illness, focusing instead on the objective manifest signs separate from the reality they represent. These authors emphasize that hearing the voice of madness requires *radical hearing ability* and capacity. Illness speaks not only to the individual, but also to the community surrounding him.

The Voice of Illness—Spoken to the Individual

Larchet stresses that illnesses represent "providential ways to salvation," and they should never be mistaken for "some native notion of punishment." This is because when illness is accompanied by faith, it leads the person in light of his vulnerable position and the misery of his body to seek reconciliation with God. This leads one to reflect on the "illness of their soul" and estrangement from God. Illness has the power to call the afflicted and those around him to repentance. This is amplified when medicine and natural remedies prove to be helpless—such as in the case of "schizophrenia." These cases are reminders to oneself and others "of the fundamental, ontological link that unites illness, suffering and death to the sin of everyone."[91] Paul took pride in participating in Christ's suffering. He counted all that he had lost as "rubbish" so that he would know Christ and "the fellowship of His suffering," in order that he would "attain the resurrection from the dead" (Phil 3:8–11).

As I argued in the chapter 1, a person cannot share the glory of resurrection without sharing the pain of crucifixion. Frame says, "God preserves

90. Laing, *The Divided Self*, 34.

91. Larchet, *Theology of Illness*, 51.

His people through persecution and honors their suffering by uniting it to the suffering of Christ," that they may unite with him in his resurrection.[92] As Booth views it, the death of every human being uniquely portrays the message of crucifixion. It is the end of the mortal body and personal endeavors on "the cross of the superpersonal *law*, the law of biological existence." It is the "dignity" of the sufferer, which is "expressed by the voice of illness and death," by participating—at times unconsciously—in the suffering of Christ even as the two thieves did.[93] From that viewpoint, illness is far more than a physical encounter; it is a *theological* reality.

In illness one experiences the weakness of one's earthly being, one's fragility and inadequacy; it humbles the spirit like nothing else, forcing an encounter with one's own mortality. Larchet notes that illness undermines the person in the core of his being and challenges his "former false equilibrium." It reveals the vanity of our attachments by showing that none can help and one's essential needs surpass the limits of those attachments. If illness is understood and experienced from this perspective, it will not crush the person under the weight of his physical calamity; rather it will turn the person toward God. The intensity of the illness intensifies the process of transformation in the person and speeds the unification process with Christ through brokenness and faith.[94] Platt points out that God works in ways that "puts his people in positions where they are desperate for his power," and then he reveals himself to them and "shows his provision in ways that display his greatness."[95] It is only in deepest darkness that the intensity of God's light can be experienced.

These theologians share the belief that God knows what is needed to lead each person toward salvation. Larchet draws on St. John Climacus, stressing that the pain of illness is very similar to the use of medicine: "It is only subjectively an evil; objectively, it serves for the good of the person it affects."[96] Thus, illness is medicine for the soul. God makes the person, by virtue of the "evil" that afflicts his body, aware of a greater evil that may not be "apparent" and yet afflicts his soul. For in the comfort of a healthy body, the person would remain indifferent or insensitive to the state of his soul.

It appears that the forces that heal and the forces that destroy are inseparably entangled. Illness is hidden in strength and healing is hidden

92. Frame, *Doctrine of God*, 284.

93. Booth, "The Voice of the Body," 23

94. Larchet, *Theology of Illness*, 59–60.

95. Platt, *Radical*, 48.

96. Larchet, *Theology of Illness*, 62.

in weakness. Booth argues that illness was often seen as a weakness, but through experience in many fields of encounter with illness, researchers have learned that the sources of strength in a person is precisely what is most susceptible to illness: "Disease may be considered the punishment for having favored one's strongest function."[97] Illness assails that part of personality that is the strongest in meeting the demands of society and bringing feelings of self-sufficiency. This corresponds to Scripture's claim that God sets his eye on one's source of pride: "I shall also make the pride of the strong ones cease" (Ezek 7:24).

Luther encountered God in the darkness of his mental afflictions. God was no longer a goal for him to reach, but a personal God who moved inside him. Luther gives the church a great example of human struggle for a good conscience when faced with guilt and shame. He "expresses so boldly the illness both of his own being and of his own time," says Siirala. Luther's healing ultimately came through "his sickness" and "not in escape from it."[98] It was in confronting the dark parts of his soul that he found a new identity. Erikson believes that it was the power of Psalms in which Luther immersed himself that helped him to overcome his battle; for in the prayer of the psalmists, man's heart is exposed before God to see all his being with all its conflicts and darkness:

> The theology as well as the psychology of Luther's passivity is that of man in the *state of prayer*, a state in which he fully means what he can say only to God: *Tibi soli peccavi*, I have sinned, not in relation to any person or institution, but in relation only to God, to *my* God . . . Luther warns of all those well-meaning (*bone intentionarii*) religionists who encourage man "to do what he can": to forestall sinning by clever planning . . . and to be secure in the feeling that they are as humble and as peaceful as "it is in them to be." Luther, instead, made a virtue out of what his superiors had considered a vice in him (and we, a symptom), namely, the determined search for the rock bottom of his sinfulness: only thus, he says, can man judge himself as God would.[99]

Many of Luther's symptoms are now considered "psychiatric disorders" clearing a path for modern psychiatrists and psychologists to label him "insane." "Was Luther crazy?" asks R. C. Sproul. "Perhaps," Sproul

---

97. Booth, "Variety in Personality and its Relation to Health," 404; cited in Siirala, *The Voice of Illness*, 187 n. 77.

98. Siirala, *The Voice of Illness*, 130.

99. Erikson, *Young Man Luther*, 202, 205–6.

responds to his own question, "But if he was, our prayer is that God would send to this earth an epidemic of such insanity that we too may taste of the righteousness that is by faith alone."[100] Sproul points to the fact that Luther had already distinguished himself as "one of the brightest young minds in Europe in the field of jurisprudence," even before he entered the monastery. There was nothing wrong with Luther's brain; he was brilliant. It was his brilliance that led him to see the depth of his sinfulness against the law of God. It was his judicial genius that convinced him he had no hope of meeting the law of God. It was the contrast of his sinfulness to the majesty and the holiness of God that brought him deep despair; and in that despair, he experienced God and heard his voice like never before. In that despair, God equipped him to change the history of humankind.[101]

The Voice of Illness—Spoken to the Community

According to Tillich, illness points to a "distorted relationship" between a person and his "social group." Therefore, healing entails the "restitution" of a coherent relationship to the particular social group. If sickness is perceived this way, it may well be that "it is a healthy reaction against a sick society."[102] When heard, the voice of illness often expresses the illness of a community; a clue that the conquest of the disease is also dependent on that community. Marshall points out, that whilst "God allows sickness in the lives of His own people . . . for the maturing of his saints," in many occasions it is for a much "higher purpose." In many instances, sickness is brought in a "vicarious" sense; that is, "it is for the sake of others rather than the person who is sick."[103] This is why a community cannot afford to turn away from the sickness of its members.

Zilboorg examines the history of mental illness as a phenomenon that reflects the inner pains and inner struggles of the cultural and social life of various times. He points out that by assigning physical hypotheses to many of the symptoms, one was "relieved . . . from the discomfort of looking into the obscure recesses of psychological problems." The community's attitude toward mental illness expresses who it is, fundamentally. In fact, in every historical era, the challenge of mental illness has been dealt

100. Sproul, *The Holiness of God*, 94–95.

101. Ibid., 86–87.

102. Tillich, Foreword, v.

103. Marshall, *Healing from the Inside Out*, 14–15.

with in a manner reflecting "the spirit of the age."[104] The voice of mental illness, Siirala contends, whether "stifled, avoided, or heeded," points to the foundational values the community is built upon. Listening to the language of mental illness perturbs the equilibrium that has been gained through isolation and avoidance of the mentally ill.[105]

Juli McGruder is an anthropologist who has conducted extensive cross-cultural research on "schizophrenia." She writes: "What we say about mental illness reveals what we value and what we fear."[106] We claim "this cannot be God's doing," because if we give God that much power, it has implications that ripple through our lives in ways we cannot accept. Or we say, "it certainly cannot be about demons," because that renders us powerless; the existence of a spiritual realm, and entities such as angels and demons, take away one's sense of control. A person with "schizophrenia" challenges one's "commonly accepted version of reality." She points out that the public fears people with "schizophrenia," not only for their "occasional but overrated and over-publicized physical dangerousness—a statistically small threat,"[107] but also because it represents a "reversal" of what that society has come to accept as the "essence of human nature." The

104. Zilboorg and Henry, *Medical Psychology*, 256, 459–60.

105. Siirala, *The Voice of Illness*, 72.

106. McGruder, "Life Experience is Not a Disease," 64.

107 The concept of abundant violence by those suffering from "schizophrenia" has been touted in popular media without strong scientific foundation. Peter Roger Breggin has reported in his research that psychiatric drugs are the culprit behind the violence by those who suffer from "mental illness." He discusses "The Role of Psychiatric Drugs in Cases of Violence, Suicide, and Crime." Breggin, *Medication Madness*, 384. It is valid to question whether a person whose brain structure has been altered by the use of these drugs loses his insight and his judgment of right and wrong. I suggest that it is that loss of insight that may lead to foolish and harmful acts completely *foreign to the person's native character and values*. The scientific studies clearly show a sense of dysphoria on the part of those on antipsychotic drugs. Shitij Kapur explains that though the condemning voices and delusions may persist for years after the person has been put on medication, it has been repeatedly reported by patients that these elements don't "bother" them "as much anymore." Referring to pivotal studies in the 1950s, Kapur explains that "antipsychotics induce 'a forgetfulness of motive.' . . . This core finding has been replicated in hundreds of different paradigms over half a century and remains the single fundamental property shared by all effective antipsychotics." Kapur, *Psychosis*, 16. Contrary to psychiatry's assertion that the mentally ill have no "insight" due to their illness—a justification for compulsory treatments—I suggest it is their true insight about right and wrong that brings them to rage against the evil voices they hear. After being medicated for a while, and after having experienced structural alterations in their brain, they are not as bothered by the voices they hear, possibly because they have lost their true insight and a judgment of right and wrong. See Hessamfar, "Mental Illness, Right & Wrong, Drugs, and Violence."

Western cultures value a "certain unitariness of consciousness." McGruder notes that people become utterly hopeless when "contemplating mentation" that seems less controlled, and "more open to outside influence."[108]

Siirala stresses that the encounter with illness has to be communal. For example, common formation of symbols is a significant aspect of communal encounter with illness. The church has failed to hear the voices that have arisen in the midst of an encounter with illness speaking to the "perversions of our common life." This failure has been most dramatic in dealing with mental illness. The institution of Inquisition was the church's solution to mental illness in medieval time; in the twenty-first century, psychiatry has become a more humane solution to the same problem. In both cases, Siirala claims, the church has convinced herself that the problem is being handled in the most proper way; thus it can continue with its primary responsibility of proclaiming the Word of God.[109] When the voice of mental illness is properly heard we discern that it expresses more than an individual desperate cry for help, it is revealing the illness of the greater community; it is calling the church to repentance—to a true *metanoia*—a calling that the church cannot afford to disregard.[110]

Siirala points out that a merely "sympathetic hearing" of the person who is suffering will not lead to "an encounter with the reality of illness." Speaking of the role of a therapist, he stresses that a healing dialogue between the patient and a therapist can be effective only when a "deep crisis" takes place in both of them. If a community surrounding a patient merely offers sympathetic ears, without receiving the prophetic message of the illness targeted at them, the healing will be far from reach. Both parties must be "pulled into the whirlpools of becoming ill and becoming well."[111] If the illness has a prophetic voice, then the healing depends on the embracing of that message.

When one hears the voice of illness, it demands that one engage in dialogue between one's professed faith and one's performance in life. In the encounter with illness a decisive role is assigned to the family, the church, and the community around the person. This is because human beings are organically interrelated to their community—as the members of one's body are organically interrelated. After all, "We are members of

108. McGruder, "Life Experience is Not a Disease," 65.

109. Siirala, *The Voice of Illness*, 53–56.

110. The Greek word used for repentance in the New Testament is *metanoia*, which entails complete transformation and reorientation.

111. Siirala, *The Voice of Illness*, 83.

one another" (Eph 4:25). Siirala highlights that ironically relatives and the immediate community "begin to resist the healing of the sick in cases where healing means for them a challenge to revise their own posture." For example, in dealing with "schizophrenia," one has to face the fact that the illness points to the "schizophrenia" of the distinct cultural aspects of the community where the illness is manifest.[112] Once one grasps this interrelatedness, then it is easily seen that in reality—not merely from an empathetic point of view—the illness of one is the illness of another.

Anthropological research presents great examples of the communal nature of illness and the community's encounters with it. A classic example is the description by Knud Ramussen of the therapeutic methods of the Eskimos. In this example he describes how a healer healed a woman who was "almost totally paralyzed" in the presence of the people of the village. The most remarkable element of his story is that the community bore a collective accountability and responsibility for the problem. The healer, himself, also raises the question willingly to see whether he or his wife had violated any of the community rules. Ramussen points out that "the readiness to confess and the humble asking for forgiveness was not limited only to the patient." The whole community was willing to show vulnerability and humility to reach a solution. The key to this experience is that "Both the healer and the audience confess indirectly that they are guilty of transgressions of values; they take the patient's situation as their own and defend it." In this incident, the healer performs the interviews with great care so that "perfect purity can be reached." The audience wholeheartedly participates in confessions and the act of intercession.[113] The readiness to confess and the humble asking for forgiveness are not limited only to the patient; the patient has become the "sacrificial lamb" for the community to be awakened. David Cooper notes, "We all repeatedly die partial deaths in order that the others, for whom we are the sacrificial offerings, may live."[114]

Those who interact with the "schizophrenic" will realize that they are sharers of the split life they are encountering. If they refuse to acknowledge their role and participation in his illness, then healing will be out of reach. Wilhelm Kütemeyer, explaining the importance of participating

112. Ibid., 89.

113. Honko, "Varhaiskantaiset," 64–66; cited in Siirala, *The Voice of Illness*, 185 n. 62. We see the same principle given in James 5:14–16: "Is anyone among you sick? . . . the prayer offered in faith will restore the one who is sick, and the Lord will raise him up. . . . Therefore, confess your sins to *one another*, and pray for *one another*, so that you may be healed."

114. Cited in Ruitenbeek, *Going Crazy*, ix.

in the burden of the suffering person, points out that many incompatible forces that cannot be united are intermingled in the sick person "in a labyrinthine way." These can be disentangled when they are "taken over by another, so that one suffers for another." It is then that these forces "lose their pathological, destructive character," and bring healing both to the sick and to the companion.[115] This affirms what Paul encouraged the Galatians to do: "Bear one another's burdens, and thus fulfill the law of Christ" (Gal 6:2). It seems that when the prophetic message of illness is received by the community, and its purpose is fulfilled, the pathology loses its power.

Indeed, one of the reasons that mental illness lingers is the refusal of the immediate community to take accountability for the illness. Booth says, "Today more and more the technique is developed to make people insensitive to conflicts so that neither their own nor their neighbor's comfort will be disturbed."[116] Instead of listening to its prophetic voice, in the "pursuit of happiness," illness appears only as a threat that must be destroyed. Instead of being encouraged to embrace such troubled souls with sensitivity and care, we are directed by authorities to turn them over to those who would restrain them. The irony of this picture is that the more we try to fight mental illness—in contrast to surrendering to its message—the more power it gains over us.

The Voice of "Mental Illness"

Mental illness has always been an ingrained part of the history of humankind, and within each society contradictory perspectives are taken toward the people it afflicts. Larchet notes that those labeled as "insane" have encountered respect and reverence when they were considered as "messengers from above . . . mediators between man and God," and persecution, abandonment, and execution when considered as "slaves of evil powers."[117] Nevertheless, the nature and cause of what we call "mental illness" have always posed serious difficulties.

We have argued that "mental illness" is shaped through language, and in particular, it is the construct of discourses of medicine and science; however, as we have seen, scientific research shows that the current medical construct is fatally flawed. Meanwhile, other discourses construct

115. Cited in Siirala, *The Voice of Illness*, 186 n. 72.

116. Booth, "Physician between the Spirit and the Flesh"; cited in Siirala, *The Voice of Illness*, 108.

117. Larchet, *Mental Disorders*, 1.

illness through other images that are harder to grasp and pin down, but are exceedingly powerful. Our encounter with mental illness is bound to take us beyond the medical to theological, social, political, and ethical areas where different meanings are formed. Many in desperation and disappointment with other sources of knowledge turn to theology, with its power to give life-transforming responses, to explain and to give purpose and meaning to the experience of illness. This is the lens through which we will attempt to encounter "schizophrenia."[118]

Western societies value reason and intellect—wrapped in the word "science"—because it gives humankind some semblance of control over life, resulting in power for those who "have" it over those who "do not have" it. But Scripture teaches that the secrets of God are revealed to those who do not seem to "have it": "Jesus answered and said, 'I praise Thee O Father . . . that Thou didst hide these things from the wise and intelligent and didst reveal them to babes'" (Matt 11:25). And Paul said to the Corinthians: "Because the foolishness of God is wiser than men . . . God has chosen the foolish things of the world to shame the wise, and God has chosen the weak things of the world to shame the things which are strong, and the base things of the world, and the despised, God has chosen" (1 Cor 1:25–27). In "schizophrenia," it is indeed the weakest of the weak who are being used by God as his instruments. Our rational explanations indeed prove to be inadequate to explain the ways of God. Scripture is not bound to the socially acceptable norms of the twenty-first century, and the God of the Bible is not obligated to act as we expect him to act. Shirley Sugerman stresses that:

> An explanation of possession, trance, and other shamanistic behavior associated with these states solely in terms of psychopathology is untenable. Behavior that would be regarded as psychotic in our culture may be highly valued and have a useful social role in another.[119]

If one's behavior is considered pathological by a cultural standard, it would seem it has less to do with one's personality structure *per se* than with the way that a particular community interprets the behavior. These are essential considerations as one draws distinctions between "sanity" and "madness."

---

118. Woodward, *Encountering Illness*, 46, 42.

119. Sugerman, *Sin and Madness*, 76.

Laing, who takes issue with the medical model of madness as disease, believes that the inner-self is estranged from the outer-self, and that the belief in inner reality is lost. Thus, anyone who engages with that inner reality is perceived to be mad.[120] Laing contends we all suffer from a "divided self," which is separated from one's true self and is threatened by reality.[121] This is why "schizophrenia" scares us; because it forces us to look at ourselves in an unfamiliar mirror. In contrast to the biblical message, for the Western mind, the consciousness of reality is identical to reality itself. Siirala says, "The degree of humanity then depends primarily upon man's ability to make observations of reality."[122] What makes one "human" is to come in touch with the reality of who he is before God. Scripture clearly tells us that it is only the Spirit of God that can open up one's eyes to perceive reality (cf. Luke 24:16, 31; 1 Cor 2:11); God is the source of inner light. And it is in one's spirit/*pneuma-nous* that the inner light is kindled.

"This is a schizophrenic age," says Sugerman, "What we suffer from then is a cultural madness, a socially accepted madness."[123] What one experiences internally cannot always be talked about without making oneself the subject of mockery, as it is considered madness to express one's inner experiences. According to Laing,

> Phenomenologically the terms "internal" and "external" have little validity. . . . One of the difficulties of talking in the present day of these matters is that the very existence of inner realities is now called in question. . . . For example, nowhere in the Bible is there any argument about the *existence* of gods, demons, angels. People did not first "believe in" God: they experienced His Presence, as was true of other spiritual agencies. The question was not whether God existed, but whether this particular God was the greatest god of all, or the only God; and what was the relation of the various spiritual agencies to each other. Today, there is a public debate, not as to the trustworthiness of God, the particular place in the spiritual hierarchy of different spirits, etc., but whether God or such spirits *even exist*. . . . Sanity today appears to rest very largely on a capacity to adapt to the external world—the interpersonal world, and the realm of human collectivities . . . any personal direct awareness of the inner world has already grave risks. . . . The outer divorced from any

120. Ibid., 45.

121. Laing, *The Divided Self*.

122. Siirala, *The Voice of Illness*, 36.

123. Sugerman, *Sin and Madness*, 45, 62.

illumination from the inner is in a state of darkness. We are in an age of darkness. The state of outer darkness is a state of sin— i.e., alienation or estrangement from the *inner light*.[124]

Henri Nouwen emphasizes the value and the danger of the inner life. He says, "We hardly need emphasize how dangerous the experimentation with the interior life can be. . . . Withdrawal into the self often does more harm than good. On the other hand it also is becoming obvious that those who avoid the painful encounter with the unseen are doomed to live a supercilious, boring and superficial life."[125] He stresses the importance of the journey to be under the guidance of a spiritual leader, and he expresses the "painful fact" that "most Christian leaders" are "poorly prepared" to deal with the issues of inner life.

In Laing's view, the cause of the progression of "schizophrenia" and its chronicity is not to be found in the "patient" alone, but in the whole social context in which the psychiatric treatment is given. What happens between a patient and a psychiatrist works toward degrading the person as a human being, by pinning a label that brings about his estrangement within society. This way, the system that is meant to heal and cure in effect causes more damage and pain. If it is difficult for us to relate to individuals who experience themselves and the world in ways beyond our comprehension and incongruent with socially accepted norms, then the problem is *us* and not them.[126]

Julie McGruder draws on her personal experience as the ex-wife of an individual with mental illness, on her anthropological research, and the research of others in the field to argue that "medicalizing madness can be counterproductive to recovery." Medicalizing madness risks, and possibly guarantees, deafening the community from hearing the voice of the phenomenon, effectively tuning it out, and stripping away the meaning and moral value of the experience. McGruder believes that analogies drawn to biological diseases—such as diabetes—not only does not help but is also misleading. She points out that "experiences called symptoms" are meaningful and perceiving them as signs of disease could deny understanding of their "positive" aspects. In order to help those who are trying to recover,

---

124. Laing, *The Politics of Experience*, 115–17.

125. Nouwen, *The Wounded Healer*, 37.

126. Laing, *The Politics of Experience*, 86–90.

one "must attend to the fullness of their experiences," and not allow their "medical diagnoses" to be a distraction.[127]

Siirala explains that how we refer to an illness is an essential part of how we encounter it, pointing out that "the diagnosis is already part of the therapy." Simply put, how we name certain phenomena determines how we deal with them. A living word that does not betray its "symbolic function" enhances "communal unity," and brings hope and grace; a perverted, "diabolical word" destroys unity and harmony. Siirala calls those terminologies that bring disharmony and destruction "diabolical." The nomenclature used can be part of the problem or the solution. For example if one is assumed to be hallucinating, all effort will be put into eliminating that negative experience, but if the same person is perceived to be receiving visions from God, then the phenomenon will be treated with reverence and dignity. The language used to express the character of illness serves not only to describe it, but also to convey to others how they should react to it.[128]

Medicalizing mental illness has the adverse effect of intensifying what may have brought on the original brokenness. According to John Modrow's personal account of mental illness, when someone afflicted with the illness experiences thoughts and behavior that he himself cannot understand, it is likely that his sense of self-worth is already badly shaken. What psychiatry offers this person is a "scientific proof" that he is indeed utterly worthless and will always remain this way. Because his illness is the representation of his sick brain, his bad genes, and misguided chemistry, he is singled out among all the "normal" people around him, magnifying the helplessness that comes with not being able to do anything about his dilemma.[129]

Sally Clay, in addressing the First National Forum on Recovery from Mental Illness, said:

> Those of us who have had the experience called "mental illness" know in our hearts that something profound is missing in these diagnoses. They do not take into account what we have actually endured. Even if the "bad" chemical or the "defective" gene is someday found, madness has its own reality that demands attention.[130]

127. McGruder, "Life Experience is Not a Disease," 59–60.

128. Siirala, *The Voice of Illness*, 34, 43.

129. McGruder, "Life Experience is Not a Disease," 66–67.

130. Clay, "The Wounded Prophet," cited in McGruder, "Life Experience is Not a Disease," 67.

Jay Neugeboren, whose brother, Robert, suffers from chronic "schizophrenia," argues against "no-fault brain diseases" postulated by the field of psychiatry. He contends that this kind of biological assessment to reduce someone to their genetic configuration dismisses a life history and how a person perceives his own value and the value of his past experiences. Neugeboren argues against the "dead-end scientific materialism that would reduce Robert to a flawed heretical biological inheritance that somehow determines his behavior and his fate."[131] This denies Robert his history and his identity as a child of God.

Bert Kaplan, in his striking collection of personal accounts of mental illness, exposes "the kernel of purposefulness and intentionality" around which these illnesses are organized. He points to the problem in psychiatry of taking too seriously "only what it could observe and verify," instead of listening carefully to the voice of the patients. It is only from the outside perspective that this phenomenon is seen as "bad" and something to be eliminated.[132] In one of his cases, Norma MacDonald, who suffers from "schizophrenia," writes an account of her experience:

> Living with schizophrenia can be living in hell, because it sets one so far apart from the trend of life followed by the majority of persons today, but seen from another angle it can be really living . . . it seems to lead to a deeper understanding . . . it's an exacting life, like being an explorer in a territory where no one else has ever been. I am often glad that illness caused my mind to "awaken."[133]

In another case, Seymour Krim, who was institutionalized several times for major "psychotic episodes," defends "the vitality of his madness," and contends that it is time for psychiatry and society as a whole to reinterpret "madness," and recognize its value and meaning. It is time for the "locked doors of insanity" to be "shaken loose" and the prisoners of the old definition to be allowed to express the reality of their experience. He points out that both laypersons and psychiatrists have missed acts of expressiveness by those imprisoned in the category of "psychotics" as "flat irrationality" and not seen the "symbolic meanings" that they broadcast.[134]

---

131. Neugeboren, *Imagining Robert,* cited in McGruder, "Life Experience is Not a Disease," 67.

132. Kaplan and Murphy, *The Inner World of Mental Illness,* vii–viii.

133. Ibid., 184.

134. Ibid., 62–63, 74.

In traditional societies, the shared moral and religious values create a framework for making sense of life crises and misfortunes. But in our fragmented, pluralistic postmodern setting, these events—the loss of a loved one, personal failures, etc.—put our *psyche* out of balance. Kleinman says:

> Lacking generally agreed-upon authorization for how to interpret misfortune, there is a definite tendency in the contemporary world to medicalize such problems and therewith to turn to the cultural authority of the health professions and science for an answer to our predicaments. Taking on a medical or scientific perspective, however, doesn't help us to deal with the problem of suffering: in contemporary biomedicine . . . there is no teleological perspective on illness that can address . . . problems of bafflement, order, and evil, which appear to be intrinsic to the human condition.[135]

He points out that the "modern medical bureaucracy" is oriented to deal with suffering merely as a "mechanical breakdown requiring a technical fix." But the required interpretation is a personal endeavor to get past "simple sounds of bodily pain" and "psychiatric symptoms" into a layer deep within, into the patient's unique life story, where the voice can be faintly heard, and deciphered, if only by a language outside of our norm.[136]

For a generation now we have insisted on the biomedical notion of mental illness. Ethan Watters, in his blistering and fascinating work of reporting and analysis, profiling the work of cross-cultural researchers and anthropologists, points to a different picture. These researchers have shown that the experience of mental illness is tightly related to its cultural context. Invariably, it is the cultural beliefs, values, and stories that help us understand these diseases in non-Western cultures. "Those stories," says Watters, "whether they tell of spirit possession or serotonin depletion, shape the experience of the illness in surprisingly dramatic and often counterintuitive ways." There is valuable knowledge hidden in the diverse cultural understandings of mental health and illness that we are ignoring "at our own peril."[137]

Watters uses the example of the tsunami disaster of 2004 in Sri Lanka to explain how the West forces its values surrounding mental illness on the rest of the world. After the tsunami, a memo was sent by the faculty of the

135. Kleinman, *The Illness Narratives*, 28.

136. Ibid., 28–29.

137. Watters, *Crazy Like Us*, 5–7.

University of Colombo in Sri Lanka, pleading with the "arriving army of counselors" from the West not to diminish the experiences of survivors "to a question of mental trauma" and the people themselves as "psychological casualties." They basically rejected the arguments that "Western ideas about trauma are universal." "A victim processes a traumatic event as a function of what it means," they wrote. "This meaning is drawn from their society and culture and this shapes how they seek help and their expectation of recovery." They emphasized that trauma reactions are far more significant than "physiological reactions inside the brain," and they pointed to deeper meanings within the culture. What was a meaningful help, the professors wrote, was to listen to the voice of trauma and understand "what the affected people were signaling by this distress."[138]

Despite the common belief that with the earliest signs of distress medical help must be provided to stop the progress of the "disease," there is little evidence that such efforts help. Watters points out that the research during the 1990s—"the heyday of trauma counseling"—showed that early interventions not only did not help, but in many cases caused more harm. Many researchers concluded that, "the early interventions were actually impeding the mind's natural healing process."[139] This could be due to the fact that the stress had certain meaning and goals, which were blocked from fulfilling their purpose. In mental illness, just as in physical ailments, we can see the manifestation of the healing power of God at work. God through his providence and in ways far beyond our comprehension is constantly at work to heal and to save.

In the mental realm, Boisen says, "all that the best physician can do is to help nature in removing the obstacles to the free-flow of life-giving forces."[140] It is of vital importance that the process of healing that God begins in the person is not interrupted or violated, but rather nurtured. As an evidence for the natural process of healing in the brain, in research conducted by Professor Cyndi Shannon Weickert and her colleagues, they found a high density of neurons in deeper areas in the brains of people with "schizophrenia." "For over a decade we've known about the high density of neurons in deeper brain tissue in people with schizophrenia. Researchers thought these neurons were simply forgotten by the brain,

---

138. Ibid., 76–77.

139. Ibid., 118.

140. Boisen, *The Exploration of the Inner World*, 54. Gaiser also argues that certain biblical texts (Lev 13:18, 37; 14:3, 48) demonstrate healing, "simply through the natural passage of time." See Gaiser, *Healing in the Bible*, 32.

and somehow didn't die off like they do during development in healthy people. What we now have is evidence that suggests these neurons are derived from the part of the brain that produces new neurons, and that they may be in the process of moving. We can't be sure where they are moving to, but given their location it is likely they are on their way to the surface of the brain, the area most affected by schizophrenia." Weickert believes that in this process, "the brains of people with schizophrenia may attempt to repair damage caused by the disease."[141]

Looking through the eyes of those who live in communities where "human tragedy is still embedded in complex religious and cultural narratives," Watters asserts that modern intellectuality seems to expose Westerners as a "deeply insecure and fearful people." The great investments into psychiatric research to prove a model of biologically based mental illness is a symptom of losing all other "belief systems that once gave meaning and context to our suffering."[142] Without a belief system that offers individuals a stable pathway through life hurdles, and meaningful frameworks within which to encounter pain and affliction, society is built upon sand. Watters warns that one may be able to deal with the absence of these belief systems during times of peace and prosperity, but "truly traumatic events have the power to startle us into awareness of a heart-stopping emptiness." No wonder that society cannot hear the voice of illness anymore. It is no surprise that our anguish and trauma and hidden wounds are forced into intellectual scientific boxes. The psychiatric diagnoses may provide some transient comfort, "but in the end it is cold comfort. It cannot replace what we have lost," says Watters.[143]

It is noteworthy that these kinds of observations about psychiatry are usually made by anthropologists, journalists, social scientists, other psychiatrists, and almost never by officials of the Christian church or leaders of faith groups. "Despite their elegant appeals for political advocacy," and their attempt at the "inclusion of the mentally ill within congregational" gatherings, says Kinghorn, the church has failed to recognize the "fragile status" of the concept of "mental illness" promoted by psychiatry, "as a foundation in which to build a theological response." The church has assumed that "mental Illness" and "mental disorder" are givens. Kinghorn,

141. See Weickert's remarks on Neuroscience Research Australia, "The brains of people with schizophrenia may attempt to heal," para. 4–5, 1. The original study: Yang et al., "Increased Interstitial White Matter Neuron Density in the Dorsolateral Prefrontal Cortex of People with Schizophrenia," 63–70.

142. Watters, *Crazy Like Us*, 122.

143. Ibid, 123.

who is a Christian psychiatrist himself, disagrees with that assumption and believes that "things are not so simple." The church ought to deal with this issue through a deeper sense of theological reflection.[144] Alan Tjeltveit makes the observation that because of the church's history of embarrassing attempts to reject certain "scientific theories" that are now widely accepted, the church is timid to question psychotherapy and psychiatry on issues of mental health.[145] Yet, he agrees that it is of paramount importance for the church to draw on its wealth of theological and ethical traditions to engage in this issue. This can only be done by keeping in sight the person with all his complexity and diversity in the context of his relationship with God and his immediate community.

Juli McGruder went to Zanzibar in search of answers to a question that has perplexed cross-cultural researchers in mental illness for twenty years: "Why did people diagnosed with schizophrenia in developing nations have a better prognosis over time than those living in the most industrialized countries in the world?"[146] During her research, McGruder began to observe that the nature of emotional reaction on the part of those families encountering "schizophrenia" in Zanzibar was quite different than that of families in the industrialized world. These differences, she contended, might go a long way in explaining why someone suffering from "schizophrenia" in Zanzibar will often do better than someone diagnosed in the United States. The idea that psychotic phenomena such as those experienced in "schizophrenia" are the result of chemical imbalances or brain abnormalities had not yet been well-integrated into the mental health system in Zanzibar. "Much more salient were beliefs in spirit possession and the permeability of the human consciousness by magical forces," says Watters, who followed McGruder around Zanzibar for a period of time.[147]

Watters reports on two huge cross-cultural psychiatric studies performed by the World Health Organization (WHO) over the course of twenty-five years beginning in the 1960s. The studies had follow-up periods of two and five years, and were conducted in a dozen sites, within ten countries, and following more than a thousand "patients" around the globe. The remarkable conclusion was that people suffering from

144. Kinghorn, "Ordering 'Mental Disorder,'" 15.

145. Tjeltveit, "Psychotherapeutic Triumphalism and Freedom from Mental Illness," 135–36.

146. Watters, *Crazy Like Us*, 128.

147. Ibid., 130–32.

"schizophrenia" did much better over time in developing countries in contrast to industrialized nations. Whereas in the latter group—such as the United States and Denmark—over 40 percent of "patients" over time were considered "severely impaired," only 24 percent of the former group—such as India and Nigeria—ended up "similarly disabled." McGruder's research following on WHO's findings was set to go beyond the manifestation of "symptoms," into an existential level of explaining who these people were and how and why they experienced the illness the way they did. For her, it all came down to the cultural context of how the illness was dealt with.[148]

The research on cross-cultural study of "schizophrenia" indicates that "overly negative" Western expectation about the course of illness is not helpful and actually contributes to the chronicity of the illness.[149] Nancy Waxler states that the research in "peasant and other traditional societies" shows that psychiatric illnesses in these communities, "in spite of what many might call inadequate systems of psychiatric treatment," are often short-lived and "non-recurring." She suggests this is the result of the way the community and the family respond to the phenomenon: They look for "predictors of the course of mental illness," not within the afflicted individual, "but in the world around him."[150] Siirala echoes the same principles, and points out that in the West it is the individual who is in charge and in control of his own destiny, and the community only plays a peripheral role. When "schizophrenia" is encountered as a communal illness, one can discover "possibilities of common healing." Both the illness and the healing are dependent on the "whole community organism" rather than on one individual.[151]

All the aforementioned studies affirm the need for the participation of the community in the milieu of illness and the willingness to receive its prophetic message. This participation will open the gates of healing and bring freedom from bondage to a medical epistemology for unraveling madness. Drawing on these principles, we now turn to a theological model of "schizophrenia," intent on receiving its prophetic voice within God's redemptive framework, as a gift from him to his church.

148. Ibid., 137, 140.

149. Kleinman, *The Illness Narratives*, 229.

150. Waxler, "Is Mental Illness Cured in Traditional Societies?," 233–34.

151. Siirala, *The Voice of Illness*, 93–94.

The Voice of "Schizophrenia": A Theological Reflection

The goal of this section is to give an alternative account of "schizophre-nia" that emerges from theological reflection on the experience quite apart from what psychiatry may or may not have to say. In this exercise, my existential experience will intersect more overtly, within a reflective framework, with all that we have learned from a situational perspective about "schizophrenia" and the normative perspective given by Scripture. In one sense, we will create a new language or a new form of expressive/descriptive grammar to help Christians reframe "schizophrenia." In order to capture the complex dynamics of the new voice, it becomes necessary to change cadence and mix genres.

The manner in which one encounters his illness determines whether his historical existence will lead toward "perdition or salvation," says Siira-la.[152] In the desperation of mental illness, when all is dark, it is the salvation narrative offered by Christ that can give the promise of hope and redemp-tion. The challenge for humanity is to come to the realization that he is on the path toward destruction. As Foucault stated, "Madness fascinates because it is knowledge."[153] Paul Ricoeur points to the value of symbols forcing us into awareness, because the symbols have latent powers that could transcend the ostensive referential meaning of the phenomenon. Albeit, Ricoeur does not suggest that the symbolic meaning exhausts the text, yet he suggests that symbols offer a "gift of meaning." The search for meaning requires "patience and rigor," but the symbols have power to "give rise to thought" and thoughts can lead to interpretation. "In short, it is by *interpreting* that we can *hear* again," says Ricoeur. It is in the virtue of symbols that "man remains language through and through." In order to understand the symbols, we must first believe; and without belief we can-not understand. Therefore, for Ricoeur, our faith and our understanding are correlational. Moreover, the interpreter can never "get near to what his text says unless he lives in the *aura* of the meaning he is inquiring after." Thus, it always relies on "presuppositions."[154]

In the case of my personal experience with my daughter's "schizo-phrenia," it was the intensity of the illness impregnated with symbolic meanings that forced the family to listen. Looking at "psychotic" symbols, with the presupposition of faith in a sovereign God, who controls all

152. Ibid., 120.

153. Foucault, *Madness and Civilization*, 21.

154. Ricœur, *The Symbolism of Evil*, 348–51.

things, and who loves beyond human standards, one is forced to search for a deeper meaning. The richness of the symbols of wandering, captivity, chaos, rage, impurity, rebellion, self-hatred, and the inability to love and to be loved all speak of the situation of humankind in the world. Then the task is, as Ricoeur says, "starting from the symbols," to seek to decipher the "existential concepts."[155] It is within a theological context that the symbols can come to life through reflection and speculation, to disclose their voice based on the biblical foundation.

The authors we have studied have noted that in mental illness constructive and destructive forces are imbued with a prophetic voice; and it is the interplay of these forces that brings one to a crisis of understanding. The encounter with healing in sickness, light in the midst of darkness, grace hidden in affliction, and life in dying, opens such a new perspective that leads the person to a new realm; former interpretations of experience break down and the events of life find a new meaning. In this encounter, Siirala believes, "Events of life which have been repressed from conscious experience as meaningless become alive again"; everything will find its new meaning.[156] In this new light, the crisis that brought one down with such a violent force will become the source of life leading one to Christ, the Great Physician. This is how true repentance, real *metanoia*, can be experienced by God's grace.

As I outlined in my methodology, my personal experience with my daughter's "schizophrenia" informs my theological reflection. In search of answers, because all other explanations had proven inadequate for evaluating the rich and intense encounter with the illness, I desperately engaged in a constant dialogue of possibilities, linking them to the writings of Scripture and of other scholars and witnesses, drawing inferences and reaching conclusions. In Helia's case, and most probably in all cases of "schizophrenia," it seems as if God's purposes were at least twofold: God was doing a major work in Helia's soul (see chapter 1); and second, Helia was an instrument in the hand of God for changing the lives of those around her. In God's economy nothing goes to waste; as Paul reminds us, "We know that God causes all things to work together for good to those who love God, to those who are called according to His purpose" (Rom 8:28). In reflecting theologically on Helia's journey into madness, we heard the voice of her illness through rich biblical images. In this reflection, Scripture is used as a "mirror," following the methodology outlined in my

155. Ibid., 356.

156. Siirala, *The Voice of Illness*, 112.

Introduction, mirroring "our own lives," helping us search for answers to a deeply complex human question. The most striking images of the experience of "Schizophrenia" are portrayed through the narratives of: 1) a journey to Exile; 2) a prophetic voice; 3) a sacrificial lamb; and 4) a leper. Let us listen to these voices.

"Schizophrenia"—A Journey to Exile

In an analysis of "self-experience" in "schizophrenia," Lysaker wrote in *Schizophrenia Bulletin*, "Schizophrenia is portrayed as involving an experience of exile from oneself."[157] Indeed, what Helia experienced was a manifest example of the Exile. She, like Israel, was sent to exile to truly come to know her God; she took the whole family with her. The Exile meant the loss of everything for Israel: their wealth, their community, their peace, their identity, and seemingly their God; and so it meant for our family. It "was an era of desolation and at the same time, an era of restoration," as VanGemeren says.[158] As Israel had to leave the Land of Promise, our family, too, had lost the Promised Land with all its abundance and blessings. According to Klein, "Exile meant death, deportation, destruction, and devastation."[159] In the years of her illness, Helia was dying every day. There were no signs of life, no hope, no grace, nothing but intense darkness. This was far more than a host of physical and socio-economic problems. It was a severe theological blow to our faith. John Day notes that in the first subsection of the book of Ezekiel (chaps. 4–11), "time's up and God's gone"; and it was all because of Israel's idolatry.[160] As the "temple in Jerusalem had been burned," Helia had lost the place in her soul "where his face was to be seen."[161] She had lost her God whom she loved wholeheartedly. He was hidden. The Exile was a jolt of disillusionment for the most faithful among Israel. The same way that the exiles questioned God's trustworthiness and his faithfulness to the Davidic covenant, I questioned whether the promise of salvation in Christ was real. I was not sure if this was the God I had signed up for!

157. Lysaker and Lysaker, "Schizophrenia and Alterations in Self-Experience," 333–34.

158. VanGemeren, *Interpreting the Prophetic Word*, 57.

159. Klein, *Israel in Exile*, 2.

160. Day, "Ezekiel and the Heart of Idolatry," 21–22. Ezekiel 20:16: "because they rejected My ordinances . . . for their heart continually went after their idols."

161. Klein, *Israel in Exile*, 3.

"The Exile also had a positive impact in bringing about the unity of a godly remnant from both Israel and Judah," says VanGemeren.[162] It inaugurated an era of true transformation by the "Spirit of restoration," evidenced by a renewed devotion and fidelity to the Lord, to his wisdom in Judgment, and by a renewed hope in the full restoration. It had the same effect on our family; it unified us around Helia's illness. It is noteworthy that Jeremiah, who prophesied about the destruction and restoration of Jerusalem, continually encouraged the people to accept their state of exile, and not fight against it. He says:

> Thus says the LORD, "Behold, I set before you the *way of life* and the *way of death*. He who dwells in this city—[Jerusalem]—will die by the sword and by famine and by pestilence; but he who goes out and falls away to the Chaldeans who are besieging you will live, and he will have his own life as booty." (Jer 21:8–9; emphasis mine)

Interestingly enough, "the way of life" was to accept the life in exile; it was a call to surrender to Babylon, to say "yes to the reality and appropriateness of God's judgment—that was Jeremiah's and God's word as the shades of exile fell."[163] It was clear that God had ordained for Israel to go through the experience of exile to be transformed and find a lasting relationship with his God. Jeremiah consistently prophesied about Jerusalem's inevitable destruction and "was consequently treated as a pro-Babylonian traitor."[164] Jeremiah denounced the spiritual laziness of Israel and denounced their institutions of temple, priesthood, and kingship. Our family life suffered from the same underlying sins. Our Christianity was superficial, and our faith facile; our religious practices had become ritualistic; we had taken our God for granted.

Jeremiah spoke of a new era in which the remnant of Israel, when radically transformed, will rebuild their land. These new people will truly be blessed by God, and his laws would be written on their hearts. VanGemeren says, "At the heart of Jeremiah's message is Yahweh's freedom. Yahweh is free in wrath, judgment, vengeance, vindication, and restoration. Therefore there is hope for the godly."[165] Who were the remnants who outlasted the Exile and returned to the land to rebuild their temple

162. VanGemeren, *Interpreting the Prophetic Word*, 57.

163. Klein, *Israel in Exile*, 49.

164. VanGemeren, *Interpreting the Prophetic Word*, 308.

165. Ibid., 319.

and worship their God again? How did the exilic community live, survive, and endure? The history of the church is filled with examples of those who truly experienced the darkness and abandonment of an exile, which was a catalyst for their transformation to the image of Christ. When God seemed most hidden, the remnants drank the cup given to them by their Father, and hung on with hope to his promises in his Word. Instead of cursing the darkness, Klein claims, one must understand that "Exile is a time for hope, not triumphalism," albeit a difficult challenge.[166]

Luther is one of the best examples for the church as regards dealing with darkness and the hiddenness of God. In his state of exile, he struggled desperately in his soul to find peace with God. Luther came to know God's grace and his need for it in the pages of Scripture at the peak of his despair. That was the source of hope for our family too. It was the promises of God laid out in the pages of Scripture that kept us going. Luther found Christ hidden in the very reality of life. His despair, his abandonment, his exile, led him to find his new identity in Christ. Erikson writes:

> This paradoxical foolishness and weakness of God became a theological absolute for Luther: there is not a word in the Bible, he exclaimed, which is *extra crucem*, which can be understood without reference to the cross . . . he insists on Christ's complete sense of abandonment. . . . Luther spoke here in passionate terms very different from those of medieval adoration. He spoke of a man who was unique in all creation, yet lives in each man; and who is dying in everyone even as he died *for* everyone. . . . What he had tried, so desperately and for so long, to counteract and overcome he now accepted as his divine gift—the sense of utter abandonment, *sicut jam damnatus*, as if already in hell. . . . The passion is all that man can know of God: his conflicts, duly faced, are all that he can know of himself. The last judgment is the always present self-judgment. Christ did not live and die in order to make man poorer in the fear of his future judgment, but in order to make him abundant today: *nam judicia sunt ipsae passiones Christi quae in nobis abundant*. Look, Luther said at one point . . . how everywhere painters depict Christ's passion as if . . . we know nothing but Christ crucified. The artist closer to Luther in spirit was Dürer, who etched his own face into Christ's countenance.[167]

---

166. Klein, *Israel in Exile*, 151.

167. Erikson, *Young Man Luther*, 205, 207.

While it is heartwarming to read Luther's words, the experience of exile and darkness is anything but. Helia lost the use of most of her faculties during the years of her illness. "How could God have abandoned her to that extent?" I asked everyday. Laing sees the process of natural healing as one similar to the "ancient quest for the self," the solitary experience of the "dark night of the soul."[168] In regard to that journey, John of the Cross explains how the person has to lose the use of all faculties to be born in a new realm. All that the person depended on has to be dismantled, so that new spiritual faculties can be gained; that is why "when the soul is making most progress, it is travelling in darkness, knowing naught."[169] As the soul approaches the presence of God, "the blacker is the darkness," and "the deeper is the obscurity" that is experienced because of its weakness.[170] This is similar to a man who approaches the sun; the blinding light creates intense darkness, and the pain and affliction created is unbearable. This affirms what David says: "He made darkness His hiding place" (Ps 18:11).

"Oh, miserable is the fortune of our life," says St. John, "for that which is most clear and true is to us most dark and doubtful; wherefore . . . we flee from it."[171] He asserts that as long as the natural senses and faculties are engaged and active, they will lead the person to false light; it is only when the person is in darkness that the soul is well protected in the hand of God. The self has to go backward to be able to go forward. One has to die in order truly to live (John 11:24–25). Laing calls this a trip back to one's "lost home." He writes that he wished he could drive everyone out of their "wretched mind." He urges everyone to break through the "condition of alienation, of being asleep, of being unconscious, of being out of one's mind, [which] is the condition of the normal man," into a changed existence.[172]

Laing describes the stages of the journey from the outer reality to the inner reality as a voyage from life to dying—a death of the ego. In this journey, a descent into hell, the self dies in order to gain the true self. But he warns that if the traveler does not have a "sheet anchor which helps" him to "weather the storm," he may not make it to the other side. Laing writes, "So there should be other people who sort of look after you." He believes that this journey of madness "*is not what we need to be cured of,*

168. Sugerman, *Sin and Madness*, 60.

169. John of the Cross, *Dark Night of the Soul*, 84.

170. Ibid., 85.

171. Ibid.

172. Laing, *The Politics of Experience*, 24; Sugerman, *Sin and Madness*, 60.

but that it is itself a natural way of healing our own appalling state of alien-
ation called normality." Madness, in Laing's view, is not necessarily about
breakdown, but rather it holds the promise of breakthrough.[173] Exile held
the same promise of breakthrough for Israel. They had a chance to find
their God and their true identity again.

One of the most hurtful aspects of this exilic life was the loss of community, the way others treat you. Friends stopped coming to our house;
even in church, when Helia was mobile and we would take her, people
showed that they were not comfortable around her, as if our decision to
attend services was an imposition. The stares, the whispers, the mockings,
and the fake smiles were all signs that she was in a "foreign land." Regardless of the "caring" and "loving" masks we all know how to wear, a person
who is stigmatized by psychiatric labels will end up living a marginalized
life. She will never be considered a full member of the society with the
same rights as other citizens. Greene-McCreight writes about her feelings
of being stigmatized:

> With the darkness, I experience visions and voices. This is true
> of mental patients from time to time. But the stigma of mental
> illness, including the jokes made by the healthy about the ill,
> is worse than the visions and voices. At least the visions and
> voices teach me something about myself and about God. But
> the stigma teaches me nothing except about the proclivity of
> humanity to harm humanity.[174]

But where was God in the midst of all this? Didn't he promise that he
would be with those who are persecuted and oppressed? God had seemingly left Helia helpless and defenseless. He was the "perverse shepherd"[175]
that Jeremiah lamented about:

> He has driven me and made me walk in darkness and not in light.
> Surely against me He has turned His hand repeatedly all the day.
> He has caused my flesh and my skin to waste away;
> He has broken my bones . . .
> In dark places He has made me dwell,
> like those who have long been dead. (Lam 3:2–4, 6)

"Schizophrenia" is a true picture of life without grace, "away from the presence of the Lord and from the glory of His power" (2 Thess 1:9). God

173. Laing, *The Politics of Experience*, 134, 136; Sugerman, *Sin and Madness*, 61.

174. Greene-McCreight, *Darkness Is My Only Companion*, 56.

175. Klein, *Israel in Exile*, 12.

seemingly is nowhere to be found. It is all darkness—no sign of light, no sign of life. Greene-McCreight writes:

> [T]he most dangerous thing about mental illness is that it can lock us in ourselves, convincing us that we are indeed our own, and completely on our own, isolated in our distress. Darkness *is* my only companion. Mental illness is a veil that shrouds our consecration to God, blocking out the glory of the Holy One. Our wounds fester; our remoteness from the source of our healing increases. Mental illness shuts all windows and doors to the soul so that we cannot speak, meditate, or do anything to the glory of God, or so it seems. All is experienced as pain. We are locked in ourselves, unable to forget our pain. How does the Christian endure such remoteness from the source of our life?[176]

Exile is the reminder of a broken covenant; of a Father who has given away the child into the hand of enemy. His absence, forgetfulness, silence, and rejection seemed unrestrained. But how can one hope without him? How can one live in the land of no grace? Greene-McCreight speaks to the hiddenness of God in the midst of her darkness. She says, "God hides Himself from my suffering, in my suffering."[177] She shared that feeling with the Psalmist, Luther, and Isaiah. The Psalmist cries out: "Why dost Thou stand afar off, O LORD? Why dost Thou hide Thyself in times of trouble?" (Ps 10:1). Luther believed we know God best *sub contrario*, or in his hiddenness.[178] Isaiah said, "Truly, Thou art a God who hides Himself, O God of Israel, Savior" (Isa 45:15). Isaiah knew that though he was hidden, there was no other Savior but him.

Klein stresses that when the Lord is the Judge, only the Lord can be the hope of vindication.[179] Regardless of how the exiles felt, Jeremiah asked them to persevere because of God's promises:

> For thus says the LORD, "When seventy years have been completed for Babylon, I will visit you and fulfill My good word to you, to bring you back to this place. 'For I know the plans that I have for you,' declares the LORD, 'plans for welfare and not for calamity, to give you a future and a hope.' Then you will call upon Me and come and pray to Me, and I will listen to you. And

176. Greene-McCreight, *Darkness Is My Only Companion*, 116.

177. Ibid., 120.

178. Wengert, *The Pastoral Luther*, 16.

179. Klein, *Israel in Exile*, 56.

you will seek Me and find Me when you search for Me with all
your heart." (Jer 29:10–12)

Clearly, God had a plan for sending His people into Exile. This plan,
against all appearance, was for their good. They would finally come to
know Him and serve Him with all their hearts. Who, then, are the faithful
remnants who will possess the land? Frame says, "It is under the rule of the
righteous Branch that God's people will be gathered from all the nations."
Then they will join together to praise God for His salvation. He points
out that Israel never repents out of its "own moral strength." Instead, it
requires a "redemptive re-creation."[180] When Jeremiah prophesies about
the remnant, Frame says: "We again see the righteous branch (23:5–6),
whose name is 'The Lord Our Righteousness,'" pointing ultimately to the
only elect remnant, Jesus Christ. "He is the faithful remnant, the righteous
Branch," says Frame. "And in Christ, by His grace" alone one can "belong
to the remnant."[181] It is only those who are united with Christ who will
return to live in the Promised Land—the kingdom of God.

In his classic spiritual masterpiece, *Dark Night of the Soul*, St. John of
the Cross explains how major afflictions and pain suffered by the soul lead
to union with Christ. In the process of this journey, the person is freed
from the lust of the flesh and taken over by the Spirit of God. But in order
to get there, the soul that travels "in the darkness . . . also achieves even
greater gain and progress . . . by a way that it least understands—indeed,
it quite commonly believes that it is losing ground . . . and [this] makes
it depart recklessly from its former way of life."[182] The soul will have to
first be "brought into emptiness and poverty of spirit and purged from
all help, consolation and natural apprehension with respect to all things."
The person becomes incompetent, rejecting all reason, knowledge, and
anything he formerly depended on. He becomes "poor in spirit and freed
from the old man," so that he can receive the new life in the "state of union
with God."[183]

The purpose of Exile was to change Israel in a transformative way. It
was to put off "the old self" and to put on "the new self." Greene-McCreight
speaks of how personality is dissolved in illness: "Tastes, desires, disposi-
tions that formerly marked our personality vanish with mental illness."

180. Frame, *Doctrine of God*, 321.

181. Ibid., 322.

182. John of the Cross, *Dark Night of the Soul*, 84.

183. Ibid., 62. For further explanation of the journey toward union with Christ, see
chapter 1.

She was wondering whether she would ever have herself back. Reflecting on her experience, she concludes that "personality is relatively unimportant vis-à-vis God." In God's eyes, one is neither how one feels nor what one thinks nor even what one does. The person's significance comes from who one is in their relationship with God for the fulfillment of his purposes. And God's primary purpose is "to save us from our best yet perverse efforts to separate ourselves from his presence, from his fellowship." She acknowledges that in the Western cultures it is "not stylish" to say that personality is not what defines a person. This is because most people think of God as a "self-help device," for the purpose of enhancing our personality: "to help us quit smoking, drinking, overeating, abusing our kids." She believes we expect God to help us to "be nicer people, so we can stand to live in our own skin, to help us have more friends." She contends that religion in America is mostly about improving our way of life; that is because "most of us are functional atheists, even though we may be quite pious indeed." As she sees it, Western mentality seeks a religion that leads to the betterment of life. The question is whether the God of Scripture ever promised a better life based on Western standards. Her contention is first and foremost, "that God demands our worship and obedience."[184]

Klein says, "To say only no to exile is triumphalism; to say only yes is hopelessness. To say yes and no is to affirm the judgment, to recognize this exilic existence as one's real vocation, and yet to confess and actualize the transforming power of the Promiser."[185] Klein's assessment of exile confirms Laing's understanding of the journey through madness; it also corroborates Helia's experience. What sustained Israel in Exile was faith in their God and his promises. As Laing indicated, without an anchor, it is impossible to "weather the storm." Exile is the time of temptation to desire and pursue empty deliverances. For Helia and our family, his grace pointed us to see life through the eyes of the Cross. It was a time for self-reflection and self-examination; a time for turning to God and remembering that in his hiddenness, his fingers are at work ordering the lives of his people.

"Schizophrenia"—A Prophetic Voice

In Scripture, the prophetic revelation is seen as sent by God, and it is not intended just for the person who receives it, but rather, it is "an element in the continuing dialogue between God and man." Sugerman points out that

184. Greene-McCreight, *Darkness Is My Only Companion*, 89.

185. Klein, *Israel in Exile*, 151.

in the Western cultures, with the distinction between the "objective and the subjective," hearing a voice or seeing an image is considered as "individual aberration." But that is not the case in biblical text in which God is the source of prophetic revelation with a clear plan and purpose. In Scripture these revelations would be experienced as inspiration, or possession, or trances, and received as meaningful and consequential phenomena in the community. It is this acceptance, or lack thereof, which defines the limits within which deviant behavior receives an interpretation. If the deviant behavior is outside the socially acceptable limits, then it would be considered madness. It is based on today's socially acceptable limits that many scholars looking back to the Old Testament era consider prophets such as Ezekiel—who was subject to trances and frenzies—to be "schizophrenic."[186]

God wants his people to be his mouthpiece, living their lives prophetically. The Scripture claims that mankind has gone astray; each has turned to his own way (cf. Isa 53:6). God forces his people to listen and calls them to repentance through his prophets and the Spirit of his Son (Eph 4:11; Heb 3:7–11). Buber reminds us that God's grace comes at great cost. He does not submit himself to the desire of people to be adored by them as a great facilitator of their plans. He believes God's Word is at work in the midst of human words; yet from the perspective of those human words his Word *seems* "powerless." God does not make his Word believable, but it is the person who has to make the choice between hard truth and an easy lie. Buber stresses that God is not there to impress humanity. He does not exercise his power in order to corroborate his word to gain our trust. False prophets make it easy for man to feel good about himself. The authentic prophetic word demands man to listen. "In days of false security a shaking and stirring word of disaster is befitting," says Buber. God speaks through his prophet and points to the "historically approaching catastrophe."[187] Buber, in reference to Jeremiah as a true suffering prophet of God says:

> But no word of Jeremiah is simply personal; his sufferings, though he does not know it, are transparent into the sufferings of Israel—not the sufferings of one generation, still less of this corrupt generation, but the sufferings of the eternal people. . . . His "I" is so deeply set in the "I" of the people that his life cannot be regarded as that of an individual. In general those who tend to distinguish precisely in Scripture between the collective

186. Sugerman, *Sin and Madness*, 75–76.

187. Buber, *The Prophetic Faith*, 176–78.

and the individual "I" are mistaken. The "I" of the individual remains transparent into the "I" of the community . . . the "I" of Jeremiah passes over directly into the "I" of the people. . . . This, however, is not only because Jeremiah identifies himself in moments of inspiration with the people, but because he really bears the people within himself. The contradiction that destroys the people resides in his very self. . . . The sufferings which he bears because of Israel he bears for Israel.[188]

As Jeremiah "really bears the people within himself," so do those who are labeled with "schizophrenia." They do bear the pain of their community along with its spiritual aberrations. Moreover, like Jeremiah, those suffering from "schizophrenia" cannot help but prophesy the word that God is speaking through them in their "symptoms." It is impossible to escape from the providence of God. Jeremiah was a prophet who attempted to leave his vocation at all costs. He says:

O LORD, Thou hast deceived me and I was deceived; Thou hast overcome me and prevailed. I have become a laughingstock all day long; everyone mocks me.
For each time I speak, I cry aloud; I proclaim violence and destruction, because for me the word of the LORD has resulted in reproach and derision all day long. (Jer 20:7–8)

Buber refers to Jeremiah as one of the "martyrs" of the ancient world, who has shared with us the depth of his pain in his vocation. He says:

[Jeremiah] resisted with all his might the designation to become the central man of the catastrophe, but God "befooled" him (20, 7). He longed to live in the midst of his people, but was compelled to sit lonely under God's hand (15, 17). He refused again and again to pass sentence in YHVH's name upon his beloved people, but the word remained in his heart "like a burning fire" . . . and he was weary of the vain effort to contain it (20, 9). The divine wrath heaps itself up in him and forces him to pour it out in cursing his people, without discrimination, upon children playing in the street, upon the company of merry youths (6, 11), and moreover he feels as if he did not announce a coming disaster, but as if fire actually proceeded from his mouth and consumed the logs of his people (5, 14). He knows that the avenging God is just, even though sometimes he no longer understands His actions.[189]

188. Ibid., 181–82.

189. Ibid., 180.

And such is the destiny of those labeled with "schizophrenia." They embody the call of God to bring his people back to repentance. As Buber labeled Jeremiah, they are the "martyrs" of their immediate culture and community, so to speak.

Many have pointed to similar experiences between prophets and those suffering from "schizophrenia." Some scholars, psychologists, and psychiatrists have gone as far as trying to show that some of the prophets of the Old Testament suffered from "schizophrenia." It is not simple to assess the behavior of the prophets of the Old Testament era from a vantage culturally far removed and twenty-five hundred years later, but that has not stopped many of the critics. The similarities between the two groups should not be surprising. The Spirit of God, who spoke through his prophets of the old, continues to do his wondrous work through his chosen ones even today. God called Hosea to marry a prostitute to demonstrate God's love and grace in spite of Israel's harlotry. Hosea, through his action and way of life, was communicating God's message to his community. Isaiah was ordered to walk naked and barefoot for three years "as a sign and token against Egypt and Cush" (Isa 20:3–5). At Micah's time, many people were so insensitive to the problem of their sins that they expected nothing but favor from God. Micah's message reminded them of the consequences of national sin. He, like Isaiah, was commanded by God to go naked before Israel: "Because of this I must lament and wail; I must go barefoot and naked; I must make a lament like the jackals and a mourning like the ostriches. For her wound is incurable" (Mic 1:8–9a). How would that behavior be perceived by twenty-first century psychiatry?

Jack Miles refers to Isaiah, Jeremiah, and Ezekiel as individuals who suffered from "madness." He considers them to have been "manic," "depressive," and "psychotic."[190] This cavalier assessment has been applied to Ezekiel more than any other prophet. This is because God called him to be the most prominent example of a prophet who embodied his message in his actions. Ezekiel himself was to be the living symbol of the rebellious nation. He was to act out all that was to befall them. Ezekiel was the mouthpiece of the Lord (3:4), and the Lord's hand was strong upon him (3:14). The Lord makes him dumb (3:26) and he opens his mouth (24:27; 33:22). He is motionless and "catatonic" for an extended period (4:4–8); he is lifted up by the Spirit between heaven and earth (8:3); he engages in a very bizarre conduct (4:12; 5:1–4; 12:3–6) and he is forbidden to show any emotions and mourn the death of his wife (24:15–16). Because

---

190. Miles, *God: A Biography*, 197–98.

of the unusual behavior, Steven Shawn Tuell warns that Ezekiel has been "readily dismissed as a crank," and "his book given scant attention." He notes that the Western society "calls anyone who has visions and hears voices 'insane,'" whereas in other cultures "ecstatic behavior is part of the expected range of religious experience." Indeed, one is reminded that Jesus' own family said of him, "He is out of His mind" (Mark 3:21, NIV). Ezekiel's "sign-acts" are "vivid demonstrations of the prophet's message and authority," says Tuell, and they "would have compelled the attention of [his] audience and made [his] message more persuasive." He goes on to say: "When a prophet performs a sign-act, he embodies and participates in God's activity."[191]

Even though psychiatry is challenged to diagnose with precision a living patient in our contemporary culture, that has not stopped many scholars to confidently assign various clinical diagnoses to Ezekiel's behavior. This is because the language used by the prophet to describe his experiences resonates with the textbook classification of psychiatric disorders. Consequently, Ezekiel is identified by many "as psychic, schizophrenic, epileptic, catatonic, psychotic, or paranoid, or given other such labels," depending on the diagnostic classification "*en vogue* at the time."[192] Edwin Broome, applying Freudian analysis, concluded that Ezekiel was "a true psychotic" characterized by "a narcissistic-masochistic conflict, with attendant phantasies of castration and unconscious sexual regression," along with "schizophrenic withdrawal," and "delusions of persecution and grandeur."[193] The book of Ezekiel gives the following accounts about the prophet:

> Then I came to the exiles ... and I sat there seven days ... causing consternation among them. (3:15)

> The Spirit then entered me and made me stand on my feet, and He spoke with me and said to me, "Go shut yourself up in your house." (3:24)

> Moreover I will make your tongue stick to the roof of your mouth so that you will be dumb, and cannot be a man who rebukes them, for they are a rebellious house. (3:26)

191. Tuell, "Should Ezekiel Go to Rehab?," 289, 292, 296 n. 33.

192. Dillard and Longman, *An Introduction to the Old Testament*, 319.

193. Broome Jr., "Ezekiel's Abnormal Personality," 291–92.

> As for you, lie down on your left side, and lay the iniquity of the
> house of Israel on it; you shall bear their iniquity for the number
> of days that you lie on it. For I have assigned you a number of
> days corresponding to the years of their iniquity, three hundred
> and ninety days; thus you shall bear the iniquity of the house of
> Israel. (4:4–5)

> Now behold, I will put ropes on you so that you cannot turn
> from one side to the other, until you have completed the days of
> your siege. (4:8)

Broome analyzes these texts and concludes: "That this mutism, immobility, and feeling that bands were placed upon him . . . is a characteristic a psychotic experience is hardly questionable. . . . This catatonic state of the prophet . . . is central for our understanding of Ezekiel's personality."[194] Tuell, who opposes those who read the Book of Ezekiel as a "psychological autobiography," contends that Ezekiel is taking upon himself "the *sin* of the house of Israel." Ezekiel is a "sign" to Israel, "a sign of God's absence, and Jerusalem's abandonment."[195] Ezekiel was not "schizophrenic"; but is "schizophrenia" a powerful "sign-act" to make "schizophrenics" the Ezekiels of our time, with a message as powerful as the prophet embodied? What might that message be?

If humankind is trapped in sinfulness, without understanding the depth of its depravity, what might bring it to its senses? Maybe it is an existential experience, not a theoretical one that would awaken the human and enlighten him to his true condition. Maybe by being forced to encounter "schizophrenia" his eyes would be opened to his true picture. This is who he is; this is his destiny: living in hell day and night, in "the outer darkness," where "there shall be weeping and gnashing of teeth," with no sign of grace "away from the presence of the Lord and from the glory of His power" (Matt 22:13; 2 Thess 1:9). Anyone who has been *blessed* with the opportunity to spend an extended time with an *unmedicated* person suffering from "schizophrenia" is bound to have seen that tormenting image far too clearly. It is a true picture of hell, but it is a blessing, because it *awakens* the witness. One cannot go on to live a "normal" life after that experience. Robert Whitaker, in his foreword to *Soteria*, writes:

> Indeed, as I read this book, I felt envious of those who worked
> at Soteria. They had the opportunity to "be with" unmedicated

194. Ibid., 280–81.

195. Tuell, "Should Ezekiel Go to Rehab?," 292, 297, 300 n. 48.

people who were battling with "madness." They clearly learned a great deal from this experience. They may have found it frustrating at times and often emotionally draining, but always rewarding and meaningful.[196]

Zilboorg explains that when those with mental illness are embraced in the community, the voice of mental illness can break through. The illness elucidates the illness of the community. The illness is no longer merely the individual's illness; rather, a relationship between "mental disease" and "the whole of community life" becomes apparent.[197] In Helia's case, our family encountered our own sickness in hers. She was manifesting right before our eyes our deformities, which were covered under our masks of civility. We had no choice but to stare at ourselves with all our innate ugliness.

Studies that have considered variations of the spread of "schizophrenia" in different cultures and in different layers of the same culture have produced some eye-opening results. The data indicates the nature of illness to be directly related to the community where it manifests itself, suggesting that it is anything but an abstract meaningless disease.[198] The various expressions appear to have a voice demanding the attention of their immediate audience. McGruder found through her studies that there were enough variations to suggest that "the disease was shaped by something besides the purely genetic or biological." She noticed that the symptoms experienced by those with "schizophrenia" were often "reflections of the phobias and fascinations of specific cultures." The other interesting factor was that the symptoms were changing as times were changing. Thus, in a particular culture, the disease would manifest itself differently at different eras. "Researchers who focused on the biomedical or genetic linchpins of the disorder often dismissed these [cultural based content] differences." Stranger still, the research pointed to the manifestation of symptoms depending on the particular neighborhood. It is so pronounced that some neighborhoods in cities seem to produce more afflictions of "schizophrenia" that researchers have questioned about "the environmental pathogens that might exist in one place and not another."[199] Could these content vari-

196. Whitaker, Foreword, xiv–xv.

197. Zilboorg and Henry, *Medical Psychology*, 462.

198. Bustamante, "The Importance of Cultural Factors in Mental Hygiene," 254–55. The research shows that "schizophrenia is not found among the [Forest] Bantus . . . the reason for it is the solidity of their standards of value" (254).

199. Watters, *Crazy Like Us*, 134–36. Social inequalities and increased deprivation in a neighborhood are linked to "schizophrenia" in the following study: Kirkbride et al.,

ations point to something unique to a particular community? Could the disease be the voice of an inner sickness within a particular family, group, neighborhood, city, or nation? There seems to be an agreement around that hypothesis among many scholars.

With a striking unintended corroboration of the theological arguments stated above, in a study conducted by thirteen scientists from some of the most prestigious academic institutions, including Massachusetts Institute of Technology (MIT) and Harvard Medical School, it is shown that the "schizophrenics" take on the external stimuli from their environment, internalize it, and manifest it in the forms of "symptoms." This is because the "default mode" of their brain—the part that is "on" when one is at "rest" and is suppressed when one is attending to activities—is hyperactive and hyperconnected at all times. This means that they are always in a so-called "neutral gear" mode. They are empty themselves, and cognitively cannot direct their attention to elements of choice, but instead, the stimuli from the environment—both good and bad—travel through them without their intentional engagement. Consequently, the nature of the "default network" in people suffering from "schizophrenia" is such that it "may promote the assignment of self-relevance to unrelated external events and blur the line between internal thoughts and external events."[200]

These scientists "examined the status of the neural network mediating the default mode of brain function, which typically exhibits greater activation during rest than during task, in patients in the early phase of schizophrenia" who had not yet been affected by medication and the psychosocial consequences of their illness (i.e., stigma, isolation). They discovered that the "suppression of the default network becomes increasingly important with increasing cognitive demands." In other words, in those who apply intense intellectual cognition, the "default network" within the brain becomes suppressed, where, in a state of "task-independent" rest, the suppression of the "default mode" is low. According to Whitfield-Gabrieli, et al., "These results relate variation in default network function to variation in *personality*."[201]

In "schizophrenia" the level of suppression has a reverse relation to the intensity of the "symptoms." Thus, those with heavy "hallucinations"

"Social Deprivation, Inequality, and the Neighborhood-Level Incidence of Psychotic Syndromes in East London."

200. Whitfield-Gabrieli et al., "Hyperactivity and Hyperconnectivity of the Default Network in Schizophrenia and in First-Degree Relatives of Persons with Schizophrenia," 1280.

201. Ibid., 1279, 1283; emphasis mine.

and "delusions" have high levels of activity and connectivity and a low level of suppression in their "default network." In fact this is how the healthy brain acts in "rest," the state in which no attention is given to activities in the surroundings; the "default network" has a very low suppression and high connectivity. Speaking theologically, the person becomes an empty vessel and is at "rest" from self-driven initiatives. This is the state that many attempt to attain through meditative exercises, and it makes the person open to transcendence and spiritual influences. Therefore, at this empty state, the influences from the environment reverberate back, and at times this could be overwhelming. Whitfield-Gabrieli et al. summarize this finding as follows:

> Hyperactivation of the default network may blur the normal boundary between internal thoughts and external perceptions. Constant overengagement of the default network could lead to an exaggerated focus on one's own thoughts and feelings as well as *an ambiguous integration between one's own thoughts and feelings with events in the environment.* Thus, neutral events would seem to be imbued with exaggerated self-relevance, and the boundary between the internal world of reflection and feeling and the external world of perception and action would be weakened.[202]

Drawing on these scientific findings, it can be argued that people with "schizophrenia," who are deeply broken, emptied of themselves, disarmed of their intellectual faculties, are in a vulnerable state of "rest," exposed to the pains and ills of their surrounding. Through the exceptional state of their "personality," all that is in their environment will deeply affect them. They internalize and embody the nature of their community and will reflect back a true picture of it as "sign acts," or so-called "symptoms."

Martti Siirala, himself a psychiatrist, expresses the encounter with the person afflicted with "schizophrenia" this way:

> [W]e see the sick person as a man in whose sickness and in whose total situation our inhumanity, our unlived life, our idolatry, and our blindness become crystallized; in the encounter this total situation is brought under judgment. The sick person is manifestly a prisoner under suspicion, hate, unfaith, and hopelessness, which qualities to a great extent remain hidden in us. He is as a stone crying out. Even though he is under the burden of all this, the Creator compels the creature in him to cry out

202. Ibid., emphasis mine.

concerning his condition, if only we have ears to hear. . . . Being out of place means at the same time being a prisoner in the network common to all men. Not only the original cause of the anguish but also the continuation of it, and his increasing aloneness, are connected with our withholding our association with him. We protect ourselves from becoming entangled in his skein because what is revealed in him exposes our common guilt. . . . We try to protect ourselves even against the anticipation that what we encounter here perhaps calls into question our whole reality, our faith, our conduct, our self-understanding. Here is perhaps the deepest reason for our strong need to isolate the anguish of illness and to keep it at a distance, beyond the reach of our ears.[203]

"Schizophrenia" is an unsettling reminder of unyielding fabric of unpredictability, uncertainty, chaos, and confusion in the human condition. "Schizophrenia" forces us to confront our lack of control over our own and other's condition; it is a major blow to humanity's *pride*. It points to our failure to explain and master much in our world. Most fundamentally it forces us to stare at our true image that we so ably hide behind our everyday masks. The person with "schizophrenia" forces us to look face to face at our true self. When the illness is encountered in a loved one or a neighbor, the signs and symbols of the illness radiate such deep meanings that none can escape.

"The madness of our patients is an artifact of the destruction wreaked on them by us," says Laing. He contends the madness encountered in "patients" is "a gross travesty, a mockery, a grotesque caricature" of what we all are inside us. This is the age of no faith. He points to Amos's prophecy of a time that the Lord will send a famine on the land, "Not a famine for bread or a thirst for water, but rather for hearing the words of the Lord" (Amos 8:11). We cannot hear anymore. "That time has now come to pass," says Laing. "It is the present age." If we are not hearing as he contends, indeed "schizophrenia" and the starvation of those who go through it points to our spiritual starvation.[204]

Symptoms of mental illness, McGruder believes, are "social actions" that "create meaning from psychophysiological processes in the body *and* act out social-emotional processes in a bodily way."[205] This is exactly what Ezekiel was called to do; Ezekiel's "sign-acts" are today's psychiatric

203. Siirala, *The Voice of Illness*, 94–95.

204. Laing, *The Politics of Experience*, 118–19.

205. McGruder, "Life Experience is Not a Disease," 63.

symptoms. For example, it is neither a biological pathology, nor a meaningless act, when someone with "schizophrenia" often spends money "exorbitantly." Their behavior is a mirror of a consumerist society, "power of fetish objects," in the culture, and highly valued expressions of self-love.[206] T. M. Luhrmann, a professor of anthropology at Stanford University, argues that the experience of voice hearing for people with "schizophrenia" is closely related to their social context and the community around them. For example, the Americans suffering from "schizophrenia" are badly tortured by their voices and are often commanded to commit suicide, or are spoken to about war and violence. Whereas those suffering from the illness in India are often instructed by their commanding voices to perform domestic work, to clean up, and to bathe. At times, they too, like their American counterparts, are targets of sexual and profane tormenting voices. She concludes, "Meanwhile, it is a sobering thought that the greater violence in the voices of Americans with schizophrenia may have something to do with those of us without schizophrenia. I suspect that the root of the differences may be related to the greater sense of assault that people who hear voices feel in a social world."[207] Also, "the loss of identity of the person," says Kütemeyer, "seems to be one of the basic characteristics of our society."[208] Martti Siirala believes that the "schizophrenic" person takes our burdens upon himself and "embodies our basic splits; in him they become a manifest predicament."[209]

That is exactly what Helia manifested before our eyes. She had taken on all our sins and was acting them out in physical forms. Helia, like Ezekiel, was given many labels; and like him, she was the embodiment of our innate corruption. She had let down all the barriers; her masks and fake appearances had disappeared. She could no longer hide her wounded heart behind her attractive figure and the beauty of her face. The faculties that could mask the truth of her inner person were disengaged. She was frighteningly vulnerable. The true self, the wretched, the miserable, the poor, the naked had risen their heads and she was a revelation of who I was. The pain of our depravity had transcended the theoretical realm and stared us in the face with vivid clarity; no longer could help be found in our "sense of genius," or "flair," or "riches," or "loftiness" to rescue us from despair. Her illness was foreshadowing our destiny. Encountering her

206. Ibid.

207. Luhrmann, "The Violence in Our Heads."

208. Siirala, *The Voice of Illness*, 181 n. 42.

209. Ibid., 187 n. 74.

illness, I was forced to look at my own insanity; I was forced into naked existence; all the covers were pulled back.

Her rebellion and lack of respect for any authority was pointing at me. The strange way she decorated her room was a picture of how we were decorating all aspects of our lives in pure vanity. When she would put on ten layers of clothes, and when she carried five bags in her hand, with all the junk she had hoarded, it spoke of the greed and wastefulness in our lives. Like her, we were hoarding beyond our needs, and even beyond pleasure. Her lack of hygiene pointed to our impurities and defilement. Her starvation and her twisted body were a picture of our starved and twisted souls. Her rage, her anger, and her screams exposed our fears. Her insatiable desire to spend money pictured our covetousness. Her disorganized thoughts, her incoherence, her confusion showed our depravity. The difference was that we were still equipped with faculties that could hide our true selves. Through her I saw who I was and I did not like the picture. As Warfield says:

> It is only by knowing sin that we can know righteousness, as it is only by knowing darkness that we know light. We must know what sin is and how subtle it is before we can realize what righteousness is. . . . We must know the depth that we may appreciate the heights. . . . We must know sin in order to know judgment. We must know sin in its native hideousness that we may understand its ill desert, and perceive with what judgment the sinner must be judged. . . . Sin is made known; righteousness is revealed; judgment is laid bare. And men convicted of their sin have but a choice of the righteousness or judgment.[210]

This is heavy stuff. Yet when we face reality, when we face our faults, our sins, that is when we also begin to find the solution to our alienation and madness. There is no shortcut with God!

"Schizophrenic"—A "Sacrificial Lamb"

It is significant that a person in the face of grave adversity shows exemplary courage and often remarkable patience, and contends successfully with the unending assault of an impaired body and a broken spirit. What is the source of this strength? Warfield believes one can endure the long course of losses and threats only when it is "ultimately to the purpose of

210. Warfield, *The Person and Work of the Holy Spirit*, 19.

God."[211] The experience of abandonment in "schizophrenia," though intensely painful and dark, happens under the watchful eyes of a sovereign God. "Schizophrenia," severe depression, or other soul-tearing anguishes loudly speak of the "fellowship of suffering"[212] with Christ.

Calvin, in regards to the crucifixion of Christ, says he "took upon himself the shame and reproach of our iniquities, and in return clothed us with his purity."[213] Earlier in this study, we heard from several theologians and researchers who explained the substitutionary nature of illness, when one bears the illness of the community, as Christ did for humanity. Likewise, Helia imitated Christ by wearing our sins on her body in such a way that we had no choice but to encounter them. We could not turn our face away from staring at our sins without turning away from her. This is the burden that every person with "schizophrenia" bears, for their family, for their church, and for their greater community. Our salvation comes from Christ through his grace, but Helia and those like her are "soldiers of the cross" used by God to bring a rebellious race to their senses. Helia had become a picture of Christ—a "sacrificial lamb"—and not only to experience true life as a result of continual death in her flesh; she had also seemingly become so empty that the Spirit of God could bend her in any direction to communicate to those around her. Paul saw in his own life a reenactment of Jesus' death. He died daily in the service of Christ that the life of Jesus might be manifested in his mortal body. He also became an instrument for his church to experience the life of God: "So death works in us, but life in you" (2 Cor 4:12). He told the Ephesians: "I ask you not to lose heart at *my tribulations on your behalf*, for they are your glory" (Eph 3:13; emphasis mine). Warfield says, "The very life circumstances of Paul became a preached Gospel. . . . For the dying is for Paul and the life for his hearers."[214]

In contrast with the overwhelming weakness of the vehicle, the intensity of the message is all the more discernible. The fact that these empty vessels can endure such intense suffering is a sign of the mighty protective hand of God. Pinel, the famous French asylum physician, marveled at the "unbelievable endurance of physical hardship" by "schizophrenic" patients, and often expressed his puzzlement at the ability of "schizophrenic" women to lie naked in below freezing conditions without showing any discomfort. He wondered if such people should be considered "sick," when in

211. Ibid., 61.

212. Cf. Phil 3:10.

213. Calvin, *Institutes*, 2/16.6.

214. Warfield, *The Person and Work of the Holy Spirit*, 61.

many ways they seemed healthier and more resilient than average human beings.[215] Likewise, in the midst of her severe trial, Helia was sustained; she was "afflicted in every way, but not crushed . . . struck down, but not destroyed" (2 Cor 4:8–9). Along with Paul, she was carrying about in her body "the dying of Jesus," that his life might be manifested in her and those around her. "When we lose hope in ourselves, when the present becomes dark and future black before us, when effort after effort has issued only in disheartening failure, and our sin looms big before our despairing eyes," says Warfield, one must remember that Paul in his own battles points us "not to the victory of good over evil, but to the conflict of good with evil—not to the end but to the process—as the proof of childship to God."[216] Helia carried her cross everyday and fought that battle in fellowship with Christ.

Norman Brown, a student of psychoanalysis, likewise sees in Luther a man of prophetic stature for Western history, a man whose anguish and psychological battles paved a way for a model of an encounter with mental illness. Luther wrestled to reconcile life and death, wrath and grace; he saw victory only in the Cross. Brown writes:

> In Luther's new *theologia crucis*, the Christian, like Christ himself, must voluntarily submit to crucifixion by the Devil. "To take up the cross is voluntarily to take upon oneself and bear the hate of the Devil, of the world, of the flesh, of sin, of death." And as Christ harrowed hell by offering Himself for hell whole and entire . . . so "God leads down to hell those whom he predestines to heaven, and makes alive by slaying." Hence it is one of the signs of predestination to heaven not merely "to be resigned in very deed to hell" but even to "desire to be lost and damned." It would be hard to find a clearer illustration of the actuality and effective power of that death instinct which Freud postulated and which the non-Freudian world has ridiculed. For hell, Luther said, is not a place, but is the experience of death and Luther's Devil is ultimately personified death. Luther's new *theologia crucis* rejects the traditional Aristotalian-Thomistic goal of actualizing the potentialities of life as *amor concupiscentiae*, and calls us to experience hell on earth, to experience life on earth as ruled by the death instinct, and to die to such a death-in-life, in the hope of a more joyful resurrection.[217]

215. Foucault, *Madness and Civilization*, vii–viii.

216. Warfield, *The Person and Work of the Holy Spirit*, 108–9, 44.

217. Brown, *Life Against Death*, 215–16.

Luther's aforementioned statement, "God leads down to hell those whom he predestines to heaven" is truly remarkable. The popular twenty-first century Western Christianity could not be any further from this thinking. Kierkegaard was a theologian intensely interested in finding an answer to the question of "What it means to be a Christian—in Christendom." He gives his view on that in *Training in Christianity*—by some accounts his favorite work. The answer is centered on one concept—*"contemporaneousness with Christ."* To be a Christian is not about holding an ideology about who Christ was, nor is it to believe in its great teachings; Christianity is: "to become contemporary with Christ in His suffering and humiliation . . . in spite of the world's rejection of Him, in spite of the social and intellectual stigma involved in doing so."[218] Kierkegaard paints a picture of true Christianity that is impossible to achieve but through the fellowship of his cross.

Scripture explains the crucifixion scene like this: "Now from the sixth hour darkness fell upon all the land. . . . Jesus cried out with a loud voice, saying, 'Eli, Eli, Lama Sabachthani?' that is, My God, My God, why has Thou forsaken Me?" (Matt 27:45–46). In that hour, Frame says, Christ is "even estranged from his Father," while he bore the full burden of the sins of the world.[219] Swinton says Jesus experienced an "inner alienation" similar to what "all victims of evil" endure. There was a true experience of abandonment. "In the passion of Christ we discover such genuine identification with human suffering that Jesus undergoes precisely the abandonment and inability to feel the presence of God that is a primary mark of the human experience of evil. Jesus felt abandoned . . . and yet, ultimately He was not." Jesus' true sense of alienation from God is an affirmation for those who suffer evil, "framing" their experience as a spiritual one, "rather than a mark of doubt or faithlessness."[220] The resurrection could not have been a reality without the crucifixion. Jesus knew that it was the loving hand of God that was directing the whole drama (cf. John 18:11). This did not make the cross any easier to bear. But it is also an anthropological reality for those who are called to a divine union.[221]

The "sixth hour" when "the darkness falls on the land" and the "crucified lamb" is "forsaken by the Father," is seemingly a never-ending hour for sufferers of "schizophrenia." In the presence of fullness of sin, life is

218. Kierkegaard, "Training in Christianity," 372.

219. Frame, *Doctrine of God*, 694.

220. Swinton, *Raging with Compassion*, 163.

221. See chapter 1.

consumed in the powerful grip of darkness and sapped of its vitality; God's light is absent. Christ's words were "drawn forth from anguish deep within his heart," says Calvin. He goes on to point to the divine sovereignty in this event: "he bore the weight of divine severity, since he was 'stricken and afflicted' . . . by God's hand, and experienced all the signs of a wrathful and avenging God. . . . Therefore, by his wrestling hand to hand with the devil's power, with the dread of death, with the pains of hell, he was victorious and triumphed over them."[222] In "schizophrenia," that cosmic battle continues. Every "schizophrenic" shares Jesus' cry of dereliction. As the crowds mocked Jesus, so they mocked Luther, Helia, and millions of others who under the labels of "madness," "insanity," or "schizophrenia" have been subject to the proclivity of humankind to hate its own.

The "Schizophrenic"—the Leper of the Twenty-first Century

According to Kleinman, stigma often carries a "religious significance"—the person seen as "sinful or evil"—or as reflecting "weakness and dishonor." Thus the stigmatized person is considered an outsider, "an alien other" upon whom the community projects the attributes it rejects. By rejecting this person, the community gains a social identity with values opposite to what the stigmatized person represents. In "schizophrenia," like the leprosy of old, the individual is stigmatized, rejected, and discredited because his "bizarre actions"—his "sign-acts"—break cultural conventions. The disease invokes cultural categories the community would rather ignore: "what is ugly, feared, alien, or inhuman."[223]

The "schizophrenic" people are the lepers of our time; they are the rejected souls, who have become the "scum" of society. The culture tells us that they need to be kept at bay for our convenience and "safety." Typically, when a person contracts a disease, he receives sympathy, empathy, and all kinds of support from his church, friends, and family. In contrast, those diagnosed with "schizophrenia" are vilified. Like lepers, they are the "outcast" and the "unclean." Despite the fact that many highly esteemed biblical characters suffered from leprosy (namely, Moses [Exod 4:6–7], Miriam [Num 12:10], Naaman [2 Kgs 5], and King Uzziah [2 Chr 26:19–21]), having leprosy, according to Steven Sainsbury, "implied, and continues to

---

222. Calvin, *Institutes*, 2/16.11.

223. Kleinman, *The Illness Narratives*, 159.

connote, evil and both spiritual and physical uncleanness."[224] Lepers were never cured by medical experts; they were *cleansed* by priests; they were isolated from family and friends and were always "objects of scorn and ridicule."[225]

Although the Bible does not specifically refer to leprosy as sin, the biblical writers still seem to link the two. Sainsbury says, "Writers consistently refer to lepers as 'defiled,' a description which syntactically connects leprosy with sin." This linkage is further supported by the fact that the lepers were required to identify themselves as "unclean" before the public. Scripture clearly defines the "cure" for leprosy in "sin-related terms," and the cleansing mandated in Leviticus requires "an elaborate set of procedures" performed by priests, before they can pronounce the leper clean.[226] Diamond, drawing on Maimonides's[227] writings, contends that leprosy was considered as a "sign and wonder" whose cause could be "traced to the moral order rather than the natural one." These leprous outbreaks do not correspond to "the normal way of the world," and can be read as "miraculous" and also as "rare and unordinary."[228] Speaking of the signs, James Arthur Diamond says:

> They are distinguished by the *escalating strength* of their cautionary effects, which begin on walls, spread to furniture, then to clothing, and finally to the physical person. Each manifestation is calibrated to signal danger and afford an opportunity to avert further harm by a remorseful change in behaviour. Unless an ethical awareness is achieved, the leprosy metastasizes from building to chattel to clothing to body in a pattern of increasing exposure and isolation culminating in quarantine where the perpetrator is "segregated and identified all alone."[229]

Likewise, in many instances, those diagnosed with "schizophrenia" show mild signs of isolation or strange behavior at the onset of their problems. In most cases, instead of others receiving the voice of their illness with nurturing love, they become the subject of harsh treatment by almost everyone. Alongside severe treatments by society, mental health workers,

224. Sainsbury, "AIDS: The Twentieth-Century Leprosy," 70.

225. Ibid., 72.

226. Ibid., 73–74.

227. Maimonides was a preeminent medieval Jewish philosopher and one of the greatest Torah scholars and physicians of the Middle Ages.

228. Diamond, "Maimonides on Leprosy," 96, 101.

229. Ibid., 101; emphasis mine.

and even confused and fearful families, the intensity of the illness escalates. The aforementioned words of Diamond about leprosy could easily be applied to the cases of "schizophrenia": "These signs are distinguished by the *escalating strength* of their cautionary effects. . . . Each manifestation is calibrated to signal danger and afford an opportunity to avert further harm by a remorseful change in behaviour."

This analysis of leprosy is consistent with Susan Sontag's view of a disease being "encumbered by the trappings of metaphor."[230] She confirms that in the Middle Ages, "the leper was a social text in which corruption was made visible; an exemplum, an emblem of decay."[231] She is alarmed by the idea of these metaphors bringing rejection and abandonment to the afflicted, in an age that "we have a sense of evil but no longer the religious or philosophical language to talk intelligently about evil." Sontag believes, "As long as a particular disease is treated as an evil, invincible predator, not just a disease, most people [afflicted with the disease] . . . will indeed be demoralized by learning what disease they have." Outside of a religious context, people who suffer are "hardly helped" when their disease is mentioned "as the epitome of evil."[232] That is the problem with "schizophrenia": it is perceived as the leprosy of our time with its evil character. But, the community does not have the belief system to enable it to deal with that metaphor in a religious context that can decipher its symbolic meaning in a fruitful fashion.

Jesus stretched out his hands toward the lepers and saved them out of their hopelessness. The same way that leprosy has the illusion of being a skin disease, but represents something deeper in the biblical text, "mental illness" may have the appearance of being purely pathological, but it reflects something deeper in the person's heart and mind and in his or her surroundings. Treatment of the lepers was the jurisdiction of priests. They had to ensure their separation from the rest of the camp due to their uncleanness. However, there was an exception:

> [I]f the leprosy breaks out further on the skin, and the leprosy covers all the skin of him who has the infection from his head even to his feet, as far as the priest can see, then the priest shall

230. Sontag, *Illness as Metaphor*, 5.

231. Ibid., 58. Likewise, John Pilch of Medical College of Wisconsin argues against associating the modern-day leprosy (Hansen's disease) to the phenomenon of biblical leprosy. He draws on anthropological insights of Arthur Kleinman and Mary Douglas to suggest that "biblical leprosy . . . actually symbolizes concern for the purity and cleanliness of the social body." See Pilch, "Biblical Leprosy and Body Symbolism," 108–13.

232. Sontag, *Illness as Metaphor*, 85, 7.

> look, and behold, *if* the leprosy has covered all his body, he shall pronounce clean him who has the infection; it has all turned white *and* he is clean. (Lev 13:12–13)

This picture reflects the grace and mercy of God when all that is disharmonious within us is brought to the surface. Charles Haddon Spurgeon says:

> When a man sees himself to be altogether lost and ruined, covered all over with the defilement of sin, and no part free from pollution; when he disclaims all righteousness of his own, and pleads guilty before the Lord, then is he clean through the blood of Jesus, and the grace of God. Hidden, unfelt, unconfessed iniquity is the true leprosy, but when sin is seen and felt it has received its death blow, and the Lord looks with eyes of mercy upon the soul afflicted with it. Nothing is more deadly than self-righteousness, or more hopeful than contrition.[233]

This text offers comfort to those who are awakened to their deep sense of sin. Jesus Christ has his arms open to all who mourn and confess their sins, regardless of how dark and foul they might be. Whoever comes to him, he will certainly not cast out (cf. John 6:37). "The great heart of love will look upon those who feels [*sic*] themselves to have no soundness in them, and will pronounce them clean," says Spurgeon. The very condition that so grievously discouraged the leper is here turned on its head into a "sign and symptom of a hopeful state." It is the "thorough sense of sin," that is the beginning of *metanoia*, "one of the earliest works of grace in the heart," and the light that will lead to true healing.[234]

This phenomenon best describes what was happening to Helia in her first "psychotic episode." She was consumed by her sense of sinfulness, crying out a series of nonstop and continuous confessions, on her knees, with tears, for more than forty-eight hours. She could not be stopped; she was in a different realm, not responding to anyone around her. Similar kinds of experiences have been called by Stan and Christina Grof a "Spiritual Emergency": a term that suggests both a "crisis" and an "opportunity of rising to a new level of awareness" or "spiritual emergence."[235] It is an "emergency" because, as Isabel Clarke says, "it can take a turn for the dark and uncontrollable."[236] This experience entails a "psychospiritual transfor-

233. Spurgeon, *Morning and Evening*, 546.

234. Ibid., 546, 115.

235. Grof and Grof, *Spiritual Emergency*, x.

236. Clarke, *Madness, Mystery and the Survival of God*, 70.

mation," that memories of the past will come to surface—in a metaphoric way, leprosy covers the whole body—to be dealt with and lead the person to a "more mature and fulfilling way."[237] In biblical terms it is a rapid and intense work of sanctification done by the Holy Spirit. Because all defenses are gone and the person is completely disarmed of his intellectual faculties, the person is vulnerable to the encounters in the spiritual realm, both good and evil. Clarke stresses that a "nurturing context" within which the encounter takes place under the guide of a spiritually discerning person is "vital in ensuring a benevolent outcome in the end."[238]

We continue to contemplate what Helia's fate would have been if she had not been treated so aggressively and by force with suppressive medication after her first psychotic episode, and if her "crises of transformation" or "spiritual opening" had been supported and managed properly. Would we have prevented all that has held her captive under the shackles of darkness for the past thirteen years? We will never know! Nonetheless, what our family learned from Helia's condition is what Spurgeon concludes out of the teaching of Leviticus about leprosy:

> We must confess that we are "nothing else but sin," for no confession short of this will be the whole truth, and if the Holy Spirit is at work within us, convincing us of sin, there will be no difficulty about making such an acknowledgment—it will spring spontaneously from our lips.[239]

Indeed, confessions sprang out of Helia's mouth, nonstop for two days, until they were silenced by strong antipsychotics.

In Christ, the hope of return from exile lives, and the crucified among us can get a foretaste of resurrection of Christ and be declared clean by the Great High Priest. We serve a God who has opened the veil and called all to his throne of Grace and Mercy. In search of an answer, through theological reflection we were led to understand sin as it is traditionally defined by the Judeo-Christian tradition, and "schizophrenia" or "madness" as a more contemporary idiom, to be correlated and reflect the human condition in a similar way. Let us look deeper into madness as a reflection of human condition with the hope that we can be shaken out of our comfort zone.

---

237. Grof and Grof, *The Stormy Search for the Self,* 37–38, 40.

238. Clarke, *Madness, Mystery and the Survival of God,* 71.

239. Spurgeon, *Morning and Evening,* 546.

The Human Condition: Madness—A True Picture of Sin

Kierkegaard, by some accounts a master on the human religious *psyche*, has offered many deep reflections on the human predicament in his writings.[240] He was astonished at the erroneous nature of the Christians' facile faith and shows his disappointment about what "to be a Christian has become." It is a "mere tomfoolery, something which everyone [embodies] as a matter of course, something one slips into more easily than into the most insignificant trick of dexterity."[241] To him, faith was not something to be easily acquired and maintained; it was a lifelong process that wholeheartedly transformed the person. In fact many of us who claim to be faithful Christians cannot endure and maintain our trust in God's mysterious ways when our faith is tested by fire (1 Pet 1:7). But why is it so difficult to enter into true Christianity? Drawing on Lutheran thoughts, he says, "Christianity is and must be a sort of madness or the greatest horror." It is only the "consciousness of sin" that can push one into this "dreadful situation," coming out on the other side covered in grace. One can enter into Christianity only through the "consciousness of sin," and "by the help of the torments of a contrite heart."[242] It is only through entry into rock-bottom knowledge of one's own darkness, shame, and guilt that one can come out reborn in the land of grace. When the concept of sin is abolished and Christianity is about world history and gentle teachings of civic and ecclesiastical life—"all of which Luther would have called bosh, and which is blasphemy, since it is impudence to wish to fraternize with God and Christ"—Christian life can never be truly transformed to deep-rooted "gentleness, grace, lovingkindness, and compassion." But how might a gracious God bring about a true "consciousness of sin" among his people?

Sin is an abstract concept for most people, even for the most devout Christians. Christians take comfort that their sins are forgiven through the redeeming work of Christ. That is where most Christians end with sin and move on with their daily lives. But, is that Scripturally sufficient? Does Scripture not teach repentance as a requirement for true faith and salvation? According to Frame, repentance and faith are the two sides of the same coin: "Faith is turning to Christ; repentance is turning away from

---

240. Barrett, *Irrational Man*, 168. Barrett considers Kierkegaard as a "psychologist of religious experience" to be "without peer."

241. Kierkegaard, *Training in Christianity*, 412.

242. Ibid., 412–13; It appears that it was exactly this intense "consciousness of sin" that drove Luther, Teresa of Avila, and Helia into their journey of "madness."

sin. You cannot have one without the other."[243] Yet both faith and repentance are gifts from God. He leads his people in paths that would grant them repentance and would generate faith in their hearts.

Grudem points out that repentance is far more than "deep remorse over one's actions." It is *hatred* toward sin and realization that one's sin "has offended a holy God." That deep-rooted hatred and realization "will result in a changed life."[244] He emphasizes:

> [I]t is clearly contrary to the New Testament evidence to speak about the possibility of having true saving faith without having any repentance for sin. It is also contrary . . . to speak about the possibility of someone accepting Christ "as Savior" but not "as Lord," if that means simply depending on Him for salvation but not committing oneself to forsake sin.[245]

He contends that the "watered-down version of the gospel," encouraging the population, "Believe in Jesus Christ and be saved," without the emphasis on repentance, has created "such inadequate results today."[246] True repentance is about living with a changed perspective, and reorienting toward God, and not the world. *Metanoia* denotes a change of mind, a reorientation, a "practical *reformation*" of the self, a "*reversal* of the past" and the outlook of an individual's view of the world and of himself.[247] But, how can this transformation be achieved? Frame says, "Repentance, too, is the work of God in us."[248] How does a loving God bring a person to truly hate sin in the deepest part of his spirit and turn to God? As I have been arguing, madness brings humanity face to face with the darkness of sin; an overwhelming darkness that will shake one's being to its root. The prophetic voice of madness is a trumpet call to repentance—a voice from which there is no escape. And yet it can be quieted down through the most vehement antipsychotic drugs of the twenty-first century.

Sugerman draws on the myth of Narcissus to portray a pattern of human behavior and the underlying core of human reality. She brings the psychological understandings of our postmodern time and the wisdom of religious traditions to present a revealing interpretation of human

243. Frame, *Doctrine of God*, 73.

244. Grudem, *Bible Doctrine*, 310.

245. Ibid.

246. Ibid., 312.

247. Mounce, *The Analytical Lexicon to the Greek New Testament*, 317.

248. Frame, *Doctrine of God*, 73.

predicament. She shows that narcissism is indeed a major spiritual aberration manifested throughout human history. It is humanity's pride that has led to humanity's self-destructiveness.[249] Blaise Pascal said:

> Since man has lost the true good everything can appear equally good to him, even his own destruction. . . . Man . . . has plainly gone astray, and fallen from his true place without being able to find it again. He seeks it anxiously and unsuccessfully everywhere in impenetrable darkness.[250]

Sin has been traditionally centered in pride, in self-worship, and self-centeredness, or what is called narcissism. In Sugerman's view, sin and madness epitomize the "universal condition of *narcissism*."[251] She points out that whether we speak of "narcissism," or of the Judeo-Christian "sin of pride," or of Laing's "divided self," we are referring to a "spiritual disorder" of the individual and of all humanity. She says:

> This understanding of the flight from the self as madness and as sin and the resulting despair that issues from this state is a prior condition for its reversal. It is a call for a radical transformation of consciousness—*metanoia*, a total change of mind—which would mean the breaking of the shell of the old false self, the courage to drop the mask, a loss of the self to gain the self, death for there to be rebirth. Rather than a sanity that has been madness, we need a madness that might lead to a true sanity. For this we might give thanks, as for a special grace.[252]

Sugerman points out that Pascal's *Pensées* could have been written for a contemporary publication. She sees Laing echoing Pascal's observation, claiming that our "strategies for survival" stemming from our pride in our self-reliance seem "paradoxically to be leading us deeper into division and closer to self-destruction."[253] It is this human condition that Kierkegaard calls "impotent self-consumption"; a condition where one "cannot get rid of himself," and continues "in the sickness of the self" in deep despair.[254]

249. Sugerman, *Sin and Madness*, 15–16.

250. Pascal, *Pensées*, 425, 427; cited in Sugerman, *Sin and Madness*, 15, 11.

251. Sugerman, *Sin and Madness*, 66, emphasis mine. Interestingly enough, in DSM IV, "Narcissistic Personality Disorder" is identified as a pathological condition requiring medical attention. From the perspective of the Christian biblical tradition, this is the state of the fallen humanity.

252. Ibid., 67.

253. Ibid., 11.

254. Kierkegaard, *Training in Christianity*, 342.

Mankind is moving away from what it claims it values every day. "We preach love and do violence. We speak of peace and make war." We do not see our true selves; we speak a language that is foreign to our motives and our deeds. We claim "progress" and we experience "doom." "We are indeed divided selves in a divided world," says Sugerman. She contends that if mankind continues on the current path, "the survival of man is endangered."[255] In Kierkegaard's thoughts, when one is faced with coping with despair, "every means . . . short of religion, is either unsuccessful or demoniacal."[256]

Becker, speaking of human condition, expresses his puzzlement and disgust with the true nature of man:

> This is a dilemma that I have been caught in, along with many others who have been trying to keep alive the Enlightenment tradition of a science of man: how to reflect the empirical data on man, the data that show what a horribly destructive creature he has been throughout his history, and yet still have a science that is not manipulative or cynical. If man is as bad as he seems, then either we have to behaviorally coerce him into the good life or else we have to abandon the hope of a science of man entirely.[257]

The question is whether the symbols spoken through evil in general—as claimed by Ricoeur[258]—and madness in particular would succeed to force humanity into hearing? The German philosopher, Friedrich Nietzsche, wrote that "to have lost God means madness; and when mankind will discover that it has lost God, universal madness will break out."[259] If Nietzsche is right, then madness is a manifestation of true darkness, life without a sense of God. Could that be the reason that looking at madness makes us scared and insecure? Could it be because it reminds us unconsciously of the destructive darkness that indwells the fallen humanity? According to Laing, a person's separation from the "Presence" of God, directed by one's "ego," is true madness. That is why he calls our time an "age of darkness"; this is the "state of sin," when all are estranged "from the *inner light*."[260] In

---

255. Sugerman, *Sin and Madness*, 11, 13.

256. Barrett, *Irrational Man*, 169.

257. Becker, *Escape from Evil*, xvii–xviii.

258. Ricœur, *The Symbolism of Evil*, 348–56.

259. Kaufman, *Nietzsche*, 81; cited in Sugerman, *Sin and Madness*, 17.

260. Laing, *The Politics of Experience*, 115–17.

the biblical tradition sin is abiding in the state of darkness—a state of law-lessness and "moral evil," says Frame.[261] The "symbolism of sin" in Scrip-ture denotes a "disruption in man's relationship to God." Sin is when one turns to "false gods," which is "nothingness" leading to death.[262]

According to Sugerman, there is now a view of madness that cor-roborates the traditional concept of sin, but expresses it in a different form. This view understands madness not as pathology "but as the equivalent of sin—*a disorder of the spirit*—a disruption of man's fundamental rela-tionship to existence."[263] Likewise, Paul David Tripp claims, "Sin is the ultimate disease, the grand psychosis."[264] One cannot escape from it or defeat it on his own power. It is the source of all pain, suffering, disease, despair, and death. Sugerman claims that the interpretation of madness as sin heightens our self-understanding; it is a portrait that reveals us to ourselves. Moreover, the image of Narcissus helps us to see ourselves more vividly. Ernest Becker wrote about the idea of narcissism:

> [T]his idea is one of Freud's great and lasting contributions. Freud discovered that each of us repeats the tragedy of mythical Greek Narcissus: *we are hopelessly absorbed with ourselves.* If we care about anyone it is usually ourselves first of all . . . we feel that practically everyone is expendable except ourselves.[265]

It is good to remember, after all, that Narcissus died of that self-absorption. Sugerman notes that his myth is a "profound and penetrating comment on the human dilemma." She says:

> Narcissus, as a metaphor for the human condition—for our sin, our madness—takes us to that deeper level, that originat-ing point, at which the self divides and at which its intentions diverge, on the one hand grasping love and life, while on the other hand, in that very gesture, embracing death. Narcissism is that sin and that madness by which we unwittingly descend into that nonbeing in which we "love" ourselves to death.[266]

Narcissus presents us with a grim portrait of one who is highly de-tached, inaccessible, and self-sufficient, but none of that suffices to sustain

261. Frame, *Doctrine of God*, 168, 296.

262. Sugerman, *Sin and Madness*, 17.

263. Ibid., emphasis mine.

264. Tripp, *Instruments in the Redeemer's Hands*, 12.

265. Becker, *The Denial of Death*, 2. Emphasis mine.

266. Sugerman, *Sin and Madness*, 22.

him. His image expresses the "self-encapsulation" and "anguish" that is the outcome of failure to experience love. As Narcissus pleads with his image not to reject him to no avail—resulting in a "sense of worthlessness and of rage turned inward"—humankind is faced with the dilemma of self-rejection in the midst of its self-love. This creates an inability to be one with oneself in harmony, resulting in a "divided self." For Narcissus and also for humanity, self-love points to death.[267]

Sugerman, comparing Kierkegaard to Laing, finds similarity in their perspectives. Man in separation from God and his source of existence becomes "ontologically insecure," living "in exile," as Laing observed. In dread he is "shut up," said Kierkegaard. Narcissus/human, "in dread of rejection," and "in terror of abandonment," falls into a state of nonbeing, which is referred to as "sin" by Kierkegaard and "madness" by Laing.[268]

Humanity has been warned for centuries that his pride is leading him to death. Robert Payne says:

> [W]e are witless against pride, and it is time that our wits should be gathered together, before it is too late. We have seen pride ride like a winter wind . . . bringing in its train the evil Nemesis; and though the theologians thundered against it, and the tragic poets saw the vision of the darkness ahead, no one could ever banish it entirely from men's hearts. . . . We live in a world where the flame may consume us all. Pride . . . haunts us and may haunt us forever, though we are beginning to learn the nature of the penalty which must be paid—the evidence lies all around us in a world in ruins.[269]

There is no more shocking depiction of the penalty of sin than the torment of madness—the experience of hell. Indeed, the most awesome portrayal of madness in Scripture is the story of Nebuchadnezzar, king of Babylon, who, intoxicated with a sense of pride and self exultation, proclaimed, "Is this not Babylon the great, which I myself have built as a royal residence by the might of my power and for the glory of my majesty?" (Dan 4:30). As a result of this inordinate display of self-esteem, he became the target of God's discipline. He was driven mad, away from humankind, "and began eating grass like cattle. . . . His hair had grown like eagles' feathers and his nails like birds' claws" (Dan 4:33). His insanity continued for seven years, Scripture explains, until by God's grace he lifted up his eyes towards

267. Ibid.

268. Ibid., 23.

269. Payne, *Hubris, a Study of Pride*, 312; cited in Sugerman, *Sin and Madness*, 24.

heaven and recognized "that the Most High is ruler over the realm of mankind" (Dan 4:32). Nebuchadnezzar was not only blinded with self-absorption, but reflected the pride of his nation, "BABYLON THE GREAT, THE MOTHER OF HARLOTS AND OF THE ABOMINATIONS OF THE EARTH" (Rev 17:5). In the biblical tradition pride has been the root of all sins and "abominations"; for it is the pride of Adam and Eve that triggered their longing to be "like God" (Gen 3:5). In madness we stand denuded and glare at the frightening abyss of pride—self-absorption—and its destructive fruits. Calvin saw man's pride as his greatest hidden enemy: "For we always seem to ourselves righteous and upright and wise and holy—this pride is innate in all of us—unless by clear proofs we stand convinced of our own unrighteousness, foulness, folly, and impurity."[270]

When the grace of God "in its more active operation" is withdrawn for a period of time even from the best Christian, says Spurgeon, "there is enough of sin in his heart to make him the worst of transgressors." This is what happens in madness. We are "darkness itself," says Spurgeon, when "the Sun of Righteousness" hides his light from us.[271] It is in the hiddenness of God that humanity comes to know its true self. Proverbs 16:18 says: "Pride goes before destruction and a haughty spirit before stumbling." Spurgeon warns that "a proud heart is the prophetic prelude of evil." Thus, it is the enemy of pride that must be conquered at any cost, so that the human person can taste the true abundant life that he has been promised in Christ. "If we forget to live at the foot of the cross in deepest lowliness of spirit," says Spurgeon, "God won't forget to make us feel the pain of His rod."[272]

Sugerman's thesis is that pride does not reflect an "inordinate, exaggerated self-love," but rather, a "self-hatred" and "self-destruction." The apparent self-idolatry that manifests as "self-encapsulation," she believes, is to guard against an "overwhelming sense of worthlessness." She points to Kierkegaard's understanding of sin based on biblical tradition to confirm her interpretation. She reads Kierkegaard's definition of sin in terms of "self-destruction."[273] In a psychological analysis of the "self," Kierkegaard portrays pride as a mask, which conceals the fear of a destiny worse than death—the "sickness unto death." This sickness results from a dread of being "a nothing" before God. One can be "saved" from this sickness and be

---

270. Calvin, *Institutes*, 1/1.2.

271. Spurgeon, *Morning and Evening*, 363.

272. Ibid., 133.

273. Sugerman, *Sin and Madness*, 26–27.

brought back to health only by God's grace and his love. In the Christian understanding, death is a transition to life; thus, no earthly bodily sickness leads to death. Death might be the "last phase of sickness," but for a Christian, death is not the last thing. When Kierkegaard refers to "sickness unto death" he points to "despair" where the last thing is truly "death."[274]

Laing sees the same phenomenon as "ontological insecurity," which is wrapped in "madness." Sugerman stresses that "[i]n the works of both Kierkegaard and Laing, sin and madness emerge as ways of understanding pride."[275] Indeed, "schizophrenia" is about self-absorption, attempting to hang onto oneself, struggling to save oneself, but in reality moving toward destruction. Both sin and madness reflect separation from God, confusion, darkness, uncleanness, hopelessness, inability to love and to be loved, a sense of abandonment and loneliness. For Kierkegaard, "At the center of the sickness of the psyche is a sickness of the spirit," says Barrett.[276] Sugerman contends that religion and psychology meet in Kierkegaard's analysis of the "sickness of the human spirit," and in Laing whose analysis of the same phenomenon points to the "sickness of the psyche."[277]

Humankind has moved away from its source of life. "[M]an is a being who must *become* who he is," says Sugerman. His progress and growth "is not instinctive"; man avoids "becoming."[278] Sin is not a particular "misdeed," but it is the state man is in. As Augustine said, *non posse non peccare*—"Not able not to sin."[279] The self runs away from becoming the true self, and it "defends his unfree mode of being," in a state of bondage to sin. "The self holds on desperately to the bondage it is in" and refuses to burst into freedom, "because the good threatens him with self-destruction." He does not know that it is exactly this "unauthentic self" that he must give away to gain his true self.[280] This is what Kierkegaard calls "demoniacal personality." Pointing to the demons' reaction when faced with Jesus in the New Testament, Kierkegaard says, "The demoniacal becomes thoroughly evident only when it is touched by the good, which now comes to its confines from the outside." The demoniacal personality attempts to

---

274. Kierkegaard and Bretall, *A Kierkegaard Anthology*, 339–71.

275. Sugerman, *Sin and Madness*, 28.

276. Barrett, *Irrational Man*, 170.

277. Sugerman, *Sin and Madness*, 28.

278. Ibid., 28–29.

279. Monergism, "Augustine's Doctrine of the Bondage of the Will," para. 1.

280. Sugerman, *Sin and Madness*, 33–34.

get rid of good at any cost; because the good is after the destruction of the demoniac.[281] This is a reaction that is easily seen in those suffering from "schizophrenia": they run away from love. Laing explains: "A schizophrenic patient would not allow anyone to touch her."[282] The demonic forces at play inside the person are threatened by *love*; that is exactly why *love* is the only weapon that can overcome this enemy.

Kierkegaard's dread brings the possibility of freedom. It is only through faith that dread becomes "absolutely educative." Through its intensity, dread consumes all trivial concerns that are peripheral to the search for true self; it lays bare their deceptions. Thus, one is granted the possibility of *becoming* who he was created to be.[283] "A commitment to selfhood requires a dying away to immediacy, that is, a *shedding of his old self*," says Sugerman. This essentially means suffering: the giving up of immediate desires and dreams as an admission of surrender to God as the One who will define the purpose of one's life. At this state one is faced with his own impotence, that he "can do absolutely nothing of himself," and realizes that he is "nothing before God." Through this sense of resignation, and the awareness of his impotence, he discovers his helplessness and need for God; and in this realization he is made conscious of being a sinner.[284] This is the portrait of madness: a picture of complete impotence and incompetence. As Calvin said, "Thus, from the feeling of our own ignorance, vanity, poverty, infirmity, and—what is more—depravity and corruption" one comes to realize that "full abundance of every good, and purity . . . rest in the Lord alone."[285]

In madness, the self sheds successive layers of its hiddenness; it becomes transparent. This is a crisis, because as Kierkegaard puts it, it is a negation of a previous self—the false self that has become the accepted norm. This struggle is very painful, but the "deeper self . . . knows that this sickness is not unto death, but unto life."[286] It is the fatality of pride that has to be defeated, and the tragic paradox is that the more the self defends itself to stay who it is, the closer it gets to real death. To destroy pride is to recall the self to the faith that one needs God at all cost, because

---

281. Kierkegaard, *Kierkegaard's the Concept of Dread*, 106.

282. Laing, *The Divided Self*, 99.

283. Kierkegaard, *Kierkegaard's the Concept of Dread*, 139.

284. Sugerman, *Sin and Madness*, 39–41. Emphasis mine.

285. Calvin, *Institutes*, 1/1.1.

286. Sugerman, *Sin and Madness*, 42.

ultimately God is *love*. The picture without God is complete nothingness and chaos—the picture of madness.

Schizoid condition, the narcissistic self-entrapment, the inability to love and to receive love, says Sugerman, is the "condition in all of us." In the same way that Scripture tells us that every person is a sinner, Sugerman says, "In the schizophrenia of the human spirit we all participate in differing degrees." The "schizophrenia" of the human spirit is our state of sinfulness. Is there any hope for man's narcissism to receive treatment? Freud said no! Scripture points to Christ as the only hope for humankind. Indeed, "schizophrenia"—what Sugerman calls "the narcissistic disorder par excellence"—informs us about our true selves.[287] Sugerman is not alone in this assessment. W. Ronald Fairbairn, the famous Scottish psychiatrist, says, "according to my way of thinking, everybody without exception must be regarded as schizoid."[288] He believes "*the basic position in the psyche is invariably a schizoid position.*" This would not hold true, of course, in the case of a "theoretically perfect person whose development had been optimum"; but indeed there is "nobody who enjoys such a happy lot."[289]

Erich Fromm joins these voices in the belief that we all suffer a "pathology of normalcy," which is equivalent to a "chronic low-grade schizophrenia." He contends that the pathology of contemporary society is "alienation, anxiety, loneliness, the fear of feeling deeply, lack of activeness, lack of joy." These symptoms have taken over everyone's lives.[290] Ernest Becker goes farther and asserts that "schizophrenia" is the exaggerated form of the human condition:

> [T]he psychotic uses blatantly, openly, and in an exaggerated way the same kind of thought-defenses that most people use wishfully, hiddenly, and in a more controlled way. . . . In this sense the psychoses are a caricature of the life styles of all of us—which is probably part of the reason that they make us so uncomfortable.[291]

287. Ibid., 138, 144.

288. Fairbairn, *Psychoanalytic Studies of the Personality*, 7.

289. Ibid., 8.

290. Fromm, *The Crisis of Psychoanalysis*, 41.

291. Becker, *The Denial of Death*, 218.

It is the "hypersensitive" nature of these individuals that makes them portray the human condition in such a striking way. They absorb everything around them onto their spirit and reverberate it back. Becker says:

> The schizophrenic . . . relies . . . on a hypermagnification of mental process. . . . Schizophrenia takes the risk of evolution to its furthest point in man: the risk of creating an animal who perceives himself, reflects on himself. . . . [His]symbolic awareness floats at maximum intensity all by itself. This is really a cursed animal in evolution, an animal gone astray beyond natural limits. We cannot imagine an animal completely open to experience and to his own anxieties, an animal utterly without programmed neurophysical reactivity to segments of the world. Man alone achieves this terrifying condition which we see in all its purity at the extremes of schizophrenic psychosis. . . . No wonder this "disease" is the one that most intrigues and fascinates man. . . . It represents neurotic openness carried to its extreme of helplessness. . . . [T]his is what cultural man everywhere strove to achieve. . . . [The schizophrenic] see[s] that the fabrications of those around [him] are a lie, a denial of truth—a truth that usually takes the form of showing the terror of the human condition more fully than most men experience it.[292]

Becker's words are harsh and heart-wrenching. He intends them to be this strong to point at the ignorance and the blindness of humanity. The Preacher declares concerning the sons of men: "God has surely tested them in order for them to see that they are but beasts" (Eccl 3:18). There is no more revealing test to expose the extent of humanity's self-absorption and self destruction than madness. Becker considers "neurosis" as the "clinical" expression of the entirety of the human condition: "Men are naturally neurotic and always have been, but at some times they have it easier than at others to mask their true condition, . . . The "cure" for neurosis is difficult in our time."[293] He sees this difficulty centered on man's rejection of traditional view of God and sin. He sees the "classical sinner" and the "modern neurotic" as one and the same:

> [B]oth of them experience the naturalness of human insufficiency, only today the neurotic is stripped of the symbolic world-view, the God-ideology that would make sense out of his unworthiness. . . . Traditional religion turned the consciousness of sin into a condition for salvation; but the tortured sense of

292. Ibid., 219–20.
293. Ibid., 198.

> nothingness of the neurotic qualifies him now only for miserable extinction, for merciful release in lonely death. It is all right to be nothing vis-à-vis God, who alone can make it right in His unknown ways; it is another thing to be nothing to oneself, who is nothing.[294]

Becker points out that the neurotic person suffers from a consciousness of sin, regardless of what labels he may use for his experience of self. He shares the same existential predicament with his religious ancestors, without believing in the concept of sin and the hope of salvation out of his torment. Indeed, this makes it a sad and "neurotic" state. "Thus the plight of modern man," says Becker, is that he is "a sinner with no word for it," or even worse, "who looks for the word for it in a dictionary of psychology."[295] It is this neurotic, schizophrenic sense of abandonment and separateness of humanity from his Creator, substituting self-love for God's love that leaves us in exile.

Foucault says, "sane man could read in the madman, as in a mirror, the imminent movement of his downfall."[296] The question is who "has the ears to hear" the sound of the trumpet, and "who has the eyes" to perceive the depth of darkness in humanity when it is totally unmasked. Where are the pierced repentant hearts that would take the "burden" upon themselves, respond to the call, and run to the throne of grace to receive mercy? This is the voice of "schizophrenia": a true picture of sin—the unmasked, naked state of the fallen humanity.

The Role of Demonic Forces

If what we have argued is true, and "schizophrenia" is the depiction of sin in its intensity, then surely evil must play a role in this illness. That is a role that has not gone unnoticed by those who have encountered this phenomenon. The assumption in the mind of many Christians is that there is a link between a psychiatric illness and "demon possession." This is mostly because in the New Testament, the closest analogy to what is understood as madness is the dire conditions described in relation to those possessed by demons, and Jesus' effective deliverance of them was a symbol of the coming of the Kingdom (Matt 8:28–34, 12:28; Mark 5:1–20;

294. Ibid., 197.

295. Ibid., 198.

296. Foucault, *Madness and Civilization*, 248.

Luke 8:26–39). However, for many interpreters, the hermeneutical challenge of linking scientifically defined illnesses in the twenty-first century to demonic maladies encountered by Jesus and his disciples in the ancient world is difficult to overcome. In addition to hermeneutical difficulties, some psychiatrists and psychologists are disposed to align Jesus and religious beliefs more with those things "that contribute to mental illness" than with their therapeutic benefits.[297] On the other hand, because of the failure of the current treatments, some mental health workers are showing interest in the role of demonic concepts in the treatment of those suffering from severe mental illnesses—albeit, in most cases such enquiries point to "figurative, metaphorical 'demons'—mental, emotional or psychological traumas, memories or 'complexes.'"[298] Consequently, this issue is essential to any theological analysis of insanity. This is significant because Jesus' encounters with demons in Gospel accounts build up a narrative that integrates the nature of evil, the nature of the fallen humanity, and God's redemptive work in his creation.[299]

In regards to demonic activity in the Scripture, scholars typically entertain three possibilities:

1) It was common for people to attribute to demons diseases and unusual behavior because of their pre-scientific worldview, and their inability to explain and understand the root causes of illness.

2) Demon possession was a phenomenon limited to biblical times and for the purposes of Jesus and the apostolic ministries; these have ended, because there is no need for them anymore.

3) Demonic attacks still occur in our times as they did in biblical times.[300]

Matthew Stanford, a Christian neuroscientist, responds to these positions. In his view, the first option is problematic, because it causes one "to question Jesus' integrity (and perhaps his divinity), since he believed that

---

297. Stuckenbruck, "The Human Being and Demonic Invasion," 96–97.

298. Diamond, "The Devil Inside"; Diamond, a clinical and forensic psychologist, points out that "Hippocrates, the father of western medicine, was originally a trained exorcist. . . . Exorcism can be said to be the prototype of modern psychotherapy." He encourages his peers to pay attention to the "vital existential and spiritual questions addressed by exorcism."

299. Stuckenbruck, "The Human Being and Demonic Invasion," 104.

300. Stanford, Grace for the Afflicted, 33–34.

demons were at work." In response to the second point, he believes there is some truth to the fact that exorcism was a major component of Jesus' ministry as a sign of inbreaking of the kingdom of God. However, at no point in the New Testament is there any indication that "demonic activity would cease with the apostolic age." In contrast, there is a great emphasis on "the evil schemes of Satan and his demonic cohorts" against the church (Eph 6:11–12; 1 Pet 5:8; 2 Cor 2:10–11). Many of the church fathers, including Ignatius, Justin Martyr, Tertullian, Origen, and Athanasius, made a great effort to warn the church about demonic activity.[301]

Ronald Roschke points to Corpus Hippocraticum (CH), a compendium of medical knowledge from the Mediterranean region, for insights into the cultural contexts for healing in the ancient world. Some parts of this massive work date back to the fourth century BCE, but its completion is believed to have happened during the first or second century CE. Roschke rejects the notion that "demon possession" was the byproduct of the ancient people's ignorance about science. He suggests that the "CH shares a modern conviction that issues of illness and health can be understood . . . through observation and treatment; the approach is empirical, not supernatural." Thus he argues that ancient people could have easily analyzed illnesses without reference to demonic possession; thereby, the presence of such biblical references suggests the veracity of such phenomena.[302]

In regards to the third suggestion, Stanford believes that "demon possession" is an impossibility for those who are born-again Christians. These people belong to Christ and Satan cannot "possess" their souls. He points out that exorcism and deliverance prayers may still be appropriate for non-believers, in an effort to lead them to faith in Christ. However, Stanford suggests that it is still very common for all people, in and out of the Christian realm, to suffer from illnesses that are "demonically caused." He points out the difficulty—"if not outright impossibility"—of differentiating the original cause of an illness. This is because all illnesses will have

301. Ibid. Stanford does not address the possibility that Jesus, in his humanity, might have not known certain things and might have just spoken within the cultural norms of the time. See also Athanasius and Gregg, *The Life of Antony and the Letter to Marcellinus.* The *Life* of the hermit-monk Antony is a spiritual classic written by Athanasius; it is a vivid portrayal of how the beloved monk battled demonic attacks.

302. Roschke, "Healing in Luke, Madagascar, and Elsewhere," 461, 465. It was shown in chapter 2 that humoral theories of Hippocrates were pervasive in the medical science beginning from the fourth century BC. Medicine was then excluding the supernatural influences and health and illness could only be understood in naturalistic terms.

some physical manifestation, and consequently the medical community has no choice but "to treat all sickness the same." The healing process can always include prayer for the afflicted in addition to medical treatment.[303] Roschke, who believes demonic influences should be considered when illnesses are encountered, is alarmed by the Westerners' creation of opposition between scientific and spiritual healing, and he sees it as an impediment to wholesome healing.[304]

Vernon McCasland contends that those "disorganizations of the mind," which are called "neuroses" or "psychoses" by our modern psychiatric terminology, are the same phenomena that the "ancients" called demon possession.[305] He believes these terminology differences are the realities of evolution of language and culture. "The scientifically trained student" must not be concerned with "names or vocabulary," because they "change radically" across ages. What is of essential interest is the mental phenomena that continues to challenge humanity. McCasland claims that the contemporary analysis of mental illness provides a "graphic psychological description" to what was experienced in demon possession. The phenomena of personality are identical, but the vocabularies have changed. "The exorcist means by demon possession what the psychiatrist means by mental illness and what the layman means by insanity," says McCasland. He goes on to argue that the person who was labeled as "demon possessed" in earlier times, would today be "in our psychiatric clinics or in other institutions for the mentally ill."[306] What McCasland appears to have neglected is the fact that biblical demonic presentations reflected an invasive existence of a *foreign* being within the person's soul outside of his control, whereas contemporary mental health sciences focus on inner issues within the person himself, whose agency is a factor toward his recovery.[307]

---

303. Stanford, *Grace for the Afflicted*, 34–35.

304. Roschke, "Healing in Luke, Madagascar, and Elsewhere," 466–67.

305. McCasland, *By the Finger of God*, 26. Gaiser shares similar perspective with some caveat: "In fact . . . many, perhaps most, of what the New Testament names specifically as exorcisms would be diagnosed today as cases of 'mental illness' or spiritual or emotional disorder." It appears that he bundles mental, spiritual and emotional disorders as potentially caused by demons. However, he guards against linking the two at all times. Gaiser, *Healing in the Bible*, 135, 136 n. 10.

306. McCasland, *By the Finger of God*, 8, 27.

307. For an exposition of the biblical texts to demonstrate that *demonic possession involves the entry of an external spirit into the human body*, see Stuckenbruck, "The Human Being and Demonic Invasion."

McCasland states that ideas of demon possession in early centuries "often had the same respectable standing" that "theories of science" enjoy today. The practice of "casting out demons" was clearly a "reputable profession" that has been replaced by psychiatry. "The exorcist also was a physician; it was his function to cure disease," says McCasland. What is irreconcilable about McCasland's analysis is that he considers exorcism to be involved in "the control of supernatural powers"; and yet he equates it with psychotherapy because he believes "the feeling which accompanied the spell itself provided the psychological basis for the cure."[308] In other words, it was the psychological effect of "autosuggestion" that eliminated the demons. He clearly considers these "supernatural powers" as very obedient entities! It seems he reached that conclusion because in all cases in Scripture demons were cast out simply by a command from Jesus or the apostles.

Oesterreich, based on his extensive research of "demon possession" around the globe across the centuries, makes similar claims to McCasland. He is pleasantly surprised by the "perfect similarity of the facts" between biblical stories and his research findings. He remarks that this causes his "respect for the historic truth of the Gospels" to be enhanced to an "extraordinary degree." Based on his studies, he considers the related biblical narratives to be "entirely realistic" and of an "objective character."[309] He contends that the great difference between the modern mental illness and the old states of possession are purely psychological. "Viewed from outside," says Oesterreich, "the states are similar"; but from the psychological perspective, they are directly related to the attitude of the individual. In most cases today, patients believe that these attacks are "natural phenomena" and "pathological manifestations." Formerly—or even in cases of certain religious traditions today—the idea of possession "supervened" and influenced the person and occasioned the possibility of demonic influences. He believes the "appearance of possession," is "always" associated with "the belief in the devil." He considers the belief itself—by means of "autosuggestion"—actually nourishes possession and sustains it.[310]

---

308. McCasland, *By the Finger of God*, 13, 17–18.

309. Oesterreich and Ibberson, *Possession, Demoniacal and Other*, 4–5. Professor Oesterreich of the University of Tubingen has made an extensive survey of the history of possession from the most ancient times down to the twentieth century. Additionally, he presents a thorough survey of the existing literature on this topic in the beginning of the twentieth century.

310. Ibid., 127, 121.

It is not quite clear how Oesterreich can judge the veracity of assaults by the devil based on people's personal beliefs. As Stanford suggested earlier, it is impossible for people to know the first cause of their illness. In fact, it is never technically correct to categorize illnesses as caused by the devil, or by natural causes, since from the Christian perspective the original cause is always God, and it will always have some sort of natural manifestation. Oesterreich claims that with the age of Enlightenment, the belief in spirits lost its power among the "civilized races." In his view, this has caused the concept of possession to disappear. He attributes this to the fact that from the moment humans cease to entertain seriously the possibility of being possessed, "the necessary autosuggestion is lacking." According to him, manifestation of possession is in regression around the world even among "primitive peoples" where Christian missions have been influential. From his perspective, this is because Christianity inspires people with trust in God and frees them "from the fear of demons and their attacks on the souls of the living."[311]

Andrew Sims, a Christian psychiatrist who has worked on "diocesan teams for deliverance ministry in the Church of England," claims there is no "obvious" relationship between psychiatric disorders and demon possession. He admits that he is influenced by the Western "rationalism," because that is the "atmosphere" he lives in. At the same time, he stresses the importance for psychiatrists to take seriously how the person explains his experience of illness. He draws on a research conducted on exorcism to point out that "possession" is not as widespread as some make it; "it cannot just 'happen' unwittingly." This is not like a "common cold" that someone can "catch" unknowingly. He believes it only happens to those who put themselves in "a vulnerable position," by membership in certain cults or by personal invitation "from a despairing will."[312]

Sims believes that those who see demons everywhere are in danger of abdicating their personal responsibility by believing that all wrongs are always the fault of demons. He admits that cases of possession happen to non-Christians, but he advises against any exorcism for a "Christian believer who has never intended to have dealings with the devil nor given himself over to a deliberate way of life of evil." Sims, like Oesterreich, argues that in these cases the exorcism not only does not "reassure the subject," but due to "auto-suggestion" it may have the opposite effect and

---

311. Ibid., 378–79.

312. Sims, *Is Faith Delusion?*, 168–69, 175.

reinforce the person's belief about demonic possession and intensify his illness.[313]

To corroborate his position in support of medical nature of most mental illnesses, Sims points to a statement by John Bavington, a Christian psychiatrist, who worked in Pakistan for many years. Bavington writes:

> Attitudes to psychiatry have ranged from a dogmatic condemnation of the subject (psychiatry) as "of the Devil" to a rather cautious and reserved acknowledgement of its place and value. These (negative) attitudes . . . [are] strong among missionaries influenced more by prevailing local view of mental disturbance as "evil" or "satanic." . . . While not wishing to deny the possibility of spirit possession, from my experience of many years in Pakistan I can hardly think of a single case of alleged possession which could not, at the same time, and from a psychiatric perspective, be recognized as either epilepsy, hysteria, schizophrenia or, more rarely, some other diagnostic category. Making such a diagnosis does not, of course, exclude other possible levels of etiology.[314]

As Bavington admits himself, the etiologies of these diseases are not known. It is hard to argue with certainty that there is no demonic power behind any of these or other diseases, merely because psychiatry has chosen to name certain phenomena by specific labels. In fact, Sims himself points out that "all disease is evil," and one cannot argue for the presence of demonic power behind psychiatric disorder any more than physical illness.[315] Sims is indeed correct; Scripture clearly points out to some physical maladies caused by the devil (Luke 13:11; Matt 9:32–33). Müller notes that Scripture makes a distinction between illnesses that might be "externally caused" by demons—usually treated with the means of Jesus' touch or the application of some kind of remedy—in contrast to the phenomenon where "the demon dwells in the sick person"—in this case they need to be driven out by the power of God.[316] Moreover, Scripture is very clear that the deception of the devil targets one's mind to turn him away from God. Paul told the church in Corinth: "I am afraid lest as the serpent deceived Eve by his craftiness, your minds should be led astray" (2 Cor

---

313. Ibid., 175, 179.

314. Ibid., 168.

315. Ibid., 188.

316. Seybold and Müller, *Sickness and Healing*, 149; cited in Gaiser, *Healing in the Bible*, 134.

11:3). In Scripture, the mind—also referred to as the heart—is the seat of one's consciousness. Jesus said: "From within, out of the heart of men, proceed the evil thoughts" (Mark 7:21). The devil attacks the mind with lies and accusations to drive the person into despair and destruction (John 8:44).

Larchet explains that certain mental illnesses are purely somatic; they can be caused by ailments intrinsic to the body and cause hallucination, delirium, or other psychic manifestations. But in all those cases the physical ailment can be detected through medical technologies and clearly categorized by their markers. "The psychiatric symptoms that present themselves in such cases are not disorders of the soul except from a very superficial point of view," says Larchet. These disorders are diseases of the body. The diseases of the soul are either of demonic or of spiritual origins. He distinguishes between the two with the former being applied through instrumentation of demonic powers, and the latter coming directly from God for the purpose of sanctification.[317]

Larchet points to the story of the demon possessed Gadarenes, as a clear example of insanity (Matt 8:28–34; Mark 5:1–20; and Luke 8:26–39). He sees a similarity between that case and what many saints have experienced in the history of the church. However, due to a lack of precision and brevity of descriptions, it is difficult to classify them according to the current complex nosological categories of psychopathology. Larchet, like Roschke, objects to the common understanding today that "the attribution of demonic cause to certain forms of insanity" by the fathers was due to the inability of the medical knowledge of that time to determine natural causes. He points out that this "is to forget that medicine contemporaneous to the Patristic writings . . . envisioned things according to the same natural perspective as modern psychiatry, and just like the latter, left no place for demonic etiologies."[318]

Medicine chooses to ignore demonic causes; its scientific methodology is obligated to deny supernatural realms. Larchet emphasizes the point that though demonic actions are spiritual in nature, it is "widely expressed in the domain of the senses and can therefore be clinically apprehended by its effects." Moreover, demonic etiologies can easily be confused with organic diseases, since their manifestation is "in bodily disorders which, externally, look like standard illnesses."[319] For example, the

317. Larchet, *Mental Disorders*, 34, 39, 44ff., 89ff.

318. Ibid., 45–47; Larchet points out that many of the monks were among the most educated men of their time, even in the field of medicine.

319. Ibid., 47.

fact that neuroimaging technologies may show some "abnormal" activity in the brain by itself cannot justify a brain disease. The activity may easily be the byproduct of anxiety, confusion, and chaos induced through demonic influences.

Larchet explains that demons seek to damage the soul by working through the body and the brain. This is what makes the etiological recognition very difficult. St. John Cassian provides the following details:

> When an unclean spirit makes its way into those organs in which the soul's vigor is contained, [it] imposes an unbearable and immeasurable weight on them, and overwhelms the intellectual faculties and deeply darkens their understanding.[320]

Again, Larchet stresses that one of the greatest challenges in detecting demonic attacks is the notion that "the devil engenders psychic disturbances by provoking disturbances in the organism itself." This is why the temptation is there to see the etiology as purely psychological, or because of the "organic factors" that are observable, they could be mistaken for a physical illness. In these cases, usually some treatments of "a purely physiological nature" are applied by the psychiatrist. Such treatments could result in improvement in physical symptoms, by affecting the physical organs involved. "But these organs are only mediators," says Larchet, for this treatment "only modifies the symptoms of the disease." Larchet, like Sims, Stanford, and others, affirms that it is extremely difficult to determine the influence of demonic forces. He points to the teaching of Scripture that this can only be done through the gift of a discerning Spirit (1 Cor 12:10). He is comforted knowing that this is "allowed by God," and through it the individual is "spiritually fortified"; this is the privileged path to "spiritual progress" and "divine blessings" and "purification," that cannot be otherwise achieved.[321] Likewise, Piper believes that "GOD GOVERNS SATAN'S EVERY MOVE . . . And therefore every move of Satan is part of God's overall purpose and plan."[322]

As Sims acknowledges, the reality is that "all have sinned, and that the devil exerts his influence in subtle and different ways upon everyone."[323] The devil's influence over personal conduct and thoughts are widespread. Jesus says to Peter: "Get behind Me, Satan! You are a stumbling block to

---

320. Cassian and Ramsey, *John Cassian, the Conferences*, 12; cited in Larchet, *Mental Disorders*, 48.

321. Ibid., 48–49, 51–56.

322. Piper, *Spectacular Sins*, 47–48.

323. Sims, *Is Faith Delusion?*, 175.

Me; for you are not setting your mind on God's interests, but man's" (Matt 16:23). Jesus is recognizing that Peter is trying to keep him from obedience to his Father's plan to die on the cross. Peter is acting out the desire of Satan who is the source of that opposition. This is an indication that those who are the closest to the will of God, or those who are broken in spirit, are often targets for satanic attacks. Therefore, it behooves us to guard against stigmatizing those who are already under intense suffering, as "demon possessed," and justify their separation from the rest of the society. Gaiser explains;

> Automatically to label those who are mentally ill as "possessed,"
> as indeed has happened through much of history, would be
> the same kind of misuse of biblical terminology, producing the
> same kind of victimization of people, as automatically to label
> those with leprosy as "unclean" even beyond the biblical world.[324]

However, Gaiser's solution around this stigmatization is to appeal to some sort of medicalization. He says, "To identify demonic possession in the modern world in any kind of responsible way requires cooperation with competent medical and psychological therapy." I have already addressed the issue that while medicalizing this phenomenon may help with stigmatization it can also introduce a whole set of new problems. Alternatively, perhaps, the recognition that evil surrounds all of us in this world, and affects the most vulnerable with more intensity, should be the first step toward acceptance and tolerance.[325] Let us not forget that Satan leaves alone those who are already helping his destructive missions (John 8:44; 1 John 3:8). Instead he attacks those who are the most vulnerable and would present a threat to him. Therefore to judge the inherent character of individuals *merely* because they are targets of attacks by the forces of evil is nothing but foolishness and shows theological naïveté.

Contrary to common belief, Larchet points to the positive attitude of the church fathers toward the "possessed/insane" among them. These people were usually not considered as "someone subject to divine chastisement," but "someone undergoing a trial authorized by God in order to purify him and bring him to a superior spiritual state."[326] This is an intense

---

324. Gaiser, *Healing in the Bible*, 136 n. 10.

325. Paul reminds the church in Ephesus that the root of all its struggles is in the spiritual realm; Eph 6:12.

326. Larchet, *Mental Disorders*, 57.

"mortification" of flesh, as both Owen and Calvin discussed.[327] Larchet points to Paul's writing to the Corinthians: "I have decided to deliver such a one to Satan for the destruction of his flesh, that his spirit may be saved in the day of the Lord Jesus" (1 Cor 5:5). If the process is allowed to take its natural course, and the person is cared for with love and prayer, he comes out the other side as a truly transformed human, embarking on a path of *metamorphism*. This is the path to union with Christ accomplished only by God's grace. Jesus himself told Peter: "Simon, Simon, behold, Satan has demanded permission to sift you like wheat; but I have prayed for you, that your faith may not fail; and you when once you have turned again, strengthen your brothers" (Luke 22:31–32). It is noteworthy that Jesus does not assure Peter that Satan's request was denied because Peter is so loved by God; rather he encourages him to stay steadfast and faithful in the process.

It is normal for Christians to fear the devil; after all they are warned about his deceptive schemes throughout Scripture. But one must not ignore the significant role of the dominion of darkness in the redemptive narrative of the Bible. Brown, referring to Luther's Christian experience says, "Protestantism was born in the temple of the Devil, and it found God again in extremest alienation from God."[328] An experience of uncontrollable evil that makes man powerless led Luther to confirm with Paul that the devil is "the god of this world" (2 Cor 4:4). Luther said:

> The devil is the lord of the world. Let him who does not know this, try it. I have had some experience of it: but no one will believe me until he experiences it too. . . . We are servants in a hostelry, where Satan is the householder, the world his wife, and our affections his children. . . . Outside of Christ, death and sin are our masters and the devil our god and sovereign, there can be no power or might, no wit or understanding whereby we could make ourselves fit for, or could even strive after, righteousness and life, but on the contrary we must remain blind and captive, slaves of sin and the devil. . . . The devil lets his own do many good works, pray, fast, build churches . . . behave as if he were quite holy and pious.[329]

327. See chapter 1.

328. Brown, *Life Against Death*, 209.

329. Ibid., 211–12.

In Luther's conception of power of the devil, Brown finds seeds of life sown by grace. It is Luther's theology of death-in-life that awakens the hope of eternal life:

> The positive features in Luther are his diabolism and his eschatology. Actually the diabolism and the eschatology are two sides of the same coin. It would be psychically impossible for Luther to recognize the Devil's dominion over this world . . . without the faith that the Devil's dominion is doomed and that the history of man on earth will end in the kingdom of God, when grace will be made visible. . . . Hence the decadence of Protestantism may be measured by the decline of diabolism and eschatology. Theologies (including later Lutheranism) which lack a real sense of the Devil lack Luther's capacity for critical detachment from the world, lack Luther's disposition to fight the Devil, and end by calling the Devil's work God's work. . . . Later Protestantism substituted for Luther's vision that we are bondsmen in the Devil's hostelry the notion that our calling is divinely appointed.[330]

This dismissal of the devil will lead to what Siirala calls a "pale eschatology." If man does not accept the reality of the devil, and trusts the power of his own personal faith, he cannot grasp the need for an eschatological message that points to the kingdom of grace becoming visible. In that context, he "pretends to be outside the sick situation," and denies any struggle with forces of darkness, a.k.a. "devil, sin, and death."[331]

In explaining the devil's role in "schizophrenia," Sugerman notes that it is curious that madness "invokes both the devil . . . and the divine madness," and in reality fuses them both. This is about what God does in the soul through his divine inspiration and revelation, and at the same time, the person has to cross over the unknown dark territories where the demonic spirits dwell. This is truly a spiritual warfare as Jesus had to engage, and of which Paul warned all believers. Sugerman, drawing conclusions from Laing's work, states that what appears to us as "madness" is really a "pseudo madness," just as the sanity of most "normal" people is "pseudo sanity." The therapeutic methods that Laing suggests are rooted in ancient mysticism, which consists of a spiritual journey "into the depths of hell," encountering the "dominion of the devil" as Luther had experienced too. This is a "dangerous and ambiguous quest" to confront and defeat the

---

330. Ibid., 217.

331. Siirala, *The Voice of Illness*, 133.

enigmatic forces of darkness, in order to discover "the treasure of life, a death and rebirth, a transformed consciousness—*metanoia*—a loss of the self to receive the self."[332] Madness, then, may be seen as both a "sickness of spirit" and the essential process for cure. This pseudo madness Laing views as "the possibility of true sanity," one that will take the soul to the realm where it can face reality. For, "when the center will no longer hold, when the will can no longer will the mask of the false self, then that failure of the will becomes the possibility of the breakthrough of the alienated spontaneous self."[333]

But how could this dangerous journey be taken without faith and without God's grace? Laing himself agrees that this radical method is not for everyone, but maybe only for those who are the called. This would be *metanoia*, indeed, a madness that truly kills the false self to all its lusts and desires, and false wisdom and rationality; a madness whose truth might lead to a new birth, "to a true sanity rather than a sanity whose falseness has been madness." Moreover, Laing claims that the radical transformation that takes place in the individual demands major transformation in those in his immediate community. Thus, all have to "consent to changes of a complementary or reciprocal nature" within themselves. Clearly, major change in one person has a ripple effect in the relation of that person and others. In fact, this very one fact may motivate many to consider the individual pathological, rather than to be willing to change themselves.[334]

Teresa of Avila, the famous sixteenth-century Spanish mystic, offers us one of the most vivid portraits of a descent to Hell. She suffered from variety of illnesses and serious mental anguish all her life. Cohen, who translated her autobiography, refers to her as a "hysterically unbalanced woman, who . . . was entirely transformed by profound experiences." She was haunted by persistent hideous visions and experienced hearing inner voices. At times, she was lifted into the air to her own consternation and the amazement of those around her. Additionally, she suffered from physical pain, vomiting, heart-spasms, cramps, and partial paralysis. She was considered by most of her contemporaries to be either insane or possessed by the devil, and yet her "insanity" transformed her into one of the heroes of the Catholic Church. She combined the religious life with one of great public service in the later years of her life. She founded seventeen reformed convents against heavy oppositions, and wrestled successfully

332. Sugerman, *Sin and Madness*, 85.

333. Ibid., 86.

334. Ibid., 87; Laing, "Metanoia: Some Experiences at Kingsley Hall, London," 16.

with church authorities; she was canonized in 1622, and in 1814 she was named "the national saint" of Spain.[335] One of the most memorable experiences of Teresa was when God allowed her to experience Hell. The passage in which she relates her experience is elaborate and dramatic:

> I found myself, without knowing how, plunged, as I thought, into hell. I understood that the Lord wished me to see the place that the devils had ready for me there, and that I had earned by my sins . . . even if I should live for many years, I do not think I could possibly forget it. . . . I do not think that my feelings could possibly be exaggerated, nor would anyone understand them. I felt a fire inside my soul, the nature of which is beyond my powers of description, and my physical tortures were intolerable. I have endured the severest bodily pains in the course of my life, the worst, so the doctors say, that it is possible to suffer and live, among them the contraction of my nerves during my paralysis. . . . But none of them was in anyway comparable to the pains I felt at that time, especially when I realized that they would be endless and unceasing. But even this was nothing to my agony of soul, an oppression, a suffocation, and an affliction so agonizing, and accompanied by such a hopeless and distressing misery that no words I could find would adequately describe it . . . my soul were being continuously torn from my body. . . . I can find no means of describing that inward fire and that despair . . . greater than the severest torments or pains. . . . [I] seemed to feel myself being burnt and dismembered. . . . There is no light there, only the deepest darkness. Yet . . . it was possible to see everything that brings pain . . . it was the Lord's will that I really should feel these torments and afflictions of spirit, just as if my body were actually suffering them. . . . I quite clearly realized that this was *a great favor*, and that the Lord wished me to see with my very eyes the place from which His mercy had delivered me. . . . I can think of no time of trial or torture when everything that we can suffer on earth has not seemed to me trifling in comparison with this . . . this vision was one of the greatest *mercies* that the Lord has bestowed on me. It has *benefited me* very much, both by freeing me from fear of the tribulations and oppositions of this life, and by giving me the strength, whilst bearing them, to give thanks to the Lord, who, *as I now believe*, has delivered me from these continuous and terrible torments.[336]

---

335. Teresa, *The Life of Saint Teresa of Avila*, 1, 12–16, 19.

336. Ibid., 233–34; emphasis mine.

Teresa truly came to taste the grace of God through this experience. It was only after experiencing true darkness that the light of the Lord overtook her life. She was a changed person ready to serve her Lord. Thus, *"as I now believe,"* was her confession of true faith, a gift that finally led her on the way to be united with Christ.

According to John of the Cross, God will allow the devil to enter into a spiritual battle with the soul, by presenting it with images that might be deceiving. This produces "a certain horror and perturbation of spirit which at times is most distressing to the soul." Sometimes, the soul is able to overcome this terror quickly and free itself from the struggle. At other times "the devil prevails" and afflicts the soul in ways that are greater "than any torment in this life could be." Since this is an attack on the spirit, "it is grievous beyond what every sense can feel." All of this will pass without the soul actively doing anything. John stresses that when the devil is given permission to torment the soul, it is solely for the purpose of purifying the soul to prepare it for "some great spiritual favor." For he "never mortifies save to give life, nor humbles save to exalt." The person who endures this horror is granted a "wondrous and delectable" spiritual gift, which is loftier than can be described. This will lead the way to the "Divine union."[337]

These kinds of stories are not unique to former centuries. David Bradford, in his phenomenological investigation of "psychotic" experiences, focuses on those who encountered what they believed to be an experience of God. One of the cases is about Sarah, who had an abusive childhood, a troubling adult life, had worked periodically as a prostitute, and had been hospitalized for severe psychosis and catatonia among other things. She claimed that she was a lukewarm Christian who never took her faith seriously. Sarah believed she started hearing the voices of both God and Jesus, calling her to repentance. Apparently during that period she started being attacked by Satan to prevent her responding to God's call. These attacks consisted of "different physical things" that terrified her. Bradford, who had witnessed some of those physical effects, explains: "Her 'tongue' began 'pulling over to the side, feeling really weird,' and like she was 'going to swallow it,' and causing her to talk periodically with slurred speech." Psychiatrists had no clear explanation for those "symptoms." Sarah's explanation to Bradford was that "Satan was trying to stop her from telling" Bradford about her satanic attacks.[338]

---

337. John of the Cross, *Dark Night*, 105–7.

338. Bradford, *The Experience of God*, 273–76.

Sarah had several visions of "Judgment Day" and actually had a terrifying experience of "Hell." She explains:

> [I]t was like I was half awake and half asleep . . . like dreaming, but I wasn't asleep. Wide awake and having these dreams . . . I was locked inside my body and it was like God showing me what Hell was like. I would be shown what the punishment will be for all the sins I committed against Him all my life. I couldn't move, I couldn't talk, I couldn't do anything, and I was dead on the outside. . . . God locked me inside; I was trapped in my body—for eternity. . . . I was seeing it in my mind, but it was like seeing it with my eyes too.[339]

Her mental experience of Hell was so severe that "sores started breaking out all over Sarah's body." She also "started getting terrible pains in her bones, especially the legs and arms." Sarah understood this "to mean that God 'wanted her to feel the pain and agony his Son went through for her.'" This was a turning point for Sarah, who claimed "I suddenly realized that He loved me—He really loved me." Bradford notes, this experience convinced her that "if there's Hell, there's a heaven, and if there's heaven, there's a God; and if there's a God, then everything in the Bible is true." According to Bradford's research, Sarah had severe physical, mental, and spiritual torments, which finally led her to God and transformed her life.[340] The question here is not to what extent these images were demonic and the result of satanic assaults. The presence of evil is obvious. The more relevant point is that God can use evil for good. Satan may have meant evil against Sarah, but clearly "God meant it for good" (cf. Gen 50:20).

Given the option between the "biomedical understanding of schizophrenia and the spirit possession narrative," says Watters, "most Westerners assume the drier science-bound explanation for the disease would certainly inflame less emotion and stigma."[341] But McGruder's research showed that in Zanzibar, because people accepted the presence of spirits as part of their daily life, it made bizarre or disruptive behavior more understandable, forgivable, and meaningful. Therefore, it also decreased the sense of blame or shame carried by the family or the ill individual. In Zanzibar, it was "widely believed that spirits may take control of human bodies and that all illness, adversity and misfortune are a normal part of

---

339. Ibid., 276–77.

340. Ibid., 273–80.

341. Watters, *Crazy Like Us*, 156–57.

human existence programmed by the Almighty." Thus, when people do not assume that they are in control of all events in their lives, "they do not so deeply fear those who appear to have lost it."[342] It was understood by all that neither the individual nor the family had the ability to effectively control the "blessings and burdens of God" and the "mysteries of the spirit world." The key was that their belief system "kept the sick person within the social group."[343] In fact, instead of being scared, everyone saw symbolic meanings in "schizophrenia":

> In the family's Muslim belief, managing hardships provided a way to pay the debt of sinfulness. Illness or bad turns of fortune were seen as neither arbitrary nor a punishment. Rather, they believed that God's grace awaited those who not only endured suffering but were grateful for the opportunity to prove their ability to endure it.[344]

When people believe in God, the idea that demonic spirits have influence in this world is not an oddity. Indeed, Jesus himself talked about it. Paul, Matthew, Luke among others wrote about it. So it is the "atheist" spirit in us that finds these concepts totally unacceptable. Jesus' ministry could not start until he had encountered the devil and had overcome the temptations thrown at him by the devil. Scripture recounts that Jesus, "full of the Holy Spirit," right after his baptism "was led about by the Spirit" to encounter the devil (Luke 4:1). Grudem claims, "The tactics of Satan and his demons are to use lies (John 8:44), deception (Rev 12:9), murder (Ps 106:37; John 8:44), and every other kind of destructive activity to attempt to cause people to turn away from God and destroy themselves."[345] So demonic activity is not always linked to sin; Grudem says that "since Jesus Himself was severely tempted by Satan," *no Christian is exempt* from such attacks.[346]

Considering the intensity of darkness and the presence of evil in mental illness, it seems naïve and ignorant to reject the influence of demonic spirits. The influences, based on what we have seen, are of variegated nature, but nevertheless they exist. The spectrum of the struggle could range from intense battles as Teresa of Avila or Luther experienced,

342. McGruder, "Life Experience is Not a Disease," 65.

343. Watters, *Crazy Like Us*, 158.

344. Ibid., 154–55.

345. Grudem, *Bible Doctrine*, 176.

346. Ibid., 180 n. 8.

to accusations and deceptions targeting a broken and contrite spirit in its most vulnerable position. One thing is for certain; we cannot fight this battle with aggression and persecution. As Paul said, "Do not be overcome with evil, but overcome evil with good" (Rom 12:21). Calvin referring to this passage stresses that a Christian must always "strive to conquer evil with good."[347] Our evil acts will intensify the forces of darkness, but our expression of love and kindness will disarm the same forces.

As William James noted, "the evil facts . . . are a genuine portion of reality; and they may after all be the best key to life's significance, and possibly the only openers of our eyes to the deepest levels of truth."[348] The question of evil is bound to confront those who encounter mental illness, and regardless of one's denials and white-washing, it has "rational significance."[349] Swinton asserts, "despite frequent encounters with actions and persons often described as 'evil,' mental health carers are not presented with any therapeutic strategies or perspectives that might enable them to understand and deal constructively with evil."[350] This area holds a great potential for the church to demonstrate her leadership in claiming the inbreaking of the kingdom of God by offering practical therapeutic approaches to overcome the forces of darkness. Grudem suggests that since Christ is seated at the right hand of the Father, and the church has been raised and seated with him in heavenly places, then "*we now share in some measure in the authority that Christ has,* authority to contend against 'the spiritual hosts of wickedness in the heavenly places' . . . and to do battle with weapons that 'have divine power to destroy strongholds.'"[351] This is a challenge and a calling for the church.

Summary

In this chapter, we argued that the history of encounter with illness has proven that illnesses demand to be studied from different perspectives. All illnesses bring about both physical and psychological suffering. Moreover, all illnesses create spiritual suffering by exposing the fragility of the human condition. Severe illnesses, such as "schizophrenia," touch us in

347. Calvin, *Institutes,* 4/20.20.

348. James, *The Varieties of Religious Experience,* 152.

349. Ibid., 153.

350. Swinton, "Does Evil have to Exist to be Real?," 20.

351. Grudem, *Bible Doctrine,* 268.

our core and force us to question ourselves, our values, our way of life, our relationship with God and others. Moreover, they can bring us face to face with our inadequacy, and with the lack of control we have over our lives. They humble the spirit like nothing else, forcing an encounter with our own mortality and destroying our false sense of equilibrium. They not only have the power to free us from that innate self-reliance and pride that renders us weak in our walk with God, but also have the force to call the afflicted and those around him to repentance. Therefore, illnesses are both *theological* and *teleological* by nature.

Based on anthropological and theological research, we argued that the encounter with illness has to be communal. For example, common formation of symbols is a significant aspect of a communal encounter with illness. When one hears the voice of illness, it demands one engage in dialogue between one's professed faith and one's performance in life. In the encounter with illness a decisive role is assigned to the family, the church and the community around the person. This is because human beings are organically interrelated to their community—as the members of one's body are organically interrelated.

The church has failed to hear the voices that have arisen in the context of an encounter with illness speaking to the "perversions of our common life."[352] This failure has been most dramatic in dealing with mental illness. We saw in this chapter that the methods of treatment and socially formed presumptions could deafen us to the voice of illness. These studies—principles advocated by Siirala, McGruder, Ramussen, and Kütemeyer—affirm the need for the participation of the community in the milieu of illness and indeed to be willing to receive its prophetic message. This participation will open the gates of healing and bring freedom from "entrapment in a medical epistemology" for understanding madness.[353] With the help of psychotropic drugs psychiatry may remove the "symptoms" of personal disorders; it is, indeed, far easier for a society to depend on medication as the treatment of choice. It requires much less of us as a community. Unfortunately, this will certainly distort the voice of illness, if not completely silence it.

Building on insights drawn from the treatment of "schizophrenia" in different communities, we saw that the illness throws a unique light on the illness of the community character. Those who deal with the "schizophrenic" will realize that they are "a part of that split life which they are

352. Siirala, *The Voice of Illness*, 53.

353. McGruder, "Life Experience is Not a Disease," 77.

encountering." If they refuse to acknowledge "their participation in the milieu of his illness," then healing will be out of reach. Indeed, one of the reasons that mental illness lingers is the refusal of the immediate community to take accountability for the illness. Instead of listening to its prophetic voice, illness appears only as a threat that must be destroyed. The irony of this picture is that the more we try to fight mental illness—in contrast to surrendering to its message—the more power it gains over us.[354]

Drawing on these principles, we turned to a theological model of "schizophrenia," intent on receiving its prophetic voice as a gift from God within his redemptive framework. I argued that the schizoid condition, the narcissistic self-entrapment, the inability to love and to receive love, is the human condition. Based on Sugerman's research, I argued for a fresh view of madness that corroborates the traditional concept of sin, but expresses it in a different form. In this perspective, madness is not understood as disease, but "as the equivalent of sin—a disorder of the spirit— a disruption of man's fundamental relationship to existence."[355] One cannot escape from it or defeat it by his own power. It is the source of all pain, suffering, disease, despair, and death. This interpretation of madness as sin is to heighten our self-understanding; it is a portrait that reveals us to ourselves.

In order to help Christians grasp the depth and intensity of the experience of "schizophrenia," I offered an alternative account of the illness that emerges from a theological reflection on the phenomenon quite apart from its psychiatric classification. In search of biblical images that would "mirror" this soul-wrenching experience, I reframed the illness in terms of the following narratives: 1) a journey to Exile; 2) a prophetic voice; 3) a sacrificial lamb; and 4) a leper. And such is the destiny of those labeled with "schizophrenia": They are the broken and contrite vessels—abandoned as a contemporary leper, exiled from friends, family, society at large and seemingly God, emptied of themselves and "martyred" as "sacrificial lambs"—who cannot help but embody a "prophetic" message that is to awaken their community. "Schizophrenia," "madness," "insanity," or whatever label we put on it, is no longer a tragic disturbance from which to escape, but it brings forth an opportunity to detect in those we've labeled with "schizophrenia" something of the disharmonies that stain the texture of the whole community. What is revealed in them exposes our common

354. Siirala, *The Voice of Illness*, 94.

355. Sugerman, *Sin and Madness*, 17.

guilt; there is no escape from it, even though it calls into question our whole reality, our faith, our conduct, and our self-understanding. The evil forces giving life to this illness can only be conquered when we embrace it as our own illness. God, who longs to bring back his children into his arms, does not cease calling them by a variety of voices in his created nature—some whispered, and some thunderous. Surely, it is time for the church to respond to this call!

4

A Path Forward

Healing Together

This is My commandment, that you love one another,
just as I have loved you.

John 15:12

Bring my soul out of prison, So that I may give thanks
to Thy name; The righteous will surround me,
For Thou will deal bountifully with me.

Psalm 142:7

Let love of the brethren continue. Do not neglect to show
hospitality to strangers, for by this some have entertained
angels without knowing it. Remember the prisoners,
as though in prison with them, and those who are ill-treated,
since you yourselves also are in the body.

Hebrews 13:1–3

In the last chapter, I argued that illnesses are not purely meaningless bio-logical phenomena. Particularly, with regards to mental illness (an area where medical science has been severely challenged to offer satisfactory explanations of the experience), the voice of illness ought to be heard in

the context of the sufferer's community. In reference to a psychotic experience Aderhold et al., remind us that, "It is not the psychosis—whatever
this might be—that is being treated, but a human being in the midst of an
altered experience" who should be "supported and accompanied, realizing
that each individual is very different from the other, and consequently
there can be no 'universal recipe' and no universal diagnosis."[1]

The question confronting us is: "What constitutes a faithful Christian
response to a person in the midst of a psychotic experience?" This chapter
explores that appropriate response, by suggesting a model of care centered
on hearing and embracing the voice of the illness in a way that can lead to
healing together. While learning from successful projects both inside and
outside the church, the model is built upon the notion that relationships in
Christ provide the fertile ground where the seeds of hope, love, grace, and
faith will bear fruits of healing and transformation, where the unexpected
and the unimaginable could nevertheless become possible.

In recent times, there is much talk in theology and literary theory of
understanding "otherness" and accepting those who are different from us.
The attempt is to avoid oppression of that which we do not comprehend, or
that makes us uncomfortable. In spite of all that rhetoric, Marion Carson
points to the unfortunate reality that, "Psychotics are still the 'ununderstandable' (Jaspers' neologism), and so must be sidelined, excluded as useless, if not downright dangerous." They are truly the modern lepers, exiled
away from their communities. Carson draws a parallel between reactions
to the book of Revelation in the Christian canon and the psychotic people:
"Both have been isolated and abused, both subjected to surgery, analyses
and strange theorizing. Both have been classed as 'ununderstandable' and
dangerous, and thus marginalized, neglected and abandoned."[2]

There have been many interpretations of the book of Revelation
throughout Christian history. Its darkness, its "otherness," and its "strange-
ness" have fascinated the reader and caused a sense of terror and fear; its
content has been called "mad," and "morally *inferior*." Carson asks, "After
all, are not such images of many headed dragons, of bloody battlefields,
of plagues, of earth and sky fleeing away the stuff of psychosis, evidence
that the author . . . was deranged, possibly even dangerous?"[3] But understanding it in its historical context makes it clear that the author was not

1. Aderhold et al., "Soteria: An Alternative Mental Health Reform Movement,"
155.

2. Carson, "Fine Madness," 361.

3. Ibid., 362.

psychotic and the content is anything but "mad." Its imagery points us to a future hope, glory of God, and the ultimate triumph of Good over Evil.

Carson draws on the work of Richard Hays, who portrays Revelation as a "prophetic confrontation of all earthly pretentions to power, all symbolic orders other than that of the Lamb that was slaughtered,"[4] and explains that the same dynamics are at play in psychosis. In spite of major suffering and distress associated with psychosis, much research is showing that it is "actually a very important part of our humanity . . . and that this mode of 'otherness', were it not to exist, would leave our world considerably poorer." The line between madness and sanity is a very fine line and easy to cross. In the same way that the strange world of Revelation with its "visions and dreams" and intriguing "madness and creativity" forces us to "be taken out of ourselves and to look up," we need "psychoticism" in the "normal life," accepting its mystery and allowing its content to lead us on to new heights in "understanding of both humanity and theology."[5]

Scripture speaks in powerful language of the relevance of madness to the whole community. All are called "stupid," "devoid of knowledge" and "insane" (Jer 51:17; Eccl 9:3). Siirala explains that Scripture speaks of power of salvation over illness, and that "the conquest of the powers which cause mental illness is seen as a sign of the messianic age."[6] He points out that by contrast to Scripture, the history of the church is filled with "isolation and persecution of the mentally ill." Society's and the church's treatment of the mentally ill has been colored by oppressive policies and behavior. Indeed, the church has at best abandoned and neglected, and at worst, abused and persecuted the insane.

Some might wonder if it is fair and even wise to ask the church to take an active role in the care of the insane—after all, this is the twenty-first century, the age of science and technology! Woodward suggests that we as members of the body of Christ are faced with the challenge of how we might become "agents of healing for God." Practitioners of medical science will always come up with explanations stemming from their understanding of human biology. But issues related to faith in God are far broader than the questions physicians are trying to answer. Jesus' approach to healing was "to evoke latent attitudes of faith" and to connect them with the "healing power of God." Sometimes it was the faith of others that made a difference—the paralytic's friends, for example (Matt 9:2). It was

4. Ibid., 363.

5. Ibid., 364.

6. Siirala, *The Voice of Illness*, 51.

not always the question of the faith of the sufferer or what he personally did; "healing is a shared enterprise." Is the church able to act as a "body"? In biological reality the health of the body depends on the health of each member. The church cannot escape this fundamental biblical teaching and expect fruitfulness. Jesus offers an opportunity for the faith of the community and God's power "to coalesce in creating a new order."[7]

Insofar as madness is recognized as a phenomenon, both *theological* and *teleological*, with a deep prophetic voice, one that exposes our state of sinfulness and calls the church into repentance, how is the church to encounter it effectively and faithfully? I argued in the previous chapter that the evil forces giving life to the experience of insanity could only be conquered when the immediate community embraces it as its own illness. In the context of that outlook, what matters most is that when Christians encounter a person who is ill, oppressed, confused, and tormented, they take it upon themselves to "*make space* in their lives" to care for those persons as if they were caring for Christ himself.[8] Shuman suggests that the cross of Christ is not simply the symbol for the "redemption of suffering" but it is also "the basis of the communion that constitutes the body."[9] For in Christ the enemies, i.e., the Jews and Gentiles, are made "into one new man" that he "might reconcile them both in one body to God *through the cross*" (Eph 2:15–16; emphasis mine). In fact John Zizioulas goes so far as to declare, "Communion with the other requires the experience of the cross."[10] He is suggesting that only through the sacrifice of one's own desires for the sake of the other can the glory of Christ and the power of his work on the cross manifest in history. Dietrich Bonhoeffer explains, "It is the fellowship of the Cross to experience the burden of the other. If one does not experience it, the fellowship he belongs to is not Christian."[11] In short, the one who refuses to bear the burden of another is indeed denying the "law of Christ" (Gal 6:2).

If madness has a voice ordained by God, then the target audience is first and foremost God's covenantal people, the church. It behooves us to listen to that voice, instead of shutting it off. By constraining the insane, we are violating their God-created existence, damaging their personality. To

7. Woodward, *Encountering Illness*, 94.

8. Shuman, *The Body of Compassion*, xvi.

9. Ibid., 103.

10. Zizioulas, "Communion and Otherness," 14; cited in Shuman, *The Body of Compassion*, 104.

11. Bonhoeffer, *Life Together*, 101.

bear another's burden means experiencing that person's pain, weaknesses, and oddities, everything that tries our patience at every turn and generates friction, conflict, and collisions. Now we must ask if it is sufficient to encounter the insane simply with an outwardly kindness. After all, is it not too much to ask to truly love such individuals?[12] Does the church or common humanity even have the capacity for such a self-sacrificial love? Kierkegaard explains that when one encounters another one suffering from insanity—he calls it "demoniacal" personality—one is overwhelmed by the intensity of the phenomenon.[13] The encounter invokes a sense of fear and guilt in the observer; he knows deep inside, whether he admits it or not, that this is the fate he deserves and that may befall him. Therefore, in order to spare oneself from a sense of guilt, he may offer compassion to such a person. That kind of self-serving compassion, the kind that sees the person in despair as "other," Kierkegaard claims, has no value for the sufferer. As Becker reminded us earlier, the one suffering from "schizophrenia" is very much attuned to sensing the lack of authenticity in those around him; he knows "the fabrications of those around [him] are a lie." He is not fooled by a superficial "compassion." Kierkegaard notes:

> Only when the compassionate person is so related by his compassion to the sufferer that in the strictest sense he comprehends that it is his own cause which is here in question, only when he knows how to identify himself in such a way with the sufferer that when he is fighting for an explanation he is fighting for himself, renouncing all thoughtlessness, softness, and cowardice, only then does compassion acquire significance, and only then does it perhaps find a meaning.[14]

It appears that Kierkegaard is suggesting that only when one is awakened and embraces the problem of the sufferer as his own, pointing to his own depravity, then and only then is he truly bearing the sufferer's burden, and only then has his compassion any healing power.[15] Along the same lines,

12. Paul commands the Romans: "Let love be without hypocrisy" (Rom 12:9).

13. Kierkegaard defines a demoniacal personality as one that "is in the evil and is in dread of the good." The good threatens the force of evil in the person, because it "signifies to it the reintegration of freedom, redemption, salvation, or whatever name one would give it." Kierkegaard, *Kierkegaard's the Concept of Dread*, 106.

14. Ibid., 107.

15. The same principle was discussed earlier by Siirala, emphasizing that a healing dialogue between the patient and a therapist can be effective *only* when a "deep crisis" takes place in both of them. Siirala, *The Voice of Illness*, 83. Referring to a variety of scientific studies, Kapur points to a patient's "heightened sensory receptiveness," and

Henri Nouwen, speaking of care in an *authentic* Christian community, speaks of the miracles that can happen when people are willing to "break through paralyzing boundaries," and risk stepping into emptiness to be filled by God.[16] He declares:

> To care means first of all to empty our own cup and to allow the other to come close to us. It means to take away the many barriers which prevent us from entering into communion with the other. When we dare to care, then we discover that nothing human is foreign to us, but that all the hatred and love, cruelty and compassion, fear and joy can be found in our own hearts. When we dare to care, we have to confess that when others kill, I could have killed too. . . . By the honest recognition and confession of our human sameness we can participate in the care of God who came, not to the powerful but powerless, not to be different but the same, not to take our pain away but to share it. Through this participation we can open our hearts to each other and form a new community."[17]

For Nouwen, it is the "participation" in one another's pain that will bring about true communion and opens the gates of healing.

The Apostle Paul, speaking of the mystical body of Christ, commands the church: "On the contrary, it is much truer that the members of the body which seem to be weaker are necessary. . . . God has so composed the body, giving more abundant honor to that member which lacked . . . that the members should have the same care for one another. And if one member suffers, all the members suffer with it" (1 Cor 12:22–26). The principal biblical response for Christians is to receive the affliction of another member of the body of Christ as a blow to themselves. Indeed Paul Tripp, pointing to the whole body metaphor, argues that it is impossible to read Paul in Ephesians 4 and 1 Corinthians 12 and "conclude that sanctification is an individual concern." There is a demand for "accountability and submission to a fellow believer" that would shape the whole body into the "fullness of Christ."[18] This appears to mean that if for nothing else but

---

explains that in the case of people suffering from schizophrenia, "From days to years . . . patients continue in this state of subtly altered experience of the world, accumulating experiences of aberrant salience without a clear reason or explanation for the patient." Kapur, "Psychosis," 15.

16. Nouwen, *Out of Solitude*, 41.

17. Ibid., 42–43.

18. Tripp, *Instruments in the Redeemer's Hands*, 327.

the desire for personal growth in holiness and sanctification, one must embrace such encounter with weaker members.

Drawing on Zizioulas's work, Shuman stresses that the differences among the members of the body are not limited to "roles adopted in one situation or another," but rather that the differences are "ontological." He is speaking about who these people are created to be. The differences are "irreducible" and are meant to be "for the good of the body *and* of its members." These differences exist as an essential requirement to bring "wholeness through interdependence." In fact, Paul is adamant that the fullness of Christ can only be accomplished through the interconnection of *all* members: "But now there are many members, but one body. And the eye cannot say to the hand, 'I have no need of you;' or again the head to the feet, 'I have no need of you'" (1 Cor 12:20–21). As Shuman points out, "It is not simply suffering that is shared within the body but the solution to the suffering as well."[19] In other words a person might assume that his care of the afflicted is leading him toward recovery, where all along both have been instruments in God's hand for the purposes of mutual healing, sanctification, and transformation.

The "schizophrenic" is created as a unique member of the body entrusted with a unique prophetic gift, employed as a special instrument in the hand of God for the benefit of others. For in our fallen world "schizophrenia" can be "God's megaphone," to an individual, to a family, to a community, to a nation, to turn away our eyes from vanity of a life that, according to Carson, "functionally disowns God, no matter what we say in our creeds."[20] God is moving through the "schizophrenic," demanding attention.

The Western church has failed to live up to the radicalness of Christ's message. I argued that the insane portray us in vivid ways, as lepers covered with leprosy, and that to bring us to our senses they expose the hidden sins of our hearts through their "sign acts," revealing what we have masked so expertly under our civilized postures. Yes, it is messy to deal with them. But can we afford to avoid them as members of the church? Did Christ reject the desperate cry of the lepers? According to Tripp:

> The church is . . . a conversion, confession, repentance, reconciliation, forgiveness, and sanctification center, where flawed people place their trust in Christ, gather to know and love Him better and learn to love others *as he has designed*. The church is

19. Shuman, *The Body of Compassion*, 109.
20. Carson, *How Long, O Lord?*, 108.

messy and inefficient, but it is God's wonderful mess—the place where he radically transforms hearts and lives.[21]

Indeed, caring for a "schizophrenic" person is ministry at its messiest, most inefficient—and maybe also at its most meaningful state. It is stepping into darkness, where one can detect the light at its brightest. It is allowing oneself to become muddied and stinky, so that one experiences "the fellowship of His suffering" and gets a glimpse of what he bore on the cross. It is where, at the depth of weakness and helplessness, his "power is perfected" and his grace becomes "sufficient" (2 Cor 12:9). It is stretching out one's arms not only to touch the leper, but also to embrace him, holding him next to one's naked body, until one experiences all his burdens and wounds for oneself. Then, indeed, one has "fulfilled the law of Christ" (Gal 6:2).

Paul reminds the church in Corinth that God "reconciled us to Himself through Christ and gave us the ministry of reconciliation . . . Therefore we are ambassadors for Christ, as though God were entreating through us" (2 Cor 5:18, 20). Tripp explains that the work of an ambassador is to incarnate a leader, representing his thoughts and values in all things: "He stands in the place of the king."[22] The ambassador's work is not a part-time job, it is about everything he says and does. This is a great calling to represent the King of kings and the Lord of lords. This means that our personal agendas have to cease to exist. Tripp believes that it is through this calling that Christ "deliver[s] us from our bondage to ourselves! This is our most subtle, yet most foundational form of idolatry."[23] The church is not able to be the ambassador of the King in the world of the insane by playing only in the margins. Most humans lack the self-sacrificing love that demands so much of us. We get irritated by people who interfere with our comfort and pleasure.[24] Relationships with the insane are messy, consuming, and shattering at times. But in the midst of it, something miraculous happens: our true heart is revealed to us; that is when true repentance can take shape. As Tripp says, "moments of difficulty are moments of redemption."[25] And moments of giving are in reality moments of receiving (Acts 20:35b).

21. Ibid., emphasis mine.

22. Tripp, *Instruments in the Redeemer's Hands*, 104.

23. Ibid., 108.

24. Ibid., 120.

25. Ibid., 124.

Communities of Healing

The care of the insane has presented major challenges to Western civilization in the past sixty years. With the advancement of psychopharmacology, the insane have been sent back into communities to "live the ordinary life" within "the ordinary society." This sounds like good news, "until one looks into that ordinary society."[26] Nils Christie, who has engaged for more than twenty years with communal villages in Europe, portrays this movement back to the society as follows:

> The insane back to the families was the slogan, but those families were not the same. . . . They were not large anymore; they did not provide free service from females permanently at home. The road from the mental hospital did not lead to a home filled with life and vivacity. The road led with great regularity to a room in a boarding house in the center of the city. Or it led to an existence as a bag-lady, homeless and with all belongings in some plastic bags, strolling the streets of our glittering, modern towns. Or it led to another type of institution—to prison.[27]

Many of the mentally-distressed are quite vulnerable, and have no support system, and no caring community to lean on. In addition to their trauma, they have to deal with the loss of friends, rejection, ridicule, vanished self-esteem and utter bewilderment about what has happened to them. It is the cruelty of their new life that drifts them toward inner-cities to be "part of an anonymous street scene," hiding among the multitude of the inhabitants of "cardboard cities."[28]

The enormity of the pain that these afflicted souls and their families experience is incomprehensible for the average citizen. Stewart Govig, a professor of religion whose son suffers from chronic "schizophrenia," writes:

> For nearly two decades now we have visited him at various hospitals, halfway homes, and filthy apartments. We have cringed at his compulsive, bizarre behavior, stood mute in its presence, and witnessed an almost total social withdrawal. We have gagged at body odor and watched his teeth decay to the point

---

26. Christie, *Beyond Loneliness and Institutions*, 99.

27. Ibid., 99–100.

28. Carson, "Loving, Discernment, and Distance," 227–28.

of extraction. . . . Nevertheless, reality dictates acceptance of a long-term, gravely disabling and handicapping condition.[29]

All along, Govig's son Jay has received the best psychiatric treatment that America has to offer, but the outcome has been filled with pain and misery both for him and his family. With the aid of psychiatric drugs, some people like Jay are able to live semi-functional lives, working in their communities, but most suffer from a variety of health issues, which are the side effects of their medications. The reality of their life is that their psychiatric condition never leaves them. At best, they learn how to go through the days one after the other, coping with their illness, which has been stamped on their forehead for a lifetime. But is that the best we can do as a society and as the church of Christ? There should be no rest for Christians as long as the picture is so grim for some of our own. Fortunately, there is an alternative path, a "road less travelled," which is hopeful, transformational, beyond mere coping, targeting recovery.

"Recovery is often defined conservatively as returning to a stable baseline or former level of functioning. However, many people, including myself, have experienced recovery as a transformative process in which the old self is gradually let go of and a new sense of self emerges."[30] These are the words of Patricia Deegan, who has recovered from "schizophrenia." We have heard from a variety of accounts in this book that once one is diagnosed with "schizophrenia," people—unfortunately this includes the church and the family in addition to the mental health professionals—act as if one's fate and future is sealed with doom and hopelessness. With the diagnosis of "schizophrenia" one is handed their "book of life" that had already been written by Emil Kraepelin,[31] and is forced to be "inspired by the thought of a life spent coping" by clinging to psychiatric medications.[32] Nothing is further away from truth if faith in Jesus Christ is alive and his church resolutely embodies that faith in action, intent on fighting for a

29. Govig, "Chronic Mental Illness and the Family," 405–6.

30. Deegan, "Recovery as a Self-Directed Process of Healing and Transformation," 6.

31. Kraepelin is recognized as the father of *descriptive psychiatry*, which is used as the primary model of treatment in the westerns world. See chapter 2.

32. Deegan, "Recovery as a Self-Directed Process of Healing and Transformation," 9–10. In a recent scientific study, Zipursky et al. wrote: "Mental health professionals need to join with patients and their families in understanding that schizophrenia is not a malignant disease that inevitably deteriorates over time but rather one from which most people can achieve a substantial degree of recovery." Zipursky et al., "The Myth of Schizophrenia as a Progressive Brain Disease."

life that has meaning and purpose. The opportunity lies before the church to answer the call to partake in God's redemptive plan, to be his "fellow workers" in "building up the body of Christ," by embracing those whose spirit and personhood are under attack by forces of evil (1 Cor 3:9; Eph 4:12).

The opinions about psychiatry versus alternative methods of treatment continue to be irreconcilably divided and attract heated debates. It is enough for one to follow the conversation in the psychiatric blogosphere among the professionals in the field to get an uncomfortable dizzy feeling that by no means are we standing on solid ground. Also, with the ever-continuing expansion of psychiatric disorders, it seems as if American psychiatry is bringing an ever-increasing number of people into the "madness tent."[33] Madness, far from disappearing or "being cured," continues "to taunt and bewilder us, and to consume more and more of our resources" and "our concern."[34]

While researchers in psychiatry and neurosciences are feverishly working to discover the etiology of madness, to develop more effective drugs with fewer side effects, and design more workable treatments, millions of people around the world suffer from life-disabling, tormenting, hopeless, never-ending battles with a variety of mental disturbances. What is the alternative for these afflicted souls while the world is passing them by, leaving them just waiting? Lehmann and Stastny ask:

> Can we imagine a world which no longer espouses the currently standard psychiatric methods? A world in which a human being in dire straits need not fear to seek help, where someone looking for treatment does not risk being unexpectedly locked up, restrained, forcibly injected and only able to regain control of their life after an indeterminate period of time?[35]

Their answer to their own question is a definite "yes." To that end Lehmann and Stastny have collected a series of research papers, presented in *Alternatives Beyond Psychiatry*, depicting non-psychiatric options that have had remarkable results around the globe. They believe that if we as a society learn to be more tolerant of diversity, if we learn to create an environment "which promotes recovery" by encouraging optimism in the midst of "painful and confusing experiences and alternate realities," and if

33. Whitaker, *Mad in America*, 286.

34. Foskett, *Meaning in Madness*, 162.

35. Lehmann and Stastny, "Reforms Or Alternatives?," 406.

we respect the dignity of the human person for who one is created to be, then undoubtedly recovery is within our grasp.[36]

In 1842, long before the age of psychopharmacology, T. H. Gallaudet, the Chaplain of the Retreat for the Insane at Hartford, wrote of the care for the insane in his institution:

> That such services, if rendered in a calm, discreet, and affection-
> ate manner, are productive, under the divine blessing, of great
> good to the insane, no one acquainted with their condition and
> the effects of these services, can doubt. Every year's experience,
> both in this Institution, and other similar ones, abundantly es-
> tablishes this truth.[37]

This is the sentiment which was shared by practitioners of Moral Therapy and has been repeated throughout history when the insane have been treated with dignity and nurturing care.

Madness has been part of the human predicament from the begin-ning. My assertion has been that God speaks through the phenomenon of madness to people who witness it. I also argued that when people listen to that voice, the possibility of healing is within their grasp. If that asser-tion is true, then surely there must be contemporary communities that have witnessed healing when it was unimaginable and far from reach. They may not have consciously acted upon the arguments presented in this book, but they might have stumbled over the secret to healing in the midst of chaos.

In that belief, I embarked on finding such communities that might corroborate some of the assertions of this thesis. I was not disappointed. For wherever there is love, the Spirit of God is at work causing miracles and bringing a testimony to his faithfulness. The Apostle Paul was cor-rect: "Love never fails"! (1 Cor 13:8). Applying similar principles as Moral Therapy, a variety of environments have been founded on openness, love, empathy, interest, authentic relationships, respect, and "an integrated ap-proach to body, mind and spirit." Every one of these models is built on the "importance of understanding one's own story and the meanings con-tained in the 'symptoms.'"[38] These environments have helped a multitude of people to return to a life with meaning and purpose. There is much to

---

36. Ibid., 406–8.

37. Gallaudet, "Report of the Chaplain," 136.

38. Lehmann and Stastny, "Reforms Or Alternatives?," 408.

learn from their experiences. We will survey a few of these models as a basis for our recommendation for a path forward.

Soteria

The Soteria House treatment model was introduced by the American psychiatrist Loren Mosher, a self-proclaimed atheist,[39] a student of phenomenological/existential psychiatry who was inspired and influenced by the teachings of Ronald D. Laing. As the Chief of the Schizophrenia Center at the National Institute of Mental Health (NIMH), Mosher became increasingly convinced that "'Schizophrenic' behavior results from psychosocial experiences and is not biological in origin."[40] In order to test his hypothesis, Mosher led the creation of a community-based residential facility in a working-class neighborhood in Santa Clara, California during the 1970s. The house, offering an alternative to a mental hospital, contained twelve rooms and could house six to seven "schizophrenic" persons, plus two or three staff around the clock. They mostly focused on people suffering from their first or second psychotic episodes.

Soteria developed its philosophy based on various clinical notions. The practices advocated by the Moral Therapy in the eighteenth century played a major role in shaping the structure of Soteria. There was a significant emphasis placed on the "healing potential of human relationships" as practiced within moral therapies and advocated by some psychoanalytical pioneers such as Freida Fromm-Reichman. There was also a belief that psychosis can lead to growth and transformation if it is "treated in an open, nonjudgmental way" as preached by Laing and Karl Menninger.[41]

Soteria was distinguished in some fundamental ways from other community-based treatment facilities for mental health. First, it was not a clinical facility, and it was run by "nonprofessional" staff, and "admitted only clients who would have otherwise been hospitalized." Second, the use of psychiatric drugs was kept to a minimum and applied only as the last resort. Third, the home was an "*alternative* to hospitalization," not a place that one would go to after release from a mental hospital. The vision was to explore if one could heal more easily in a small, "homelike" setting, if not exposed to the psychiatric-based environment and treatment.[42]

39. Mosher et al., *Soteria*, 282.

40. Ibid., 301.

41. Ibid., 1, 4.

42. Ibid., 2.

The nonprofessional staff created an open, non-threatening, "unhurried" atmosphere, where the staff spent time patiently with the residents, allowing them to express their madness as they chose. The staff believed that "sincere human involvement and understanding were critical to healing interactions." Most of them worked long shifts of thirty-six to forty-eight hours to provide plenty of opportunity for relationships of trust to be developed, and avoid disruptions due to staff rotations. The staff and residents shared all household management and maintenance responsibilities.[43]

The desire was to "*be with*" the residents and allow them to be as they wished, understanding that their communication styles and behaviors were often unlike anything the staff had encountered before. Joanne Cacciatore, who works with bereaved individuals who have suffered a major loss, explains that the wounded, more than anything else, need someone who is willing to bear witness to their suffering, and pay it its due dignity and respect. She says one must be "willing to join a person in the abyss and sit with the suffering non judgmentally, without urging him or her toward healing before healing's time has come."[44] In Soteria, likewise, the staff were inspired just to "be with" the residents. "Staff came in most cases to have an experience that would leave an indelible imprint, an experience on which they would have an impact, an experience that would be reciprocally formative."[45]

Soteria's philosophy considered "schizophrenia" as an "altered state of consciousness," commonly accompanied by mystical experiences "beyond reason," which "evolved in and affected the psychosocial matrix of the entire family or other intimate group forming the disturbed person's ecology." This new state brings about major crisis not merely in the life of the person labeled "mad" but also in the life of his immediate community who are faced with an unknown phenomenon, and in return their fears intensify the "disturbed person's terror." The staff were told to tolerate and indeed appreciate the unusual state of mind and behavior and regard them as "metaphorically valid and comprehensible" in the context of their cultural and family dynamics. In fact, all residents were entitled to their own perception of reality and were given space to parade their unconventional persona.[46] The time at the house was spent on playing games, watching

43. Ibid., 7.

44. Cacciatore, "DSM5 and Ethical Relativism."

45. Mosher et al., *Soteria*, 8.

46. Ibid., 11, 12.

TV, cooking, art, music, reading to one another, yoga, gardening, and regular meetings to discuss the affairs of the household and resolve any interpersonal conflicts. All these activities were perceived as potentially "therapeutic." The only formal therapies were for the families of the residents to help them deal with their own wounds and address any family dynamics that might have contributed to the crisis. It was important to get the families involved "in the process of their offspring's healing."[47]

In Soteria, people changed not through psychotherapy or medical treatment, but instead through normal everyday interactions with the other residents and the staff. The staff involved themselves in genuine and respectful conversations with the disturbed person and suspended their own view of reality in an attempt to understand that of the other person. This was not easy, and at times would try one's patience to the extreme limits. Sometimes it was necessary to *be with* the person all night and embrace his unusual behavior, or deal with his rampage, which often did reveal deep wounds caused by hurtful family relationships, social rejections, and emotional and physical abuse. There was never any attempt to invalidate or ridicule the residents' stories. Indeed—as we have argued— it was this willingness to empty oneself and truly embrace the world of another human being that did the trick. The relationships developed at Soteria would become permanent in most cases, because they would leave an imprint on both sides.

The treatment consisted and responded to three phases: 1) The *acute state*, during which the person was accompanied by one of the staff around the clock. This was about *being with* the person and allowing him to express his madness in potentially unconventional ways; 2) The *restitution phase* was when the resident was able to get involved with daily activities and through "symmetrical peer relationship" with the staff he could learn to trust again; 3) The last phase was about *orientation to the outside world*, helping the residents develop new skills, such as planning and managing personal finances. The peer network stayed intact even after release from the house to help the person with continued recovery, with housing, job searches, education, and general reintegration back into the society. A complete or partial recovery was usually achieved within six to eight weeks, and the majority of the residents returned to their own communities after four to five months.[48]

47. Aderhold et al., "Soteria: An Alternative Mental Health Reform Movement," 148, 154, and Mosher, et al., *Soteria*, 116.

48. Aderhold et al., "Soteria: An Alternative Mental Health Reform Movement,"

Although Soteria's research was designed for first or second episode psychotics who had never been hospitalized, during the last two and a half years of the program, Soteria accepted some private clients to help with finances. These individuals were mostly "chronic schizophrenics" and had had significant hospitalization in their past. They proved to be the most difficult cases, and their "problematic behavior" was often "the result of their past treatment." In fact, Mosher refers to them as "iatrogenes" in his writings. Approximately 75 percent of this group had to continue on medication and the length of their stay at Soteria was usually much longer (about a year) and they typically did not recover fully in the way that those did who had never been medicated to begin with.[49]

Why did Soteria work? According to Mosher, the staff expected recovery for all residents and was determined to lead them that way. Residents were never treated as if they were "crazy." There was a great emphasis on "finding meaning in psychosis," which gave value and respect to the experience. A major contribution of the model was "its rehumanizing of madness" along with "demedicalizing of psychosis." This philosophy and belief system organically changed the dynamics of all relationships in the house. The staff with their attitude, flexibility, intuitiveness, and hopefulness created a home for people who were mired in confusion and despair, and helped them to see the light again. They themselves were changed by the experience forever.[50]

Soteria soon became a source of controversy and conflict between Mosher and his supervisors at NIMH. Mosher's model of minimal use of psychiatric drugs was regarded as a challenge to the drug-based model of treatment pervasive in conventional psychiatry. Whitaker says, "And while love and food and understanding proved to be good medicine, the political fate of that experiment ensured that the Soteria project would be the last of its kind and no one would dare to investigate this question again."[51] As the medical treatments over the years failed to yield recovery and as the scientific research exposed the iatrogenic effects of the antipsychotics, scientists in search of new models are pulling out Soteria files and reevaluating that project. In 2008, almost forty years after Soteria opened its doors, in an analysis published in *Schizophrenia Bulletin,* one of the

---

148–49.

49. Mosher et al., *Soteria*, 90–91.

50. Ibid., 266–74.

51. Whitaker, *Mad in America*, 220.

premier psychiatric journals, Calton et al. looked at all studies that had evaluated Soteria from its inception. They reported:

> The studies included in this review suggest that the Soteria paradigm yields equal, and in certain specific areas, better results in the treatment of people diagnosed with first-or second-episode schizophrenia spectrum disorders (achieving this with considerably lower use of medication) when compared with conventional, medication-based approaches. Further research is urgently required to evaluate this approach more rigorously because it may offer an alternative treatment for people diagnosed with schizophrenia spectrum disorders.[52]

The Soteria movement is emerging again with great vitality. Projects are implemented or are underway in Switzerland, Germany, Hungary, the Netherlands, Sweden, and Alaska. Also, a large group of activists, users, care-givers, and survivors are working on establishing Soteria homes across the UK.[53]

The Soteria model reaffirms the assertions in this study that people suffering from psychosis are better served in a homelike setting, in the company of those who show true care, patience, and respect toward their extraordinary experience. Moreover, it acknowledges the vital role played by the "entire family" and any "other intimate group" around the person.[54] The point of concern with Soteria is the question of housing several distressed individuals under the same roof. These are people who need special attention and who lack skills to deal with other overtly troubled individuals. Undoubtedly, this puts great strain on the staff, who in spite of their deep commitments could easily be overwhelmed by the challenge in hand. Also, as Mosher and his staff realized, this model may not be as helpful to people who have been suffering from chronic "schizophrenia."[55]

---

52. Calton et al., "A Systematic Review of the Soteria Paradigm for the Treatment of People Diagnosed with Schizophrenia," 181–192.

53. See the website for the Soteria Network in the UK, online: http://www.soterianetwork.org.uk/index.php.

54. Mosher, et al., *Soteria*, 11.

55. Ibid., 125–64.

The *"Healing Homes"*[56]

"Healing Homes" is an alternative model for healing mental illness through a collaborative and relational structure. The program is run by the Family Care Foundation (FCF), founded in 1987 in Gothenburg, Sweden. The funding for the program comes from The National Board of Health and Welfare, and the services are offered for free to all its clients. The program was founded by Carina Håkansson, a social worker and a licensed psychotherapist, who has been leading it passionately since its inception.[57]

Håkansson and her team have been determined to stay away from "dead descriptions (diagnoses) of living people" and minimize the use of psychiatric medications. Her description of people is never about "either-or" but rather "both-and." People can be "both happy and sad," or "both sensible and crazy." There is also a "neither-nor" element at work. What one encounters may be "neither this nor that"; it might be about "more than what we can *understand*." The belief is to recognize the diversity of personalities and value the dignity of the human spirit that might be disturbed by the blows of life. Their philosophy in a nutshell is about "consideration and concern for the other."[58]

Their program is engaged in a new way of doing therapy based on the power of collaboration and relationships. They assign people who suffer from severe emotional distress with whom the conventional psychiatry has failed—people who would normally get diagnoses such as schizophrenia or bipolar or borderline personality or drug addiction—to one of their thirty non-professional host families, usually in a farm house, where they live for several months to several years. So, contrary to Soteria, these clients are not "fresh" psychotics. "Many come to us in a crisis that has lasted for a long time. They are not only running out of strength, but also running out of hope for something better," says Håkansson.[59]

56. I am deeply grateful to Carina Håkansson and her colleagues for welcoming me to their organization and allowing me to look into their work and to spend time with several of their host families and the individuals they care for. Their vision and their dedication to their cause have been great inspirations to me.

57. Håkansson, *Ordinary Life Therapy*, 142; the program and the work of Family Care Foundation is chronicled in *Healing Homes: An Alternative, Swedish Model for Healing Psychosis,* a feature-length documentary film directed by Daniel Mackler. See http://www.iraresoul.com/dvd2.html.

58. Ibid., 14.

59. Ibid., 26–27.

The host families—some have been hosting clients for more than two decades—are selected solely for their personal characteristics. Håkansson explains:

> We seek cooperation with family homes that have room in their homes and in their lives for one or more of our so-called clients. There must be a physical space, but most of all there must be an emotional space to meet another human being. . . . How could they have the courage and the energy to let a person come into their lives who so many times before has "given up" or who so many times before has been labeled as "too difficult"? . . . However crazy this may be, it is that kind of family that we search for and the kind of family that our clients need most.[60]

There is always a therapist (referred to as the supervisor) assigned to the host family and the natural family, and one working directly with the so-called "client." The family homes, the therapists, the clients' own families, all become part of *the extended therapy room.* The family homes are given a stipend to cover the expenses of housing the client, and an insignificant salary for their services. This way those who open the door of their homes do not have to incur any additional financial burdens.[61]

The so-called clients become family members in these homes as an alternative to a psychiatric institution. They are never referred to by any psychiatric labels or even referred to as "clients." They are called only by their names. Håkansson strongly rejects the psychiatric labels:

> In my thinking, diagnosis symbolizes an us-and-them thinking that we who "know" will tell them what they are like or what kind of life they lead. It is a language of power where one speaks for the other and acts as interpreter for the other. Furthermore, to be given a diagnosis is no innocent game; on the contrary, for many it is like a verdict that you have to live with for a long time, maybe even for the rest of your life. . . . For others the diagnosis becomes an identity, something that you are: "I am a schizophrenic" or "I am an alcoholic." Lots of people have lived for years and years with their diagnosis and gradually arranged their life accordingly.[62]

There is never any use of force as one gets assigned to a healing home; everything is done in a dignified way that respects the personal desires of the

60. Ibid., 52.

61. Ibid., 25–26, 18.

62. Ibid., 87.

individual. If the individual has any children, they will be brought along into the host family to avoid separation between the parent and young children. The client's children and the host children go to school together. If the client is a troubled child, the parents are invited to come with their child and live together in the host family. These people live together, play together, work together on the farm and with the animals, and fight together, as any normal family would. They truly carry each other's burdens, and it appears that something profound takes place in all their lives. "The family home sees more possibilities than difficulties, otherwise it would not take on the task," says Håkansson.[63]

Every new person brings a new challenge that requires the love and attention of a dedicated team, with a hopeful vision that considers every person worth fighting for. Together they embark on a journey toward healing, while living an "ordinary life" attending to their daily routines. Mackler, who has profiled the Healing Homes in a feature-length documentary film, while reviewing Håkansson's book offers the following perspective:

> The magic of this book is that Håkansson shows again and again just how these "ordinary" families provide a wonderfully rich and therapeutic environment for the clients, but at times, even more so, how the clients provide a wonderfully rich therapeutic experience for the families in return. Similarly, the "professional" therapists and supervisors—and Håkansson herself, who founded and runs the organization—also gain richly from the experience.[64]

Indeed, the work is exciting, tantalizing, encouraging, and meaningful in deep-rooted ways for all involved. There is reciprocity of influence and healing. Håkansson, whose vision and leadership are the force behind this endeavor, was first inspired to do something at age fifteen. One morning, right before her fifteenth birthday, she had "a severe convulsive fit and became unconscious." Taken to the hospital for treatment, she was later told by her physician "in a grave voice" everything that from that point on she "would not be able to do." Håkansson explains:

> That verdict drastically marked my life for many years to come. . . . Later, it was proven that the convulsive fit had been an isolated phenomenon and the predicted verdict never would come true, however, it had a strong effect on me. I learned the significance of how people meet and the importance of speaking in

63. Ibid., 51.

64. Mackler, review of *Ordinary Life Therapy*.

> a way that enables understanding . . . this episode influenced me and my life thereafter, privately and later professionally. . . . Evidently this early experience bred both anger and distrust against too predetermined ideas and so-called truths. . . . [I want] to give voice to the people I have met through the years in my work, and to try to convey the strength that is there when people come together and take both themselves and the other seriously.[65]

The concept of *the extended therapy room* is a model and philosophy that enables the sharing of thought, feeling, and action in everyday life among people who have different ways of "expressing themselves," come from different experiences, and dream about different things. It is in this extended therapy room where mutual transformation takes place that has led Håkansson to believe that "almost everything is possible" through collaboration and serious relationships.[66] After a while the issues being addressed are not just the client's but everyone else's in the circle. In their interactions with the clients, the host family and even the supervisors come face to face with their own weaknesses and flaws. It is truly a collaborative healing process. Lennart, one of the host fathers, explains:

> You have to analyze yourself and your weaknesses and strengths. I don't think we'd have been the people we are today without all that we have been through in the shared work. . . . Of course you don't always feel great, but you get a totally different view of life for yourself and for others. . . . You see so many angles of a problem that you didn't see before.[67]

Ingvor, a host mother, claims, "To care about a fellow human being can't just be a job. It is a way of life."[68] Håkansson emphasizes the importance that time and a network of loving people play while one is going through severe disturbances. It takes people who are patient, gentle, and caring. She says, "[Y]ou could be fooled into believing that it is just a matter of your own will, and that you are the architect of your own fortune. . . . If it were that simple, many things would be substantially different." While Håkansson acknowledges the significance of personal "strength and will power," she attributes the successes toward recovery to the "context" created for the person that

---

65. Håkansson, *Ordinary Life Therapy*, 17.

66. Ibid., 18–19.

67. Ibid., 62.

68. Ibid., 67.

must be conducive to healing. Time is significant in building trust in each other, to take risks, to "doubt," to overcome misunderstandings, to fall and rise again, to "fuss," and "to think that the other is an altogether horrendous person, only later to discover that it was not all that bad." Håkansson says, "We believe that we, together, see, hear, and are capable of more than each one individually."[69]

In their extended therapy room, the client's own family plays a key part. The past relationships are important. There are hidden pains and secrets that need to be brought forth and dealt with. If those issues, which may have contributed to the past troubles, are not addressed, the person will never gain the strength and the trust necessary to return to an independent life. Moreover, in most cases, the families themselves have already been through hell. It is not easy to witness the loss of your loved ones as you knew them, while struggling through the health care system for their survival with no avail. It is important to remember that the cases that come to FCF are primarily those who have been given up on by the regular system. Thus, the families are tired, hopeless, and wounded. They need help as much as their loved one who is labeled as "ill."

One of the great elements contributing to the success of this program is that all costs are covered by the state. There is no discrimination based on wealth, social class, gender, race, or original nationality. Håkansson and her team of family homes and professional therapists have helped many individuals and families in severe psychiatric states for more than two decades. They have done it because they believe in the power of love and relationships. They have had disappointments and people who have left in the middle of the program because they could not wait for healing any longer. But the vision lives on and is catching.

Håkansson highlights the mysterious dimension of what they deal with and the significance of not knowing and yet pressing on "without too many assurances and guarantees of security." She points out that many therapies fail because they expect change to be easy: "We disregard the agonies that change also implies and the leap we sometimes have to take without knowing where and how we will fall." It is in times of vulnerability, surrender, selflessness and solidarity, when all come together, that Håkansson and the Healing Homes with their guests have experienced "a lightness and bouncing joy" at the sight of "miracles and little wonders."[70]

69. Ibid., 22, 51.

70. Ibid., 112, 119, 128.

This model, like Soteria, affirms the claims made in this study, that the best way to help people with mental distress is to create an environment that gives them space, respect, and love. The family homes give these people the gift of an "ordinary life" with all its ups and downs, yet under the watchful eyes of a caring family that believes in the natural ability of the human soul to recover from the blows of life. Undoubtedly, the natural settings in farms, away from the pressures of urban life, play a key role. Moreover, as witnessed by some of the host families and the staff themselves, the transformation was not only for the so-called clients but for all involved. This model recognizes the significance of bringing the family into the "*extended therapy room*"; their approach affirms our assertion that healing typically remains far from reach until deep-rooted interpersonal issues in the person's immediate community are addressed. One of the greatest facilitators of success for this model is the complete financial backing by the state—a foreign practice in the context of current treatments in the United States.

Open Dialogue Therapy

Western Lapland in Finland has experienced one of the more dramatic stories of "schizophrenia" recovery in all of Europe. Considering the size of the population, the region used to have an unusually high rate of "schizophrenia," about twice or three times the rate in the rest of Finland, or of other countries in Europe. The good news is that this grim picture has dramatically changed and today in Western Lapland, they encounter only a few new cases of the illness. Moreover, the long-term outcomes for the people who have experienced psychosis are by far the best in the Western world.[71] How did this striking shift take place?

Whitaker, who has spent time in Western Lapland to evaluate this shift, explains, "This is a medical success that has been decades in the making."[72] In 1969, Yrjö Olavi Alanen became the Chairman of the Department of Psychiatry at the University of Turku, Finland. Contrary to his colleagues, Alanen saw meanings behind the symptoms that "schizophrenia" patients experienced and believed that psychotherapy could help them. Alanen stated, "It's almost impossible for anyone meeting with these

71. Whitaker, *Anatomy of an Epidemic*, 336–37.

72. Ibid., 337.

patients' families to not understand that they have difficulties in life."[73] In his view, the role of the psychiatrists and their team was to parse the "schizophrenic's" symptoms as a key for opening up and addressing the family problems.

Based on this philosophy, Alanen in conjunction with a couple of his colleagues developed a "case specific" Need-Adapted Approach (NAA) for treatment of seriously psychotic patients based on psychodynamic principles. If needed, some were put on low doses of antipsychotics, but mostly the treatment revolved around a "group family therapy" of a unique "collaborative" style. The treatment teams, referred to as the "psychosis teams," made no attempt to eliminate the psychotic symptoms, but the focus was on understanding the experience and discussing the past "successes" in the person's life hoping to lead him to get a "grip on life," and imagine a constructive future.[74]

During the 1970s and 1980s, Alanen's work started bearing fruit. Even chronic patients were experiencing improvement and many were released from the hospital. This success generated great interest in the rest of the psychiatric community, and between 1981 and 1987, Alanen led the Finnish National Schizophrenia Project to introduce the NAA nationally. It was becoming obvious that psychotherapy and family therapy were helping recovery from "schizophrenia." But, in order to settle the question of antipsychotics usage, beginning in 1992 a study was conducted among people with first-episode of psychosis in six centers. All centers provided NAA treatment, but in three "experimental" centers, no antipsychotic drugs were given in the first three weeks, and only if there were no improvements after that period, were neuroleptics prescribed. After two years, those individuals in the "experimental" centers who had never been put on any antipsychotics (about 43 percent of the cohort) had the most positive outcome.[75]

Although most of Finland continued with the application of antipsychotics for the treatment of psychosis, one of the three "experimental" sites—Tornio, in Western Lapland—inspired by NAA, developed a more innovative family therapy model called "Open Dialogue." In the national study, Tornio enrolled thirty-four psychotic patients, of whom twenty-five were never given any antipsychotics. It was at this site that the hospital staff came to experience the positive progression of unmedicated psychosis in

73. Whitaker, *Anatomy of an Epidemic*, 337.

74. Ibid.

75. Ibid., 338.

conjunction with "need-adapted" treatment. Whitaker says, "And they found that while recovery from psychosis often proceeds at a fairly slow pace, it regularly happens."[76] The Open Dialogue therapy, founded on assertive community treatment, resembles NAA in terms of "stressing family-centeredness, home visits, and team work," but does not rely on psychotherapeutic methods in the same way that NAA did.[77]

Jaakko Seikkula, professor of psychotherapy at the University of Jyväskylä in Finland, who also worked at Keropudas Hospital in Tornio for close to twenty years, has been the lead investigator on several studies of psychotic patients in West Lapland. For a long time "Keropudas Hospital was occupied by dozens of long-term patients who had been considered 'incurable,'" says Seikkula. The need-adapted therapy without the use of psychiatric drugs created "a more optimistic treatment model," which took advantage of a "patient's own psychological resources" toward healing.[78] Under Open Dialogue therapy, Seikkula reports, in a two-year follow up of first-episode psychotic patients for two consecutive periods, between 1992–93 and 1994–97, "it was found that 81% of patients did not have any residual psychotic symptoms, and that 84% had returned to full-time employment or studies. Only 33% had used neuroleptic medication."[79] The study was repeated again in 2003–2005 to "determine whether the outcomes were consistent 10 years after the preliminary period." The results were "as good as" the 1990s.[80]

Today, Western Lapland psychiatric facilities consist of the fifty-five-bed Keropudas hospital and five outpatient clinics. All mental health workers have received training in family therapy, and today Open Dialogue is a well-established and tuned-up method of care, with a constancy of trained staff, many of whom have been there for decades. "Their conception of psychosis is quite distinct in kind, as it doesn't really fit into either the biological or psychological category," says Whitaker. They see psychosis as the fruit of "severely frayed social relationships." Tapio Salo, one of the psychologists who practices Open-Dialogue therapy, explains, "Psychosis does not live in the head. It lives in the in-between of family members, and

76. Ibid., 339–40.

77. Seikkula et al., "The Comprehensive Open-Dialogue Approach in Western Lapland," 193.

78. Seikkula, "Becoming Dialogical," 180.

79. Seikkula et al., "The Comprehensive Open-Dialogue Approach in Western Lapland," 192.

80. Ibid.

the in-between of people. . . . It is in the relationship, and the one who is psychotic makes the bad condition visible. He or she 'wears the symptoms' and has the burden to carry them."[81] This way, the person with psychosis is truly a "sacrificial lamb" in his community. Indeed, this corroborates the view that the encounter with illness has to be *communal* and that illness points to a "distorted relationship between the individual and [a] social group." Therefore, healing entails the "restitution" of a coherent relationship to the particular social group.[82]

Within the Open Dialogue model the response to the psychotic episode is of great urgency for everyone. The difficult mysteries hidden in hallucinations must be reflected upon in the first few days, because they may "easily fade away" and the opportunity to have access to them "may not reappear."[83] All are trained that when one is contacted for help, a meeting will be organized within twenty-four hours, preferably at the patient's home. There will be at least two or three constant staff members present who will become the "team" dedicated to the family. The team may consist of a psychiatrist, a psychologist, and a nurse. The patient, his family, friends, other key members of his social network, even his boss, are invited to the meeting to discuss all the relevant issues. No one walks into the meeting with any preconceived notions about the problem; but all will promote an "open dialogue" in which everyone can express his or her thoughts. Seikkula explains that "the 'right' diagnosis *emerges* in joint meetings . . . [and] that the process of understanding, that is, arriving at a full and practical understanding in a dialogic manner by all concerned of what has happened, can itself be a very therapeutic process."[84]

In this ongoing open dialogue, problems become evident. This approach does not allow for any fixed "treatment planning with stable plans"; instead, the flow of dialogue in every meeting leads to a new process. In other words, the treatment is constantly re-planned as needs arise and as new narratives are generated. The essential element is for all involved to tolerate "uncertainty" and allow the open dialogue to stay alive.[85] The sufferer "reaches for something unreachable by others in their surroundings," says Seikkula. "The aim of the treatment becomes the expression

---

81. Whitaker, *Anatomy of an Epidemic*, 341.

82. Siirala, *The Voice of Illness*, 53; Tillich, Foreword, v.

83. Seikkula and Alakare, "Open Dialogues," 229.

84. Seikkula, "Becoming Dialogical," 181.

85. Ibid., 182–84.

of experiences that did not have words or a shared language."[86] As was previously shown through Ramussen's research among Eskimos, when the community of friends and family felt collective responsibility for the illness, their readiness to confess and ask for forgiveness was the key to bringing about healing. It appears that the same basic principles are at work in the Open Dialogue therapy.

There is a great emphasis on hearing everyone's voice and creating a safe environment for inner feelings to come out. Seikkula explains, "Therapists and clients live in a joint, embodied experience that happens before the client's experiences are formulated in words. In dialogue an intersubjective consciousness emerges."[87] This process enables all to find their hidden voices, and soon they will become respondents to themselves. The concept of intersubjective consciousness no longer frames individuals as subjects of their lives, "in the sense that the coordinating centre of our actions exists within the individual." It gives rise to the concept of the "polyphonic self" that is constructed based on "response and responsiveness." No longer is the individual there by himself; it is the network of his community together that emerges as the new self—the polyphonic self.[88] Even though they do not attribute their model to any Christian principles, it appears as if the participants truly become "one body" and individually "members of one another." The process is highlighting that humans are relational beings and in that context, Seikkula explains:

> Nothing more is needed than being heard and taken seriously and it is this which generates a dialogical relation. And when— after a crisis—we again return to dialogical relations, the therapeutic task is fulfilled because agency is regained.[89]

Speaking of the hope that the staff inspires in the sufferer and the family, Birgitta Alakare, one of the lead psychiatrists in the program, says, "The message that we give is that we can manage this crisis. We have experience that people can get better, and we have trust in this kind of possibility." Even though they are confident about the promise of their approach, they admit that in some cases the process may take several years before the person can get his "grip on life" and for his "relationship to society" to be

---

86. Seikkula and Alakare, "Open Dialogues," 229.

87. Seikkula, "Becoming Dialogical," 186.

88. Ibid., 187.

89. Ibid., 191.

repaired. This is about restoring health in the community surrounding the person, and it requires patience and a steady effort.[90]

"Open Dialogue" therapy has been a great success. For the past two decades or so "the picture of the psychotic population" in Western Lapland has dramatically changed. Since 1992–1993 when Tornio was selected as one of the "experimental" sites to test the need for medication, "not a single first-episode psychotic patient has ended up chronically hospitalized." Today, the cost of psychiatric care in the region is the lowest in all Finland. In a multinational Nordic study conducted in 2002–2006, among the first-episode psychotic patients in Tornio, 84 percent of patients were fully functional, working, or studying at the end of the two years, and only 20 percent were on psychiatric medication. "Most remarkable of all, schizophrenia is now disappearing from the region," says Whitaker. This is due to the fact that a diagnosis of schizophrenia will be given usually after the patient has suffered from the symptoms for at least six months. With the current model of care the psychotic symptoms are abated fairly quickly.[91]

According to Whitaker, "Only two or three new cases of schizophrenia appear each year in western Lapland, a 90 percent drop since the early 1980s." This is a remarkable success story that has drawn the attention of mental health providers in other parts of Europe. Even in the strongly drug-captivated US, similar experimental projects are beginning to take shape. "This really happened," says Seikkula, speaking of their success. "It's not just a theory." Whitaker, who sat through several therapy meetings, called it "a bit mystifying." None of the staff could give him an explanation as to why the process worked so effectively. "The severe symptoms begin to pass," said Salo, "We don't know how it happens, but [open-dialogue therapy] must be doing something because it works."[92] Throughout this book I've tried to show that when the community takes the burden of illness as its own and authentically participates in search of answers by

90. Whitaker, *Anatomy of an Epidemic*, 342–43.

91. Ibid., 343.

92. Ibid., 343–44. A multi-disciplinary team at the University of Massachusetts Medical School, led by Douglas Ziedonis and Mary Olson of the Department of Psychiatry, is collaborating with Jaakko Seikkula and his colleagues in Finland to adapt "Open Dialogue" for the purpose of implementing it in the US. For more information on that project see online: http://www.umassmed.edu/psychiatry/globalinitiatives/opendialogue.aspx. Additionally, the Institute for Dialogical Practice is the US-based training facility for Finnish Open Dialogue and dialogical therapy, established in Haydenville, Massachusetts, in 2012. See online: http://www.dialogicpractice.net.

confessing its own sins, the evil forces at work are disarmed, and God's grace, forgiveness, and healing power begin to flow. It appears as if the same principles are at work in the Open Dialogue model.

Seikkula et al. discuss the change in the overall culture of West Lapland in respect to mental health. It seems that psychosis is not as stigmatized as it is in other places. This is partially due to the fact that the staff treats psychosis as something meaningful to be understood rather than as something to eliminate. Also the involvement of a large number of people in these group dialogues is helpful. Every year, about 1,500 people suffering from psychotic incidents are treated through Open Dialogue. In each case, at least the close family members participate in the treatment. "It can thus be estimated that every year about 4,500–7,000 people participate in joint therapy meetings, amounting to as much as 5–10% of the population," says Seikkula. The actual number is probably higher than this due to the large network of participants. This removes the stigma, creates "increased openness in participating psychiatric treatment," and encourages people to initiate treatment with the earliest signs and receive help. Consequently, "psychotic symptoms are less entrenched" than is the case in other societies where the stigma prevents people speaking up and seeking treatment.[93]

Seikkula and others involved in Open Dialogue strongly oppose "generalized models for psychiatric treatment." They believe these crises point to deep-rooted human issues, which can only be respectfully and properly dealt with within the local and cultural context of the person's life. Each treatment approach must be relevant to the person's unique case.[94] Seikkula claims:

> The positive outcomes in Open Dialogue may indicate that psychosis no longer needs to be seen as a sign of illness, but can be viewed as one way of dealing with a crisis and after this crisis, many or most people are capable of returning to their active social life. And when so few actually need neuroleptic drugs, we can ask whether our understanding of the problem itself should be changed. Perhaps it is not the biochemical state of the brain that causes hallucinations, but, instead, hallucinations include real incidents of life and are one possible response to

93. Seikkula, "The Comprehensive Open-Dialogue Approach in Western Lapland," 201–2.

94. Seikkula and Alakare, "Open Dialogues," 238.

severe stress. This can occur in every one of us and no specific biological vulnerability is needed.[95]

This model portrays the arguments of this thesis in regards to the significance of hearing everyone's voice within their cultural context in a vivid fashion. Their great emphasis on family therapy and addressing the root communal issues calls for the person to stay at home and the therapy to be brought to him and his immediate community. However, it is clearly necessary for the team of therapists to have been trained in the specific methods of Open Dialogue. This model, while offering a much more structured approach, emphasizes flexibility in shaping the treatment based on each individual's unique situation.

Fifohanza, the Awakening Movement—The Toby Model

The Toby Model of ministry that is practiced in the northern region of Madagascar—an island nation off the southeast coast of Africa—integrates conventional medical treatment with prayer, pastoral care, exorcism, preaching, and Christian education to help people suffering from illnesses, all "*in a setting of Christian community and Christian love.*"[96] The root of this program, implemented by the Lutheran church in Madagascar, goes far back to the 1940s and 1950s to a "visionary prophetess" named Volahavana Germaine—more commonly referred to as Nenilava (Tall-Mother)—who as a child received repeated revelations and instructions from Jesus to develop a healing ministry. She was directed to establish a healing and care model based on the teachings of New Testament on illness.[97]

Ronald Roschke, who went to Madagascar to evaluate this "visionary healing movement," was surprised at the importance of this ministry within the Malagasy Lutheran church, which has allocated a major organization for its oversight and coordination. "At the heart of Nenilava's revelation was the creation of *toby*," says Roschke. "*Toby* (pronounced 'too-bee') is the Malagasy word for a 'compound' or 'settlement.'" Toby is

---

95. Ibid., 237.

96. Rakotojoelinandrasana, "Holistic Approach to Mental Illnesses," 182. Daniel Rakotojoelinandrasana wrote his DMin dissertation on *Toby Ambohibao*, Madagascar, presenting it as a potential model of healing ministry for the church to approach the problem of mental illness.

97. Roschke, "Healing in Luke, Madagascar, and Elsewhere," 459–60.

a place of rest, a community built with the aim of bringing holistic healing to Christians. Today, there are dozens of Tobys operational across Madagascar. According to Roschke, "Each *toby* is a community of healing to which anywhere from a dozen to several hundred people might come. Some live in the compound a few weeks; some spend most of their lives there."[98] Toby is designed with a vision of biblical healing in mind, where all residents and staff learn to live the "Christian lifestyle," in a community that is centered on loving one another, accepting each other unconditionally, praying together, and growing in the knowledge of Scripture and its application in daily life.[99]

The Toby of Ambohibao, which is dedicated to the care of the mentally ill, is located in the suburb of Madagascar's capital city, Antananarivo, next to the Lutheran Hospital of Ambohibao. The Toby and the hospital work in close partnership with each other, and emphasize a marriage between "scientific medicine" and "biblical methods." The model, drawing on the teachings on healing ministry in the New Testament, acknowledges the reality of "spirit-related disorders" that could cause disruption in people's lives through both bodily and mental afflictions. Malagasy Christians believe that in order to conform to the model of Jesus' ministry, the church needs to engage the world of spirits—"more precisely, to proclaim the kingdom of God, to heal the sick, and to cast out demons (Matt 10:7–8)."[100]

The healing practice is centered on healing services that are conducted up to two or three times a day, consisting of prayer, Scripture reading, songs of worship, and some preaching. In every service they read the four biblical texts that were emphasized in Nenilava's visions (Matthew 18:18–20; Mark 16:15–20; John 14:12–17, 20:21–23). Each Toby is staffed by a team of lay individuals who have received two years of biblical training on issues of healing; these staff persons are called *mpiandry*, or shepherds. While medical doctors attend to the physical problems of the patients, the shepherds attend to their spiritual and relational health. The team of shepherds conducts the healing services under the direction of their pastor. Roschke explains:

> During prayer, the shepherds put on their white robes and then begin a general exorcism of the congregation. With commanding voices and waving arms the shepherds announce in the name of Jesus that all evil spirits must leave. Persons who are ill

98. Ibid.

99. Rakotojoelinandrasana, "Holistic Approach to Mental Illnesses," 183.

100. Ibid., 182–83.

and possessed come forward and the shepherds deal with them individually, casting out demons with convulsive force. After the expulsion, prayer with laying on of hands invites the Holy Spirit to take possession of the petitioner.[101]

Roschke admits that this dramatic scene with its intense and emotional liturgies is "a challenge to the sensibilities of many twenty-first-century Westerners steeped in a postmodern scientific world-view."[102] But, is it biblical, and does it work? Roschke believes this healing experience in Malagasy is a much closer reflection of the biblical worldview in the Gospels than what is found in "the laboratories, hospitals, and doctors' offices of contemporary North America." He rejects the notion that "health," "healing," and "disease" are universal constructs. These terms are deeply attached to cultural understandings of reality and it is this lens through which one perceives one's problems and seeks out solutions. He points out that among many non-Western cultures, "healing" is not necessarily about eliminating "disequilibrium" in bodily organs; it is, rather, "an attempt to provide personal and social meaning for the life problems created by sickness."[103]

As was previously argued, the medical knowledge of the biblical time, based on the Corpus Hippocraticum (CH) "does not identify evil spirits as a factor in illness." In fact, the causes of illness, according to the CH, are detectable merely by observation and knowledge of the "physical reality of our bodies."[104] Roschke believes that Luke, in spite of being a physician himself, took the demonic ideas of Mark's Gospel seriously enough to use them in his own writing:

> If the author of Luke has fused the positivist categories of medical knowledge of his day with Mark's story of a cosmic battle between Good and Evil, it teases us to consider whether such a fusion might be possible—and desirable—in our own era. Scientific Westerners will need some help to make this leap. We can find assistance from contemporary cultures in which a scientific practice of medicine coexists with belief in demonic possession and the practice of exorcism—in places like Madagascar.[105]

101. Roschke, "Healing in Luke, Madagascar, and Elsewhere," 460.

102. Ibid.

103. Ibid., 461.

104. Ibid., 464.

105. Ibid., 466–67.

The Ambohibao Toby cares for the mentally ill based on categorizing these patients into those suffering from 1) a "spirit-related disorder (SRD)" caused by demon possession or magic; 2) mental illnesses of organic nature with clear pathological biomarkers; 3) some combination of the first two categories. The work of ministry, performed by the shepherds, can be described as: 1) "church activities": these are the basic services related to the ecclesiastical operations (worship, sacraments, biblical education, training of the shepherds, etc.); 2) "The ministry of work and empowering" is focused on the individual care of the patients who have to live in the toby and receive care according to their needs; 3) "The ministry of counseling," which covers the elements of pastoral care for the patient and their families to get to the root causes of the mental disturbance, such as issues of sin, guilt, relational conflicts, "magico-religious practices," lack of forgiveness, and the need for repentance; 4) "Other ministries and activities," where other activities related to work, schooling, farming, etc. are managed.[106]

Roschke emphasizes the radical integration of science and spirit in the Toby model, where even a patient with tuberculosis can first be treated in a local hospital with intravenous drugs, and then to be sent to live in a Toby, "where he is surrounded by a supportive and encouraging community, takes part in the services of healing and exorcism, and . . . 'God heals him.'" In this movement, people reject an "opposition between scientific and spiritual healing." They see God as the ultimate healer; in fact their motto is: "We treat; God heals."[107] And it is both science and spirit that are tools in their toolbox to be applied toward all treatments. Most medical doctors who work at Toby Ambohibao are also shepherds and have had training in "spirit-related disorders." This necessity of cross-training is being realized even among the Western psychiatrists. Bradley Lewis, both a practicing psychiatrist and a humanities scholar at New York University, writes:

> I believe in psychiatry. I believe that secular cultures need the services psychiatry can provide. . . . These clinicians should have a broad education and be aware of the multiple dimensions of human suffering and human flourishing. . . . To nurture that kind of clinician, psychiatry must reconsider its basic priorities,

106. Rakotojoelinandrasana, "Holistic Approach to Mental Illnesses," 183–84.

107. Roschke, "Healing in Luke, Madagascar, and Elsewhere," 467; For an exposition of this principle of human agency directed by God's sovereign power as the ultimate healer, see Gaiser, *Healing in the Bible*, 33.

as that caliber of clinician requires scholarly resources beyond the sciences. . . . It is difficult these days to find well-rounded and intellectually nuanced psychiatrists. The best way to correct this imbalance toward science and rationality is to develop alliances on both sides of campus that will bring the tools and insights of the humanities to bear on the training of psychiatrists.[108]

He makes these assertions because he believes, "Of all the medical specialties, psychiatry is the least consistent thematically with scientific methods (in spite of the new psychiatry's recent claims) and the closest in subject matter to the arts and humanities."[109] It is also noteworthy that Lewis emphasizes the need for psychiatry in "secular cultures." The implication of his message is that people of faith have their own resources to comfort them in the midst of anxiety and suffering, but psychiatry has the potential to serve those who have no access to such resources. Regrettably, in Western cultures, even the people of faith have mostly lost insight into possibilities that their faith traditions offer in time of mental distress.

Likewise, Ronald Pies wrote:

> I believe psychiatrists must reclaim and reinvent our role as holistic healers—doctors who are as comfortable with motives as with molecules, and as willing to employ poetry as prescribe pills. When guided by sound evidence, this is not promiscuous eclecticism, but rather what I have termed, "polythetic pluralism." I favor an expansion of the psychiatry residency to 5 years, so that residents may receive enhanced training in psychotherapy and the humanities, eg, literature, comparative religion, and philosophy.[110]

Pies is clearly affirming that clinical psychiatry is much more than medical treatment. For that reason he also advocates the reduction of pure and generic "medical school training from 4 to 3 years, with substantial streamlining and condensation of the pre-clinical curriculum."

Lewis and Pies's suggestions align with the paradigm within which Ambohibao's pastors and psychiatrists work. As psychiatrists are trained to deal with SRDs, the pastors and shepherds are also trained to differentiate between organic disorders and the spiritual ones. The diagnoses are made based on the following criteria: 1) The patient's life history and evaluation of any occult activities; 2) Evaluation of the disorder's "symptomatology,"

---

108. Lewis, *Moving Beyond Prozac, DSM, & the New Psychiatry*, xiii.

109. Ibid., 64.

110. Pies, "How American Psychiatry Can Save itself."

and the possible correspondence to any pathological standards; 3) The discernment of presence of any demonic spirits that would require exorcism; 4) The person's reactions to the exorcism ceremonies—"Improvement is often drastic for people who have SRD as opposed to people who have classic mental disorders."[111]

Regardless of the psychiatric or spiritual dimension of the disorder, the treatment will always engage the problem through "medical, sociopsychological, and spiritual and religious"[112] angles. The medical treatment including the use of psychiatric drugs and electroshock therapy are applied as necessary. Rakotojoelinandrasana explains how the shepherds in Ambohibao recognize that a person has been healed of demonic oppressions:

> The sign of certitude is when the person expresses true relief and joy, almost ecstasy, then is able to call upon the name of Jesus for salvation, mercy and thanksgiving, and from then on her/his behavior and attitude will be consistent with a Christian normal life. In the practice of the revival, a person who is still demonized is incapable and unwilling to call on the name of Jesus.[113]

Rakotojoelinandrasana stresses that the rejection of the possibility of demonic influences in mental disorders, due to the doctrines of biological psychiatry, has done a disservice to those suffering from these afflictions in the Western world. He states:

> Contrary to the prediction of the Enlightenment that the advent of science would remove demonism from our society, one sees a resurgence of demonism in our postmodern world. Demon possession is a universal phenomenon, found not only in tribal cultures. The Western world, and the church in particular, needs to be ready for its challenge.[114]

Phillip Sinaikin claims, "Despite being a psychiatrist for twenty eight years and having had jobs where I worked with extremely ill patients, I still find psychosis shocking. It truly is like demonic possession, the degree to which the delusions and hallucinations take over."[115] Stewart Govig, whose

111. Rakotojoelinandrasana, "Holistic Approach to Mental Illnesses," 184–85.

112. Ibid., 185.

113. Ibid., 186.

114. Ibid., 187.

115. Sinaikin, *Psychiatryland,* 242. Sinaikin, who is very critical of the direction his profession has taken, believes "schizophrenia" is one of the few "mental disorders" that

son Jay suffers from "schizophrenia," is an advocate of biological psychiatry and has found its treatment, though not perfect, helpful in support of his son's condition. However, he admits: "Looking back on Jay's acute episodes at the onset of his illness, I am still mystified by the rantings I heard about Satan, wizards, and even Lucifer. Demon possession, when I see it in the New Testament scriptures, has an uncomfortable familiarity."[116] He admits that in spite of familiar imagery, he does not know what to do with those biblical texts in relation to his own son. Govig is correct that "schizophrenia" in many facets reflects the images drawn by the demoniacs in Scripture. But it is imperative for the church to be humble and discerning, and not make judgments hastily in this regard. Speaking of "exorcism and spiritual healing" as a model for healing madness, Foskett stresses, "Whatever the alarms and uncertainties about this model, and there are many who have suffered terribly at its hands, there are others for whom it has brought healing and relief."[117] Exorcism and spiritual healing must be included in the church's toolbox, but applied with tremendous care guided by the discerning power of the Holy Spirit. Moreover, it is essential for the act of exorcism to be practiced *only* by those who have been anointed for such a ministry by God. Fighting the forces of darkness is not a casual task to be taken lightly (Acts 19:13–15).

Undoubtedly, within the Toby model in Ambohibao, demonic influences are accepted as anything but confusing and mythical. They have seen repeated deliverances of people who have gained their wholeness by the power of the Spirit of God who has brought them out of darkness. Rakotojoelinandrasana claims that the revival experiences in Madagascar affirm the reality of demonic attacks and remind the church of the "christological truth" that has been ignored conveniently; the fact that "the Son of God has come into the world to destroy the work of the Devil (1 John 3:8)." This is a promise that brings hope, healing, and liberty to those who have been rejected by all sources of hope in this world. The Toby model is about "a holistic salvation, a salvation that does not just save people

---

is truly a biological illness. However, he readily admits that the question of "schizophrenia" is a very complex one for everyone involved, and affirms that "the biological basis and underlying cause of psychotic disorders is not known." Admitting the absence of any proof for a biological etiology, it appears that his view of "schizophrenia"-as-a-biological-illness is only due to the fact that antipsychotics are able to control some of the symptoms; 240–42.

116. Govig, *Souls are made of Endurance*, 93.

117. Foskett, *Meaning in Madness*, 135.

from sin, in view of the other world, but a salvation that also addresses the predicaments of the present world."[118]

Roschke claims that our "modernist bifurcation of physical and spiritual reality" handicaps our ability to treat our illnesses "holistically." It is also our individualistic perspective in medicine that "closes the door to social realities that affect our well-being." It is shortsighted on the part of the Western culture to ignore "the network of relationships" surrounding the person, which for sure are both "part of the disease" and "its resolution." The West also needs to learn "how to speak about evil and its power among us."[119] Scripture is quite clear about the influence of evil as opposing powers that the church has to overcome by putting on the armor of God through the power of Christ (Eph 6:11–12). This is a difficult but necessary element to be taken on by the church in its struggle toward "holistic" healing.

Among the four models studied for this thesis, the Tobys model is the only faith-based structure. Ironically, this is the model that subscribes to the medical treatment of mental illness more than any of the others. However, the Toby practicioners too believe in communal healing and the power of relationships that are authentic, caring, and respectful. While they believe in "spirit-related disorders" and exorcism, they put emphasis on radical integration of science and spirituality. This is done under the watchful pastoral supervision, which enforces biblical teachings about what a faithful Christian life ought to be.

In the Fellowship of His Suffering: The Road to Healing

The church in the West can learn much from the aforementioned models of treatment for those who are afflicted by the life-disabling phenomenon of madness. It is not a matter of choice to embrace the psychotics in our immediate community; it is a call of God knocking at our doors. Bonhoeffer stresses, "We must be ready to allow ourselves to be interrupted by God. God will be constantly crossing our paths and canceling our plans by sending us people" who are disruptive to our pre-planned affairs. We may turn our face away from them, "preoccupied with our more important tasks" as the priest and the Levite did toward the man who was beaten by

118. Rakotojoelinandrasana, "Holistic Approach to Mental Illnesses," 187–88.

119. Roschke, "Healing in Luke, Madagascar, and Elsewhere," 467–68.

the robbers and left to die. "When we do that," says Bonhoeffer, "we pass by the visible sign of the Cross raised athwart our path to show us that, not our way, but God's way must be done."[120]

If there was one element common to all the models that have been successful in dealing with the mentally ill, undoubtedly it was nurtured relationships that are meaningful and ingrained in daily lives. Whitaker reminds us that if we truly want to help these people we cannot think of them as those with "broken brains"; rather, we have to think of them as the Quakers did when they established the York Retreat—as "brethren."[121] Bonhoeffer explains, "The exclusion of the weak and insignificant, the seemingly useless people, from a Christian community may actually mean the exclusion of Christ; in the poor brother Christ is knocking at the door."[122] This is a knock that we cannot afford to ignore. In the meek and the broken, he is asking to dine with us. Would we invite him in? (Rev 3:20).

Based on the reality of life for these broken, afflicted, and oppressed children of God the church has to step in as Christ's ambassador and incarnate his love and care for these "lepers" of our time. In order to accomplish that, I propose a model of care consisting of the following elements: 1) A place one can call home; 2) Pastoral care and counseling structure for the person suffering and his family; 3) A partnership with the psychiatric community; 4) Operational management. We call this model "Healing Together" due to its emphasis on communal responsibility both for the illness and the healing.

A Place One Can Call Home

In all the models presented here there is a great emphasis on family counseling, because all have realized that the family as a whole is wounded and requires healing. As we have already seen the research clearly confirms that Expressed Emotions (EE) in the family can cause a relapse of the symptoms and is a barrier to full recovery.[123] Many of the psychotic symptoms are aiming at the family. Lori Schiller, who suffers from "schizophrenia,"

---

120. Bonhoeffer, *Life Together*, 99.

121. Stastny et al., *Alternatives Beyond Psychiatry*, 12.

122. Bonhoeffer, *Life Together*, 38.

123. Tarrier, *The Family Management*, 254–82.

explains the intensity of her emotions toward her family whenever they visited her:

> I loved them so much. I was so proud of them. I was so glad to see them. And I couldn't wait for them to leave. They stirred up in me a whirlwind of violent emotions that I didn't understand, and had to struggle mightily each and every visit to control until they were gone.[124]

It is difficult if not impossible to expect a family to go through this journey with disciplined behavior, a low level of emotions and no sense of anger, guilt, and shame. And yet, all these elements are contributors to worsening the psychotic symptoms. Also, families themselves need healing, which is hard to accomplish while they have to endure the day-to-day stress of caring for their loved one in his new state, constantly being reminded of their loss. After all, as the saying goes, "It is hard to change a tire while the car is running." The person who is not well has to live away from home until wounds are healed, both for the person and the family. Phyllis Vine, a historian, explains, "In some instances families can sustain a relative's chronic demands only when the person does not live with them. One form of assistance that families need most is access to residential housing they can rely upon."[125] In many cases, the lack of sufficient and effective care structure has led to criminalization of people with mental illness, mostly for relatively minor offenses. "In desperation, some family members charge their loved one [with crimes] in the hope that they will be able to access service through the forensic psychiatry system," explains Dr. Chaimowitz. "Unfortunately the price of this uncertain access is the criminalization of the individual."[126]

There is a real need for Christian families that have "room in their homes" and "room in their lives," who can receive the person with all his challenges and welcome him into their lives for as long as it might be necessary. This is very similar to the model of "Healing Homes" in the countryside of Sweden. The distinction is the Christian emphasis here. The ideal is to have a family within the person's congregation open their doors and welcome the guest as a new addition to their family that they might

---

124. Schiller and Bennett, *The Quiet Room*, 210.

125. Vine, *Families in Pain*, 93; cited in Govig, *Souls are made of Endurance*, 51.

126. "Action Needed to Address the Increasing Criminalization of People with Mental Illness Say Canadian Psychiatrists," online: http://www.digitaljournal.com/pr/610008#ixzz1oFlYYFiQ.

serve their God and become the "instruments in the Redeemer's hands."[127] Contrary to the conventional wisdom, most of the insane are quite harmless when they are treated humanely, with dignity and respect. One must remember the words of Philippe Pinel, who transformed French psychiatry by treating the mad with affection and care and saw a different outcome. Describing them, he used words like "affectionate," "impassioned," "pure," "exalted," "tenderness," and "virtue."[128] These words are certainly not common in our western collective consciousness when we think of the insane. This might be the consequence of our own insecurities, which have been intensified by images engraved in our thoughts by the "cruel and false 'psycho' media sterotypes [sic]"[129]; we certainly do not regard them as "brethren." Most of the insane are not "unusually bizarre, dangerous, mercurial," says Richard Erickson, who is a theologian and a clinical psychologist. He says many might have "difficulty relating with other people, in organizing their lives, and in effectively responding to stressful events," but the quality of their lives could be significantly improved through "[w]ell-conceived assistance" from within their communities.[130]

To be effective in this undertaking, the host families have to approach it compassionately, yet without illusion. Winifred Overholzer, the superintendent of St. Elizabeth's Hospital in Washington D.C., insightfully commented about the insane: "The mentally ill are just like us, only more so."[131] They truly are an intense picture of our true selves, which is the greatest gift they could offer us—a mirror where we are forced to gaze at ourselves. The insane will bring their messiness as a sanctifying fire along with promises of reward beyond one's grasp. The author of Hebrews reminds the Christians: "Let love of the brethren continue. Do not neglect to show hospitality to strangers, for by this some have entertained angels without knowing it. Remember the prisoners, as though in prison with them, and those who are ill-treated, since you yourselves also are in the body" (Hebrews 13:1–3). Grudem refers to this as an "inspection visit," like "the newspaper's restaurant critic who disguises himself and visits a new restaurant." He believes this should encourage the faithful to "minister to the needs of others whom we do not know."[132]

127. Tripp, *Instruments in the Redeemer's Hands*, 360.

128. Quoted in Whitaker, *Mad in America*, 21.

129. Govig, "Chronic Mental Illness and the Family," 406.

130. Erickson, "Serving the Needs of Persons with Chronic Mental Illness," 157.

131. Ibid., 156.

132. Grudem, *Bible Doctrine*, 173.

The Swedish experience has proven that these homes are best suited to be in the countryside, or in small towns away from the hustle and bustle of big cities. This will provide the opportunity for spending time in nature, freedom to walk around without being disturbed, and ideally to work with animals on a farm. More important than the location of the house is the presence of the Spirit of God in our proposed model. The ideal host families are those that are reasonably stable, calm, gentle, interested in their own growth, zealous for serving God, and whose union is built upon the foundation of faith in Christ and his revelation in Scripture as a roadmap for life. It is only in that setting that the challenges will be reframed as opportunities for self-reflection and for living a life that is gratifying beyond temporary pleasures. Obedience to the teachings of Scripture led by the anointing of the Spirit of Christ is the key to success and fruitfulness in this battle against darkness. James teaches: "Submit therefore to God. Resist the devil and he will flee from you" (James 4:7). Vanier says, "The spirit of evil is powerless against humility."[133] Love, humility, patience, and obedience to God disarm forces of evil that are provoked by pride.

It is the sanctifying power of this journey that brings one face to face with the darkness of one's own heart and the depth of one's sinfulness. Living with and caring for the insane opens our eyes to the realm of darkness not merely at an intellectual level, but one will be able to apprehend experientially the "out of measure" nature of sin. "Never, until sin is seen and sorrowed for as the greatest evil, will Christ be seen and rejoiced in as the greatest Good," says Jeremiah Burroughs.[134]

Burroughs believes that humanity is "cheated to their own destruction," because they only know of sin through the "false mediums" of this world. He says, "Could we but lay our ears to hell and hear the howlings and yellings of those damned spirits aggravating sin, we should then have a true comment upon the subject in hand."[135] The "howlings and yellings" of the insane are a picture of that destiny to awaken those who do not take sin seriously. The voice of insanity will open any deaf ears and any blind eyes to know sin like they never knew, and by gazing at its depth of darkness one comes to his senses to get a grip of his own fallenness. And it is in that realization that the glorious grace of God is manifest to grant repentance, regenerate new life, and shine light over darkness. This is a hardship from which only the faint of heart and the foolish will run.

133. Vanier, *Community and Growth*, 218.
134. Burroughs, *The Evil of Evils*, xviii.
135. Ibid., xix.

The pain and the hardship are seeds that can grow into a fruitful life where healing is possible not only for the afflicted, but also for all who surround him "to be" with him (Heb 12:11). Jean Vanier says, "There is something prophetic in people who seem marginal and difficult; they force the community to become alert."[136] It is these people who force the community around them to change, because they sense false behavior, and more than anything else they demand authenticity. If people of all kinds of background like those in Soteria house or the Swedish "Healing Homes" have the capacity to care for the "schizophrenics," then surely faithful Christians who are endowed with the power and grace of God are up to the task. As Bonhoeffer explains, one who has been justified by God's grace is surely willing and able "to accept even insults and injuries without protest, taking them from God's punishing and gracious hand." As we have heard from the experience of others, the "schizophrenics" in most cases are harmless, confused, and very lonely. The best someone can do for them is to integrate them into an environment where they are taken seriously, respected, and listened to, regardless of how odd their language may sound at times. He who is not able to listen to his brethren "will soon be no longer listening to God either," says Bonhoeffer.[137]

According to Vanier, nothing is more therapeutic than "authentic relationships" combined with "work" and "true spiritual life." Work could be as simple as responsibilities around the household or on the farm. These elements combined will bring about "hope," "self-acceptance," and "motivation."[138] Swinton speaks of the "friendships of Jesus," which target those who are broken and marginalized, and offer hope and dignity to them. For example, when Jesus encountered the Samaritan woman (John 4) who was "heavily stigmatized and outcast" in the Jewish community, he treated her as a person worthy of conversation and attention. Swinton says, "In speaking with her and sharing her drinking vessel, Jesus makes Himself marginalized and unclean. However, in doing this he takes her into the community of God, resurrects her personhood, and heals her brokenness."[139]

Building relationships with the "schizophrenics" is a bit tricky, though. In fact, the person suffering from "schizophrenia" is not able to establish relationships easily, because he is so consumed by his inner

136. Vanier, *Community and Growth*, 274.

137. Bonhoeffer, *Life Together*, 96, 98.

138. Vanier, *Community and Growth*, 279.

139. Swinton, *Resurrecting the Person*, 142.

world. Carson suggests, "those who undertake to care for someone with the disorder should not impose themselves upon the person, but provide a discreet and patient resource for them."[140] This is a relationship that demands a selfless unconditional servant attitude. When love is the unconditional love of Christ, then it is not directed to the other person for one's own sake. It doesn't seek affirmation or reciprocal relationship. It is very difficult for the "schizophrenic" to love back. In fact often he will reject all acts of love. What an amazing picture of how we reject God's love! Bonhoeffer explains:

> Human love desires the other person, his company, his answering love, but it does not serve him. On the contrary, it continues to desire even when it seems to be serving. . . . [H]uman love cannot love an enemy, that is, one who seriously and stubbornly resists it. . . . [W]here it can no longer expect its desire to be fulfilled . . . it turns into hatred, contempt, and calumny. . . . Human love makes itself an end in itself. . . . Spiritual love, however, comes from Jesus Christ, it serves him alone; it knows that it has no immediate access to other persons. Jesus Christ stands between the lover and the others he loves.[141]

It is in this servitude toward the "unlovable" that we come to learn the depth of God's love—how he loved us when we were "dead in our transgressions" (Eph 2:5) and rejected him at every turn. It is only then that what we had accepted intellectually will become real in our soul.

Pastoral Care Structure

The primary purpose of the pastoral care function is to help the person and his immediate community—this includes his church—to hear the voice of his illness. In dealing with madness, as Foskett suggests, "The metaphor of revelation is a better vehicle for describing the goal of pastoral care and counseling than is the metaphor of healing."[142] It is important to note that in the Christian model, the psychotic experience, though it afflicts an individual in an extraordinary fashion, is not merely a personal problem. It ought to be seen as a blow to the body of Christ for which the church community should take responsibility. In this journey, Foskett believes, all

140. Carson, "Loving, Discernment, and Distance," 232.

141. Bonhoeffer, *Life Together*, 34–35.

142. Foskett, *Meaning in Madness*, 168.

involved will come to recognize that the answers, if there are any, lie ahead of them, and that together they "could go and look for them."[143]

Psychosis is a phenomenon that has pushed the person beyond normal boundaries of personal mind, caused by circumstances in life and the ensuing relationships. Isabel Clarke notes, "[T]he assumption that the individual person is complete, self sufficient and shut into their physical being, that we are separate little entities whizzing around and knocking into each other" is to look at a human being as a "billiard ball."[144] But, the human mind is far more than that: it is connected to the other members of the body of Christ and to one's Creator through one's spirit. This deep connection to the other members is what facilitates the manifestation of deep-rooted problems in the body through a vessel that has been emptied by severe brokenness, such that it can project all that flows through him from the rest.

As scholars such as Siirala, Laing, and Larchet have argued, wrapped in socially formed presumptions and methods of treatment the church can easily be deafened to the voice of "schizophrenia." Those who subscribe to the medical model of mental illness run the risk of losing the ability to interpret the phenomenon, focusing instead on the objective manifest signs separate from the reality they represent. Larchet claims that in the "divine economy," God uses illnesses as "providential ways to salvation" for the ill person and those around him.[145] Open Dialogue therapy in Finland has proven, as Siirala and Tillich have argued, that it is the distorted relationship between the sufferer and his immediate community that has brought about the illness. Therefore, healing entails the "restitution" of a coherent relationship to the particular social group, and more importantly addressing the root causes of those problems to prevent them from recurring. If sickness is understood this way, then the "sickness" is not as "sick" as some might perceive; rather "it is a healthy reaction against a sick society."[146] This is why the significance of the function of pastoral care—an interpretative function that would discern, shine light, and guide—in this encounter cannot be overestimated.

These illnesses are ours; they speak to our struggles, our fragility, our failures, our despair, and our confusions. "And as God's people, in particular, such waywardness and woe is exactly what our Bible is about," says

---

143. Ibid., 76.

144. Clarke, *Madness, Mystery and the Survival of God,* 17.

145. Larchet, *Theology of Illness,* 47, 51.

146. Tillich, Foreword, v.

David Powlison. "This is what Jesus comes to do something about. This is what church and ministry are intended to tackle."[147] Unfortunately, most pastors perceive their work to be centered on their preaching, and a series of religious activities that would invite the non-believers into the church or cause the growth of the local denomination. But the result for the church in the West has been anything but impressive. David Platt, reflecting on what has happened to the church, says, "I could not help but think that somewhere along the way we [have] missed what is radical about our faith and replaced it with what is comfortable. We [are] settling for a Christianity that revolves around catering to ourselves when the central message of Christianity is actually about abandoning ourselves."[148]

Christianity is about transformed lives, broken vessels emptied of themselves, instead filled by the Spirit of Christ, working in union together to bring glory to God. Has the church missed the calling on counseling the body in its personal contexts, helping each one to fulfill his destiny and to be transformed to the image of Christ? This is indeed what the Great Commission is about: the work of discipleship, to help people to be baptized by the fire of sanctification, and come out on the other side in the image of Christ "to observe all that [He] commanded" (Matt 28:19–20).[149] Is the church willing to hear the voice of the Lord, which comes from the midst of the fire? We read in Deuteronomy, that at Mount Sinai when the Lord spoke directly to his people: "the mountain burned with fire to the very heart of the heavens: darkness, cloud and thick gloom. Then the LORD spoke to you from the midst of the fire" (Deut 4:11–12a). Is the church willing to listen to the Voice that is coming from the midst of the "darkness, cloud and thick gloom"? Or, will she run away in fear as Israel did?

Powlison wonders how the church could have missed on this calling, and delegated the responsibility of counseling her members onto the "secular mental-health professionals." He says:

> Make no mistake: according to Scripture, Christian faith and life are occupied with all the gritty, grimy, sad, or slimy things that make for human misery. Jesus came to start making right all that has gone wrong. And we are his living body put to work

147. Powlison, Foreword, 12.

148. Platt, *Radical*, 7.

149. Powlison, "The Great Commission is a Great Place to Begin to Understand Biblical Counseling."

here on earth to keep making right whatever is wrong. And
never forget: we are part of what is wrong.[150]

Thus, if attending to the miseries of life and guiding people to hear the
voice of God in the midst of darkness are the primary responsibilities of
the pastoral care and counseling, how shall one go about this in dealing
with "schizophrenia"?

Support of an Acute Psychosis

One of the most frightening and confusing human experiences is when
one crosses the normal boundary of the human mind into "what is
popularly known as madness," and technically referred to as "psychosis."
Clarke explains that this could also be associated with certain religious
experiences, or even "the idea of possession."[151] Grof and Grof have written extensively on the idea of "spiritual emergency" as a "transformational
journey of spiritual development . . . a crisis in which the changes within
are so rapid and the inner states so demanding that, temporarily, these
people may find it difficult to operate fully in everyday reality."[152]

When a loved one experiences psychosis, families have no clue what
they are encountering. The church has been completely ignorant and absent in such scenes. In the Western world, the person is usually taken to an
emergency room and the mental health care workers will take over. Govig,
who recalls the first time his son experienced a psychotic episode and the
experience of "chaos and confusion" for his family, sadly claims that the
medical professionals and social workers who had taken over "formed"
his "church" at that point. He explains, "psychiatrists were the priests,
health professionals were the staff support, and other parents [of those
suffering from mental illness] the fellow congregational members. Faith
was in science."[153] At the onset of the crisis it was the psychiatric ward that
offered a "respite" to the "anxious parents and a vulnerable, sick youth."
Consequently, it was the doctrines of psychiatry that set the road map for
a lifelong journey that they embarked on, a journey that continues today.

150. Powlison, Foreword, 12.

151. Clarke, *Madness, Mystery and the Survival of God*, 23–24.

152. Grof and Grof, *The Stormy Search for the Self*, 1.

153. Govig, "Chronic Mental Illness and the Family," 406.

Govig says of the challenges of that moment, "The stage was set for rehospitalization and a downward spiral toward chronicity."[154] In all that despair, the church was absent, "aloof and silent" and it even "seemed irrelevant." Initially their expectation was that "Salvation would come from science and drug therapy,"[155] but over the years, he realized that the health care professionals, in spite of all their efforts and good intentions, could not bring recovery to his son. He laments, "The ministry of my church of science began to wear thin over the years. I began to look back upon my 'regular' church. Its weakness, I concluded, was not so much a result of hypocrisy as an outcome of long-standing ignorance and avoidance habits."[156] After all, one might ask, "what could the church do in this situation other than maybe offer up some prayers?" This is a medical issue, and why would one want to burden the pastors and the congregation with something they do not understand and that is not in the realm of their competency? Right? Not so right!

Isabel Clarke paints a different picture for us. She argues that the effect of the supernatural on the human mind could be both "ecstatic and demonic," and causes phenomena that are "the stuff of the origins of religious and spiritual movements," and "they are equally the stuff of madness."[157] Clarke portrays the psychotic experiences of several individuals and demonstrates that the outcome appears to be always dependent on how that first episode is encountered. She believes that a loving and supportive environment, which respects the experience and allows it to take its course, leads to recovery and a transformation in most cases. Clarke's claim about the significance of the appropriate treatment at the onset of psychosis, which is also confirmed by Seikkula in the practice of Open Dialogue, cannot be the end of the story. As we have seen, the "Healing Homes" in Sweden have successfully helped many of those who were treated unsuccessfully by the mainstream psychiatry. Nevertheless,

154. Ibid.

155. Ibid., 410.

156. Ibid., 408. See also Waterhouse, *Strength for His People*, 97. Waterhouse, a theologian and a supporter of the medical model of mental illness, whose brother suffers from "schizophrenia," documents the visible weakness of the church in supporting the families of those who suffer from "schizophrenia." He points out, "In 1983 the California Alliance For the Mentally Ill conducted a survey to determine the source to which families went for help and the value of any help received. Of twelve common sources, clergy ranked last in helpfulness," 9.

157. Clarke, *Madness, Mystery and the Survival of God*, 55, 47.

it appears as if the treatment of the first psychotic episode will determine the course of the illness.

One of the cases cited by Clarke belongs to Annabel, who experienced several psychotic episodes. The first one happened when she was in India, and because her host family was familiar with such phenomena, they treated it calmly and gently. It is significant that she acknowledges, "I am able to write positively about my journey because I have reached a place of deep healing in my present life."[158] Annabel explains her first episode while she was staying with a family in Northern India:

> At first, I entered a space of deep grief in which I was unable to stop crying, and I intuited that I was connecting into the grief of the earth. . . . My hosts took me along to my bedroom and as I lay down, I experienced a golden light pouring into the crown of my head and with it the invitation to dream up a New Earth. . . . Although my hosts were close to me it felt very important that they did not disturb me at this moment. . . . As I lay, I heard music which arose from within my being, though seemed to be coming from the outside. . . . I recall seeing a snatch of TV in which a woman voiced "They have dropped a bomb" which was weird and synchronous. . . . On a physical level I was quite active, not sleeping much for two to three days. Awareness of my hosts' presence was generally limited. I recall one occasion when the grandmother and head of the household, Mama, was sitting close to my head as I lay. On leaning my head back I saw her face transform into that of an owl with laser-like beams coming from her eyes and into mine. On the whole the relationship between me and my hosts was co-operative and peaceable, though on an occasion when I became less than calm they tried to limit my movements, and I recall ripping off my clothes so they could not use them to constrain me. The urge not to be controlled by anyone other than myself was powerful and I had the sense that my freedom had been curtailed in the distant past. . . . Although much of the process was internal and invisible to others there were episodes in which my outward behavior was clearly bizarre. My hosting family, whose spiritual roots were deep, instinctively trusted the process and though alarmed by my behavior, kept me at home under close and loving watch. I had only one visit to a psychiatrist in which I was given two doses of anti-psychotic medication. What could be described as the acutely psychotic phase only lasted two to three days.[159]

158. Ibid., 65.

159. Ibid., 66–68.

The detailed account of Annabel's experience highlights many features shared by others who have had a psychotic episode. Her behavior was clearly alarming and bizarre at times, and her host family demonstrated faith in the process and "strong nerve" at a personal level. Clarke, who has worked as a clinical psychologist for more than fifteen years, admits that psychosis is not anything to be "sentimental" about. However, she emphasizes that the outcome, though dependent on "a number of factors"—not least the strength of the person to withstand the intense encounter—undoubtedly can be managed much better in an "affirming and nurturing context," versus by force and compulsory commitment in a psychiatric ward.[160]

It is this need for a safe and supportive environment that could be fulfilled by a pastoral team at the person's home during similar crises—as the Open Dialogue practitioners do for the sufferers of psychosis. A family who has never known about such phenomenon would naturally overreact with anxiety, fear, and despair. How wonderful it would be if the church had a supportive team of caregivers who could be called upon at a moment of crisis like this, to put the family's fears to rest, spend time with them, pray with them, and help them to "draw near with confidence to the throne of grace" and receive comfort (Heb 4:16). Erickson explains that "the routine work of mental health worker is far more commonplace than outsiders are led to believe . . . it is a mistake to assume that aspects of their knowledge are too exotic, their interventions too intricate, and the problems they commonly address too complicated to be understood."[161]

In fact, the Soteria project insisted that all staff be hired from a pool of people with no training in psychiatry or psychology. They paid more attention to the personal traits of their potential staff, looking for people who were caring, gentle, patient, and who had the ability to listen and were not attached to psychiatric dogmas. Loren Mosher believed,

> [T]hat the inexperienced and psychologically unsophisticated can adopt useful interpersonal-phenomenological stances vis-à-vis psychosis more easily than highly trained MDs or PhDs, because the former work from no theory of "schizophrenia"— psychodynamic, organic, or both. Because they are unburdened by preconceived theories, nonprofessional staff members are

160. Ibid., 71.

161. Erickson, "Serving the Needs of Persons with Chronic Mental Illness," 158.

free to be themselves, to follow their untutored responses, and
to be spontaneous with psychotic individuals.[162]

This affirms that Christians could easily qualify to care for each other at
times of mental crises. In fact, since they are armed with the promises of
Scripture, and endowed with the power of the Holy Spirit, they are far better equipped to attend to the wounds of their brethren with a discerning
touch. As we have seen from a variety of research, the acute phase, when
treated properly, usually subsides in a matter of days or weeks. Yet, there
remain further issues that need attention and care. At this juncture the
sufferer needs to be allocated to a host family and a dedicated team of
counselors, attuned to the voice of illness, led by the power of the Holy
Spirit, to begin the process of healing for all involved.

Ongoing Care and Counsel

Recovery takes distinct shape and content for each individual. It is never a
linear process, and will require discernment and flexibility to attend to the
issues as they surface. In the proposed model here, counselors should be
appointed to the host family, the individual, and the natural family. This
is very similar to the model implemented in "Healing Homes" in Sweden.
Carina Håkansson attributes a big part of their success to the ongoing support that the team of therapists offers to the host families. Without that,
Håkansson believes it would be difficult to find any families who are willing to sign up for such a challenge. But knowing that they have a support
system around the clock that they can lean on makes it possible for many
families to take the leap of faith and welcome distressed people into their
lives. There is an ongoing need for supervision of the families to ensure
they can cope effectively with the daily pressures of life as they interact
with their new family member. In the context of befriending those with
mental illness, Swinton suggests the need for "teaching people basic relational skills, such as the importance of listening, coping with frustration,
boundaries, and empathy."[163] These are essential skills for any effective relationship and could enhance the capacity of the host families to manage
the dynamics of their expanded household.

It is significant that models such as "Healing Homes," Soteria, or Tornio's Open Dialogue, which are founded on a variety of belief and value
systems, have accomplished so much. Powlison suggests that Christians

162. Mosher et al., *Soteria*, 45.

163. Swinton, *Resurrecting the Person*, 186.

ought to be better than any other groups "at both receiving and giving" counseling. This is true because "No one else's explanation of human misery" compares with the depth of the Christian view. They don't have a concept of sin, and they do not understand that "we suffer within a context of meaningfulness." Other value systems do not take into account that "actual persons are made and sustained by God and are accountable to God, searched out and weighed moment by moment."[164]

The Christian message is based on the promise of redemption and a new life for the cure of souls—"the root meaning of *psychotherapy*." Powlison believes that only through biblically based Christian counseling can one "heal deeply," for "intentional, life-transforming discipleship is a Christian distinctive." He warns against the "Band-Aids" that are essentially to "augment self-reliance." A healed life is a life that is dependent on God and a healed heart is a heart after the heart of God. Powlison reminds the church of her "unique and significant counseling calling," which he suggests the church has failed to fulfill by being "foolish," "rigid," "inept," applying "pat answer[s]" and "snap judgment[s]" lacking "wisdom."[165] It is truly noteworthy that those outside of the church have demonstrated far more compassion and conviction toward the mentally ill than Christians with the claim of being indwelled with God's love and Spirit.

Every theory and approach to human suffering exposes the "author's core personal faith." It offers a context for "interpreting and then reconfiguring humanness," based on the author's system of personal beliefs. Secular institutions might be successful in helping people become happier and more constructive, but can never change one's heart. Nothing short of that is acceptable in the Christian realm. "The Lord interprets personal struggles and situational troubles through a *very* different set of eyes," says Powlison.[166] The church has indeed failed to bring that interpretative lens to those who are mentally ill and their community, and has delegated that task to secular health care professionals. The healing in mental illness comes wrapped in revelation. When the revealed message is unwrapped, then the healing can be fruitfully accessed. Powlison warns counselors not be content with superficial healing, remembering how Jeremiah spoke of Israel's priests and prophets: "And they have healed the brokenness of My people superficially, saying, 'Peace, peace,' but there is no peace" (Jer 6:14).

---

164. Powlison, Foreword, 12.

165. Ibid., 13–14.

166. Ibid., 16, 14.

Facing the ongoing anguish of having a loved one suffering from "schizophrenia," Govig cites a parent's cry for answer in the midst of confusion and guilt:

> What did we do to create this situation? Were we too lenient and lacking in discipline? Were we too strict? Did we love our children enough? Did we hold on too tightly and identify ourselves with them? Am I perpetuating the illness? Are we doing enough now? Is there a better hospital, a better doctor, a better treatment?[167]

These self-reflections are common among those whose loved ones are suffering. This is when God is knocking at the door of those who are hurting, awakening them. These moments are the openings for God's Spirit to penetrate and bring out all that would need healing. It is in moments like this that the parents can be assured that they have done nothing worse than any other parent would have done given their personal history and circumstances. For we all have fallen short of his glory (Rom 3:23), and we all have sinned in our own unique contexts. "Indeed, there is not a righteous man on earth who continually does good and who never sins" (Eccl 7:20). This is not time for shame and guilt; rather it is time to open the door and invite the "Wonderful Counselor" in for a heart to heart conversation, reframing the moment of crisis as a moment of blessing. As the book of Job declares, "He delivers the afflicted in their affliction, and opens their ear in time of oppression" (Job 36:15). This journey is a chance to grab hold of the truth of how fallen we are and how mighty he is to save. Piper says, "Oh, how often God works this way! He takes the very sins of the [people] and makes them the means of the [people's] deliverance."[168]

I have argued throughout this book that encounter with illness has to be communal and that it would be a mistake to observe the phenomenon as an individual medical problem. The "symptoms" of those labeled as "schizophrenics" speak to our shared guilt and common disease of spirit. These afflicted souls are gifts to the church to bring us to an awareness of our depravity, and the particular "disorders" of the immediate community that require attention and examination. As Viktor Frankl, the famous Austrian neurologist and psychiatrist—as well as a Holocaust survivor—said, "That which is to give light must endure burning."[169] The function of pas-

---

167. Govig, "Chronic Mental Illness and the Family," 407.

168. Piper, *Spectacular Sins*, 78.

169. Cacciatore, "DSM5 and Ethical Relativism."

toral care in this context is to help everyone—including themselves—to observe the reality and see clearly with the eyes of God.

In this process the authenticity of everyone is essential. It is of critical importance for all to be cared for as they take collective responsibility for the revelations coming through and allow the light to shine on the "illness of the community organism." Siirala emphasizes:

> The further one follows the patient into his split reality, the more obvious becomes the network of common guilt in which human beings are entangled. The encounter with schizophrenia shows that the split life has emerged in a world where the communal nature of illness is denied; healing can be effected only through experiencing the illness as held in common. When schizophrenia is encountered as a common illness one discovers that there are also hidden in it possibilities of common healing. Both becoming ill and healing are events in the whole community organism.[170]

The reality of "schizophrenia" forces everyone to listen. The pastoral team must keep that attitude as a centerpiece of the whole counseling process. The unceasing examination of the "symptoms" leads to illumination and dialogue, which leads to repentance, and ultimately leads to reconciliation. It is in this process that everyone receives God's counsel in their own context. All become his disciples, learning to look at themselves as God sees them. Powlison explains that as one enters "into God's counseling process," little by little, "God's take on things becomes yours. You increasingly come to live in reality, leaving the shadowlands behind, forsaking the imaginary virtual realities."[171] This is a gift that many Christians long for, but may never experience its realization.

Partnership with the Psychiatric Community

Throughout this book I have argued that biological psychiatry's attempts at treatment have not always helped, or perhaps they have succeeded in "symptom" reduction at a very great expense to other facets of the person's life. However, there is evidence that some psychiatric illnesses have biological etiologies. There could be dementia, brain tumors, Huntington's disease, Wilson's disease, steroid-induced psychosis, infections,

---

170. Siirala, *The Voice of Illness*, 94.

171. Powlison, Foreword, 15.

neuropathological lesions, recreational drug use, or hormonal imbalances that may cause psychiatric effects. Such cases are detectable via imaging technologies or blood and urine tests. Therefore, they represent clear cases of biological ailment in need of medical treatment.

There are also more extreme cases of psychosis or anxiety that may not subside by themselves after a few weeks or months, and may require intervention by a psychiatrist to reduce the level of suffering and allow the person to establish dialogue with his social network. Therefore, within an effective care model, access to caring and humane psychiatric help is necessary. As we saw in the models in Soteria, "Healing Homes," Tornio's Open Dialogue, and the Tobys in Madagascar, psychiatrists were always available for special cases. It was clearly essential to have access to psychiatric help through physicians who had bought into such alternative models of treatment and were committed to the value systems on which they were founded. For example, at Toby Ambohibao, psychiatrists were trained in Spiritual Related Disorders (SRD) and believed in demonic influences as possible causes of the "symptoms."

Thus, it is necessary to incorporate the services of committed Christian psychiatrists into the Healing Together model. The administration of psychiatric drugs requires careful handling to avoid gross overmedicating of basic emotional reactions to normal pains and hurts of life. The question of when and how psychiatric drugs are used should not be answered casually. In all the successful models investigated in this research, psychiatric medication was used far more sparingly, judiciously, and wisely, on a case-by-case basis, as the last option to manage the level of distress. In most of those cases, the medication was given at a very low dosage, and for a short while to avoid chronicity and severe side effects.

More important, there is a need for psychiatrists who truly buy into the philosophy of Healing Together—like many we have heard from in this study, e.g., Kinghorn, Carlat, Mosher, Sinaikin, and Siirala—who while they understand the benefits of drugs in alleviating the "symptoms" of the more extreme psychoses, take issue with the current mindset of biopsychiatry, consumed by prescribing a surfeit of pills in response to human challenges, often to the detriment of their clients. John McNeill stresses the need for psychiatrists who appreciate the spiritual dimension of one's mental experiences. Building on the work of Fritz Künkel, McNeill says, "the nonreligious psychiatrist is as incompetent to deal with religious experiences as a blind man to interpret a work of art."[172] Clearly,

---

172. McNeill, *A History of the Cure of Souls*, 322.

there is a need for enlightened psychiatric presence in partnership with all other players in the model. It is important to note that there are many conscientious psychiatrists who are speaking up against the current system and are fighting for the rights of their clients and the dignity of their profession. There is great potential and hope for recovery, and psychiatry can be invited to the table, but the current biases that govern most of the Western psychiatric practices—i.e., pharmaceutical imperialism—must be rejected.

Operational Management

The model of Healing Together can be implemented either as part of a local church or as a parachurch organization. The important element is the focus, the awareness, and the priority that this ministry should be given. The congregations' consciousness must be raised to understanding the *theological* and *teleological* significance of this undertaking. This demands education, inspiration, and advocacy. These functions plus the overall management of the program, such as the recruitment of host families, fundraising, financial management, and public relations, require capable leadership and an effective operational infrastructure.

The ideal structure would be for the host families to be recruited and selected from one's congregation. In real life this may not always be possible. It might be difficult for those who live in big cities to create the necessary restful environment conducive to healing. The factors that will play a role in the selection of these families consist of, first, the dynamics and the character of the family unit, then, their past experiences, their geographic location, and their willingness and enthusiasm about serving God in this particular way. In the "Healing Homes" model, many families who take on the host family responsibility do it out of their deep desire to pay back. Many of them have dealt with serious challenges in the past and have been delivered by the helping hands stretched out to them by others.

The financial needs of such an environment can be significant. The key is that no individual should be rejected solely based on his financial capacity to pay for the services. In the models we reviewed in this study (with the exception of Toby, which is mostly supported by the Lutheran Church) all were mainly supported by the state. In our proposed model, there will be a need for fundraising from private sources, and an attempt must be made to secure funds from the state where the existing health care laws permit that. Most important, this is an opportunity for Christians who cannot directly participate in caring for the mentally ill to help the organization through their financial contributions. This is an undertaking that requires charismatic leadership, conviction, and education.

The key is to make congregations aware of the false beliefs they have formed through degrading images in the media, and deceptive pharmaceutical advertisements. In fact, the educational process is mostly about *unlearning* the concepts that have already been imprinted on their minds. The Christians need to be reminded that each person is "fearfully and wonderfully made" (Ps 139:14). They need to be educated through biblical teachings that all Christians are "competent to counsel."[173] Since the most effective help and comfort comes from the work of the Holy Spirit—the *paracletos*, the helper, and the comforter—those who are endowed with the power of the Spirit can bring genuine comfort and help to those in need. The church should not ignore this gift and dismiss this responsibility.[174]

There is also a great need for powerful voices to advocate for the rights and the needs of the mentally ill and their families through establishment of effective social policies and investments. Swinton explains, "An advocate is someone who cares for others so deeply that he or she is willing to stand up for them in the face of oppressive forces that seek to harm those who, for whatever reason, are vulnerable." He compares the role of an advocate to the role of a prophet, claiming that they both seek "to speak God's word into situations of injustice and oppression and, in so doing, move toward a form of transformation that reflects the will of God."[175] Those who are mentally ill cannot speak for themselves, and even when they do, they are rarely taken seriously. This is an injustice of great proportion. The words of Lemuel, in the book of Proverbs, commands the faithful: "Open your mouth for the dumb, for the rights of all the unfortunate. Open your mouth, judge righteously, and defend the rights of the afflicted and needy" (Prov 31:8–9).

"Compulsory treatment is *the* major problem in psychiatry," says Marc Rufer.[176] This is a sentiment that is shared by almost all users of psychiatry and many of the professionals in the field. Therefore, it is of great importance that Christian communities take a stand against compulsory inhumane psychiatric commitment, especially when the person

173. Adams, *Competent to Counsel.*

174. Ibid., 20.

175. Swinton, *Resurrecting the Person,* 173–74.

176. Rufer, "Psychiatry: Its Diagnostic Methods, its Therapies, its Power," 385.

is presumed incompetent merely based on his refusal of treatment. This is a blow at the dignity of his suffering and his humanity. Rufer explains,

> When necessary, a "contingency plan" is employed for compulsory treatment: as many as eight aides willing to exercise physical violence face a single helpless patient. Involuntary commitments, often carried out by the police, are frequently a dramatic occurrence involving "take-downs" and physical restraint. In terms of their traumatic nature, these interventions can be compared to rape, torture and sexual abuse.[177]

Rufer contends that the effect of compulsory treatment stays with one for the rest of his life. For most people it is impossible to regain their dignity, and their sense of trust and confidence in the people around them. Even in the best of circumstances coercion is always intrinsically damaging to one's mental health.[178]

This is clearly an area where the weak and the voiceless have been ruled by the powers of society to control them, and not to a great outcome in most cases. There is a great need for advocacy in fighting for people's rights, and creating an environment where their voices can be heard. In addition, there might be a need for interaction with the state and advocacy at the sociopolitical level. Swinton suggests that Christian communities must use their "potentially powerful political voice" to "take a solid stand against aspects of policy, practice, and public attitudes that may be causing

---

177. Ibid., 386.

178. Elyn Saks—profiled in chapter 2—has written passionately about her traumatic experiences and vigorously argues against compulsory psychiatric treatment. See Saks, *Refusing Care*, 304. Considering all the research evidence about the value of supportive community living, and the desire for healthy integration of the mentally ill into the society, Barbara Fawcett's research points to the clear tensions between the claims of psychiatry about the need for compulsory intervention to contain "risk," and the increasing pressure of a "citizenship and social justice agenda" advocated by "psychiatrists involved in the development of 'postpsychiatry', as well as by service users/survivors." See Fawcett, "Consistencies and Inconsistencies," 1027–42 (quote from 1027). Also, a report on torture, presented to the United Nations Human Rights Council in Geneva, called for a ban on "confinement or compulsory treatment in mental health settings, including through guardianship and other substituted decision-making," and deprivation of liberty based on mental illness, including when it is motivated by desire "to protect the safety of the person or of others"; Mendez, *Special Rapporteur on Torture and Other Cruel, Inhuman Or Degrading Treatment Or Punishment* (quotes from 2 and 5). A recent study conducted in the UK reports that in no ways the imposition of compulsory treatment helps with the course of illness: "We found no support in terms of any reduction in overall hospital admission to justify the significant curtailment of patients' personal liberty." Burns et al., "Community Treatment Orders for Patients with Psychosis (OCTET)."

harm to people with mental health problems and their families."[179] The church has a responsibility to call on the society and the culture when they astray from just practices. As ambassadors of Christ, Christians must promote social change, which in this case includes a more humane treatment of the mentally ill.

The success of Healing Together requires a structure that facilitates communication, sharing of experiences, and mutual support among all families. There is a need for a culture of solidarity, providing opportunities for fellowship and celebration, offsite retreats, picnics, Christmas parties, or any activities that may increase the sense of community and connect host families, individuals under their care, and their biological families. This would facilitate a sense of trust to call upon each other and help each other as unique challenges arise. This sense of community was a great element of what I observed among the people I met at the Family Care Foundation in Sweden. It is that sense of greater community that could hold the body together, and encourage it to keep going; a sense that is bound to be magnified among Christian families who are empowered by the Spirit of Christ.

Summary

In his chapter, I argued that since madness is both *theological* and *teleological* by nature, the church has a great responsibility and opportunity to embrace those suffering from this mysterious human phenomenon. This is for the purpose of caring for the most broken and forsaken members of the church, receiving the prophetic call of God to the community, and building up the body of Christ to its potential fullness.

Building on the findings of the previous chapters, we searched for communities that have been successful in implementing some of the concepts presented earlier in this book. We looked at the Soteria model, a housing community for those in their first or second episodes of acute psychosis; the Family Care Foundation's "Healing Homes," a Swedish care community for those who have been given up by psychiatry; the Finnish Open Dialogue Therapy, a treatment method focused on family therapy and the discovery of an intersubjective consciousness in the community; and the Awakening Movement's Toby Model, in northern region of Madagascar, which integrates conventional medical treatment with spiritual healing based on biblical principles. Based on the overall findings,

179. Swinton, *Resurrecting the Person*, 176.

I offered the Healing Together model as a proposed path by which the church might take responsibility for the care of souls who are encountering the extraordinary experience of madness.

Healing Together is about members of the body coming to one another's aid, bearing each other's burdens, and breaking all barriers of cultural and societal conventions. The church is called to "*incarnating Christ*" in the life of others. Incarnation is about making God's glory and presence manifest.[180] From this perspective, to be part of "Christ's life-giving work," the church has to lay down her own life and incarnate the love of Christ.[181] For by their having love for one another, as Jesus commanded, the world will know his true disciples (John 13:35). The question of caring for the insane is truly a "What Would Jesus Do?" moment. The Apostle John declares: "By this we know that we are in Him: The one who says he abides in Him ought himself to walk in the same manner as He walked" (1 John 2:5b–6). By touching the lepers, Jesus was breaking the barriers around them—the social estrangement they experienced. Can the church walk in his footsteps and be an instrument for his glory to shine through?

Govig, whose son Jay continues to suffer from chronic "schizophrenia," laments about his son's "profound, joyless apathy." He says, "To me, mental illness carries an ultimate: it hints at the yawning, formless void present at the beginning before God's wind swept over and brought light to original disorder (Gen 1:1–3)."[182] Indeed, it is the power of "God's wind" *alone*, his Holy Spirit, that can consume this chaotic disorder, and bring light into darkness. As we have shown, there may be all sorts of treatments, empowered by God's common grace, that can help, but the journey out of madness, a deep healing of the inner *spirit*, can only manifest in Christ and by his Spirit—the only true "Wounded Healer."[183] Moreover, in Healing Together, not only is a broken soul cared for, but the church can grow to a mature stature, truly imitating Christ (Eph 4:12–13).

180. Tripp, *Instruments in the Redeemer's Hands*, 97.

181. Ibid., 119.

182. Govig, *Souls are made of Endurance*, 83.

183. Nouwen, *The Wounded Healer*, 100.

5

Conclusion

But as for me I will watch expectantly for the LORD;
I will wait for the God of my salvation.
My God will hear me.
Do not rejoice over me, O my enemy.
Though I fall I will rise;
Though I dwell in darkness, the LORD is a light for me.

He will bring me out to the light,
And I will see His righteousness.

Micah 7:7–9

The Situational Context

In this study we observed that the experiences of those suffering from mental illness call into question our collective Western understanding of these phenomena. Historically, how the experiences are named determined the types of treatment that were deemed to be appropriate. The church has participated in this process, but laterally, the naming, framing and responding to those experiences have become the terrain of psychiatry. Psychiatry has a questionable history and has been the location for various political, economic, and professional power struggles as the discipline has developed and has sought to offer a rationale for its existence.

The twentieth century saw an astronomical rise in the popularity of sciences as explanatory frameworks for everything. Science has served humanity in remarkable ways, yet one should beware of dangers of scientism[1]—the view that science is the supreme authority over all human questions and the solution to all human problems. For the past two centuries, psychiatry has harnessed neuroscience to aid in psychiatric treatments. Instead of focusing on issues of personal history, their focus has shifted to the study of organic causes of mental illness. Treatments, particularly in the United States, have turned increasingly to medications.

An increasing chorus of people, including psychiatrists, psychologists, social scientists, and journalists, have spoken against the reductionist model of medical psychiatry, where the psychological functioning of the human mind is reduced to the functions of neurons that make up the physical brain. This is particularly troublesome because, as we have shown, "*no direct evidence of neuronal dysfunction in emotional disorders has ever been discovered.*"[2] Ironically, in spite of all "psychiatric advancements," mental illness has become the pathology of our times and psychiatric drugs are the number one selling drugs in the United States.[3]

I argued that our interpretive paradigm of biopsychiatry is severely flawed and is built upon a fragile unproven foundation. A careful critique of "chemical imbalance" and genetic models of mental illness revealed deep flaws and contradictions. Worse, we saw that engaging in the types of practices and interventions that emerge from such explanatory frameworks is deeply damaging, particularly with regard to pharmacological interventions. Many chronic mental illnesses may even be *iatrogenic* in

---

1. C. S. Lewis, who respected science, compared scientism to magic. He claimed that "both function as alternative religions. . . . Both discourage healthy skepticism by elevating 'experts' and 'authorities' to a level above criticism. . . . Both crave power. To the high priests of scientism, nothing is sacred—including human life itself." Quoted in the Aeropagus, "The Magician's Twin: C. S. Lewis on Science, Scientism, and Society." See online: http://www.theareopagus.org/blog/2012/10/november-forum-the-magicians-twin-c-s-lewis-on-science-scientism-and-society/#more-1028.

2. Sinaikin, *Psychiatryland*, xix.

3. According to a government study published by Center for Disease Control, antidepressants and antipsychotics have become the most commonly prescribed drugs in the United States. They're prescribed more than drugs to treat high blood pressure, high cholesterol, asthma, or headaches. See Whitaker, *Mad in America*, 303, and Elizabeth Cohen, "CDC: Antidepressants most Prescribed Drugs in U.S.—CNN."

nature and are made more complicated by neurological damages caused by such treatments.

The bias for medical treatment is so strong and pervasive that the voices in support of any other method are easily silenced and dismissed. Even though scientific studies have drawn attention to the loss of functionality and "drug-induced brain damage" as a consequence of the use of antipsychotics, millions of people, some under the age of eighteen, continue to receive them around the globe. Reviewing competing views, David Pilgrim notes, "If this scale of iatrogenic brain damage existed in a non-psychiatric population, the drug involved would probably be banned, or its use strictly controlled." Sadly, it is due to society's desire to control the mad, along with the inability of the insane to protest against their treatment, that "this prevalence of medically induced brain damage is considered acceptable by professionals and their employers."[4]

The fact that the brains of people who suffer from "schizophrenia" are different from the brains of ordinary people is not significant on its own; the challenge is to discover what these differences mean. Researchers have failed to offer any explanations for how the brain "abnormalities" they have observed might cause the actual "symptoms" experienced by patients. Despite all the impressive progress in neuroimaging technologies, Stefan J. Borgwardt, a psychiatrist, neuroscientist, and professor of neuropsychiatry at the University of Basel, states, "nearly three decades after Johnstone et al.'s first computerized axial tomography of the brain of individuals with schizophrenia, no consistent or reliable anatomical or functional alterations have been unequivocally associated with psychosis or schizophrenia and no clinical applications have been developed in psychiatric neuroimaging."[5] American psychiatrist Simon Sobo says:

4. Pilgrim, "Competing Histories of Madness," 228. Contrary to some suggestions—on the part of those who are seeking a compromised solution—these antipsychotics even at a low dosage may not be helpful. According to *Shorter Oxford Textbook of Psychiatry*, "These drugs are sometimes prescribed for their anxiolytic effect. In low dosage that do not lead to side effects . . . they are generally no more effective than Benzodiazepines. . . . However, even low-dose antipsychotic treatment, if maintained, is not free from the risk of tardive dyskinesia." See Gelder et al., *Shorter Oxford Textbook of Psychiatry*, 658.

5. Johnstone et al., "Cerebral Ventricular Size," 924–26 and Borgwardt and Fusar-Poli, "Third Generation Neuroimaging," 270–72. Also, Sederer and Erlich, from the Department of Psychiatry at Columbia University, speaking of neuroimaging scans, say, "But, these scans are not employed for initial psychiatric diagnosis. Instead, scans are used to determine the *absence* of a neurological lesion, rather than pointing out the *presence* of a behavioral condition. MRI's cannot diagnose schizophrenia or bipolar disorder, but they can identify a tumor or a stroke that may have similar psychiatric

> Unfortunately, the search for the "real" diagnosis in psychiatry is often unfruitful therapeutically. . . . We are not discovering what is really wrong. Simply finding a label; then another label; and another. . . . But at this stage, the proper question is *not* should we exclusively use treatments that have proven superior to placebo? It *is* what is the best way to formulate treatment strategies when now, and in the foreseeable future, science can't offer answers that we need?[6]

This failure to bring about fruitful outcomes stems from various conflicting forces such as the humanity of distressed and fragile souls along with their complexity and diversity, the economic interests of multinational pharmaceutical giants, the self-interests and professional aspirations of practitioners, the cultural and political interests of society to keep the mad at bay, and the forces of oppression to silence what is feared and cannot be understood, all entangled in a labyrinth with no end in sight.[7]

There are scientists, such as Kirsch, who, while objecting to the current model of medical psychiatry, still point to the brain as the culprit where "mental illness" is rooted. He says, "All subjective states—sadness, joy, apprehension, delight, fear, and boredom—are rooted in the brain."[8] We have argued that the claim that depression or "schizophrenia" have some biological roots in the brain does not equate with them being a disease in need of a cure. The differences in the brain may be the consequence of environmental distress or life tribulations, rather than some lesion or genetic deformity. In fact, Kirsch agrees, they may result from a "normally functioning brain, containing neural networks that have been shaped by life events."[9] It may be the circumstances of life that trigger a sense of loss, despair, and confusion. We may be dealing with a brain that is functioning as it was designed to function in the face of life events; none of these need necessarily mean that the underlying mechanism of the brain is broken.

It is this blurriness of the line between madness and sanity and the ultimate inability to untangle the complex correlation between an

---

manifestations. While we are seeing truly fascinating results from neuroimaging—from unraveling complicated brain depression networks to staging dementia—it has yet to serve as an anchor for psychiatric diagnosis." See Sederer and Erlich, "How Thoughts Become a Psychiatric Diagnoses."

6. Sobo, "Does Evidence-Based Medicine Discourage Richer Assessment of Psychopathology and Treatment?"

7. Kinghorn, "Medicating the Eschatalogical Body," 129–30.

8. Kirsch, *The Emperor's New Drugs*, 100.

9. Ibid.

individual's biochemistry and his social context that has brought about decades of ferocious debates.[10] At the same time researchers such as Bert Kaplan and Gordon Claridge outline an immense body of evidence against all doubts that psychosis and "normal" traits are distinct points on the spectrum of valid human behavior. These studies show that "the tendency towards psychotic behavior is distributed along a series of continua which connect madness with ordinary mental life."[11]

Kaplan, who has collected a dramatic series of first-person accounts of madness, explains that contrary to the psychopathological model, madness is organized around a "kernel of purposefulness and intentionality." This is incomprehensible for those who are watching "psychosis with its attendant suffering, humiliation, and alienation" from outside. He claims that this is the reason that the common "cure" offered by psychiatrists falls short. The question is whether it is justified to consider these states pathological and whether it is acceptable for society to be so willing to apply harmful techniques to stop such encounters. In Kaplan's view, "The cure, or solution, must be neither a return to the so-called normality that preceded the illness nor a negation of the illness. The new state must rather involve a genuine moving to a new solution, a movement which we can see would have been impossible without the illness."[12] In other words the cure is hidden within the illness and starts with the madness itself. It is only after the illness has fulfilled its purpose that the person can return to sanity.

Thus, as of 2014, the scientific community seems to be scratching its head, as perplexed and puzzled as those in centuries past about the specific connection between someone's biology, his environment, his life history, and his experience of madness.[13] With studies of epigenetics, they have shown that someone's life events can cause alterations in gene expressions without any changes in DNA sequence. The fact that someone

---

10. Staub, *Madness is Civilization*, 9.

11. Bentall, "Concluding Remarks: Schizophrenia—A Suitable Case for Treatment?" 284.

12. Kaplan and Murphy, *The Inner World of Mental Illness*, vii, x–xii.

13. Facing the publication of DSM-5 right around the corner, Thomas Insel, director of NIMH, wrote: "The strength of each of the editions of DSM has been 'reliability'—each edition has ensured that clinicians use the same terms in the same ways. The weakness is its lack of validity. . . . That is why NIMH will be re-orienting its research away from DSM categories." Insel is implementing yet another new medical framework for research, hoping to solve the biological riddles behind madness. Insel, "Transforming Diagnosis."

is born with certain gene sequences that express themselves distinctly in different environments would mean that they are created with built-in potential to respond in individual ways to their life conditions—or to their calling. What an amazing testimony to God's providence!

Based on Jeremiah 1:5 and Galatians 1:15, Zodhiates notes that "both Paul and Jeremiah were selected for their ministries before their births," by God.[14] Both Jeremiah and Paul were created with their whole being set for their unusual experiences in their mission. In fact, Jeremiah was one of the "saddest" prophets, "because his burden was so heavy." The mere fact that they were born with certain biologies, which positioned them for their missions—albeit a mission filled with "colorful" and extraordinary manifestations—does not make them pathological. However, the way we treat these individuals has the potential for significant damage and the risk of turning their unique gifts into pathology.

Proposed Solutions

I proposed an appropriate Christian response to the phenomenon of "schizophrenia" in a model of care centered on hearing and embracing the voice of the illness in a way that would lead to *healing together* in accordance with God's redemptive purposes in Christ. While learning from successful projects both inside and outside the church, the model is built upon the notion that relationships in Christ provide the fertile ground in which the seeds of hope, love, and faith will bear fruits of healing and transformation.

In so far as madness is recognized as a phenomenon, both *theological* and *teleological*, with a deep prophetic voice, exposing our state of sinfulness and calling the church into repentance, how is the church to encounter it effectively and faithfully? I argued that the evil forces giving life to the experience of insanity could only be conquered when the immediate community embraces it as its own illness. In the context of that outlook, what matters most is that when Christians encounter one who is ill, oppressed, confused, and tormented, they take it upon themselves to "*make space* in their lives" to care for those persons as if they were caring for Christ himself.[15]

The question of improvements in the quality of life for those on psychiatric drugs is hotly debated. There are individuals who have been

14. Zodhiates, *Hebrew-Greek Key Word Study Bible*, 985.

15. Shuman, *The Body of Compassion*, xvi.

helped by these treatments and would rather live with their side effects than go back to their madness. And there are those who have been seriously damaged by forced treatments and continue with daily struggles. However, it is clear that the drugs are mostly given as "chemical restraints" so that a society that does not have a capacity for tolerance, unconditional love, and self-reflection does not have to change its course. Thomas Insel, Director of NIMH, himself comments on the importance of alternative models of treatment:

> While psychosocial interventions have received much less marketing attention than pharmacological treatments, the results are arguably more encouraging. For people with schizophrenia, assertive community treatment, family psychoeducation, and supported employment have substantial effects on functional recovery and relapse rates. . . . However, few patients actually receive evidence-based psychosocial treatments.[16]

I have argued it is time to remember what worked with moral therapy as practiced by the Quakers in York, England, or by Thomas Kirkbride at the Pennsylvania hospital. It was their belief in their patients' "God-given capacity for recovery" and their ability to help nature through their "humanitarian and optimistic" outlook that helped many get well.[17] Jane Doller of Cornell University Medical College, who was the psychiatrist who led Lori Schiller to recovery, points out that "Lori Schiller's story helps remind us of something we may have lost in our rush to embrace science: Mental illness is not just about drugs and biology. It is about people. It is Clozapine that made Lori's final recovery possible. What made her recovery so successful is Lori herself."[18]

I built on the work of many scholars such as Siirala, Larchet, Sugerman, and McGruder to argue that the encounter with madness opens our spiritual ears to a profound prophetic voice about the human condition. I stated that the "symptoms" of "schizophrenia" are not void of meaning, and that the interpretation of that meaning has to be undertaken by patients, families, and those who provide the care. Indeed, the medical model of madness distorts the picture and will not allow one to hear the voice of illness, and focuses instead on the objective manifest signs separate from the reality they represent. To hear the voice of madness requires

16. Insel, "Translating Scientific Opportunity into Public Health Impact," 129.

17. Whitaker, *Mad in America*, 288.

18. Doller, Foreword.

radical hearing ability and capacity. Those who subscribe to the reduction-ist medical model of mental illness are in danger of losing the ability to interpret the phenomenon as something in relationship and unique to the particular individual and his community.

I argued that the voice of illness often expresses the illness of a com-munity—a clue that the conquest of the disease is also dependent on that community—and for that reason said that a community cannot afford to turn away from the sickness of its members. Listening to the language of madness shakes the communities' positions of false equilibrium and challenges their version of reality. When the voice of "schizophrenia" is properly heard we discern that it expresses more than an individual des-perate cry for help; it reveals the illness of the greater community; it is calling the church to repentance, a calling that the church cannot afford to disregard. The healing depends on us embracing the prophetic message of the illness. The insane portray us in vivid ways exposing the hidden sins of our hearts through their "sign acts," revealing what we have masked so expertly under our civilized postures, to bring us to our senses.

I finally proposed Healing Together, as a care model for the mentally ill within a Christian structure. Based on the basic principles of Moral Therapy and of those who have successfully cared for the sufferers of mental illness, such as Soteria house, "Healing Homes" of the Family Care Foundation in Sweden, Finnish Open Dialogue Therapy, and the Tobys of Madagascar, I recommended a model for the church to take direct re-sponsibility for the members of the body of Christ who are afflicted with mental illness. This model is built on the belief that in dealing with the mentally ill, nurtured relationships empowered by the Spirit of Christ that are meaningful and ingrained in daily lives, have a healing power. In this model the church will be involved from the onset of psychosis and will take responsibility for leading the person and his immediate community toward healing. Instead of treating suffering as an individual problem, which would lead to "self-absorbed temptations," we look at it as partici-pating in the sufferings of Christ. After all, even "our suffering belongs to the Lord," says Tripp. "Suffering does not mean that God's plan has failed. It is the plan."[19]

---

19. Tripp, *Instruments in the Redeemer's Hands*, 153.

Significance and Implications of this Study

"Schizophrenia" haunts us with its unforgiving images and lays bare "hell's pitiless truth."[20] "*Madness*" is the picture of *sin,* indeed. It is in madness that sin is portrayed to us in its odious colors so that we may genuinely hate it. It is the triumph of madness that brings to light the real problems we have buried in the deepest part of our soul. In the madness of those afflicted, a mirror is provided "in which we can catch ourselves" in the midst of our distractions and maybe "gaze long enough" to be shaken out of our comfort zones. This mirror one can hope will force us to begin to counteract "what seems to be our fate," against which we have successfully "anesthetized ourselves"; a fate that all are destined to share, not only those we consider "pathological."[21]

There was a time in which our understanding of human personality, mind and consciousness, and acceptable behavior were shaped by philosophical and religious beliefs, but today we look through the lens of the DSM to define what behaviors are acceptable and what require intervention; who is sane and who is insane; who has the right to be treated with civil privileges and who should be regarded as incompetent and subjected to various authorities. Psychiatry has convinced many of us that our joy and peace, grief and despair, and our sense of personhood are all the by-products of our brain chemistry. It appears as if the destiny of humankind, our happiness and sadness, is at the mercy of the neurotransmitters in the brain. As Porter indicated earlier, "the keys of St. Peter" have been "replaced by the keys of psychiatry."[22] Most important, Whitaker notes,

> [O]ur children are the first in human history to grow up under the constant shadow of "mental illness" . . . today, children diagnosed with mental disorders—most notably, ADHD, depression, and bipolar illness—help populate the schoolyard. These children have been told that they have something wrong with their brains and that they may have to take psychiatric medications the rest of their lives, just like a "diabetic takes insulin." The medical dictum teaches all of the children on the playground a lesson about the nature of humankind, and that lesson differs in a radical way from what children used to be taught.[23]

20. Foucault, *Madness and Civilization*, 23.

21. Sugerman, *Sin and Madness*, 13, 24.

22. Porter, *Madness*, 122.

23. Whitaker, *Anatomy of an Epidemic*, 10–11.

Is this picture acceptable to the Christian church? Have Christians ever paused and thought this through to have a sense of where this would lead? Does the church realize that the very personhood of our next generation is at stake? Are we oblivious to the fact that we are appropriating from psychiatry not only scientific hypotheses but certain normative depictions of human fulfillment that are often sociologically naïve, philosophically questionable, and theologically indefensible? It is hardly an exaggeration to say that most Christians are as happily indifferent as the pharmaceutical and mental health industries to the cultural and religious implications of these trends. The church, for the most part, has solemnly folded her hands and stood silently by, while the soul of the next generation is becoming enslaved to the consumption of mind-altering drugs.[24]

Regardless of all attempts, society cannot afford to turn away from encountering madness, which so profoundly speaks about the fragility of humanness. Madness is far beyond a mere scientific experiment. With the epidemic of mental illness in America, perhaps it is time for the church to awaken to its responsibility of "care of souls." It is time for the church to call "schizophrenia" what the experience of the sufferers has proven it to be: a true experience of hell and slavery to forces of evil, rather than what we *wish* it to be—a pathology that excuses us from any responsibility and accountability. It is important to remember that those suffering from mental illness, more than any other people, suffer from lack of a spiritual sense of God's presence. They seemingly have no access to God's grace and are taken over by darkness.[25] These are truly souls in need of care and redemption. If the church ignores this responsibility, then it may as well close shop!

Final Personal Reflections

According to Piper, we need "a vision of God into our lives that will not let us down in the worst of times . . . really bad times. Horrific times."[26] This

24. Browning, "Pastoral Theology," 91. See Kramer's warning about "cosmetic psychopharmacology"; Kramer, *Listening to Prozac*, 97.

25. Foucault, Gutting explains, saw a significant role for madness in Christian thought: "the mad are those who have reached the lowest human depths [i.e., the state of Sin in its vividness]. But this is precisely why madness can function as the unique sign of the extent of divine mercy and the power of grace." Madness is a testimony to how far mankind might fall without God's grace, whilst caring for the mad is an exhibition of how far God's mercy can reach. See Gutting, *Foucault*, 59.

26. Piper, *Spectacular Sins*, 14.

resonates deeply with the truth of what I experienced in Helia's journey through madness. At times of horrific pain, it all comes down to who and what we believe and who we lean on. If the house is built on sand, it will be washed away by the storms of evil, but a house built on the Rock will stand the beating of such forces.

In my life nothing could break into my prideful nature; I was proud of my family, my network of friends, my successes in the world, and who I was. Helia's madness was what destroyed that house of cards. Foucault is right: "madness appears . . . as the comic punishment of knowledge and its ignorant presumption."[27] Nothing can humble a proud heart as madness can with its incomprehensible forces. God cleared away most of the idolatrous clutter in my life because of Helia's illness; I lost a lot: my dreams, my career, my sense of pride about my accomplishments, my worldly identity, and my worldly riches. I truly travelled through the "valley of shadow of death," swallowed by evil, rising up in the morning with no hope, and going to bed with such despair, hoping I would never have to open my eyes again. But, in that journey something miraculous happened: I saw myself depicted in Helia's "sign acts" or "symptoms"; I came face to face with the depth of my own depravity and my need for a savior. I was freed from my "pious Christian sentimentality"[28] and I came to experience the reality of the cross. With Helia as an instrument in God's hand, many were healed of their hidden diseases in our extended family. I learned, with Luther, that there is no other way to know God but through the cross and nothing has the power to create a worshipful soul and a grateful heart but horrific suffering; because it humbles the flesh like nothing else can and sets the heart longing for union with Christ.

27. Foucault, *Madness and Civilization*, 26.

28. Tchividjian, *Glorious Ruin*, 177.

Bibliography

A Country Doctor. "Treating pain without addressing suffering." http://www.kevinmd. com/blog/2013/12/treating-pain-addressing-suffering.html.

Adams, Jay Edward. *Competent to Counsel: Introduction to Nouthetic Counseling.* The Jay Adams Library. Grand Rapids: Zondervan, 1986.

Aderhold, Volkmar, Peter Stastny, and Peter Lehmann. "Soteria: An Alternative Mental Health Reform Movement." In *Alternatives Beyond Psychiatry*, edited by Peter Stastny, Peter Lehmann, and Volkmar Aderhold, 146–60. Berlin: Peter Lehmann, 2007.

Amundsen, Darrel. "Medicine and Faith in Early Christianity." *Bulletin of the History of Medicine* 56:3 (Fall 1982) 326–50.

Anderson, Ray Sherman. *On Being Human: Essays in Theological Anthropology.* Grand Rapids: Eerdmans, 1982.

———. *The Shape of Practical Theology : Empowering Ministry with Theological Praxis.* Downers Grove, IL: InterVarsity, 2001.

Andreasen, Nancy C. *Understanding Mental Illness: A Layman's Guide.* Religion and Medicine Series. Minneapolis: Augsburg, 1974.

Angell, Marcia. "The Epidemic of Mental Illness: Why?" *The New York Review of Books.* http://www.nybooks.com/articles/archives/2011/jun/23/epidemic-mental-illness-why/.

———. *The Truth About The Drug Companies: How They Deceive Us And What To Do About It.* New York: Random House, 2005.

Aquinas, Thomas. *Summa Theologica.* Christian Classics Ethereal Library. http://www. ccel.org/ccel/aquinas/summa.toc.html.

Athanasius, and Robert C. Gregg. *The Life of Antony and the Letter to Marcellinus.* The Classics of Western Spirituality. New York: Paulist Press, 1980.

Atkinson, David John. *The Message of Genesis 1–11: The Dawn of Creation.* The Bible Speaks Today. Downers Grove, IL: InterVarsity, 1990.

Atkinson, Jacqueline M. "The Patient as Sufferer." *British Journal of Medical Psychology* 66:2 (1993) 113–20.

Augustine. "Augustine's Doctrine of the Bondage of the Will." http://www.monergism .com/thethreshold/articles/onsite/augustinewill.html.

Bakken, Kenneth L. "Holy Spirit and Theosis: Toward a Lutheran Theology of Healing." *St. Vladimir's Theological Quarterly* 38:4 (January 1, 1994) 409–23.

Barrajon, A. Pedro. "The Soul in Theology: Critical Reflections on Non-Reductive Physicalism." *Alpha Omega* 7:3 (2004) 457–63.

Barrett, William. *Irrational Man: A Study in Existential Philosophy.* Garden City, NY: Doubleday, 1962.

Barth, Karl. *Church Dogmatics*. 2nd ed. Edited by Geoffrey William Bromiley and Thomas F. Torrance. Edinburgh: T. & T. Clark, 1975.

————. *The Humanity of God*. London: Collins, 1961.

Baumeister, Alan A., and Jennifer L. Francis. "Historical Development of the Dopamine Hypothesis of Schizophrenia." *Journal of the History of the Neurosciences* 11:3 (2002) 265–77.

Beck, James R., and Bruce A. Demarest. *The Human Person in Theology and Psychology: A Biblical Anthropology for the Twenty-First Century*. Grand Rapids: Kregel, 2005.

Becker, Ernest. *The Denial of Death*. New York: Free Press, 1973.

————. *Escape from Evil*. New York: Free Press, 1975.

Bentall, Richard P. "Concluding Remarks: Schizophrenia—a Suitable Case for Treatment?" In *Reconstructing Schizophrenia*, edited by Richard P. Bentall, 283–96. London: Routledge, 1992.

————. *Doctoring the Mind: Why Psychiatric Treatments Fail*. London: Penguin, 2010.

————. *Madness Explained: Psychosis and Human Nature*. London: Penguin, 2004.

Bentall, Richard P., Sophie Wickham, Mark Shevlin, and Filippo Varese. "Do Specific Early-Life Adversities Lead to Specific Symptoms of Psychosis? A Study from the 2007 the Adult Psychiatric Morbidity Survey." *Schizophrenia Bulletin* (April 10, 2012) 734–40.

Berkhof, Louis. *Systematic Theology*. Grand Rapids: Eerdmans, 1996.

Berkouwer, G. C. *Man: The Image of God*. Studies in Dogmatics. Grand Rapids: Eerdmans, 1962.

Blackwell, Benjamin Carey. "Christosis: Pauline Soteriology in Light of Deification in Irenaeus and Cyril of Alexandria." PhD diss., Durham University, 2010. http://etheses.dur.ac.uk/219/.

Boice, James Montgomery, and Philip Graham Ryken. *The Doctrines of Grace: Rediscovering the Evangelical Gospel*. Wheaton, IL: Crossway, 2002.

Boisen, Anton T. *The Exploration of the Inner World: A Study of Mental Disorder and Religious Experience*. New York: Harper & Brothers, 1952.

Bonhoeffer, Dietrich. *Creation and Fall: A Theological Interpretation of Genesis 1–3*. New York: Macmillan, 1959.

————. *Life Together*. New York: Harper, 1954.

Bonner, Gerald. "Augustine's Conception of Deification." *Journal of Theological Studies* 37:2 (1986) 369–86.

Booth, Gotthard. "Physician between the Spirit and the Flesh." Manuscript.

————. "Variety in Personality and its Relation to Health." *Review of Religion* 10 (1946) 385–412.

————. "The Voice of the Body." In *The Voice of Illness: A Study in Therapy and Prophecy*. 2nd ed., 1–25. New York: Edwin Mellen, 1981.

Borgwardt, Stefan, and Paolo Fusar-Poli. "Third-Generation Neuroimaging in Early Schizophrenia: Translating Research Evidence into Clinical Utility." *The British Journal of Psychiatry* 200:4 (April 1, 2012) 270–72.

Bowers, Malcolm B., Jr. "Central Dopamine Turnover in Schizophrenic Syndromes." *Archives of General Psychiatry* 31:1 (July 1, 1974) 50–54.

Boyd, Jeffrey H. "A Biblical Theology of Chronic Illness." *Trinity Journal* 24:2 (2003) 189–206.

————. "Losing Soul: How and Why Theologians Created the Mental Health Movement." *Calvin Theological Journal* 30:2 (1995) 472–92.

————. "What DNA Tells Us about the Human Soul." *Calvin Theological Journal* 33:1 (1998) 142–59.

Boyle, Mary. "The Non-Discovery of Schizophrenia?" In *Reconstructing Schizophrenia*, edited by Richard P. Bentall, 3–22. London: Routledge, 1990.

Bradford, David Terry. *The Experience of God: Portraits in the Phenomenological Psychopathology of Schizophrenia*. American University Studies. Series 8, Psychology. Vol. 4. New York: Lang, 1984.

Breggin, Peter Roger. *Medication Madness: A Psychiatrist Exposes the Dangers of Mood-Altering Medications*. New York: St. Martin's, 2008.

————. *Toxic Psychiatry: Why Therapy, Empathy, and Love must Replace the Drugs, Electroshock, and Biochemical Theories of the "New Psychiatry."* New York: St. Martin's, 1991.

Brennand, Kristen J. et al. "Modeling Schizophrenia using Human Induced Pluripotent Stem Cells." *Nature* 473:7346 (2011) 221–25.

Broome, Edwin C., Jr. "Ezekiel's Abnormal Personality." *Journal of Biblical Literature* 65:3 (1946) 277–92.

Brown, Warren S. "Conclusion: Reconciling Scientific and Biblical Portraits of Human Nature." In *Whatever Happened to the Soul?: Scientific and Theological Portraits of Human Nature*, edited by Warren S. Brown, Nancey C. Murphy, and H. Newton Malony, 213–28. Minneapolis: Fortress, 1998.

Brown, Norman Oliver. *Life Against Death: The Psychoanalytical Meaning of History*. Middletown, CT: Wesleyan University Press, 1959.

Brown University. "Schizophrenia (DSM-IV-TR #295.1–295.3, 295.90)." http://www.brown.edu/Courses/BI_278/Other/Clerkship/Didactics/Readings/Schizophrenia.pdf.

Browning, Don S. "Pastoral Theology in a Pluralistic Age." In *The Blackwell Reader in Pastoral and Practical Theology*, edited by James Woodward, Stephen Pattison, and John Patton, 89–103. Malden, MA: Blackwell, 2000.

Brunner, Emil. *Man in Revolt: A Christian Anthropology*. London: n.p., 1939.

Buber, Martin. *The Prophetic Faith*. New York: Macmillan, 1949.

Bultmann, Rudolf, and Kendrick Grobel. *Theology of the New Testament*, vol. 2. New York: Scribner, 1951.

Burns, Tom et al. "Community Treatment Orders for Patients with Psychosis (OCTET): A Randomised Controlled Trial." *The Lancet* (March 26, 2013). doi:10.1016/S0140-6736(13)60107-5.

Burroughs, Jeremiah. *The Evil of Evils: Or the Exceeding Sinfulness of Sin*. Edited by Don Kistler. Grand Rapids: Soli Deo Gloria, 2008.

Burt, David R., Ian Creese, and Solomon H. Snyder. "Antischizophrenic Drugs: Chronic Treatment Elevates Dopamine Receptor Binding in Brain." *Science* 196:4287 (April 15, 1977) 326–28.

Bustamante, Jose Angel. "The Importance of Cultural Factors in Mental Hygiene." *International Journal of Social Psychiatry* 6:3-4 (September 1960) 252–59.

Cacciatore, Joanne. "DSM5 and Ethical Relativism." http://drjoanne.blogspot.com/2012/03/relativity-applies-to-physics-not.html.

Calton, Tim, Michael Ferriter, Nick Huband, and Helen Spandler. "A Systematic Review of the Soteria Paradigm for the Treatment of People Diagnosed with Schizophrenia." *Schizophrenia Bulletin* 34:1 (January 1, 2008) 181–92.

Calvin, John. *Institutes of the Christian Religion*. Library of Christian Classics. Translated by Ford Lewis Battles, edited by John T. McNeill. London: SCM, 1961.

Bibliography

Caplan, Paula J. "Psychiatry's Bible, the DSM, is Doing More Harm than Good." *Washington Post*, April 27, 2012.

Carlat, Daniel J. *Unhinged: The Trouble with Psychiatry—A Doctor's Revelations about a Profession in Crisis*. New York: Free Press, 2010.

Carlson, Arnold E. "Luther and the Doctrine of the Holy Spirit." *Lutheran Quarterly* 11:2 (1959) 135–46.

Carrel, Alexis, 1873–1944. *Man the Unknown*. New York: Harper & Bros., 1935.

Carson, D. A. *How Long, O Lord?: Reflections on Suffering and Evil*. 2nd ed. Grand Rapids: Baker Academic, 2006.

Carson, Marion. "Fine Madness: Psychosis, Faith Communities and the Rehabilitation of the Christian Apocalypse." *The Expository Times* 117:9 (June 1, 2006) 360–65.

Carson, Marion L. S. "Loving, Discernment, and Distance: Pastoral Care in Schizophrenia." *Journal of Pastoral Care & Counseling* 60:3 (September 1, 2006) 227–39.

Cassian, John, and Boniface Ramsey. *John Cassian, the Conferences*. Ancient Christian Writers 57. New York: Newman, 1997.

Chouinard, Guy, and Barry Jones. "Neuroleptic-Induced Supersensitivity Psychosis: Clinical and Pharmacologic Characteristics." *American Journal of Psychiatry* 137:1 (January 1980) 16–21.

Christie, Nils. *Beyond Loneliness and Institutions: Communes for Extraordinary People*. Eugene, OR: Wipf and Stock, 2007.

Claridge, Gordon. "Can a Disease Model of Schizophrenia Survive?" In *Reconstructing Schizophrenia*, edited by Richard P. Bentall, 157–83. London: Routledge, 1990.

Clark, Kelly James. *When Faith is Not enough*. Grand Rapids: Eerdmans, 1997.

Clarke, Isabel. *Madness, Mystery and the Survival of God*. Hants, UK: O Books, 2008.

Clay, Sally. "The Wounded Prophet." Paper presented at the First National Forum on Recovery from Mental Illness, National Institute of Mental Health and Ohio Department of Mental Health, April 1994. Unpublished Manuscript.

Cohen, Elizabeth. "CDC: Antidepressants most Prescribed Drugs in U.S.—CNN." http://articles.cnn.com/2007-07-09/health/antidepressants_1_antidepressants-high-blood-pressure-drugs-psychotropic-drugs?_s=PM:HEALTH.

Colwell, John. *Why Have You Forsaken Me?: A Personal Reflection on the Experience of Desolation*. N.p.: Paternoster, 2010.

Constantelos, Demetrios J. "Irenaeus of Lyons and His Central Views on Human Nature." *St Vladimir's Theological Quarterly* 33, no. 4 (January 1, 1989) 351–63.

Cook, Christopher C., M.D., Andrew S. Powell, Andrew C. P. Sims, and Royal College of Psychiatrists. *Spirituality and Psychiatry*. London: RCPsych, 2009.

Cooper, D. G. *Psychiatry and Anti-Psychiatry*. London: Paladin, 1970.

Cooper, John W. *Body, Soul, and Life Everlasting: Biblical Anthropology and the Monism-Dualism Debate*. Grand Rapids: Eerdmans, 2000.

Corduan, Winfried. *Mysticism: An Evangelical Option?* Grand Rapids: Zondervan, 1991.

Cortez, Marc. "Embodied Souls, Ensouled Bodies: An Exercise in Christological Anthropology and its Significance for the Mind/Body Debate." PhD diss., St. Mary's College, University of St. Andrews, 2006.

Cullmann, Oscar. *Immortality of the Soul Or Resurrection of the Dead? The Witness of the New Testament*. Ingersoll Lectures. London: Epworth, 1958.

Dammann, Eric J. "The Myth of Mental Illness: Continuing Controversies and their Implications for Mental Health Professionals." *Clinical Psychology Review* 17:7 (1997) 733–56.

Day, John N. "Ezekiel and the Heart of Idolatry." *Bibliotheca Sacra* 164:653 (2007) 21–33.

Deegan, Patricia E. "Recovery as a Self-Directed Process of Healing and Transformation." In *Recovery and Wellness: Models of Hope and Empowerment for People with Mental Illness*, edited by Catana Brown, 5–21. New York: Haworth, 2001.

Deniker, Pierre. "From Chlorpromazine to Tardive Dyskinesia (Brief History of the Neuroleptics)." *Psychiatric Journal of the University of Ottawa: Revue De Psychiatrie De l'Université d'Ottawa* 14:1 (1989) 253–59.

Diamond, James Arthur. "Maimonides on Leprosy: Illness as Contemplative Metaphor." *Jewish Quarterly Review* 96:1 (2006) 95–122.

Diamond, Stephen. "The Devil Inside: Psychotherapy, Exorcism, and Demonic Possession." *Psychology Today* (January 17, 2012). No pages. Online: http://www. psychologytoday.com/blog/evil-deeds/201201/the-devil-inside-psychotherapy-exorcism-and-demonic-possession.

Dillard, Raymond B., and Tremper Longman. *An Introduction to the Old Testament.* Grand Rapids: Zondervan, 1994.

DNA Learning Center. "DSM-IV Criteria for Schizophrenia." http://www.dnalc .org/view/899-DSM-IV-Criteria-for-Schizophrenia.html.

Doller, Jane. Foreword to *The Quiet Room: A Journey Out of the Torment of Madness*, edited by Lori Schiller and Amanda Bennett. New York: Warner, 1994.

Dreifus, Claudia. "Using Imaging to Look at Changes in the Brain." *The New York Times*, September 15, 2008.

Dreyfus, Hubert L. "Foucault's Critique of Psychiatric Medicine." *The Journal of Medicine and Philosophy* 12:4 (1987) 311–33.

Duncan, Laramie E., and Matthew C. Keller. "A Critical Review of the First 10 Years of Candidate Gene-by-Environment Interaction Research in Psychiatry." *American Journal of Psychiatry* 168:10 (October 2011) 1041–49.

Eccles, John C. *Facing Reality: Philosophical Adventures by a Brain Scientist.* Heidelberg Science Library, vol. 13. New York: Longman, 1970.

Eichrodt, Walther. *Theology of the Old Testament.* Philadelphia: Westminster, 1961.

Elkes, Joel. "Effects of Chlorpromazine on the Behavior of Chronically Overactive Psychotic Patients." *British Medical Journal* 2 (1954) 560–65.

Epstein, Leon, Richard D. Morgan, and Lynn Reynolds. "An Approach to the Effect of Ataraxic Drugs on Hospital Release Rates." *American Journal of Psychiatry* 119 (July 1962) 36–47.

Erickson, Millard J. *Christian Theology.* Grand Rapids: Baker, 1983.

Erickson, Richard C. "Serving the Needs of Persons with Chronic Mental Illness: A Neglected Ministry." *Journal of Pastoral Care* 44:2 (1990) 153–62.

Erikson, Erik H. *Young Man Luther: A Study in Psychoanalysis and History.* London: Faber, 1959.

Fairbairn, W. Ronald. *Psychoanalytic Studies of the Personality.* Florence, KY: Routledge, 1994. http://site.ebrary.com/lib/aberdeenuniv/docDetail.action?docID=5001593.

Farde, Lars et al. "Positron Emission Tomographic Analysis of Central D1 and D2 Dopamine Receptor Occupancy in Patients Treated with Classical Neuroleptics and Clozapine: Relation to Extrapyramidal Side Effects." *Archives of General Psychiatry* 49:7 (July 1, 1992) 538–44.

Fava, Giovanni A. "Should the Drug Industry Work with Key Opinion Leaders? No." *BMJ* 336:7658 (June 21, 2008) 1405.

Fawcett, Barbara. "Consistencies and Inconsistencies: Mental Health, Compulsory Treatment and Community Capacity Building in England, Wales and Australia." *British Journal of Social Work* 37:6 (September 2007) 1027–42.

Ferguson, Sinclair B. "The Reformed View." In *Christian Spirituality: Five Views of Sanctification*, edited by Donald Alexander and Sinclair B. Ferguson, 47–76. Downers Grove, IL: InterVarsity, 1988.

Foskett, John. *Meaning in Madness: The Pastor and the Mentally Ill.* New Library of Pastoral Care. London: SPCK, 1984.

Foucault, Michel. *Madness and Civilization: A History of Insanity in the Age of Reason.* New York: Vintage, 1988.

Fowler, James W. "Practical Theology and Theological Education: Some Models and Questions." *Theology Today* 42:1 (April 1, 1985) 43–58.

Frame, John M. "A Primer on Perspectivalism." http://www.frame-poythress.org/frame_articles/2008Primer.htm.

———. "In Defense of Something Close to Biblicism: Reflections on Sola Scriptura and History in Theological Method." http://www.frame-poythress.org/frame_articles/Biblicism.htm.

———. *The Doctrine of God.* A Theology of Lordship. Phillipsburg, NJ: Presbyterian and Reformed, 2002.

———. *The Doctrine of the Knowledge of God.* A Theology of Lordship. Phillipsburg, NJ: Presbyterian and Reformed, 1987.

Frances, Allen. "A Warning Sign on the Road to DSM-V: Beware of its Unintended Consequences." *Psychiatric Times,* June 26, 2009.

Friedman, Richard A. "A Call for Caution on Antipsychotic Drugs." *New York Times,* September 24, 2012.

Fromm, Erich. *The Crisis of Psychoanalysis.* London: Cape, 1971.

Gaiser, Frederick J. *Healing in the Bible: Theological Insight for Christian Ministry.* Grand Rapids: Baker Academic, 2010.

Gallaudet, T. H. "Report of the Chaplain—1842." *Journal of Pastoral Care* 33:2 (1979) 136–38.

Gaudin, Sharon. "Kurzweil: Computers Will Enable People to Live Forever." *InformationWeek* (November 21, 2006). http://www.informationweek.com/kurzweil-computers-will-enable-people-to-live-forever/d/d-id/1049093?

Geddes, John, Nick Freemantle, Paul Harrison, and Paul Bebbington. "Atypical Antipsychotics in the Treatment of Schizophrenia: Systematic Overview and Meta-Regression Analysis." *BMJ* 321:7273 (December 2, 2000) 1371–76.

Gelder, Michael G., Richard Mayou, and Philip Cowen. *Shorter Oxford Textbook of Psychiatry.* Oxford Medical Publications. 4th ed. Oxford: Oxford University Press, 2001.

Goff, Donald C. "Antipsychotics and Shrinking Brain." *Psychiatric Times,* May 3, 2011. No pages. Online: http://www.psychiatrictimes.com/articles/antipsychotics-and-shrinking-brain.

Gottesman, Irving I., James Shields, and Daniel R. Hanson. *Schizophrenia, the Epigenetic Puzzle.* Cambridge: Cambridge University Press, 1982.

Govig, Stewart D. "Chronic Mental Illness and the Family: Contexts for Pastoral Care." *Journal of Pastoral Care* 47:4 (1993) 405–18.

———. *Souls are made of Endurance: Surviving Mental Illness in the Family.* Louisville: Westminster John Knox, 1994.

Green, Joel B. "Bodies—that is, Human Lives: A Re-Examination of Human Nature in the Bible." In *Whatever Happened to the Soul?: Scientific and Theological Portraits of Human Nature,* edited by Warren S. Brown, Nancey C. Murphy, and H. Newton Malony, 149–73. Minneapolis: Fortress, 1998.

Greenberg, Gary. "Inside the Battle to Define Mental Illness." *Wired.* http://www .wired.com/magazine/2010/12/ff_dsmv/all/1.

Greene-McCreight, Kathryn. *Darkness Is My Only Companion: A Christian Response to Mental Illness.* Grand Rapids: Brazos, 2006.

Grof, Christina, and Stanislav Grof. *The Stormy Search for the Self: Understanding and Living with Spiritual Emergency.* Classics of Personal Development. London: Thorsons, 1995.

Grof, Stanislav, and Christina Grof. *Spiritual Emergency: When Personal Transformation Becomes a Crisis.* New Consciousness Reader. New York: Putnam, 1989.

Grudem, Wayne A. *Systematic Theology: An Introduction to Biblical Doctrine.* Grand Rapids: Zondervan, 1994.

———. *Bible Doctrine: Essential Teachings of the Christian Faith.* Edited by Jeff Purswell. Grand Rapids: Zondervan, 1999.

Guthrie, Shirley C., Jr. "Pastoral Counseling, Trinitarian Theology, and Christian Anthropology." *Interpretation* 33:2 (1979) 130–43.

Gutting, Gary. "Foucault and the History of Madness." In *The Cambridge Companion to Foucault,* edited by Gary Gutting, 47–70. Cambridge: Cambridge University Press, 1994.

Hacking, Ian. "Making Up People." *London Review of Books* 28:16 (17 August 2006). http://www.lrb.co.uk/v28/n16/ian-hacking/making-up-people.

———. *Rewriting the Soul: Multiple Personality and the Sciences of Memory.* Princeton, NJ: Princeton University Press, 1995.

Håkansson, Carina. *Ordinary Life Therapy: Experiences from a Collaborative Systemic Practice.* Chagrin Falls, OH: Taos Institute, 2009.

Haracz, John L. "The Dopamine Hypothesis: An Overview of Studies with Schizophrenic Patients." *Schizophrenia Bulletin* 8, no. 3 (1982) 438–69.

Harrison, Nonna Verna. "Greek Patristic Foundations of Trinitarian Anthropology." *Pro Ecclesia* 14:4 (2005) 399–412.

Healy, David. "Pioneers in Psychopharmacology." *The International Journal of Neuropsychopharmacology* 1:2 (1998) 191.

Herzfeld, Noreen. "Creating in our Own Image: Artificial Intelligence and the Image of God." *Zygon* 37:2 (2002) 303–16.

Hessamfar, Elahe. "Mental Illness, Right & Wrong, Drugs, and Violence." http://www. madinamerica.com/2013/10/mental-illness-right-wrong-drugs-violence/.

Ho, Beng-Choon et al. "Progressive Structural Brain Abnormalities and their Relationship to Clinical Outcome: A Longitudinal Magnetic Resonance Imaging Study Early in Schizophrenia." *Archives of General Psychiatry* 60:6 (June 1, 2003) 585–94.

Ho, Beng-Choon et al. "Long-Term Antipsychotic Treatment and Brain Volumes: A Longitudinal Study of First-Episode Schizophrenia." *Archives of General Psychiatry* 68:2 (February 1, 2011) 128–37.

Honko, Lauri. "Varhaiskantaiset taudinselitykset ja parantamisnäytemä." In *Jumin Keko,* edited by Jouko Hautala, 64–66. Helsinki: Suomalisen Kirjallisuuden Seura, 1990.

Hunsinger, Deborah van Deusen. *Theology and Pastoral Counseling: A New Inter-disciplinary Approach*. Grand Rapids: Eerdmans, 1995.

Hyman, Steve. "Initiation and Adaptation: A Paradigm for Understanding Psychotropic Drug Action." *American Journal of Psychiatry* 153:2 (February 1996) 151–62.

Insel, Thomas. "Transforming Diagnosis." *National Institute of Mental Health*. (April 29, 2013). http://www.nimh.nih.gov/about/director/index.shtml#p145045.

———. "Translating Scientific Opportunity into Public Health Impact: A Strategic Plan for Research on Mental Illness." *Archives of General Psychiatry* 66:2 (February 1, 2009) 128–33.

Irenaeus. "Church Fathers: Against Heresies (St. Irenaeus)." http://www.newadvent.org/fathers/0103.htm.

Isaac, Rael Jean. "Thomas Szasz: A Life in Error." *American Thinker* (September 23, 2012). http://www.americanthinker.com/2012/09/thomas_szasz_a_life_in_error.html.

Jabr, Ferris. "The Newest Edition of Psychiatry's 'Bible,' the *DSM-5*, is Complete." *Scientific American,* January 28, 2013. http://www.scientificamerican.com/article/dsm-5-update/.

James, William. *The Varieties of Religious Experience: A Study in Human Nature*. Charleston, SC: BiblioBazaar, 2007.

Jenson, Alex. "Review—Psychiatryland." *Metapsychology Online Reviews* 16:9 (February 28, 2012). http://metapsychology.mentalhelp.ntet/poc/view_doc.php?type=book&id=6428.

Jin, Hua et al. "Comparison of Longer-Term Safety and Effectiveness of 4 Atypical Antipsychotics in Patients Over Age 40: A Trial using Equipoise-Stratified Randomization." *Journal of Clinical Psychiatry* (November 27, 2012). doi:10.4088/JCP.12m08001.

John of the Cross. *Dark Night of the Soul*. Mineola, NY: Dover, 2003.

Johnstone, Eve C. et al. "Cerebral Ventricular Size and Cognitive Impairment in Chronic Schizophrenia." Abstract. *The Lancet* 308:7992 (1976) 924–26.

Joseph, Jay. "The 'Missing Heritability' of Psychiatric Disorders: Elusive Genes Or Non-Existent Genes?" *Applied Developmental Science* 16:2 (2012) 65–83.

Joy, Bill. "Why the Future Doesn't Need Us." *Wired* 8:4 (April 2000). http://archive.wired.com/wired/archive/8.04/joy.html.

Kaiser, Walter C., and Moisés Silva. *Introduction to Biblical Hermeneutics: The Search for Meaning*. Grand Rapids: Zondervan, 2007.

Kaplan, Bert, and Gardner Murphy. *The Inner World of Mental Illness: A Series of First-Person Accounts of what it was Like*. Edited by Bert Kaplan. New York: Harper and Row, 1964.

Kapur, Shitij. "Psychosis as a State of Aberrant Salience: A Framework Linking Biology, Phenomenology, and Pharmacology in Schizophrenia." *American Journal of Psychiatry* 160:1 (January 1, 2003) 13–23.

Karlberg, Mark W. "On the Theological Correlation of Divine and Human Language: A Review Article." *Journal of the Evangelical Theological Society* 32:1 (1989) 99–105.

Karow, A., D. Naber, M. Lambert, and S. Moritz. "Remission as Perceived by People with Schizophrenia, Family Members and Psychiatrists." *European Psychiatry* 27:6 (2012) 426–31.

Kaufman, Walter. *Nietzsche*. Meridian, 1960.

Kempe, Margery et al. *The Book of Margery Kempe*. Early English Text Society. Original Series 212. London: Oxford University Press, 1940.

Kendell, R. E. et al. "Diagnostic Criteria of American and British Psychiatrists." *Archives of General Psychiatry* 25:2 (August 1, 1971) 123–30.

Kendler, Kenneth S. "Toward a Philosophical Structure for Psychiatry." *American Journal of Psychiatry* 162:3 (March 1, 2005) 433–40.

Khin, Ni A. et al. "Exploratory Analyses of Efficacy Data from Schizophrenia Trials in Support of New Drug Applications Submitted to the US Food and Drug Administration." *Journal of Clinical Psychiatry* 73:6 (May 2012) 856–64.

Kierkegaard, Søren. *Kierkegaard's the Concept of Dread*. Translated and edited by Walter Lowrie. London: Oxford University Press, 1946.

———. *Training in Christianity*. In *A Kierkegaard Anthology*, translated by Walter Lowrie and edited by Robert Bretall, 372–418. London: Oxford University Press, 1947.

Kierkegaard, Søren, and Robert Bretall. *A Kierkegaard Anthology*. Translated by Walter Lowrie, edited by Robert Bretall. London: Oxford University Press, 1947.

Kim, Hyun-Sook. "The Hermeneutical-Praxis Paradigm and Practical Theology." *Religious Education* 102:4 (September 1, 2007) 419–36.

Kinghorn, Warren Anderson. "Ordering 'Mental Disorder': Theology and the Disputed Boundaries of Psychiatric Diagnosis." Durham, NC, Society for Spirituality, Theology and Health, June 17, 2010.

———. "Medicating the Eschatalogical Body: Psychiatric Technology for Christian Wayfarers." PhD diss., Duke University, 2011.

Kirk, Stuart A., and Herb Kutchins. *The Selling of DSM: The Rhetoric of Science in Psychiatry*. Social Problems and Social Issues. New York: A. de Gruyter, 1992.

Kirkbride, James B., Peter B. Jones, Simone Ullrich, and Jeremy W. Coid. "Social Deprivation, Inequality, and the Neighborhood-Level Incidence of Psychotic Syndromes in East London." *Schizophrenia Bulletin* (December 12, 2012). http://schizophreniabulletin.oxfordjournals.org/content/40/1/169.full.pdf+html.

Kirsch, Irving. *The Emperor's New Drugs: Exploding the Antidepressant Myth*. New York: Basic Books, 2011.

Klein, Ralph W. *Israel in Exile, a Theological Interpretation*. Overtures to Biblical Theology. Philadelphia: Fortress, 1979.

Kleinman, Arthur. *The Illness Narratives: Suffering, Healing, and the Human Condition*. New York: Basic, 1988.

Koenig, Harold George, Michael E. McCullough, and David B. Larson. *Handbook of Religion and Health*. Oxford: Oxford University Press, 2001.

Kramer, Peter D. *Listening to Prozac*. New York: Penguin, 1997.

Kuhn, Thomas S. *The Structure of Scientific Revolutions*. International Encyclopedia of Unified Science. Foundations of the Unity of Science, v. 2, no. 2. 2nd ed. Chicago: University of Chicago Press, 1970.

Kupfer, David J., Michael B. First, and Darrel A. Regier. *A Research Agenda for DSM-V*. Washington, D.C.: American Psychiatric Association, 2002.

Kurzweil, Ray. *The Singularity Is Near: When Humans Transcend Biology*. New York: Viking, 2005.

Kutchins, Herb, and Stuart A. Kirk. *Making Us Crazy: DSM: The Psychiatric Bible and the Creation of Mental Disorders*. New York: Free Press, 1997.

Laing, R. D. *The Divided Self*. New York: Pantheon, 1969.

————. *The Politics of Experience, and, the Bird of Paradise*. Harmondsworth: Penguin, 1967.

————. "Massacre of the Innocents." *Peace News* (January 22, 1965) 7.

————. "Metanoia: Some Experiences at Kingsley Hall, London." In *Going Crazy: The Radical Therapy of R. D. Laing and Others*, edited by Hendrick Marinus Ruitenbeek, 11–21. New York: Bantam, 1972.

Laing, R. D., and Aaron Esterson. *Sanity, Madness, and the Family: Families of Schizophrenics*. 2nd ed. Harmondsworth: Penguin, 1990.

Larchet, Jean-Claude. *Mental Disorders & Spiritual Healing: Teachings from the Early Christian East*. Hillsdale, NY: Sophia Perennis, 2005.

————. *Theology of Illness*. Crestwood, NY: St. Vladimir's Seminary Press, 2002.

Lee, Tyrone, Philip Seeman, W. W. Tourtellotte, Irene J. Farley, and Oleh Hornykeiwicz. "Binding of 3H-Neuroleptics and 3H-Apomorphine in Schizophrenic Brains." *Nature* 274:5674 (1978) 897–900.

Lehmann, Peter, and Peter Stastny. "Reforms Or Alternatives? A Better Psychiatry Or Better Alternatives?" In *Alternatives Beyond Psychiatry*, edited by Peter Stastny, Peter Lehmann, and Volkmar Aderhold, 402–11. Berlin: Peter Lehmann, 2007.

Leucht, S., G. Pitschel-Walz, D. Abraham, and W. Kissling. "Efficacy and Extrapyramidal Side-Effects of the New Antipsychotics Olanzapine, Quetiapine, Risperidone, and Sertindole Compared to Conventional Antipsychotics and Placebo. A Meta-Analysis of Randomized Controlled Trials." *Schizophrenia Research* 35:1 (1999) 51–68.

Levitt, Pat, and John March. *Transformative Neurodevelopmental Research in Mental Illness: Report of the National Advisory Mental Health Council's Workgroup*. Bethesda, MD: National Institute of Mental Health, 2008.

Lewis, Bradley. *Moving Beyond Prozac, DSM, & the New Psychiatry: The Birth of Postpsychiatry*. Corporealities. Ann Arbor, MI: University of Michigan Press, 2006.

Leyshon, David. *Sickness, Suffering and Scripture*. Edinburgh: Banner Of Truth Trust, 2008.

Lockhart, Liz. "More replication study needs to be carried out on mental health research." http://www.mentalhealthy.co.uk/news/859-more-replication-study-needs-to-be-carried-out-on-mental-health-research.html.

Loewenthal, Kate Miriam. "Religious Beliefs about Illness." *International Journal for the Psychology of Religion* 7:3 (1997) 173–78.

Longden, Eleanor. "Eleanor Longden: The Voices in my head." http://www.ted.com/talks/eleanor_longden_the_voices_in_my_head.html.

Lossky, V. *The Mystical Theology of the Eastern Church*. Crestwood, NY: St. Vladimir's Seminary Press, 1997.

Louth, Andrew. "The Place of Theosis in Orthodox Theology." In *Partakers of the Divine Nature: The History and Development of Deification in the Christian Traditions*, edited by Michael J. Christensen and Jeffery A. Wittung, 32–44. Grand Rapids: Baker Academic, 2008.

————. *The Origins of the Christian Mystical Tradition from Plato to Denys*. Oxford: Oxford University Press, 1981.

Luhrmann, T. M. "The Violence in Our Heads." *The New York Times* (September 19, 2013). http://www.nytimes.com/2013/09/20/opinion/luhrmann-the-violence-in-our-heads.html?_r=0.

Lysaker, Paul H., and John T. Lysaker. "Schizophrenia and Alterations in Self-Experience: A Comparison of 6 Perspectives." *Schizophrenia Bulletin* 36:2 (March 1, 2010) 331–40.

Mackay, Angus V. P. et al. "Increased Brain Dopamine and Dopamine Receptors in Schizophrenia." *Archives of General Psychiatry* 39, no. 9 (September 1, 1982) 991–97.

Mackler, Daniel. Review of *Ordinary Life Therapy* by Carina Håkansson. http://www.amazon.com/Ordinary-Life-Therapy-Experiences-Collaborative/product-reviews/0981907628/ref=sr_1_1_cm_cr_acr_txt?ie=UTF8&showViewpoints=1.

Marshall, Tom. *Healing from the Inside Out.* Lynnwood, WA: Emerald, 1991.

Marshall, I. H. "Being Human: Made in the Image of God." *Stone-Campbell Journal* 4:1 (2001) 47–67.

McCasland, S. Vernon. *By the Finger of God: Demon Possession and Exorcism in Early Christianity in the Light of Modern Views of Mental Illness.* New York: Macmillan, 1951.

McDonald, Suzanne. "The Pneumatology of the 'Lost' Image in John Owen." *Westminster Theological Journal* 71:2 (2009) 323–35.

McFarland, Ian A. *The Divine Image: Envisioning the Invisible God.* Philadelphia: Fortress, 2005.

McGruder, Juli. "Life Experience is Not a Disease, Or Why Medicalizing Madness is Counterproductive to Recovery." In *Recovery and Wellness: Models of Hope and Empowerment for People with Mental Illness,* edited by Catana Brown, 59–80. New York: Haworth, 2002.

———. "Madness in Zanzibar: 'Schizophrenia' in Three Families in the 'Developing' World." PhD diss., University of Washington, 1999.

McNeill, John T. *A History of the Cure of Souls.* London: SCM, 1952.

Melville, Kate. "Schizophrenia Created in a Petri Dish." http://www.scienceagogo.com/news/20110912213323data_trunc_sys.shtml.

Mendez, Juan E. *Special Rapporteur on Torture and Other Cruel, Inhuman Or Degrading Treatment Or Punishment.* Geneva: The United Nations Human Right Council, 2013. http://www.madinamerica.com/wp-content/uploads/2013/03/torture.pdf.

Menninger, Karl A. *Whatever Became of Sin?* Ecclesia Books. London: Hodder and Stoughton, 1973.

Merkel, Larry. "The History of Psychiatry." University of Virginia. http://www.scribd.com/doc/41930822/History-of-Psychiatry.

Miles, Jack. *God: A Biography.* New York: Knopf, 1995.

Miller, Gavin. "R.D. Laing's Theological Hinterland: The Contrast between Mysticism and Communion." *History of Psychiatry* 23:2 (June 1, 2012) 139–55.

Mirowsky, John. "Subjective Boundaries and Combinations in Psychiatric Diagnosis." *The Journal of Mind and Behavior* 11:3–4 (Summer and Autumn 1990) 407–24, 161–78.

Miyar, Jose, and Clive E. Adams. "Content and Quality of 10000 Controlled Trials in Schizophrenia Over 60 Years." *Schizophrenia Bulletin,* January 30, 2012. http://www.ncbi.nlm.nih.gov/pmc/articles/PMC3523927/.

Monergism. "Augustine's Doctrine of the Bondage of the Will." http://www.monergism.com/thethreshold/articles/onsite/augustinewill.html.

Moreland, J. P. "Restoring the Substance to the Soul of Psychology." *Journal of Psychology and Theology* 26:1 (1998) 129–43.

———. "Restoring the Soul to Christianity." *Christian Research Journal* 23:1 (2000) 23–27.

Moreland, James Porter, and Scott B. Rae. *Body & Soul: Human Nature & the Crisis in Ethics*. Downers Grove, IL: InterVarsity, 2000.

Morrison, Anthony P., Paul Hutton, David Shiers, and Douglas Turkington. "Antipsychotics: Is it Time to Introduce Patient Choice?" *The British Journal of Psychiatry* 201:2 (August 1, 2012) 83–84.

Mosher, Loren R., Voyce Hendrix, and Deborah C. Fort. *Soteria: Through Madness to Deliverance*. Bloomington, IN: Xlibris, 2004.

Mounce, William D. *The Analytical Lexicon to the Greek New Testament*. Grand Rapids: Zondervan, 1993.

Mowrer, Orval Hobart. *The Crisis in Psychiatry and Religion*. Insight Books. Princeton: D. Van Nostrand, 1961.

Murphy, Nancey. "I Celebrate Myself: Is there a Little Man Inside Your Brain?" *Books and Culture: A Christian Review* 5:1 (January–February 1999) 24–26.

———. "Human Nature: Historical, Scientific, and Religious Issues." In *Whatever Happened to the Soul? Scientific and Theological Portraits of Human Nature*, edited by Warren S. Brown, Nancey C. Murphy, and H. Newton Malony, 1–29. Minneapolis: Fortress, 1998.

Nee, Watchman. *The Breaking of the Outer Man and the Release of the Spirit*. Anaheim, CA: Living Stream Ministry, 1997.

———. *The Spiritual Man*. New York: Christian Fellowship, 1977.

Nellas, Panayiotis, and Norman Russell. *Deification in Christ: Orthodox Perspectives on the Nature of the Human Person*. Contemporary Greek Theologians. Crestwood, NY: St. Vladimir's Seminary Press, 1987.

Neugeboren, Jay. *Imagining Robert: My Brother, Madness, and Survival: A Memoir*. New York: Henry Holt, 1998.

Neuroscience Research Australia. "The Brains of People with Schizophrenia may Attempt to Heal from the Disease." http://www.neura.edu.au/news-events/news/ brains-people-schizophrenia-may-attempt-heal-disease.

Newberg, Andrew B., Eugene G. D'Aquili, and Vince Rause. *Why God Won't Go Away: Brain Science and the Biology of Belief*. New York: Ballantine, 2001.

Niebuhr, Reinhold. *The Nature and Destiny of Man : A Christian Interpretation*. London: Nisbet & Co., 1941.

NIMH. "Questions and Answers About the NIMH Clinical Antipsychotic Trials of Intervention Effectiveness Study (CATIE)—Phase 1 Results." http://www.nimh .nih.gov/trials/practical/catie/phase1results.shtml.

———. "Sequenced Treatment Alternatives To Relieve Depression (STAR*D) Study." http://www.nimh.nih.gov/trials/practical/stard/index.shtml.

———. "Systematic Treatment Enhancement Program for Bipolar Disorder (STEP-BD)." http://www.nimh.nih.gov/trials/practical/step-bd/index.shtml.

Nouwen, Henri J. M. *Out of Solitude: Three Meditations on the Christian Life*. Notre Dame, IN: Ave Maria, 2001.

———. *The Wounded Healer: Ministry in Contemporary Society*. New York: Doubleday, 1979.

Novartis. "Highlights of Prescribing Information." Online: http://www.pharma. us.novartis.com/product/pi/pdf/Clozaril.pdf.

Oesterreich, Traugott Constantin, and Dora Ibberson. *Possession, Demoniacal and Other, among Primitive Races, in Antiquity, the Middle Ages, and Modern Times.* Authorized Translation by D. Ibberson. London: Kegan Paul & Co., 1930.

Overstreet, R. L. "Man in the Image of God: A Reappraisal." *Criswell Theological Review* 3:1 (2005) 43–70.

Owen, John. *The Mortification of Sin: A Puritan Guide.* Lexington, KY: Feather Trail, 2009.

———. *The Works of John Owen.* Edited by William H. Goold. 24 vols. London: Johnstone & Hunter, 1850–1855.

Owen, John, William Orme, and Thomas Russell. *The Works of John Owen, D.D.* London: 1826.

Pascal, Blaise. *Pensées.* New York: Dutton, 1958.

Patterson, JoEllen. *The Therapist's Guide to Psychopharmacology: Working with Patients, Families, and Physicians to Optimize Care.* New York: Guilford, 2010.

Pattison, Stephen. *Alive and Kicking: Towards a Practical Theology of Illness and Healing.* London: SCM, 1989.

———. "Mentally Ill People: A Challenge to the Churches." *Modern Churchman* 29:1 (January 1, 1986) 28–38.

Payne, Robert. *Hubris, a Study of Pride.* Harper Torchbooks. The Academy Library. New York: Harper, 1960.

Penfield, Wilder. *The Mystery of the Mind: A Critical Study of Consciousness and the Human Brain.* Princeton, NJ: Princeton University Press, 1975.

Perceval, John Thomas. *Perceval's Narrative: A Patient's Account of His Psychosis 1830–1832.* Edited by Gregory Bateson. New York: Morrow, 1974.

Pies, Ronald W. "How American Psychiatry Can Save itself: Part 2." *Psychiatric Times* (March 1, 2012). http://www.psychiatrictimes.com/articles/how-american-psychiatry-can-save-itself-part-2.

Pilch, John J. "Biblical Leprosy and Body Symbolism." *Biblical Theology Bulletin: A Journal of Bible and Theology* 11:4 (November 1, 1981) 108–13.

Pilgrim, David. "Competing Histories of Madness: Some Implications for Modern Psychiatry." In *Reconstructing Schizophrenia,* edited by Richard P. Bentall, 211–33. London: Routledge, 1990.

Pinel, Philippe, and David Daniel Davis. *A Treatise on Insanity . . . Translated from the French by D. D. Davis, etc. (Facsimile of London 1806 Edition).* History of Medicine Series. No. 14. New York: Hafner, 1962.

Piper, John. *Contending for Our All: Defending Truth and Treasuring Christ in the Lives of Athanasius, John Owen, and J. Gresham Machen.* Wheaton, IL: Crossway, 2006.

———. *Spectacular Sins: And their Global Purpose in the Glory of Christ.* Wheaton, IL: Crossway, 2008.

Piper, John, and Justin Taylor. *Suffering and the Sovereignty of God.* Wheaton, IL: Crossway, 2006.

Plantinga, Alvin C. "On Heresy, Mind, and Truth." *Faith and Philosophy* 16:2 (1999) 182–93.

Platt, David. *Radical: Taking Back Your Faith from the American Dream.* Colorado Springs, CO: Multnomah, 2010.

Porter, Roy. *Madness: A Brief History.* Oxford: Oxford University Press, 2002.

Post, Robert M., Ed Fink, William T. Carpenter Jr, and Frederick K. Goodwin. "Cerebrospinal Fluid Amine Metabolites in Acute Schizophrenia." *Archives of General Psychiatry* 32:8 (August 1, 1975) 1063–69.

Powlison, David. Foreword to *The Biblical Counseling Movement After Adams,* by Heath Lambert. Wheaton, IL: Crossway, 2012.

———. "The Great Commission is a Great Place to Begin to Understand Biblical Counseling." *CCEF* (March 04, 2013). http://www.ccef.org/blog/great-commission-great-place-begin-understand-biblical-counseling.

Pratt, Richard L. "Pictures, Windows, and Mirrors in Old Testament Exegesis." *Westminster Theological Journal* 45:1 (1983) 156–67.

Purves, Andrew. *Reconstructing Pastoral Theology: A Christological Foundation.* Louisville: Westminster John Knox, 2004.

Raison, C. L., and A. H. Miller. "The Evolutionary Significance of Depression in Pathogen Host Defense (PATHOS-D)." *Molecular Psychiatry* (January 31, 2012).

Rajkumar, A. P. et al. "National Suicide Rates and Mental Health System Indicators: An Ecological Study of 191 Countries." *International Journal of Law and Psychiatry* 36:5–6 (September–December 2013) 339–42.

Rakotojoelinandrasana, Daniel. "Holistic Approach to Mental Illnesses." *Word & World* 24:2 (2004) 182–89.

Ricœur, Paul. *The Symbolism of Evil.* Religious Perspectives 17. Boston: Beacon, 1967.

Robinson, H. Wheeler. *Redemption and Revelation in the Actuality of History.* The Library of Constructive Theology. London: 1942.

Robinson, John A. T. *The Body: A Study in Pauline Theology.* Studies in Biblical Theology 5. London: SCM, 1961.

Rollin, Henry R. "The Dark before the Dawn." *Journal of Psychopharmacology* 4:3 (1990) 109–14.

Roschke, Ronald W. "Healing in Luke, Madagascar, and Elsewhere." *Currents in Theology and Mission* 33:6 (2006) 459–71.

Rosen, George. *Madness in Society: Chapters in the Historical Sociology of Mental Illness.* Chicago: University of Chicago Press, 1980.

Rosenhan, D. L. "On being Sane in Insane Places." *Science* 179:4070 (January 19, 1973) 250–58.

Rosmarin, David H. "Religious Coping among Psychotic Patients: Relevance to Suicidality and Treatment Outcomes." *Psychiatry Research* 210:1 (November 30, 2013) 182–87.

Rufer, Marc. "Psychiatry: Its Diagnostic Methods, its Therapies, its Power." In *Alternatives Beyond Psychiatry,* edited by Peter Stastny, Peter Lehmann and Volkmar Aderhold, 382–99. Berlin: Peter Lehmann, 2007.

Ruitenbeek, Hendrik Marinus. *Going Crazy: The Radical Therapy of R. D. Laing and Others.* New York: Bantam, 1972.

Rush, Benjamin. *Medical Inquiries and Observations upon the Diseases of the Mind.* 3rd ed. Philadelphia: J. Grigg, 1827.

Russell, Norman. *The Doctrine of Deification in the Greek Patristic Tradition.* The Oxford Early Christian Studies. Oxford: Oxford University Press, 2004.

Sainsbury, Steven J. "AIDS: The Twentieth-Century Leprosy." *Dialogue* 25, no. 3 (1992) 68–77.

Saks, Elyn R. *The Center Cannot Hold: My Journey through Madness.* New York: Hyperion, 2007.

———. *Refusing Care: Forced Treatment and the Rights of the Mentally Ill.* Chicago, IL: University of Chicago Press, 2002.

Sarbin, Theodore R. "Toward the Obsolescence of the Schizophrenia Hypothesis." *The Journal of Mind and Behavior* 11:3–4 (Summer and Autumn 1990) 259–84, 13–38.

Savage, Timothy B. *Power through Weakness: Paul's Understanding of the Christian Ministry in 2 Corinthians.* Monograph Series/Society for New Testament Studies, 86. New York: Cambridge University Press, 1996.

Schiller, Lori, and Amanda Bennett. *The Quiet Room: A Journey Out of the Torment of Madness.* New York: Warner, 1994.

Scull, Andrew T. *The Most Solitary of Afflictions: Madness and Society in Britain, 1700–1900.* New Haven, CT: Yale University Press, 1993.

Scull, Andrew T. *Social Order/Mental Disorder.* Medicine and Society. Berkeley, CA: University of California Press, 1989.

Sederer, Lloyd, and Matthew Erlich. "How Thoughts Become a Psychiatric Diagnoses." *The Atlantic* (July 18, 2012). http://www.theatlantic.com/health/archive/2012/07/how-thoughts-become-a-psychiatric-diagnosis/260012/.

Seikkula, Jaakko. "Becoming Dialogical: Psychotherapy Or a Way of Life?" *The Australian and New Zealand Journal of Family Therapy* 3:3 (2011) 179–93.

Seikkula, Jaakko, and Birgitta Alakare. "Open Dialogues." In *Alternatives Beyond Psychiatry*, edited by Peter Stastny, Peter Lehmann, and Volkmar Aderhold, 223–39. Berlin: Peter Lehmann, 2007.

Seikkula, Jaakko, Birgitta Alakare, and Jukka Aaltonen. "The Comprehensive Open-Dialogue Approach in Western Lapland: II. Long-term Stability of Acute Psychosis Outcomes in Advanced Community Care." *Psychosis* 3:3 (October 1, 2011) 192–204.

Seybold, Klaus, and Ulrich B. Müller. *Sickness and Healing.* Biblical Encounters Series. Nashville: Abingdon, 1981.

Shorter, Edward. *A History of Psychiatry: From the Era of the Asylum to the Age of Prozac.* New York: Wiley, 1997.

————. "Trouble at the Heart of Psychiatry's Revised Rule Book." http://blogs.scientificamerican.com/streams-of-consciousness/2012/05/09/trouble-at-the-heart-of-psychiatrys-revised-rulebook/.

Shults, F. LeRon. *Reforming Theological Anthropology: After the Philosophical Turn to Relationality.* Grand Rapids: Eerdmans, 2003.

Shuman, Joel James. *The Body of Compassion: Ethics, Medicine, and the Church.* Radical Traditions. Boulder, CO: Westview, 1999.

Siirala, Aarne. *The Voice of Illness: A Study in Therapy and Prophecy.* 2nd ed. New York: Edwin Mellen, 1981.

Sims, A. C. P. *Is Faith Delusion?: Why Religion is Good for Your Health.* London: Continuum, 2009.

Sinaikin, Phillip. *Psychiatryland: How to Protect Yourself from Pill-Pushing Psychiatrists and Develop a Personal Plan for Optimal Mental Health.* Bloomington, IN: iUniverse, 2010.

Sobo, Simon. "Does Evidence-Based Medicine Discourage Richer Assessment of Psychopathology and Treatment?" *Psychiatric Times*, April 5, 2012. http://www.psychiatrictimes.com/major-depressive-disorder/does-evidence-based-medicine-discourage-richer-assessment-psychopathology-and-treatment.

Song, Choan-Seng. "Oh, Jesus, here with Us." In *Asian Faces of Jesus*, 131–48. Maryknoll, NY: Orbis, 1993.

Sontag, Susan. *Illness as Metaphor.* London: Allen Lane, 1979.

Southard, Samuel. "Sin Or Sickness." In *Wholeness and Holiness: Readings in the psychology/theology of Mental Health*, edited by H. Newton Malony, 143–48. Grand Rapids: Baker, 1983.

Spitzer, Robert et al. "DSM-III Field Trials: I. Initial Interrater Diagnostic Reliability." *American Journal of Psychiatry* 136:6 (June 1, 1979) 815–17.

Sproul, R. C. *The Holiness of God*. 2nd ed. Wheaton, IL: Tyndale, 1998.

Spurgeon, Charles Haddon. *Morning and Evening: Daily Readings*. Peabody, MA: Hendrickson, 2008.

Stanford, Matthew S. *Grace for the Afflicted: Viewing Mental Illness through the Eyes of Faith*. Colorado Springs, CO: Paternoster, 2008.

Stastny, Peter, Peter Lehmann, and Volkmar Aderhold. *Alternatives Beyond Psychiatry*. Berlin: Peter Lehmann, 2007.

Staub, Michael E. *Madness is Civilization: When the Diagnosis was Social, 1948–1980*. Chicago: University of Chicago Press, 2011.

Stefansson, Hreinn et al. "Common Variants Conferring Risk of Schizophrenia." *Nature* 460 (August 6, 2009) 744–47.

Stip, Emmanuel. "Happy Birthday Neuroleptics! 50 years Later: La Folie Du Doute." *European Psychiatry* 17:3 (May, 2002) 115–19.

Stuckenbruck, Loren T. "The Human Being and Demonic Invasion: Therapeutic Models in Ancient Jewish and Christian Texts." In *Spirituality, Theology & Mental Health: Multidisciplinary Perspectives*, edited by Christopher C. H. Cook, 94–123. London: SCM, 2013.

Styron, William. *Darkness Visible: A Memoir of Madness*. New York: Vintage, 1990.

Sugerman, Shirley. *Sin and Madness: Studies in Narcissism*. 2nd ed. San Rafael, CA: Barfield, 2008.

Swinburne, Richard. *The Evolution of the Soul*. Rev ed. Oxford: Oxford University Press, 1997.

Swinton, John. "Does Evil have to Exist to be Real?: The Discourse of Evil and the Practice of Mental Health Care." *Royal College of Psychiatrists Spirituality and Psychiatry Special Interest Group Newsletter* 7 (April, 2002). No pages. Online: http://www.rcpsych.ac.uk/pdf/swinton.pdf.

———. *Raging with Compassion: Pastoral Responses to the Problem of Evil*. Grand Rapids: Eerdmans, 2007.

———. *Resurrecting the Person: Friendship and the Care of People with Mental Health Problems*. Nashville: Abingdon, 2000.

Swinton, John, and Harriet Mowat. *Practical Theology and Qualitative Research*. London: SCM, 2007.

Swope, John D. "Toward a Spirit-to-Spirit Model of Christian Union with God: Exploring the Anthropological Dimension in Biblical and Theological Perspective." PhD diss., Trinity Evangelical Divinity School, 2010.

Szasz, Thomas Stephen. *The Myth of Mental Illness: Foundations of a Theory of Personal Conduct*. New York: Harper Perennial, 2010.

Tarrier, Nicholas. "The Family Management of Schizophrenia." In *Reconstructing Schizophrenia*, edited by Richard P. Bentall, 254–82. London: Routledge, 1990.

Taylor, Jill Bolte. *My Stroke of Insight: A Brain Scientist's Personal Journey*. New York: Viking, 2008.

Tchividjian, Tullian. *Glorious Ruin: How Suffering Sets You Free*. Colorado Springs, CO: David C. Cook, 2012.

Teresa. *The Life of Saint Teresa of Avila by Herself.* Penguin Classics. New York: Viking Penguin, 1957.

———. *The Interior Castle.* The Classics of Western Spirituality. London: SPCK, 1979.

Thornley, Ben and Clive Adams. "Content and Quality of 2000 Controlled Trials in Schizophrenia Over 50 Years." *BMJ* 317:7167 (October 31, 1998) 1181–84.

Tillich, Paul. *Systematic Theology.* Chicago: University of Chicago Press, 1951.

———. Foreword to *The Voice of Illness: A Study in Therapy and Prophecy,* by Aarne Siirala, v–vi. 2nd ed. New York: Edwin Mellen, 1981.

Tjeltveit, Alan C. "Psychotherapeutic Triumphalism and Freedom from Mental Illness: Diverse Concepts of Mental Health." *Word & World* 9:2 (March 1, 1989) 132–39.

Tomes, Nancy. *A Generous Confidence: Thomas Story Kirkbride and the Art of Asylum-Keeping, 1840–1883.* Cambridge History of Medicine. Cambridge: Cambridge University Press, 1984.

Torrey, E. Fuller, and Judy Miller. *The Invisible Plague: The Rise of Mental Illness from 1750 to the Present.* New Brunswick, NJ: Rutgers University Press, 2001.

Tripp, Paul David. *Instruments in the Redeemer's Hands: People in Need of Change Helping People in Need of Change.* Resources for Changing Lives. Phillipsburg, NJ: Presbyterian and Reformed, 2002.

Trosse, George, and A. W. Brink. *The Life of the Reverend Mr. George Trosse.* Montreal: McGill-Queen's University Press, 1974.

Tucker, Gene M. "Creation and the Fall: A Reconsideration." *Lexington Theological Quarterly* 13:4 (October 1, 1978) 113–24.

Tuell, Steven Shawn. "Should Ezekiel Go to Rehab? The Method to Ezekiel's 'Madness.'" *Perspectives in Religious Studies* 36:3 (September 1, 2009) 289–302.

Turner, Erick H., Annette M. Matthews, Eftihia Linardatos, Robert A. Tell, and Robert Rosenthal. "Selective Publication of Antidepressant Trials and its Influence on Apparent Efficacy." *N Engl J Med* 358, no. 3 (January 17, 2008) 252–60.

Underhill, Evelyn. *Mysticism: A Study in Nature and Development of Spiritual Consciousness.* 12th ed. Stilwell, KS: Digireads.com, 2005.

Urbina, Ian. "Addiction Diagnoses may Rise Under Guideline Changes." *The New York Times,* May 12, 2012.

Van Huyssteen, J. Wentzel. *Alone in the World? Human Uniqueness in Science and Theology.* The Gifford Lectures, 2004. Grand Rapids: Eerdmans, 2006.

Van Kooten, Geurt Hendrik. *Paul's Anthropology in Context: The Image of God, Assimilation to God, and Tripartite Man in Ancient Judaism, Ancient Philosophy and Early Christianity.* Wissenschaftliche Untersuchungen Zum Neuen Testament. Tübingen: Mohr Siebeck, 2008.

Van Praag, Herman M. "Enlightenment and Dimmed Enlightenment: Psychiatrists, Cast Off Your Distrust of Faith." *Psychiatric Times* 29:3 (March 2, 2012). http://topics.searchmedica.com/insights/content/article/10168/2041346.

Van Putten, Theodore. "Why do Schizophrenic Patients Refuse to Take their Drugs?" *Archives of General Psychiatry* 31:1 (July 1, 1974) 67–72.

VanGemeren, Willem. *Interpreting the Prophetic Word: An Introduction to the Prophetic Literature of the Old Testament.* Grand Rapids: Zondervan, 1996.

Vanier, Jean. *Community and Growth.* Rev. ed. London: Darton, Longman, and Todd, 1989.

Vine, Phyllis. *Families in Pain: Children, Siblings, Spouses, and Parents of the Mentally Ill Speak Out.* New York: Pantheon, 1982.

Wade, Nicholas. "Hoopla, and Disappointment in Schizophrenia Research." *The New York Times.* Tierney Lab Blog (July 1, 2009). http://tierneylab.blogs.nytimes. com/2009/07/01/hoopla-and-disappointment-in-schizophrenia-research/?_ php=true&_type=blogs&_r=0.

Warfield, Benjamin B. *The Person and Work of the Holy Spirit.* Amityville, NY: Calvary, 1997.

———. *Selected Shorter Writings of Benjamin B. Warfield.* Nutley, NJ: Presbyterian and Reformed, 1970.

Waterhouse, Steven. *Strength for His People: A Ministry for Families of the Mentally Ill.* Amarillo, TX: Westcliff, 2002.

Watson, Francis. *Text and Truth: Redefining Biblical Theology.* Grand Rapids: Eerdmans, 1997.

Watters, Ethan. *Crazy Like Us: The Globalization of the American Psyche.* New York: Free Press, 2010.

Waxler, Nancy E. "Is Mental Illness Cured in Traditional Societies? A Theoretical Analysis." *Culture, Medicine and Psychiatry* 1 (1977) 233–53.

Welch, Edward T. *Blame it on the Brain? Distinguishing Chemical Imbalances, Brain Disorders, and Disobedience.* Resources for Changing Lives. Phillipsburg, NJ: Presbyterian and Reformed, 1998.

Wengert, Timothy J. *The Pastoral Luther: Essays on Martin Luther's Practical Theology.* Lutheran Quarterly Books. Grand Rapids: Eerdmans, 2009.

Whitaker, Robert. *Anatomy of an Epidemic: Magic Bullets, Psychiatric Drugs, and the Astonishing Rise of Mental Illness in America.* New York: Crown, 2010.

———. *Mad in America: Bad Science, Bad Medicine, and the Enduring Mistreatment of the Mentally Ill.* New York: Basic Books, 2010.

———. Foreword to *Soteria: Through Madness to Deliverance,* by Loren R. Mosher, Voyce Hendrix, and Deborah C. Fort, xiv-xv. Bloomington, IN: Xlibris, 2004.

Whitfield-Gabrieli, Susan et al. "Hyperactivity and Hyperconnectivity of the Default Network in Schizophrenia and in First-Degree Relatives of Persons with Schizophrenia." *Proceedings of the National Academy of Sciences* 106:4 (January 27, 2009) 1279–84.

Williams, A. N. "Mystical Theology Redux: The Pattern of Aquinas' Summa Theologia." *Modern Theology* 13:1 (January 1, 1997) 53–74.

Wittgenstein, Ludwig, and G. E. M. Anscombe. *Philosophical Investigations: The German Text, with a Revised English Translation.* 3rd ed. Malden, MA: Blackwell, 2001.

Woodward, James. *Encountering Illness: Voices in Pastoral and Theological Perspective.* London: SCM, 1995.

Woodward, James, Stephen Pattison, and John Patton. *The Blackwell Reader in Pastoral and Practical Theology.* Malden, MA: Blackwell, 2000.

Wunderink, Lex et al. "Recovery in Remitted First-episode Psychosis at 7 years of Follow-up of an Early Dose Reduction/Discontinuation or Maintenance Treatment Strategy: Long-term Follow-up of a 2-year Randomized Clinical Trial Recovery in Remitted First-episode Psychosis Recovery." *JAMA Psychiatry* 40:9 (July, 2013). doi:10.1001/jamapsychiatry.2013.19.

Yan, Jun. "Epigenetics Links Nature and Nurture." *Psychiatric News* 45:5 (March 2010) 12.

Yang, Yang et al. "Increased Interstitial White Matter Neuron Density in the Dorsolateral Prefrontal Cortex of People with Schizophrenia." *Biological Psychiatry* 69:1 (January 1, 2011) 63–70.

Youngs, Fredrick W. "The Place of Spiritual Union in Jonathan Edwards's Conception of the Church." *Fides Et Historia* 28:1 (December 1, 1996) 27–47.

Zilboorg, Gregory, and George W. Henry. *A History of Medical Psychology*. New York: Norton, 1941.

Zipursky, Robert B., Thomas J. Reilly, and Robin M. Murray. "The Myth of Schizophrenia as a Progressive Brain Disease." *Schizophrenia Bulletin* (November 20, 2012). http://schizophreniabulletin.oxfordjournals.org/content/early/2012/11/20/schbul.sbs135.full.pdf+html.

Zizioulas, John. "Communion and Otherness." *Sobornost: The Journal of the Fellowship of St. Alban and St. Sergius* 16:1 (1994) 7–19.

Zodhiates, Spiros. *Hebrew-Greek Key Word Study Bible: New American Standard Bible.* Chattanooga, TN: AMG, 1990.

Subject Index

A

abandonment, 59, 72, 172, 187, 197, 204, 206, 209, 217, 219, 223

abnormal thoughts, commonality of, 86

abnormality, postulated to fit a drug, 90

absolute Truth, God's knowledge as, 12

abyss, 3, 218, 257

acute, 70, 93, 99, 258, 279, 289, 293, 301

Adam, 25, 39, 40, 41, 45, 46, 151, 152, 218

adam, generic humanity, 26

Adams, Clive, 119, 121

Adams, Jay Edward, 299n173

ADHD, diagnosis of, 105, 311

advocate, defined, 299

agranulocytosis, 93

akathisia, 138

Alakare, Birgitta, 269n83, 270, 272n94

Alanen, Yrjö Olavi, 266, 267

Ambohibao Toby, 273n96, 274, 276, 277, 279, 297

American Medico-Psychological Association, 80

American Psychiatric Association (APA), 7n4, 8, 68, 76, 81, 103, 112–13, 116n210, 118n217

Amos, 201

amphetamines, 98

Amundsen, Darrel, 153

Ananias, sudden death of, 154

Anderson, Ray, 20n1, 36n65, 39n80, 40n82, 41n84, 43–44, 49, 64n183, 152–53

Andreasen, Nancy, 9n12, 107–8

Angell, Marcia, 89, 89n104–90n104, 105, 121–23

animal/appetitive power, 56

Anna, 63

anomalies, contradicting existing theories, 141

anthropological research, presenting examples of the communal nature of illness, 171

anticholinergic drugs, side effects, 92

antidepressants
arrival of, 90
commonly prescribed in the United States, 304n3
little more than active placebos, 98n135
number of people taking, 105

antipsychiatry movement, 124–31

antipsychotics, 89
adverse effects underestimated, 108n180
agitating the neurotransmitter system, 106
arrival of, 90
atypical, 90, 93, 120
commonly prescribed in the United States, 304n3
contributing to brain tissue volume decrement, 108
drug-induced brain damage from use of, 305

antipsychotics (*continued*)
  first generation believed to block
    the dopamine receptor, 92
  inducing a forgetfulness of
    motive, 169n107
  inducing "a pathological
    deficiency in dopamine
    transmission," 97
  not helpful even at a low dosage,
    305n4
  producing therapeutic effects, 95
  regulatory approval from FDA,
    91
  second generation, 93
  sense of dysphoria on the part of
    those on, 169n107
  use of, 105–6
Antony (monk), 225n301
Aquinas, Thomas, 28, 40, 52
armed forces, psychiatric problems
    encountered by, 112
Artificial Intelligence (AI), 21
Association of Medical
    Superintendents of
    American Institutions for
    the Insane (AMSAII), 79, 80
asylum medicine, as a specialty, 79
asylum reform, in France, 73
Athanasius, 49, 52, 225, 225n301
Atkinson, David John, 151n37
Atkinson, Jacqueline, 156
Augustine, 39, 39n78, 40, 52, 219
authenticity, 248, 285, 296
authority, to contend against
    wickedness, 240
auto-suggestion, 227, 228
axon, 88

B

bara, stressing initiation of the
    object, 26, 27
Barrajon, A. Pedro, 31–32
Barrett, William, 212n240, 219
Barth, Karl, 20, 36–37, 43, 44, 55
Battie, William, 74–75
Bavington, John, 229
Beck, James, 26

Becker, Ernest, 146, 215, 216, 221,
    222, 223, 248
Bedlam, 72n27
"being in Christ," Pauline expression
    of, 54
being with, the person, 258
believers, becoming like Christ, 48
Bentall, Richard P., 105, 112, 125,
    126, 127, 127n250, 129
Berkhof, Louis, 27, 62–63
Berkouwer, G. C., 29, 45–46
Bethlem hospital in England, 72
biblical characters, suffered from
    leprosy, 207
biblical demonic presentations, 226
biblical leprosy, 209n231
biblical time, medical knowledge
    of, 275
biblical writers, linking leprosy and
    sin, 208
biological concept of madness,
    pervasive in medicine from
    the fourth century BC, 69,
    commonly believed by the
    church, 147
biological etiologies, of some
    psychiatric illnesses, 296–97
biopsychiatry, 17, 22, 297, 304. *See
    also* organic psychiatry
bipolar disorder, 95, 95n125, 101,
    117, 136, 156, 157, 261,
    305n5, 311
Blackwell, Benjamin, 47–49, 55, 59,
    61–62, 64
Bleuler, Eugen, 9, 84
blood-letting, 69, 70, 71, 77, 79
bodily humors, 68
body of Christ, 155, 246, 249, 254,
    286–87, 301, 310
body/soul debate, 23, 33, 35
body-soul dualism, evidence in Paul
    for, 30, 58
Boisen, Anton T., 179
Bonhoeffer, Dietrich, 152n39, 247,
    280–81, 285, 286
Bonner, Gerald, 39n78, 48n114
book of Revelation. *See* Revelation
    (book of)

Booth, Gotthard, 145, 147, 148n24–
149n24, 162, 166–67, 172
Borgwardt, Stefan J., 305
born-again Christians, 159, 225
Bowers, Malcolm, 99
Boyd, Jeffrey, 22, 32, 138, 161n78
Boyle, Mary, 84–85
Bradford, David, 237, 238
brain
    causing "mental illness," 35
    chemistry of, 88
    differences in, 141, 305
    functioning like a major
        network, 33
    of a person with schizophrenia
        attempting to repair damage,
        180
    reigning supreme in psychiatry,
        34
brain "abnormalities," not linked to
    actual "symptoms," 305
brain cells, complexity of
    interactions among, 33
brain chemistry, 88, 311
brain development, having a lot
    to do with environmental
    factors, 103
brain disease, 5, 84, 130, 177, 231,
    253n32
brain neurons, structural
    changes when exposed to
    antipsychotic drugs, 107,
    108n180
brain states, 33
brain tissue, 99, 100, 107, 108, 179
breath of God, soul of man came to
    life through, 27
Breggin, Peter Roger, 96, 169n107
brethren, 75, 76, 244, 281, 283, 285,
    293
Broome, Edwin, 196, 197
Brown, Norman, 205, 233, 234
Brown, Warren, 31
Browning, Don S., 312n24
Brunner, Emil, 21, 45
Buber, Martin, 193–94, 195
Bultmann, Rudolf, 58

burdens
    bearing another's, 172, 202, 247,
        251
    carrying each other's, 263, 302
Burroughs, Jeremiah, 284

C

Cacciatore, Joanne, 257
California Alliance For the Mentally
    Ill, 290n156
Calvin. John, 20n2, 40, 41, 42, 52–
    53, 59, 60, 61, 62, 158, 204,
    207, 218, 220, 233, 240
cancer, 9, 140, 148n24–149n24,
    161–62
Caplan, Paula J., 115
Cappadocians
    on *imago Dei*, 39
    on Participation in divine life,
        51n129
    union with God, 56
care
    meaningful and practical
        approaches for, 17
    practices from a Christian
        perspective, 7
    of souls, 302, 312
caregivers, 5, 131, 292
caring, 76, 128, 146, 189, 247, 251,
    252, 264, 266, 280, 284,
    292, 297, 299, 301, 302, 308,
    312n25
Carlat, Daniel, 95, 101, 102, 111,
    113, 114, 117, 122, 123, 297
Carlsson, Arvid, 95, 98
Carrel, Alexis, 82
Carson, D. A., 152, 153, 155, 158,
    159, 163, 250
Carson, Marion, 245, 246, 286
catatonic (state)
    central for understanding of
        Ezekiel's personality, 195–97
    in regards to Helia, 6
    in regards to the
        "schizophrenics," 81
CATIE study, 95, 95n125
Chaimowitz, Dr., 282

character of illness, 147, 176

chastisement, God's present in our illness, 158

"chemical imbalance," myth of, 97–101, 109, 304

chemical restraints, 79, 309

chemical-imbalance hypothesis, 89

chemical-imbalance theory, of mental illness, 97, 100

"cherry picking," 123

Chiarugi, Vicenzio, 74

childhood trauma, development of schizophrenia and, 127n250

Chlorpromazine (brand name Thorazine)
 effects of, 93, 94
 facilitated de-institutionalization of the insane, 90
 first of neuroleptics, 92
 introduction of, 91
 therapeutic effects of, 89

Chouinard, Guy, 106, 107

Christ. *See also* Jesus
 ambassadors for, 251, 301
 chief exemplar of personhood, 63
 "contemporaneousness with," 206
 deification through participation in, 48
 estranged from his Father, 206
 fullness of, 249, 250
 having hope in, 158, 221, 245
 image of, 59, 62, 65, 67, 159, 187, 288
 law of, 142, 172, 247, 251
 as medicine, 158
 modeling, 61–62
 redeeming work of, 212
 sacrificial work of, 60, 204
 as Savior, 146
 spiritual realm directing, 37
 the Great Physician, 184
 the only elect remnant, 191
 union with, 54–55, 54n140, 58, 159, 166, 191, 233, 237, 313

"Christ in us," Pauline expression of, 54

Christian community, care in an authentic, 249

Christian epistemological framework, 11

Christian framework, for interpreting "schizophrenia," 2

Christian God, as one God comprising three persons, 12

Christian mysticism, in the Roman Catholic tradition, 52

Christian response, to "schizophrenia," 308

Christian Trichotomists, 27–28

Christianity
 about abandoning ourselves, 288
 inspiring people with trust in God and freeing them from the fear of demons, 228
 revolving around catering to ourselves, 288
 salvific revelation is unique to, 11
 as a sort of madness or the greatest horror, 212
 through the consciousness of sin, 212

Christians
 facile faith of, 212
 in a potentially miraculous world prior to the Enlightenment, 146–47
 qualified to care for each other at times of mental crises, 293

Christie, Nils, 252

Christification, 36

christoformity, journey of, 65

Christosis, 48

church
 accepted a reductionist anthropology offered by medicine, 147
 assuming mental illness as a given, 22
 called to "incarnating Christ" in the life of others, 302
 called to repentance, 170, 310

delegated responsibility of
counseling, 288
history of filled with "isolation
and persecution of the
mentally ill," 246
ignored responsibility to apply
gifts in the context of
pastoral care, 127
intervention in mental illness, 9
model to take direct
responsibility for the
members of the body of
Christ, 310
of no help in the midst of
intense suffering, 4
reconsidering interpretations of
Scripture, 14
response to mental illness
delegated, 1
standing silently by, 312
church fathers, positive attitude
toward "possessed/insane,"
232
Claridge, Gordon, 86, 307
Clarke, Isabel, 210, 211, 287, 289,
290, 291, 292
classical sinner, as the modern
neurotic, 222
classifying, people into boxes, 67
Clay, Sally, 176
clinical psychiatry
descriptive, 83, 84, 114, 253n31
much more than medical
treatment, 277
clinical research, 121
clinical trials, for psychiatric drugs,
118, 122
Clozapine (trade name Clozaril), 93,
95–96, 135, 309
Cohen, J. M., 235
collaborative healing process, 264
Colwell, John, 16n33, 58, 156
"common grace," bestowed upon
humanity, 41, 60, 302
communal encounter, with illness,
170, 241, 269

communal interdependence, for
discovery of truth, 13
communion
with God, 42
with the other, 247, 249
community
bearing the illness of, 204
built with the aim of bringing
holistic healing to
Christians, 274
conquest of disease dependent
on, 310
feeling a collective responsibility
for the illness, 270
of healing, 252–80
human beings organically
interrelated to, 170
loss of, 189
need for the participation of,
182, 241
refusal to take accountability for
mental illness, 172
sense of, 301
taking the burden of illness as its
own, 271–72
voice of illness spoken to,
168–72
"Community Treatment Orders
for Patients with Psychosis
(OCTET)," 300n178
compassion, self-serving, 248
complexifying, the situation, 15
compulsory commitment, 292
compulsory treatment, 130,
169n107, 299–300, 300n178
confinement, during seventeenth
century, 71
conflict, of good with evil, 205
Connecticut State Medical Society,
lobbied to build a local
asylum, 78
consciousness
altered state of, 257
experiencing, 21
faculties of, 28, 63
intersubjective, 270, 301
mind/ heart as the seat of, 230

consciousness (*continued*)
> as *nous*, 56
> of sin, 212
> sense of identity, 2, 8
> transformation of, 214, 235

Constantelos, Demetrios, 51

contemporaneousness, with Christ,
> 206

context, created for recovery,
> 264–65

"contradiction, between Creation
> and Sin," 45

covenant theology, 11

Cooper, David, 125, 171

Cooper, John, 29, 30, 32–33, 35, 62

copy number variations (CNVs),
> 102

Corpus Hippocraticum (CH), 225,
> 275

correlation, not the same as
> causation, 140

Cortez, Marc, 20n5, 24n16, 36n65,
> 37

"cosmetic psychopharmacology,"
> 149

counseling, receiving and giving,
> 294

counselors, appointing to the host
> family, the individual, and
> the natural family, 293

covenantal relationship, with God,
> 20, 24, 24n18, 247

creation, image at the time of, 40

Creator-creature relationship, 25

criminalization, of people with
> mental illness, 282

crises
> care for each other at times of,
> > 293
> making sense of life, 178
> pastoral care during, 292
> as something that points to
> > human issues, 272
> of transformation, 211

cross-cultural research, on mental
> illness, 169, 178, 181, 182,
> 198, 198n198

crucified Christ, leading us to the
> exalted One, 65

crucifixion
> by the Devil, 205
> of Jesus, 204, 206
> leads to resurrection, 62
> participation in his, 52

cultural context, of how illness was
> dealt with, 182

cultural needs, influencing evidence
> scientists attend to, 101

cultural standard, behavior
> considered pathological by,
> 173

cure
> hidden within the illness, 235,
> > 307
> lack of, 131, 139
> for neurosis, 222
> of souls, 294

Cyril of Alexandria, 47, 48

D

damaging side effects, of
> antipsychotics, 96, 98, 104

Dark Night of the Soul, 191

Day, John, 185

death
> on being like God, 152n39
> of every human being, 166
> as God's doing, 153–54
> as punishment in case of Adam's
> > disobedience, 151
> stark reality becoming more
> > graspable, 148
> as a transition to life, 219

death instinct, effective power of,
> 205

death-in-life, Luther's theology of,
> 205, 234

Deegan, Patricia, 253

default mode, of their brain, 199

default network, 199, 200

Degler, Carl, 101

deification, 39n78, 47, 48, 50, 57,
> 61n169

Delay, Jean, 94, 95

deliverance, from captivity and
  illness, 145–46
delusion(s), 7n4, 9, 16n33, 85,
  86n92, 94, 98, 169n107, 196,
  200, 278
Demarest, Bruce, 26
dementia praecox, 83, 84, 85. *See
  also* "schizophrenia"
demon(s)
  casting out, 227, 275
  dwelling in the sick person, 229
  seeking to damage the soul, 231
demon possession, 70, 225
demoniacal personality, 219–20,
  248, 248n13
demonic attacks, reality of, 279
demonic etiologies, confused with
  organic diseases, 230
demonic forces
  extremely difficult to determine
    the influence of, 231
  role of, 223–40
  threatened by love, 220
demonism, resurgence of, 278
demuth, 39
dendrites, 88
denial of ourselves, 61
Denifle, Heinrich, 160
Deniker, Pierre, 94, 95, 97
depravity, pain of, 202
depression
  evolutionary significance of,
    145n9
  framed as lack of serotonin or
    norepinephrine, 89
  low-serotonin theory of, 100
  managing symptoms of, 90
  not cured by medication,
    98n135
  suffering from, 158
descriptive psychiatry, 84
father of, 253n31
desire to be lost and damned, 205
despair, Luther's, 168
Deuteronomy, 154, 288
deviant behavior, 193
devil

dismissal leading to a "pale
  eschatology," 234
exerting influence upon
  everyone, 231
as the god of this world, 233
presenting deceiving images,
  236
provoking disturbances in the
  organism itself, 231
diabolical word, destroying unity
  and harmony, 176
diabolism, in Luther, 234
diagnosis
  already part of the therapy, 176
  becoming an identity, 262
  psychiatrists not settling on a
    concrete, 3
*Diagnostic and Statistical Manual of
  Mental Disorders (DSM)*
  As the "Bible of Psychiatry," 110
  classification of disorders, 110
  criteria, 115
  defining acceptable behaviors,
    311
  diagnoses as "operational
    definitions," 110
  official categorization of
    schizophrenia, 7n4
  symptoms cataloged in, 7
  understanding the nature of,
    110–18
*Diagnostic and Statistical Manual of
  Mental Disorders (DSM-I)*,
  112
*Diagnostic and Statistical Manual of
  Mental Disorders (DSM-II)*,
  112
*Diagnostic and Statistical Manual of
  Mental Disorders (DSM-III)*,
  113, 114
*Diagnostic and Statistical Manual
  of Mental Disorders (DSM-
  III-R)*, 115
*Diagnostic and Statistical Manual of
  Mental Disorders (DSM-IV)*,
  115, 214n251

Diagnostic and Statistical Manual of Mental Disorders (DSM-IV-TR), 115
Diagnostic and Statistical Manual of Mental Disorders (DSM-5), 116, 307n13
Diamond, James Arthur, 208–9
Diamond, Stephen, 224n298
Dillard, Raymond B., 196n192
disability numbers, with treatments increasing, 105
disease
    as always illness, 144
    of the body, 230
    conquest of dependent on the community, 168
    considered as punishment, 167
    defined, 8
    defining as something destructive, 162
    as evil, 229
    new, 148
    Satan's ability to cause, 160–61
disorder of the spirit, 216, 242
distorted relationship, between a person and his "social group," 168
"divided self," 174, 214, 217
Divided Self (Laing), 126
divine breath, transfer of, 27
divine economy, 287
divine nature, partaking of, 46, 47n110
divine participation, 49, 52
divine sovereignty, doctrine of, 11, 207
Divine union, leading the way to, 236
Doller, Jane, 136, 309
dopamine, making the brain supersensitive to, 106
dopamine blockade, inducing symptoms, 92, 95
dopamine hypothesis, of "schizophrenia" in 1967, 98
dopamine imbalance theory, of "schizophrenia," 98
dopamine malfunction, 98

dopamine transmission, drug-induced deficiency, 97
Douglas, Mary, 209n231
dread, Kierkegaard's, 217, 218, 220, 248n13
drug revolution, promise of a "cost-effective" method of treatment, 90–91
drug-based model of treatment, 259
drug-based paradigm of care, 106
drugs
    causing permanent damage in the brain, 109
    testing of, 122
DSM. *See Diagnostic and Statistical Manual of Mental Disorders (DSM)*
dualism, 23, 27, 29, 32
dualistic interactionism, 32n54
dualistic views, 28
Duncan, Laramie, 103

E

Eccles, John C., 32, 32n54
economic Trinity, 24, 25n20, 65
ecstatic behavior, 196
ego, death of, 188
Eichrodt, Walther, 27
Elkes, Joel, 94
Erlich, Matthew, 305n5–306n5
embracing the world, of another human being, 258
emotional space, to meet another human being, 262
empty state, 200
encephalitis lethargica (EL), 84, 85
Enlightenment, 43, 146, 147, 215, 228, 278
environment
    creating to help people with mental distress, 266
    deeply affecting people with "schizophrenia," 200
    loving and supportive, 290
    need for a safe and supportive, 292
epigenetics, 103, 307

Erickson, Millard, 54–55, 54n144
Erickson, Richard, 283, 292
Erikson, Erik H., 160, 167, 187
eschatological, 23, 38n76, 48, 146,
    164, 234
eschatological view, of salvation
    from sin, 164
eschatology, in Luther, 234
Eskimos, therapeutic methods of
    the, 171
events of life, becoming alive again,
    184
everybody, as schizoid, 221
evidence-based medicine (EBM),
    110, 119
evil
    affects the most vulnerable, 232
    giving life to the experience of
        insanity, 308
    as opposing power, 280
    powerless against humility, 284
    presence of in mental illness,
        239, 240
    primal cause of suffering, 152
    surrounds all of us, 232
exemplar, Jesus as, 36, 59
Exile, positive impact bringing
    about unity, 186
exile
    darkness and abandonment of as
        a catalyst, 187
    meaning death of, 185
    as a reminder of a broken
        covenant, 190
    as a time for hope, 187
exilic existence, as one's real
    vocation, 192
existential, interpretation of *imago
    Dei*, 38n76
existential perspective, 12, 14–15
exorcism (s), ix, 160n76, 224n298,
    225, 226n305, 227, 228, 274,
    275, 276, 278, 279, 280
exorcist, 224n298, 226, 227
Expressed Emotions (EE), in the
    family, 127, 281

expressive/descriptive grammar,
    helping Christians reframe
    "schizophrenia," 143
extended therapy room, 262, 264,
    265, 266
extrapyramidal syndrome (EPS),
    92, 96
Ezekiel, 46, 185, 193, 195, 196, 197,
    201, 202

F

Fairbairn, W. Ronald, 221
faith
    confession of true, 236
    connecting with the "healing
        power of God," 246
    sustaining in the midst of evil
        and suffering, 156
    tested by fire, 212
    as turning to Christ, 212
Fall of Adam, 45, 152
false beliefs, from media, and
    deceptive pharmaceutical
    advertisements, 299
false prophets, 193
false self, 220
families
    defining "normal," 127
    encountering "schizophrenia" in
        Zanzibar, 181
    getting involved in their own
        offspring's healing, 258
    needing healing, 282
    potential negative influence, 126
Family Care Foundation (FCF), 261,
    301, 310
family dynamics, role in the
    outcome of the psychotic
    experience, 127
family homes
    given a stipend to cover
        expenses, 262
    giving the gift of an "ordinary
        life," 266
famine, for hearing the words of the
    Lord, 201
Father and Spirit, "in" the Son, 12

"father of American psychiatry," 76

Fava, Giovanni, 124

Fawcett, Barbara, 300n178

fellow believer, accountability and submission to, 249

fellow workers, in building up the body of Christ, 254

fellowship of suffering, with Christ, 204

Finland, "schizophrenia" recovery in Western Lapland, 266–73

Finnish National Schizophrenia Project, 267

First National Forum on Recovery from Mental Illness, 176

Fischer, Diane, 135

forced treatment, abstaining from, 109

forces of darkness
  fighting, 279
  struggle with, 234

Foskett, John, 6, 279, 286

Foucault, Michael, 71, 71n20, 72, 73, 81, 81n70, 125–26, 183, 223, 312n25, 313

Fowler, James, 10

Frame, John, 11–16, 24, 45, 46, 150, 151, 165–66, 191, 206, 212, 213, 216

Frances, Allen, 115, 116, 117

Frankl, Viktor, 295

Franklin, Benjamin, 76

Freud, Sigmund, 90, 124, 164, 205, 216, 221

Freudian, 87, 114, 196

friendships of Jesus, 285

Fromm, Erich, 221

Fromm-Reichman, Freida, 256

fullness of Christ, 249, 250

functional holism, 35

functional interpretation, of *imago Dei*, 38

G

Gadarenes, demon possessed, 230

Gaiser, Frederick J., 153n45, 160n76, 163, 179n140, 226n305, 232

Gallaudet, T. H., 255

Gehazi, 154

Genesis, 25, 26, 46, 151n37–152n37, 152

genetics, of mental illness, 101–4

Germaine, Volahavana, 273

"gift of meaning," symbols offering, 183

gifts, turning unique into pathology, 308

giving moments, in reality moments of receiving, 251

glorification, image at the time of, 40

God
  as almighty, with Satan on a short leash, 161
  canceling our plans by sending us people, 280
  created Adam, 25
  created humans as holistic entities, 35
  demanding our worship and obedience, 192
  employing illness as fatherly discipline, 158
  existence of, 174
  forming the human person, 26
  gender inclusive language in reference to, 10
  hidden for an oppressed spirit, 58
  knowing best *sub contrario* or in his hiddenness, 190
  knowledge of putting illnesses in the right perspective, 150
  leading down to hell those whom he predestines to heaven, 206
  ordained for Israel to go through the experience of exile, 186
  ordaining our illnesses, 157
  perceived absence of, 156
  power of, 24
  "pruning" his people, 159
  purpose in all things is his own glory, 159
  regenerating his people, 46

sending his people into Exile, 191

of sentimentality masquerading as "love," 157

setting his eye on one's source of pride, 167

source of all power, 159

source of goodness and mercy, 158

as Spirit, 63

story of our relationship to, 151n37

ultimate cause behind all illnesses, 161

ultimate healer, 276

using evil for good, 238

using Satan as an instrument, 161

God the Creator, 25

God the Lifegiver/Sanctifier, 25

God the Redeemer, 25

God-fearing life, health-giving benefits of, 158

godly persons, in Scripture suffering illness and untimely death, 155

God's grace, coming at great cost, 193

God's people, eternal salvation of, 159

God's pleasure, living for, 61

God's providence, cause and effects under, 155

God's Spirit, connecting through the inner man, 64

God's Wisdom, seeking, 24

good and evil, 151, 211, 275

good, overcome evil with, 240

gospel of humanism, 148

Govig, Jay, 253, 279, 302

Govig, Stewart, 252–53, 278–79, 289–90, 295, 302

grace
    common, 41, 60, 302
    of God, 43, 50, 193, 210, 218, 237, 284, 285
    God exercising, 153
    life without, 189

no access to, 312

repentance, real *metanoia* experienced by, 184

sense of divinity given by, 60

transformation brought about by, 52

Great Commission, 288

Greek fathers, 39n78

on *imago Dei*, 39

Green, Joel, 30

Greene-McCreight, Kathryn, 157, 158, 189, 190, 191

Gregory of Nazianus, 56

Grof, Stanislav and Christina, 210, 289

group family therapy, 267

Grudem, Wayne, 25, 28, 46–47, 54, 62, 151, 213, 239, 240, 283

Guthrie, Shirley, 25n20

Gutting, Gary, 312n25

H

Hacking, Ian, 9, 67

Håkansson, Carina, 261, 262, 263, 264, 265, 293

Hallucination(s), 7n4, 85, 86n92, 92, 94, 98, 134, 199, 269, 272, 278

Handbook of Religion and Health, 149n28

Hansen's disease, 209n231

Haracz, John, 99

Harrison, Nonna Verna, 38–39, 51n129

Hartford Retreat, recovery rate, 77

Hawking, Stephen, 20

Hays, Richard, 246

healed life, dependent on God, 294

healing
    among non-Western cultures, 275
    characteristic of Jesus' ministry and identity, 160n76
    communities of, 252–80
    as a foreshadowing of salvation, 164
    hidden in weakness, 166–67

healing (*continued*)
   pointing to the ultimate
      Messianic salvation, 164
   praying for, 161
   road to, 280–301
   as a shared enterprise, 247
   superficial, 294
   together as a path forward,
      244–302
   traditions of, 164
"Healing Homes" model, 261–66,
   282, 290, 298
"Healing Homes" clients
   becoming family members, 262
   costs, covered by the state, 265
   own family playing a key part,
      265
healing interactions, 257
healing power of God at work, 179
healing practice, centered on healing
   services, 274
healing together, leading to, 245, 308
Healing Together model, 281
   as a care model for the mentally
      ill, 310
   described, 302
   incorporating services of
      committed Christian
      psychiatrists into, 297
   success requiring a structure,
      301
health
   enduring hope of perfect, 148
   giving a false impression of self-
      sufficiency, 146
   perspectives on, 145
health and sanity, reduced to
   chemistry, 145
healthy brain, acting in "rest," 200
healthy reaction, against a sick
   society, 287
heart, as the seat of one's
   consciousness, 230
heightened sensory receptiveness, a
   patient's, 248n15
Helia, 3–7, 16, 184, 185, 186, 188,
   189, 192, 198, 202–3, 204,
      205, 207, 210, 211, 212n242,
      313
Hell
   experience of, 238
   vivid portraits of a descent to,
      235
hermeneutical circle, use of, 12
Herod, 154, 155n49
heroic self-image, achieving, 146
"hibernation therapy," 94
hidden voices, finding, 270
hiddenness of God
   humanity coming to know its
      true self, 218
   Luther dealing with, 187
   in the midst of darkness, 190
Hippocrates, 68, 70, 224n298,
   225n302
historicity, of the Genesis message,
   151
holiness, not "happiness" as chief
   end of man, 63
holistic dualism, 30, 35
holistic healers, psychiatrists as, 277
holistic integration, of the body and
   the soul, 63
holistic-dualistic position,
   interpreting from, 58
Holy Spirit. *See also* Spirit of God
   can consume the chaotic
      disorder, 302
   caused the Son's imaging of God,
      36n38
   Christians are endowed with the
      power of, 293
   conformed to *imago Dei* by the
      work of the, 62
   convincing us of our sin, 211
   crucial role in Paul's soteriology,
      55
   as the "efficient cause of all
      external divine operations"
      in our lives, 43
   God bearing all the
      characteristics of, 60
   God's mysteries revealed
      through, 14
   inviting after exorcism, 275

knowing God through, 16

most effective help comes from, 299

power of, 302

revealing God's mysteries, 14

sanctifying work of the, 43, 211

as the Spirit of the Son and of the Father, 12

union with Christ through, 46

homeless, 71, 252

homovanillic acid (HVA), for dopamine, 89

Hornykiewicz, Oleh, 98

Hosea, 195

hospitalization

alternative to, 256

forced, 3

neuroleptics extend the length of, 94

host families

approaches by, 283

coming face to face with own weaknesses and flaws, 264

ideal, 284

recruiting and selecting, 298

selected solely for their personal characteristics, 262

howlings and yellings, of the insane, 284

human, as a unified entity, 28

human behavior, spectrum of valid, 142n2

human being(s). *See also* man

defining, 19–20

fallen into sin, 60

knowledge limited, 13

in the midst of an altered experience, 245

presuppositions about the constitutional nature of, 21–22

reducing to one substance removing complexity, 31

true nature revealed within Scripture, 23

human body, best picture of the human soul, 147

human condition

madness as a reflection of, 212–23

"schizophrenia" as the exaggerated form of, 221

transformation experienced by believers in Christ, 49

human evil, root causes of, 146

human existence, reductionist view of, 21

human lives, purpose and significance of, 25

human love, making itself an end in itself, 286

human mind, 45, 287

human nature

Aristotelian concepts of, 40

biblical writers' focus on, 20

human needs, theology's role to meet, 16

human ontology, 27–37, 55

human person

in bondage of sin, 45

elemental construct of, 23

God forming the, 26

holistic entity created by God in a dualistic fashion, 62

of Jesus, 55

as a multidimensional unity, 145

human phenomenon, mystery of madness as, 143

human questions, looking at Scripture in search of, 13

human relationships, healing potential of, 256

human sameness, honest recognition and confession of, 249

human soul, 2, 32n54, 60, 63, 143, 147, 162, 266

human species, computer technology displacing, 20

human spirit, 1, 8, 9, 17, 25, 50n125, 51, 55, 62, 147, 219, 221, 261

human suffering, 149, 206, 276, 294

human transformation, 52

humanism, growing, 70

humanitarian and optimistic outlook, 309

humanity
    goal of, 46
    on the path toward destruction,
        183
    warned for centuries about
        pride, 217
humanity's pride
    leading to humanity's self-
        destructiveness, 214
    major blow to, 201
humankind. *See also* human
        being(s)
    created as two sexes, 26
    destined to contend with nature
        for survival, 152
    faced with the dilemma of self-
        rejection, 217
    moved away from its source of
        life, 219
    proclivity to hate its own, 207
    trapped in sinfulness, 197
    understanding the nature of, 20
humoralism, 69
Hyman, Steve, 107
hyperactivation, of the default
        network, 200
Hyssteen, Van, 38

I
iatrogenes, 259
iatrogenic brain damage, scale of,
        305
iatrogenic effects
    of antipsychotics, 259
    chronic mental illness may be,
        304
    epidemic, 106
    increase in receptors, 100
    of treatment, 108
idealism, 23, 29
Ignatius, warning about demonic
        activity, 225
illness
    attributing a purpose to, 163
    attributing to one's sinful nature,
        153
    as both theological and
        teleological, 241
    bringing about both physical
        and psychological suffering,
        240
    calling afflicted and those
        around to repentance, 165
    coming from sin, 69
    as a consequence of an
        imbalance between bodily
        humors, 68
    culturally shaped, 144
    deciphering the message of, 163
    defining, 8
    "demoniacally caused," 225
    designed by God for "good," 163
    encounter with having to be
        communal, 170
    experience of, 163
    expressing the soul, 147
    God "sanctioning," 155
    hidden in strength, 166
    humbling the spirit, 166
    as innate "human experience of
        symptoms and suffering,"
        144
    intensity of, 166
    "meaning" of in respect to one's
        relationship with God, 163
    as medicine for the soul, 166
    not necessarily diseases, 144
    as an occasion to serve God and
        to grow in virtues, 154
    original cause of, 151–62
    as punishment for sin that is
        imposed for conversion, 153
    representing "providential ways
        to salvation," 165
    self-examination an essential
        response to, 159
    severe, making people feel
        abandoned by God, 156
    subject matter of, 143
    as theological by nature, 148
    theology of, 142–243
    theory developed by natural
        sciences, 147

as a threat that must be
destroyed, 172, 242
understanding in naturalistic
terms, 69
voice heard best when mingled
with faith, 163
voice of, 162–72
image(s)
deceiving, 237
demonic, 238, 279
God in their own, 157
made by the Father in his, 25
in media, 299
of Narcissus, 216
of "schizophrenia," 185, 242, 311
our true, 201
seeing, 193
various views of, 40–42
of the wicked, 150
image of Christ, 41, 46, 48, 59, 62,
67, 159, 187, 288
image of God, 24, 26, 27, 37, 38,
39n78, 41, 42, 43, 44, 46, 49,
50, 52n131, 57, 59, 61, 67,
imaging of God, modeling, 62
imaging technologies, 23, 107, 297
imago Dei
describing humans in their
current state, 44
pointing to Jesus, 38
process of reviving, 46
restoration of, 44
in Scripture, 37
immaterial dimension, focal point of
Pauline anthropology, 58
immediate judicial consequence, of
a particular sin, 154
impatience, syndrome of, 138
impersonal theology, as an outright
impossibility, 16
"The Importance of Cultural
Factors in Mental Hygiene,"
198n198
impotent self-consumption, 214
incarnation, 39n78, 50, 55, 302
individual, voice of illness spoken
to, 165–68

individual "I," transparent into the
"I" of the community, 194
"Industrialization of Psychiatry," 114
Ingvor (host mother), 264
inner alienation, Jesus experienced,
206
inner light, estrangement from, 175,
215
inner man
deepest part of the soul, 64
distinct from the physical outer
man, 58
subject to great turmoil, 59
inner self
estranged from the outer-self,
174
Laing acting out, 129
innermost faculty, concept of, 58
Inquisition, church's solution to
mental illness in medieval
time, 170
insane
bringing their messiness as a
sanctifying fire, 283
condition of at home, 72
constraining, violating their
God-created existence, 247
harmless when treated
humanely, 283
inability to protest against their
treatment, 305
mistreated as less-than-human,
72
portraying us in vivid ways, 250,
310
sending back into ordinary
society, 252
skyrocketing growth in the
number of, 80
treating with dignity and
nurturing care, 255
treating with torture and
torments, 71
insanity
appearing to be still mysterious,
103
of Nebuchadnezzar, 217–18
systematic categorization of, 112

insanity (*continued*)
  voice of opening deaf ears and
    blind eyes to know sin, 284
"insanity defense," in the justice
    system, 130
Insel, Thomas, 104, 105, 139, 140,
    307n13, 309
inspection visit, 283
Institute for Dialogical Practice,
    271n92
institutionalization paradigm, 82
instrument in the hand of God, 185
intellect (*nous*), 56
intercourse, called unto a true, 42
interior life, experimentation with as
    dangerous, 175
intermediate state, doctrine of, 29
International Classification of
    Diseases (ICD), 112, 115
International Pilot Study of
    Schizophrenia (IPSS),
    conducted by WHO, 113
intersubjective consciousness, 270
involuntary commitments,
    compared to rape, torture
    and sexual abuse, 300
Irenaeus, 39, 40, 51, 153
Isaac, Rael Jean, 130
Isaiah, 190, 195
Israel
  harlotry of, 195
  promise of breakthrough for,
    189
  requiring a "redemptive re-
    creation," 191
  sent to exile, 185
  spiritual laziness of, 186
  is warned beforehand, 154

J

James, William, 142, 240, 284
Jehoram, 154
Jeremiah, 158, 186, 189, 190–91,
    193–94, 308
Jesus, 231–32, 233, 234. *See also*
    Christ

arms open to all who mourn
    and confess their sins, 210
deliverance of those possessed
    by demons, 223
encounter with the Samaritan
    woman, 285
on entering the kingdom of
    God, 49
as the faithful remnant, 191
learned obedience from the
    things which he suffered,
    159
led about by the Spirit to
    encounter the devil, 239
made of body and Spirit, 63
on the man born blind, 154
own family said of him, "He is
    out of His mind.," 196
sense of alienation from God,
    206
sent to die on behalf of
    humanity, 60
stretched out hands toward the
    lepers, 209
as the true image of the invisible
    God, 38
Job, 158, 161, 295
John, the Apostle, 302
John of the Cross, 188, 191, 236
John the Baptist, beheaded by
    Herod, 155n49
Johnstone, Eve C., 305
Jones, Barry, 106
journey, from the outer reality to the
    inner reality, 188
Joy, Bill, 20
Judd, Lewis, 96
"Judgment Day," visions of, 238
Judicial model, of union, 54
Justin Martyr, 225

K

Kaiser, Walter C., 13n25
Kaplan, Bert, 177, 307
Kapur, Shitij, 86n92, 169n107,
    248n15
Keller, Matthew, 103

Kempe, Margery, 70
Kendler, Kenneth, 35, 141
Keropudas Hospital, 268
keys of St. Peter, replaced by the
        keys of psychiatry, 311
Kierkegaard, Søren, 206, 212, 214,
        215, 217, 218, 219, 220, 248,
        248n13
King of kings, representing, 251
Kinghorn, Warren Anderson, 22,
        180, 297
Kirk, Stuart, 114, 116, 118
Kirkbride, Thomas, 79–80, 81, 309
Kirkbride, James, 198n199
Kirsch, Irving, 89, 97, 101, 122, 123,
        306
Klein, Ralph W., 185, 187, 190, 192
Kleinman, Arthur, 8, 132, 144, 162,
        178, 207, 209n231
Kleinman's definition, defining
        illness, 144
knowing God, as a personal journey,
        16
knowledge
        explanation of, 14
        God's, 12
        three kinds of, 14
        Frame's perspectives on, 12
Koenig, Harold, 149n28
Kraepelin, Emil, 83, 84, 85, 87, 109,
        112, 114, 253
Kramer, Peter, 101, 149, 312n24
Krim, Seymour, 177
Kurzweil, Ray, 20–21
Kuhn, Thomas, 141
Künkel, Fritz, 297
Kutchins, Herb, 116, 118
Kütemeyer, Wilhelm, 171–72, 202

L

Laing, Ronald D., 125, 126, 127–29,
        128n254, 165, 174–75, 188,
        189, 192, 201, 214, 215, 217,
        219, 220, 234, 235, 256, 287
language of power, where one
        speaks for the other, 262

Larchet, Jean-Claude, 56n151, 57,
        146, 148, 163, 165, 166, 172,
        230, 231, 232, 233, 287
law, knowledge of, 14
law of Christ
        denying, 247
        fulfilling, 251
lawlessness, lust for, 46
lay analysts, psychotherapy by as
        superior, 124
Lazarus, illness and death, 159
Lehmann, Peter, 254
Lemuel, 299
Lennart (host father), 264
lepers
        Jesus touching, 302
        "schizophrenics" as twenty-first
            century, 207–11
Leprosy, 154, 207–9, 210, 211, 232,
        250
Levin, Cathy, 136–37
Leviticus, 208, 211
Lewis, Bradley, 6n2, 276–77
Lewis, C. S., 304n1
Leyshon, David, 157, 158, 159, 163
life circumstances, of Paul, 204
life conditions, responding in
        individual ways to, 308
life crises and misfortunes, putting
        our psyche out of balance,
        178
life events, causing alterations in
        gene expressions, 307
*The Life of Antony and the Letter to
        Marcellinus*, 225n301
life without grace, 189
life-giving Spirit, human being and,
        49–59
light of the Lord, only after
        experiencing true darkness,
        236
likeness
        of Christ, 55
        differences between image and,
            39
literary analysis, Scripture as the
        canon is the object of, 13
Lithium, introduction of, 90

living soul
    with a body and a spirit, 27
    created by God, 64
living word, enhancing "communal unity," 176
Longden, Eleanor, 85n90
Longman, Tremper, 196n192
looping effect, 67
Lord of lords, representing, 251
Lossky, Vladimir, 57
Louth, Andrew, 40, 50, 56
love
    distorted, 46
    spiritual coming from Jesus Christ, 286
    without hypocrisy, 248n12
Luhrmann, T. M., 202
Luke, 30, 63, 239, 275
lunatics, visiting, 73
Luther, Martin, 40–41, 160, 167, 168, 187, 190, 205–6, 207, 212, 212n242, 233, 234, 239, 313

M

MacDonald, Norma, 177
Mackler, Daniel, 261n57, 263
Madagascar, 273, 274, 275, 279, 297, 301, 310
madhouses, giving rise to modern psychiatry, 71
madness
    bringing humanity face to face with the darkness of sin, 213
    corroborating the traditional concept of sin, 242
    discerning meaning in, 7
    as disorder of the spirit, 242
    as the equivalent of sin, 216
    to express one's inner experiences, 174
    first-person accounts of, 307
    as great business in England, 72
    hearing the voice of, 165
    humbling a proud heart, 313
    as an illness of the *nous*, the spirit, 143
    journey of, 6, 188
    leading to a true sanity, 214
    as a manifestation of true darkness, 215
    opening our spiritual ears, 309
    organized around a "kernel of purposefulness and intentionality," 307
    as the picture of sin, 311
    portrait of, 220
    providing a mirror, 311
    as punishment of knowledge, 313
    pursuit of answers to the mysteries of, 6
    recognizing its value and meaning, 177
    religious experience of, 70
    role for in Christian thought, 312n25
    as a sane reaction to insane social conditions, 125
    seen as both a "sickness of spirit" and the essential process for cure, 235
    shocking depiction of penalty of sin, 217
    significance of, 6
    as sin, 216
    as testimony to how far mankind might fall without God's grace, 312n25
    as a theological and a teleological phenomenon, 2, 247, 308
    as a trumpet call to repentance, 213
    view of corroborating the traditional concept of sin, 216
    vitality of, 177
Madness and Civilization (Foucault), 125, 126
"madness tent," bringing more people into, 254
madwomen, La Salpêtrière horrific treatment of, 73

magic, scientism compared to, 304n1

Maimonides, 208, 208n227

major tranquilizers, 90

making up people, engines for, 67

man. *See also* human being(s)
    avoiding "becoming," 219
    continuing to possess image
        (*tselem*) of God but lost his
        likeness (*demuth*), 39
    remaining language through and
        through, 183
    true nature of, 215

management of the mind
    (*traitement morale*), 74

manic-depressive, 83, 136, 165

man-woman relationship, as image
    of God, 44

Mark's Gospel, demonic ideas of,
    275

Marshall, Tom, 57, 168

martyrs, of immediate culture and
    community, 195

materialistic monism, 138

materialists, viewing humans
    as made of chemical
    substances, 21

matter, underlying qualities of, 68

Matthew, 239

McCasland, Vernon, 226, 227

McDonald, Suzanne, 41–42

McGruder, Juli, 169, 170, 175–76,
    181, 182, 198, 201, 238, 241,
    309

McLean Hospital, recovery rate, 77

McNeill, John, 149, 297

"the Meaning of Health," a paper by
    Tillich, 145

medical approach, to psychiatric
    disorders, 141

medical disability, of our time, 1

medical doctors, intrusion into
    asylums, 79

medical model
    of madness, 174, 309
    providing distortion, 165

medical practices, depersonalization
    of, 148

medical remedies, brought back, 79

medical science, objectifying illness,
    144–45

medical treatment
    bias for, 305
    biological ailment in need of,
        297

medicalizing
    madness, 175
    mental illness, 176

medications
    chronic administration causing
        alterations in neural
        functions, 107
    making negative symptoms
        worse, 92
    image of people with
        "schizophrenia" shaped by,
        97
    side effects of, 92, 253
    those staying off far more
        functional in the long term,
        109
    appropriate usage of, 297

medicine
    choosing to ignore demonic
        causes, 230
    grabbed hold of moral
        treatment, 78

medieval concepts, of mental illness,
    69

meditative exercises, 200

meek and the broken, asking to dine
    with us, 281

melancholia, 69

members of the body, differences
    among, 250

Menninger, Karl, 65n185, 256

mental afflictions, of Luther, 167

mental anguish, crippling
    individuals in variety of
    ways, 9

mental disorder(s), 2, 9, 67, 68, 74,
    75, 76, 83, 101, 103, 104,
    116, 117, 124, 180, 278

mental distresses, as "fictitious
    illnesses," 129

mental experience, of Hell, 238

mental health care, American
system of, 7
mental health carers, dealing
constructively with evil, 240
mental health treatment, increased
correlating with suicide
rates, 106n173
mental health workers
routine work of, 292
showing interest in the role of
demonic concepts, 224
mental illness
Americans suffering from
debilitating, 7
appearance of being purely
pathological, 209
causing personal and social
disruption, 8
challenge to all healing systems,
8
as chemical imbalance in the
brain, 97
children growing up under the
shadow of, 311
community's attitude toward,
168
as a cultural construct, 126
deeper meaning behind, 7
epidemic fueled by psychiatric
drugs, 104
exponential growth in the US, 1
extra-biblical sources of
knowledge about, 15
"fragile status" of the concept of,
180–81
genetics of, 101–4
healing coming wrapped in
revelation, 294
hearing properly, 170
as a human phenomenon, 19
in case of chronic may be
iatrogenic, 304–5
as illness of *nous*, the spirit, 65
lack of knowledge about the
etiology of, 7
listening to the language of, 169
locking us in ourselves, 190

medical treatments for severe,
148–49
no consensus on what
constitutes, 8
of organic nature, 276
as an oxymoron, 130
as the pathology of our times,
304
personal experience with, 2
predictors of the course of, 182
premature death related to, 140
related to cultural context, 178
shaped through language, 172
stigma of, 189
those suffering from having no
access to God's grace, 312
voice of, 172–223
mental phenomena, continuing to
challenge humanity, 226
mental turmoil, causing changes in
the brain, 33
mentally ill
automatically labelled as
"possessed," 232
dismissed as unreliable, 132
on medication, 138
rarely asked and taken seriously,
132
working among, 6
Merkel, Larry, 69, 72
meta-analysis, 119, 120, 120n224,
122
metabolites, 89, 99
metamorphism, embarking on a
path of, 233
metanoia, 213
call for, 214
Greek word used for repentance
in the New Testament,
170n110
loss of the self to receive the
self, 235
madness whose truth might lead
to a new birth, 235
sense of sin beginning of, 210
metaphysical, 32, 35
model of union, 54
methodology, in this book, 10–16

Micah, 156–57, 195
Miles, Jack, 195
Mills, Hannah, 75
mind
    affecting the brain, 33
    in danger to be usurped by the
      brain, 34
    as the seat of one's
      consciousness, 230
    as something matter does, 29
mind-brain interrelationship, 35
ministry, 11, 17, 160n76, 228, 239,
    251, 273, 274, 276, 279, 288,
    290, 298
Miriam, 207
Mirowsky, John, 86
misfortune, medicalizing, 178
Miyar, Jose, 121
"models of madness," 6n2
models of treatment, importance of
    alternative, 309
Modrow, John, 176
money, spending exorbitantly as a
    "symptom," 202
monism, 27, 29
monotheistic faith, Israel's strong,
    154n45
mood stabilizers, 90
moral therapy
    creation of a home-like
      environment, 80
    with emphasis upon community
      life, 75
    first nonmedical asylum based
      on, 77
    good results of, 81
    practiced by the Quakers in
      York, England, 309
    practices advocated by, 256
    sentiment shared by
      practitioners of, 255
moral treatment, presented
    physicians with a clear
    threat, 78
Moreland, J. P., 28, 29, 32, 32n54, 62
Morrison, Anthony, 108n180
mortal beings, 144. *See also* human
    being(s)

mortality, denying, 146
mortification, 43, 62, 233
The Mortification of Sin (Owen),
    43n96
Moses, 161, 207
Mosher, Loren R., 129n257, 256,
    260, 259, 292–93, 297
Mount Sinai, 288
Mowat, Harriet, 15
Mowrer, O. Hobart, 65n184
mpiandry (shepherds), 274
Müller, Ulrich B., 229
Murphy, Nancey, 30–31, 32–33, 36
mutual indwelling, 50
"mutual within-each-otherness,"
    of different perspectives of
    illness, 145
mystical model, of union, 54
"mystical union," with Christ, 53

N

Naaman, 207
NAMI (National Alliance on Mental
    Illness), 23n14
nanobots, 20–21
narcissism, 214, 216, 221
"Narcissistic Personality Disorder,"
    in DSM IV, 214n251
Narcissus, myth of, 213–14
The National Board of Health and
    Welfare (Sweden), 261
National Institute of Mental Health
    (NIMH), 7, 95, 96, 99, 104,
    105, 107, 129n257, 256, 259,
    307n13, 309
"the national saint," of Spain, 235
National Survey of Children's
    Health, 104
natural healing, process of, 188
natural man, as truly "insane," 46
natural nature (image), vs
    supernatural nature
    (likeness) in Irenaeus'
    thought, 40
Nazi psychiatry, deemed
    schizophrenics ripe for
    elimination, 84

Nebuchadnezzar, 217–18
Nee, Watchman, 58
Need-Adapted Approach (NAA),
    267
Nenilava (Tall-Mother), 273
network of relationships,
    surrounding the person, 280
Neugeboren, Jay, 177
Neugeboren, Robert, 177
neural networks, 199, 306
neuroimaging scans, not employed
    for initial psychiatric
    diagnosis, 305n5
neuroleptic(s), 87, 90, 94, 95, 96,
    98, 100, 118, 119, 120, 267,
    268, 272
Neuroleptic Malignant Syndrome, 92
neuronal dysfunction, 304
neurons, 88, 179–80
neurosciences
    advances generating enthusiasm,
        131
    psychiatry harnessing, 304
neuroses
    as "clinical" expressions of
        entirety of human condition,
        222
    compared to demon possession,
        226
neurosyphilis, discovery of, 112
neurotic person, suffering from
    a consciousness of sin
    (Becker), 223
neurotransmitters, fluoresced
    different colors, 99n143
neurotransmitter(s), 88, 89, 106,
    107, 311
New Drug Applications (NDAs),
    120n224
"the new self," putting on, 191
Nicodemus, 49
Niebuhr, Reinhold, 44
Nietzsche, Friedrich, 215
NIMH, re-orienting its research
    away from DSM categories,
    307n13
"no-fault brain diseases," 177
"no-fault brain disorders," 23n14

non-reductive physicalism, 30
normal everyday interactions,
    people changing through,
    258
"normal" people, relearning how to
    live in the world of, 135
normality, 117, 189, 307
normative perspective, 12, 14, 183
nous (the spirit). *See also* spirit
    illness of, 58, 65, 143
    innermost part of the person,
        28n35, 174
    meaning of, 56–57
    an organ of mystical union
        (Louth), 57
    point of union, 56
Nouwen, Henri, 175, 249
nurtured relationships, in daily lives,
    281
nurturing context, 211
nurturing environment, potential
    for healing, 74

O

Obsessive Compulsive Disorder
    (OCD), diagnosis of, 4
Oesterreich, Traugott Constantin,
    227, 228
off-label prescriptions, 124
Olson, Mary, 271n92
ongoing care and counsel, 293–96
ontological holism, 35
ontological insecurity, 219
ontological monism, 30
open dialogue, promoting, 269
Open Dialogue therapy, 267–73, 287
operational management element, in
    Healing Together, 298–301
ordinary families, providing a
    therapeutic environment,
    263
ordinary life, living, 263
organic psychiatry, 86, 88, 93. *See
    also* biopsychiatry
orientation, to the outside world,
    258

Origen, warning about demonic activity, 225

original cause, of illness is always God, 228

otherness, understanding, 245

ourselves, hopelessly absorbed with, 216

outcomes, failure to bring about fruitful, 306

Overholzer, Winifred, 283

Owen, John, 36n68, 41, 42–43, 62, 233

P

pain and suffering, serving to bring about a good end, 155

Palamas, St. Gregory, 153

panpsychism, 29

parents, cry for an answer, 295

Parkinsonian sequelae, of encephalitis lethargica, 84

parkinsonian symptoms, 92

participation
  in the archetype, 38–39
  in Christ, 48, 62
  in divine life, 51n129
  of His divinity, 52
  in (with) God, 39n78, 47, 51, 52
  in illness, 171, 182, 241, 242
  in his life, 49
  in one another's pain, 249
  in the Spirit, 39n78, 51
  as (and) union, 49, 51

partnership with the psychiatric community, in *Healing Together*, 296–98

Pascal, Blaise, 214

pastoral care structure, in *Healing Together*, 286–96

pastoral team, at the person's home during crises, 292

pathologies, speaking more prominently about our human condition, 147

"pathology of normalcy," 221

patients
  following into split reality, 296

listening carefully to the voice of, 177

observing and listening to, 74

voice of, 132–39

patristic, 39, 47, 51, 56, 230

Patterson, JoEllen, 92

Pattison, Stephen, 8

Paul (Apostle), 30, 32n54, 41, 45, 48, 152, 155, 155n49, 159, 165, 172, 173, 204, 205, 229, 233, 234, 239, 240, 248n12, 249, 250, 251, 255, 308

Payne, Robert, 217

peer network, after release from Soteria, 258

Penfield, Wilder, 34

Perceval, John Thomas, 70

Pensees, Pascal's, 214

Persian Zoroastrianism, influence of, 160n76

personal identity, in a "disembodied intermediate state," 28

personal reflections, the author's, 312–13

personal sin(s)
  consequences of in the lives of others, 154
  as the root of humanity's contradiction, 64

personal traits, of potential staff at Soteria, 292

personalities
  changing, 67
  dissolved in illness, 191–92
  not defining persons, 192
  recognizing the diversity of, 261
  reconstruction of, 149
  variation in, 199

personhood, about being created by God, 63

person's life, local and cultural context, 272

perspective
  God's governing, 13
  in Frame's method, 12–14

perverse shepherd, God as, 189

perversions, of our common life, 170

Peter (Apostle), 46, 47, 231–32, 233
pharmaceutical (companies)
    advertising techniques by, 101
    depend on it to set direction for
        their research, 115
    hiding studies, 122
    increasing corruption of, 123
    lifelong customers for, 95
    new drugs having far greater
        revenues, 120
    rewarding doctors, 124
pharmaceutical imperialism,
    rejecting, 298
pharmacological interventions, 104,
    304
phenothiazines, developed as
    synthetic dyes, 93
phlebotomy, 69
physical and spiritual reality,
    modernist bifurcation, 280
physical hardship, endured by
    "schizophrenic" patients,
    204
physical restraints, 73, 79
physicalism, 23, 29
physicians, 3, 4, 71, 75, 76, 78,
    79, 82, 91, 101, 121, 148,
    208n227, 246, 297
Pies, Ronald, 277
Pilch, John, 209n231
Pilgrim, David, 305
Pilgrim State Psychiatric Hospital,
    80n66
Pinel, Philippe, 73–74, 204, 283
pious Christian sentimentality, freed
    from, 313
Piper, John, 49–50, 161, 162, 163,
    231, 295, 312
a place one can call home, as part of
    Healing Together, 281–86
Plantinga, Alvin C., 32n54
Plato, 52–53
Platt, David, 150–51, 288
pneumatological approach, to
    imago, 40
The Politics of Experience (Laing),
    128
polyphonic self, 270

"pooled analyses," of various trials,
    123
Porter, Roy, 72, 75, 80, 81, 82, 91, 93,
    104, 311
positive causal link, between
    health and certain religious
    practices, 149
Positron Emission Tomography
    (PET), 95
possession, 69, 145, 173, 178, 181,
    193, 223, 224, 225, 226, 227,
    228, 229, 232, 238, 275, 276,
    278, 279, 289
Post, Robert, 99
postsynaptic neuron, 88, 89, 99,
    100, 106
power of reason, 56
powers, in the soul, 56
Powlison, David, 288–89, 293–94,
    296
practical theology, described, 10
*The Practice of Physick: Two
    Discourses Concerning the
    Soul of Brutes* (Willis), 71
Pratt, Richard, 13
prayer for the afflicted, healing
    process including, 226
prefrontal cortex, slowly atrophying,
    108
"Presence" of God, person's
    separation from, 215
presuppositions, suspending non-
    biblical, 14
presynaptic neuron, 88, 89, 106
pride, 11, 151, 153, 159, 165, 167,
    201, 214, 217, 218, 219, 220,
    241, 284, 313
prideful nature, destroyed by
    madness, 313
"Primitive State," as a state of
    perfection (for Augustine),
    40
private sources, fundraising from
    (for *Healing Together*), 298
prolactin, increase in, 92
prophetic message of illness,
    received by the community,
    172

prophetic voice, 2, 170, 172, 182, 184, 185, 192–203, 213, 242, 247, 308, 309

prophets
compared to advocates, 299
of the Old Testament suffering from "schizophrenia," 195

propositional language, conveying information *about* God, 16

Protestant ethics, valued ability to work, 72

Protestantism, 233, 234

Prozac, 91, 149n26

pruning, done by God (Leyshon), 159

Psalms, Luther immersed himself in the power of, 167

pseudo madness, madness as, 234

pseudopatients, 87

psyche, 22, 28, 75, 113, 128, 178, 212, 219, 221

psychiatric classification, meaninglessness of, 130

psychiatric diagnoses, 110, 111, 180

psychiatric diseases, as collections of symptoms, 111

psychiatric disorders
as complex multilevel phenomena, 141
ever-continuing expansion of, 254
Luther's symptoms now considered as, 167
naming, 111

psychiatric drugs
administration of requires careful handling, 297
"billions of dollars are at stake" with, 123
criticism of (Breggin), 96
culprit behind violence by those who suffer from "mental Illness," 169n107
"epidemic of disabling mental illness" fueled by (Whitaker), 104
hotly debated, 308–9

interfering with process of communication among neurons, 89
Mosher's model of minimal use of, 259
need-adapted therapy without the use of, 268
producing long-lived alterations in brain function, 107
question of improvements in the quality of life for those on, 308–9
receive their approval to market based on clinical trials, 118
some people are able to live semi-functional lives with, 253
use of at Soteria, 256
use of in *Toby* model, 278

psychiatric history, from earlier times, 68–81

psychiatric illness
link with demon possession, 223
some have biological etiologies, 296
in peasant and other traditional societies, 182

psychiatric labels
Håkansson strongly rejecting, 262
person stigmatized by, 189

psychiatric medications
causing the brain to function abnormally, 107
minimizing, 261

psychiatric research, sponsored by pharmaceutical companies, 122

psychiatric therapeutic techniques, designed to dull the intellect, 87

psychiatric treatment
increased openness in participating (Open Dialogue), 272
against the patient's will (Helia), 3

psychiatric treatment (*continued*)
    chronicity is not to be found
        social context in which given
        (Laing), 175
psychiatric trials, quality and
    reliability of, 118–24
psychiatrists
    American, aggressive in
        diagnosing "schizophrenics,"
        86–87
    available for special cases, 297
    dissident, 125
    mistrust of, 125
    needing to truly buy into the
        philosophy of Healing
        Together, 297
    reduced to acting as society's
        policemen, 82
    testimony in court, 130
    victims of their own
        propaganda, 81
psychiatry
    versus alternative methods of
        treatment, 254
    creating a framework for
        "mental illness," 67
    denying significance and even
        evidence of soul or spirit, 22
    historical analysis of, 68–83
    least consistent thematically
        with scientific methods, 277
    medical model of, 17
    normalizing human behavior
        based on scientific theories,
        2
    questionable history of, 303
    removing the "symptoms" of
        personal disorders, 241
    resorting to meta-analysis, 119
    rise of modern, 83–88
    scientific basis of, 109–24
psychic functions, splitting of, 9
psychoanalysis, 91, 114, 126, 162,
    205
psychopharmacology, age of,
    88–109
psychosis
    beyond normal boundaries of
        personal mind, 287
    as a caricature of life styles of all
        of us, 221
    compared to demon possession,
        226
    demedicalizing, 259
    dynamics at play in, 246
    finding meaning in, 259
    as the fruit of "severely frayed
        social relationships," 268
    leading to growth and
        transformation, 256
    living in the in-between of
        family members, 268–69
    no longer needs to be seen as a
        sign of illness, 272
    as a normal reaction to life, 129
    positive progression of
        unmedicated, 267–68
    settling into the brain because of
        drugs, 106
    support of an acute, 289–93
psychosis teams (Open Dialogue),
    267
psychosocial treatments, 309
psychospiritual transformation,
    210–11
psychotheraphy, 87, 124, 132, 163,
    164, 181, 224n298, 227, 258,
    266, 267, 268, 294
psychotic behavior, 173, 307
psychotic episode, 210, 269, 292
psychotic experiences, 236, 245
psychotic illnesses, categories of, 83
psychotic symbols, looking at, 183
psychotic symptoms, 86, 88, 108,
    126, 267, 268, 271, 272, 281,
    282
psychoticism, needing in the
    "normal life," 246
psychotics, as modern lepers, 245
psychotropic drugs, 91, 93, 241
psychotropic medications, long list
    of, 92
public, fearing people with
    "schizophrenia," 169
"publication bias," 122

Purves, Andrew, 11, 53n138
Pussin, Jean Baptiste, 73

Q

Quakers, 75, 76, 77, 78, 141, 281,
309
challenge to the medical
establishment, 75

R

radical transformation, taking place
in the individual, 235
Rae, Scott B., 32
Rakotojoelinandrasana, Daniel,
273n96, 278, 279
Ramussen, Knud, 171
rational beings, treating patients
as, 77
reason
one of the "powers" in the soul
56
made man superior to animals
(Locke, Newton), 71
reason and intellect, wrapped in the
word "science," 173
rebellion, root of pain (Carson), 152
recovery, 15, 70, 75, 76, 77, 78, 79,
80, 83, 85n90, 94, 105, 107,
109, 122, 133, 135, 175, 176,
179, 226, 250, 253, 253n32,
255, 258, 264, 266, 267, 268,
281, 290, 293, 298, 309
Redeemer, 25, 45, 46, 283
redeeming son, human being and,
45–49
redemption, act of, 45
reductionist model
of Anthropology, 147
of medical psychiatry, 34, 35,
304
of mental illness, 310
reductionist view, of human beings,
29
reflective discipline, practical
theology as, 10
regeneration, 25, 40, 41, 46, 47, 62

Regier, Darrel, 117
rehumanizing, of madness, 259
relational beings, humans as, 270
relational interpretation, 38
relationships
building with "schizophrenics,"
285–86
man's capacity for personal, 43
reliability, of each of the editions of
DSM, 307n13
Relics of imago, 41
religion
as a constant principle of
coercion, 81n70
given only lip service in Western
medicine, 150
relation to psychotherapy and
medicine, 163
religious activities
central to cure, 70
good and helpful to health, 149
religious orders, care of the mentally
ill, 70
remission, 88, 121, 132
reparation, of the damage brought
about in the Garden, 152
repentance, real *metanoia*
experienced by God's grace, 184
turning away from sin, 212–13
residents at Soteria
entitled to their own perception
of reality, 257
never treated as if they were
"crazy," 259
restitution phase (Soteria), 258
Retreat for the Insane at Hartford,
255
reuptake process, 89
revelation
biblical, 143
experiencing, 193
as the inspired Scripture, 10–11
prophetic, 192
Revelation (book of), 245, 246
Ricoeur, Paul, 183, 184, 215
Ridderbos, Herman, 29
righteous Branch, 191
Risperdal, 93, 106, 136–37

Robinson, Wheeler, 145, 164

"The Role of Psychiatric Drugs in Cases of Violence, Suicide, and Crime," 169n107

Rollin, Henry, 91

Roschke, Ronald W., 225, 226, 230, 273, 274, 275, 276, 280

Rosen, George, 8

Rosenhan, David, 86–87

Rufer, Marc, 299–300

Rush, Benjamin, 76–77

Russell, Norman, 47

S

sacramental model, of union, 54

"sacred wedlock," 53

sacrificial lamb
    Helia became, 204
    patient has become for the community, 171
    person with psychosis as, 269
    "schizophrenic" as, 185, 203–7

sacrificial work, of Christ, 60

safe environment, creating, 270

Sainsbury, Steven, 207, 208

saints, autobiographical depiction of madness by, 70

Saks, Elyn, 132–33, 300n178

"salami slicing," withholding negative studies, 123

Salo, Tapio, 268

salvation
    eternal, 159
    God is the source of eventual, 158
    healing points to and foreshadows, 163
    interrelated with healing of the sick, 146
    narrative offered by Christ, 183
    as an objective divine act, 164
    power over illness, 246
    Scripture teach repentance as a requirement for, 212
    soteria, means, 145
    ultimate eschatological, 146

salvific revelation, unique to Christianity, 11

Samaritan woman, Jesus' encounter with, 285

sanctification, 24, 43, 46, 47, 54n140, 211, 230, 250, 288

sanity
    blurriness of the line with madness, 306
    compared to "madness," 173
    distinguishing from "insanity," 87
    line between madness and, 246

Sanity, Madness, and the Family (Laing), 126

Sapphira, sudden death of, 154

Sarah, hearing voices of both God and Jesus, 237–38

Sarbin, Theodore R., 89n92

Sargant, William, 90

Satan
    ability to cause diseases, 160–61
    attacking those most vulnerable, 232
    every move of, part of God's overall purpose and plan, 231
    evil schemes of, 225
    as an instrument used by God, 161
    as a real person, 160n76
    tactics of, 239

Savage, Timothy, 61

"Savior," saving pointing to, 146

Scheel, Otto, 160

Schiller, Lori, 133–36, 281–82, 309

schizoid condition, 165, 221, 242

"schizophrenia"
    as an "altered state of consciousness," 257
    a "dreadful condition," 9
    concordance rate, between twins, 101
    deeper meaning behind, 7
    devil's role in, 234
    directly related to the community where it manifests itself, 198

encountered as a communal
illness, 182
as an expression of human
variation and not pathology,
140
forcing everyone to listen, 296
forcing us to look at ourselves in
an unfamiliar mirror, 174
as God's megaphone, 250
hearing the voice of, 310
of the human spirit, 221
impossible to reliably identify as
a valid syndrome, 139
as journey to exile, 185–92
laying bare "hell's pitiless truth,"
311
leading to prolonged disability
and intense personal
suffering, 2
medical model of, 5n2–6n2
most striking images of the
experience of, 185
MRI's cannot diagnose, 305n5
high density of neurons in
deeper brain tissue in people
with, 179–80
not a single disease, 102
not sharing any of the
phenomena described by
Kraepelin and Blueler, 84
official categorization of, 7n4
origin of the term, 9
perceived as the leprosy of our
time, 209
pointing to distinct cultural
aspects of the community,
171
problems created by the drugs,
100
as prophetic voice, 192–203
psychiatry limiting diagnostic
criteria to elusive mental
symptoms, 84
as a psychobiological
disturbance of function, 86
recovery from, 253
reframed, to help Christians
grasp the depth and

intensity of the experience,
242
resulting from "overactive
dopaminergic pathways," 89
symbolic meanings in, 239
symptoms shared among several
other mental illnesses, 7
those labeled with, bearing the
pain of their community,
194
those suffering from, running
away from love, 220
through theological reflection,
17
touching on the most
fundamental fragilities of
the human soul, 2, 143
true annual cost of, 105
as a true experience of hell and
slavery to forces of evil, 312
as a true picture of sin, 223
as an unsettling reminder of the
human condition, 201
as a variation of human
expression rather than as
pathology, 142
voice of as a theological
reflection, 183–85
"schizophrenic" behavior, resulting
from psychosocial
experiences, 256
"schizophrenic"
caring for as ministry at
its messiest and most
meaningful state, 251
created as unique members of
the body, 250
evaluating relapse rate, 126–27
findings not supporting
presence of elevated
dopamine turnover in the
brains, 99
as harmless, confused, and very
lonely, 285
as lepers of our time, 207
relying on a hypermagnification
of mental process (Becker),
222

"schizophrenic" (*continued*)
symptoms as a key for opening up and addressing the family problems, 267
taking on external stimuli from their environment, 199
taking our burdens upon himself, 202
unmedicated with normal level of dopamine metabolites, 99
sciences
creating kinds of people, 66
as explanatory frameworks for everything, 304
as "tools of theology," 14
scientific secularism, cultural shift from religion to, 82
scientific theories, church's history of attempts to reject certain, 181
scientism, dangers of, 304
scientists, pointing to the brain as the culprit for mental illness, 306
Scripture
a book about redemption from sin, 45
claims that mankind has gone astray, 193
demonic activity in, 224
discern the voice of this illness through the guidance of, 17
divine authority of encounters a person in his concrete circumstances, 16
fullness of God's revelation in, 13
God's special grace revealed in, 64
his ways, as revealed in, provide us a roadmap, 159
as master guide in pastoral ministry, 11
points to Christ as the only hope for humankind, 221
speaking of the relevance of madness, 246

the spiritual realm, as clearly presented in, 32
transforming the personality of the people of God, 67
true nature of the human being as revealed within, 23
using as a "mirror," 13, 184–85
as the Word of God driving all theological work, 11
Scull, Andrew, 71, 78
secular cultures
living by the standards of, 151
need for psychiatry in, 277
secular institutions, never changing hearts, 294
Sederer, Lloyd, 305n5–306n5
Seeman, Phillip, 99
Seikkula, Jaakko, 268, 269, 270, 271, 271n92, 272, 290
self
having to go backward to be able to go forward, 188
shedding successive layers of, 220
self-absorbed temptations, 310
self-absorption
destructive fruits of, 218
madness exposes the extent of humanity's, 222
Narcissus died of, 216
Pride represents, 218
"schizophrenia" is about, 219
self-denial, 61
self-destruction, exposing the extent of humanity's, 222
self-determination, human capacity for, 56
self-encapsulation, 217, 218
self-help device, God as, 192
selfhood, commitment to, 220
self-love, pointing to death, 217
self-righteousness, nothing more deadly than, 210
self-sacrificing love
capacity for, 248
demanding so much of us, 251
sense and sensibility, split between, 9

sense of divinity, given by God's common grace, 60

sensus plenior (fuller meaning), 13n25

servant attitude, selfless unconditional, 286

servitude, toward the "unlovable," 286

shedding, of old self, 220

Shorter, Edward, 67–68, 71, 72, 75, 76, 77, 78, 81, 82, 91, 117

Shults, LeRon, 38

Shuman, Joel James, 146, 149, 247, 250

sickness
  as a healthy reaction against a sick society, 168
  treating all the same, 226
  unto death, 144, 218

side effects, 84, 90, 92–93, 95–96, 98n135, 104, 106, 109, 120, 131, 135–36, 138, 158, 253–54, 297, 305n4, 309

sign to Israel, Ezekiel as, 197

sign-acts
  breaking cultural conventions, 207
  exposing the hidden sins of our hearts, 250
  Ezekiel's, 196, 201–2
  revealing what we have masked, 310
  saw myself depicted in Helia's, 313

Siirala, Aarne, 8–9, 147, 147n17, 148, 164, 167, 169, 170, 171, 174, 176, 182, 183, 184, 200, 202, 234, 241, 246, 248n15, 287, 296, 297, 309

Siirala, Martti, 147n17, 200–201, 202

silent communication, really listening to, 6

Silva, Moisés, 13n25

Sims, Andrew, 22, 34, 74, 228, 229

sin
  abiding in the state of darkness, 216
  as an abstract concept, 212
  bondage of, 45
  confessing to one another and praying for one another, 171n113
  consequences in this life, 155
  end of, 152
  fallibility due to, 13
  God's planned judgment against, 153
  Kierkegaard's definition of, 218
  by knowing we can know righteousness, 203
  madness as, 212–23, 242, 311
  presence of fullness of, 206
  source of death, 152
  state of bondage, 219
  traditionally centered in pride, 214

Sinaikin, Phillip, 111, 113–14, 278, 278n115, 297

sinfulness, consumed by sense of, 210

sinner, with no word for it, 223

situational context, 303–8

situational perspective, 12, 14, 66

situations, happening in a context, 15, 66

sloth (*acedia*), clinical profile of, 69

Sobo, Simon, 110, 305–6

social actions, symptoms of mental illness as, 201

social change, Christians promoting, 301

social sciences, influence on theological studies, 10

social structure, connection with individual psyche, 128

society, pathology of contemporary, 221

solutions, proposed, 308–10

Son, "in" the Father, 12

Son of God, 279. *See also* Jesus

sons of God, adoption as, 47

Sontag, Susan, 209

sorrow, God "sanctioning," 155

Soteria House, 129n257

Soteria model, 197–98, 256–60

Soteria project, staff with no
training in psychiatry or
psychology, 292
Soteria, "salvation," 145
soteriological Truth, 11
soul
approaching the presence of
God, 188
called by different names, 22
diseases of, 230
doing a major work in, 185
in dualistic views, 28
like a mirror, 50
purifying, 236
traveling in the darkness, 191
in trichotomism, 28
sozo "to save," 145
space, making in their lives to care
for persons, 308
spirit, 56. *See also nous* (the spirit)
compared to soul, 63
in dualistic views, 28
kindling the inner light, 174
in trichotomism, 28
Spirit of God. *See also* Holy Spirit
born of, 25, 49
continuing to do wondrous
work, 195
opening up one's eyes to
perceive reality, 174
true union between the and the
human spirit, 25
union with the, 39
at work causing miracles, 255
Spirit of restoration, true
transformation by, 186
"spirit-related disorder (SRD)," 274,
276
spirits, existence of, 174
Spirit-to-spirit connection, 55, 62
"Spirit-to-spirit" model, Swope, 56
Spirit-to-spirit union, 50, 55
spiritual dimension, 7
spiritual disorder, of the individual
and of all humanity, 214
"Spiritual Emergency," Stan and
Christina Grof, 210
"spiritual emergency," idea of, 289

spiritual experiences, 34
spiritual healing, 279
spiritual love, coming from Jesus
Christ, 286
Spiritual model, of union, 54
spiritual realm, 32, 169
Spiritual Related Disorders (SRD),
297
spiritual suffering, illnesses creating,
144
spiritual warfare, 234
spirituality, centered on human
beings' feelings, 150
Spirituality and Psychiatry, book
concerned with issues of,
150n31
Spitzer, Robert, 113–14, 116
split life, 296
"split mind," 9
Sproul, R. C., 167–68
Spurgeon, Charles Haddon, 210,
211, 218
St. Basil, 51n129, 57, 146, 153
St. Elizabeth's Hospital, in
Washington D.C., 283
St. Gregory of Nazianus, on health,
146
St. John Cassian, 231
St. John Climacus, 166
staff, Soteria run by nonprofessional,
256–57
Stanford, Matthew, 224–25, 228, 231
STAR-D study, 95, 95n125
Stastny, Peter, 254
state of prayer, man in, 167
Staub, Michael, 125, 128, 129, 131
STEP-BD study, 95, 95n125
stigma, 117, 189, 199, 206, 207, 238,
272
stigmatized person, 207
Stip, Emmanuel, 118, 119, 120, 121
strangers, showing hospitality to,
283
stress, response to severe, 272–73
stress-buffering effect, of religion,
149n28
Stuckenbruck, Loren T., 224n297,
224n299, 226n307

Styron, William, 158
"subjective well being," patient's
        priority on, 132
substance dualism, 28
substantive interpretation, of image,
        38
sufferer, 248, 287
suffering
    of Christ, 310
    in contemporary biomedicine,
        178
    end of, 152
    humbling the flesh, 313
    necessity of, 48
    no way out of random, 158
    research methods to creating
        knowledge about, 132
    as a sign of God's anger, 157
Sugerman, Shirley, 173, 174, 192–
        93, 213–14, 215, 216, 217,
        218, 219, 220, 221, 234, 242
Sullivan, Harry Stack, 87–88
supernatural, effect on the human
        mind, 290
supernatural nature (likeness), of a
        human, 40
support system, around the clock,
        293
Swinburne, Richard, 32, 32n54
Swinton, John, xi, 15, 156, 206, 240,
        285, 293, 299, 300
Swope, John D., 50–51, 52, 56, 58,
        59
symbols
    common formation of, 170
    forcing us into awareness, 183
    formation of, 241
    radiate such deep meanings, 201
    spoken through evil, 215
symmetrical peer relationship, with
        the staff, 258
symptoms
    confusing psychiatrists, 4
    not void of meaning, 309
    reflections of the phobias and
        fascinations of specific
        cultures, 198

saw myself depicted in Helia's,
        313
speaking to our shared guilt and
        common disease of spirit,
        295
unceasing examination of, 296
synapses, 88
synaptic clefts, 88
Szasz, Thomas, 125, 129–31,
        131n267

T
taboo, against regarding role of
        environmental influences in
        the onset of psychosis, 127
talk therapy, 133
tardive dyskinesia (TD), 92, 100,
        137, 305n4
Tarrier, Nicholas, 127n249, 281n123
Taylor, Jill Bolte, 33n57
Teresa of Avila, 235–37
Tertullilan, warning about demonic
        activity, 225
theologia crucis, Luther's, 205
theological anthropology
    contextually-driven, 16, 20
    of suffering, 59–64
"theological being," man as, 41
theological context, nature of health
        and illness in, 143
theological framework, 23–59
theological model, of
        "schizophrenia," 183–85
theological perspective, voice of
        illness from, 143
"theological progress," achieving, 14
theological reality, illness as, 166
theologian, suffering from "bipolar
        disorder," 156
theology
    within a certain context, 16n33
    of illness, 142–243
    intensely personal nature of, 15
    Laing's, 128n254
    transcending statement of
        biblical doctrines, 13

theory and practice, integration of, 10
theosis, 39, 47
therapeutic methods, suggested by Laing, 234
therapeutic Parkinsonism, 97
therapeutic processes, Christian-based, 70
therapies
    based on power of collaboration and relationships, 261
    failing because change is expected to be easy, 265
therapist(s)
    assigned to the host family, 262
    and clients live in a joint embodied experience (Open Dialogue), 270
    an effective, 248n15
    gain richly from the experience, 263
    role of, 170
Thorazine, 89, 117
thought, disorder, 133, 165
Tillich, Paul, 44, 145, 163–64, 168
Tjeltveit, Alan, 181
Timothy, suffering from frequent illnesses, 155n49
toby, creation of, 273
Toby Model of ministry, 273–80
Toby of Ambohibao
    dedicated to the care of the mentally ill, 274
    categorizing patients, 276
Toby
    is about a holistic salvation, 279
    activities performed by shepherds, 276
    communal healing and the power of relationships, 280
Todd, Eli, 78
Training in Christianity, 206
transformation
    achieving, 213
    a loving and supportive environment leads to recovery and a, 290
    of the human condition, 47

of human nature into divine (Irenaeus), 51
    the intensity of the illness intensifies the process of, 166
    to the new life, 59
    that reflects the will of God (Swinton), 299
    redeeming, 46
    relationships in Christ will bear fruits of healing and, 308
    of the soul, 62
    taking place via "participation" in the "substance of God," 52
transformative powers, Prozac's, 149n26
trauma counseling, interventions not helping, 179
traumatic event, victims processing, 179
treatments
    aggressive of people suffering from "schizophrenia," 84
    constantly re-planned (Open Dialogue), 269
    increased in violence to tame the patients, 81
    justification for compulsory, 169n107
    psychological and humane, advocated by Pinel, 73–174
    some helped and some damaged by, 309
    in the United States, have turned increasingly to medications, 304
triads, in the Bible, 12
trichotomism, 23, 27
trichotomists, on Paul's language, 58
trinitarian framework, 24–25
Trinitarian model (Frame), 12
Trinity, 12, 24, 39, 54, 65
triperspectivalism, 12
Tripp, Paul David, 216, 249, 250–51, 310
Trophimus, 155n49
Trosse, George, 70
trust

for most people it is impossible
to regain their sense of, 300
placing more radical in God's
self-disclosure (Fowler), 10
relationships of, 257
time is significant in building,
265
Truth, accessibility to, 11
tselem, 39
tsunami disaster, of 2004 in Sri
Lanka, 178–79
Tuell, Steven Shawn, 196
Tuke, William, 75
twofold nature, of man, 27

U

unauthentic self, 219
uncertainty, tolerating, 269
unhealthy health, outcome of, 145
unheard-of ambiguity, Bonhoeffer
introduces, 152n39
union
"adequate" models of, 54
between the Spirit of God/
Christ and the human spirit,
25
with Christ, 43, 47, 48, 49, 50,
52, 53, 54, 62, 159, 191, 233,
313
with the divine nature, 49
with divine Spirit, 52
divine, 206, 237
with God, 51, 53, 55, 56, 59, 191
as image, 51
mystical, 53, 57
as participation, 51
nous as an organ of mystical, 57
point of (*nous*), 56
with the Spirit of God, 39
as a "Spirit-to-spirit"
connection, 55, 55n146
spiritual, 53n139, 54
as trinitarian, 54n144
United States, harsh treatment of the
insane pervasive in, 76
University of Jyväskylä in Finland,
268

University of Massachusetts Medical
School, 271n92
University of Turku, Finland, 266
unmedicated person, suffering from
"schizophrenia" as a true
picture of hell, 197
unusual thoughts, as pathological,
85–86
us-and-them thinking, 262
US-UK Diagnostic Project, 113
Uzziah, 207

V

Valium (diazepam), 91
Van Kooten, Geurt Hendrik, 58
Van Praag, Herman M., 34
Van Putten, Theodore, 138
Van Rossum, Jacques, 98
VanGemeren, Willem, 185, 186
Vanier, Jean, 284, 285
vegetative syndrome, drug induced,
94
vegetative/vital power, 56
venesection, 69
vesicles, 88
Vine, Phyllis, 282
violence, by those suffering from
"schizophrenia," 169n107
Vital model, 54
voice, hearing everyone's, 270, 273
voice hearing, experience closely
related to social context, 202
The Voice of Illness, 163
voice of illness
expressing the illness of a
community, 310
spoken to the community,
168–72
spoken to the individual, 165–68
from a theological perspective,
17
von Economo, Constantin, 84–85
voyage, from life to dying, 188

W

Wade, Nicholas, 102–3

Warfield, Benjamin B., 11, 203, 204, 205
Waterhouse, Steven, 290n156
Watters, Ethan, 150, 178, 179, 180, 181, 238
Waxler, Nancy E., 182
"the way of life," to accept the life in exile, 186
weakest of the weak, being used by God as his instruments, 173
Weickert, Cyndi Shannon, 179, 180
Welch, Edward T., 29n41
West Lapland, change in the overall culture in respect to mental health, 272
Western church, abandoning her most unfortunate and oppressed, 82–83
Western expectation, "overly negative," 182
Western mentality, seeking a religion leading to the betterment of life, 192
"What Would Jesus Do?" moment, caring for the insane as, 302
Whitaker, Robert, 72, 73, 75, 76, 78, 79, 81, 85, 93, 97, 98, 104, 106, 107, 136, 197–98, 259, 266, 268, 271, 281, 311
Whitfield-Gabrieli, Susan, 199, 200
wholeness through interdependence, 250
wicked, image of portrayed by the psalmist, 150
Willis, Thomas, 70–71

Wittgenstein, Ludwig, 147
woman, having sickness caused by a spirit, 161
"Wonderful Counselor," inviting in for a heart to heart conversation, 295
Woodward, James, 146, 246
Woodward, Samuel, 78
Word-Faith Movement, 155
World Health Organization Global Burden of Disease study, 104
World Health Organization (WHO), cross-cultural psychiatric studies performed by, 181–82
Wunderink, Lex, 109n181

Y

Yahweh (Lord), 24
Yahweh's freedom, at the heart of Jeremiah's message, 186
yatsar (to form, to sculpt), in contrast to *bara*, 27
York Retreat, 75–76
Yun, Jun, 103

Z

Zanzibar, people accepting presence of spirits, 238
Ziedonis, Douglas, 271n92
Zilboorg, 168, 198
Zizioulas, John, 247
Zodhiates, 308

Scripture Index

OLD TESTAMENT

Genesis

1:1–3	302
1–3	152n37
1:26	37–38, 44
1:26–27	26
1:27	27, 44
1:31	26
2:7	26
3:5	218
7:22	27
50:20	238

Exodus

4:6–7	207
4:11	153n45, 161

Leviticus

13:12–13	210
13:18	179n140
13:37	179n140
14:3	179n140
14:48	179n140
20:26	63
25:47–53	45

Numbers

12:10	207

Deuteronomy

4:11–12a	288
6:4–5	24n18
28:28	154
28:59	154
32:39	153

1 Samuel

2:6	153n45

2 Kings

5	207

1 Chronicles

28:19	vi

2 Chronicles

26:19–21	207

Job

2:9	161
2:10	153n45, 161
36:15	295
42:11	161

Psalms

2:4	1
6:	157
8:4–5	19
10:1	190
10:4	150
18:11	188
22	157
32	158

Psalms (*continued*)

32:11	63
82	47
106:37	239
139:14	299
142:4	1
142:7	244

Proverbs

3:	158
8:	24
16:18	218
18:14	1
31:8–9	299

Ecclesiastes

3:18	222
7:20	295
9:3	46, 246
12:7	27

Isaiah

20:3–5	195
43:21	25
45:7	154n45
45:15	190
53:6	193

Jeremiah

1:5	308
5:14	194
6:11	194
6:14	294
15:17	194
20:7	194
20:7–8	194
20:9	194
21:8–9	186
23:5–6	191
29:10–12	191
51:17	246

Lamentations

3:2–4	189
3:6	189
3:31–32	158
3:38	154n45

Ezekiel

3:4	195
3:14	195
3:15	196
3:24	196
3:26	195, 196
4:4–5	197
4:4–8	195
4:8	197
4–11	185
4:12	195
5:1–4	195
7:24	167
8:3	195
11:20	46
12:3–6	195
20:16	185n160
24:15–16	.195
24:27	195
33:22	195
36:26–27	46, 47
37	50n124

Daniel

4:30	217
4:32	218
4:33	217

Amos

8:11	201

Micah

1:8–9a	195
6:8–9a	157
6:12–13	157
7:7–9	303

NEW TESTAMENT

Matthew

1:20	55n149
5:6	63
5:8	63
7:9–10	162n81
7:22–23	42n93
8:28–34	223, 230
9:2	246
9:32–33	229
10:7–8	146, 274
10:28	27
11:2–5	146
11:25	173
12:18	55n149
12:28	223
14:1–12	155n49
16:23	232
18:18–20	274
22:13	197
27:45–46	206
28:19–20	288

Mark

3:21 NIV	196
5:1–20	223, 230
7:21	230
16:15–20	274

Luke

1:35	55n149
2:36–37	63
4:1	55n149, 239
4:18	55n149
8:26–39	224, 230
8:55	27
9:1–2	146
9:6	146
9:11	146
13:1b-3	154
13:11	229

13:16	161
16	30
18	55n149
22:31–32	233
23:43	30
24:16	174
24:31	174

John

1:32	55n149
3:5	49
3:34	55n149
4	285
6:37	210
6:63	19
8:44	230, 232, 239
9:3	154
10:38	12
11:4	142, 159
11:24–25	188
12:27	28n34
13:21	28n34
13:35	302
14:10	12
14:12–17	274
15:12	244
15:26	12
18:11	206
19:5	46
20:21–23	274

Acts

4:14	146
4:30	146
10:38	160
19:13–15	279
20:35b	251

Romans

1:	11
3:23	295
6:5	48, 62
6:23	152
7:14–19	45
8	55
8:9	12

Romans (*continued*)

8:9–11	54n144
8:10	28n33
8:18–23	48
8:28	162n81, 184
8:29	46
10:9	24n18
12:9	248n12
12:21	240
14:17	63

1 Corinthians

1:25–27	173
2:11	174
3:9	254
5:5	233
6:17	50
10:31	25
11:27–31	158
12	249
12:10	231
12:12–20	53
12:20–21	250
12:22–26	249
13:8	255
15:45	46

2 Corinthians

2:10–11	225
3:	55
3:17–18	55
3:18	41, 46, 59, 61, 61n169
3:18, NIV	59
4:4	38, 46, 233
4:8–9	205
4:10	61
4:12	204
4:16	58, 64
5:1–8	27
5:1–10	30
5:6–9	30
5:18	251
5:20	251
11:3	229–230
12:2–4	30

12:7	155n49
12:9	251
13:5	54

Galatians

1:15	308
3–4	55
6:2	142, 172, 247, 251

Ephesians

1:11	159
1:11–12	25
2:5	286
2:15–16	247
3:[16]-17	54
3:13	204
4	249
4:11	193
4:12	254
4:12–13	302
4:24	41
4:25	171
6:11–12	225, 280
6:12	232n325

Philippians

1:20–24	30
3:8	49
3:8–11	165
3:10	49
3:10–11	48
3:12–13	53
4:13	159

Colossians

1:13	60
1:15	38
1:26–27	54
3:10	41

1 Thessalonians

1:6	63
5:23	27, 56n151

2 Thessalonians

1:9	189, 197

1 Timothy

5:23	155n49
6:10	46, 66

2 Timothy

3:2	46
3:4	46
4:20	155n49

Hebrews

3:7–11	193
4:12	27
4:15	159
4:16	292
5:8	159
12:8–11	156
12:11	285
13:1–3	244, 283
13:5	46

James

3:15	45
4:7	284
5:14–16	171n113

1 Peter

1:7	212
3:19	27
5:8	225

2 Peter

1:4	46, 47
2:15	46
3:13	152

1 John

2:5b-6	302
2:15	46
3:8	232, 279
5:19	60

Revelation

3:20	281
12:9	239
17:5	218
21:1	152
21:3–4	152
21:27	152